1970	1980	1990	**2000**	

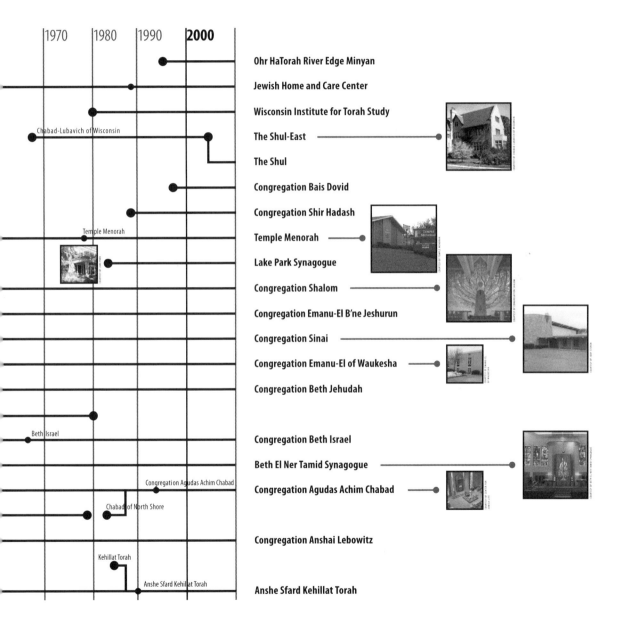

Ohr HaTorah River Edge Minyan

Jewish Home and Care Center

Wisconsin Institute for Torah Study

The Shul-East

The Shul

Chabad-Lubavich of Wisconsin

Congregation Bais Dovid

Congregation Shir Hadash

Temple Menorah

Lake Park Synagogue

Congregation Shalom

Congregation Emanu-El B'ne Jeshurun

Congregation Sinai

Congregation Emanu-El of Waukesha

Congregation Beth Jehudah

Beth Israel

Congregation Beth Israel

Beth El Ner Tamid Synagogue

Congregation Agudas Achim Chabad

Chabad of North Shore

Congregation Anshai Lebowitz

Kehillat Torah

Anshe Sfard Kehillat Torah

One People, Many Paths
A History of Jewish Milwaukee

John Gurda

Library of Congress Control Number: 2009937687
ISBN 9780982558201

Graphic Design - Market Engineers
mrkteng@att.net
Grafton, WI 53024

Printed in the United States of America
Burton & Mayer, Inc.
Menomonee Falls, WI 53051

 22

Introduction

In October 2007, when the research for this book was still in its early stages, I was asked to describe my progress to date for Koach, a senior citizens' group that meets at Milwaukee's Jewish Community Center. "My, what a big tent you have," I began. In the previous few months, I had attended services at most of the area's synagogues (visiting three on a single Rosh Hashanah), and I was slowly making the rounds of the community's non-religious institutions. I had met everyone from full-bearded rabbis in big fur hats to a self-described "third-generation atheist." I had discovered the historic split between German Jews and their eastern European cousins in my archival research and, as the only *Wisconsin Jewish Chronicle* subscriber on my block in Bay View, I was beginning to grasp the complexities of today's community.

Even before I could tell a minyan from a minhag, the theme of this book practically announced itself: the interplay of unity and diversity, both past and present. Milwaukee's Jewish community, like those elsewhere, has always been marked by a powerful sense of peoplehood on the one hand—the big tent—and equally imposing internal divisions on the other. Those divisions are most visibly religious—within the major movements as well as between them—but they carry over into the social and cultural spheres. You can meet Jews who are fervently observant or militantly secular, committed to the community or barely attached, absorbed in the life of the mind or immersed in the world of the marketplace, happily married to non-Jews or horrified at the very thought, ideologues or aesthetes, idealists or nihilists. No single set of characteristics is adequate to describe what it means to be a Jew in America, today or at any time in the past. The Jewish people encompass an unusually broad range of human possibilities, and yet they acknowledge a common ancestry and a shared identity—separate, to be sure, but at the same time inseparable.

Telling the story of this complex community has called for a tolerance of ambiguity and an ear for nuance. For someone with a native interest in all things ethnic and an equally strong curiosity about varieties of religious expression, it has also been nothing less than fascinating. I am grateful to Marianne and Shel Lubar, first of all, for opening the Jewish world to me. They are the community pillars who conceived the idea for this book and saw it through to completion. Three readers—historian Jane Avner, journalist Alan Borsuk, and educator Jody Hirsh—served as an editorial board that never met. Their individual diligence spared the author a number of goyish gaffes and generally made the text both more readable and more reliable. Jay Hyland, the Jewish Museum Milwaukee's exemplary archivist, demonstrated a command of his collection and an eagerness to help that aided this project immeasurably. And graphic designer Jim Price of Market Engineers made my words look good, just as he has for the last twenty years. To all, my gratitude.

John Gurda

Publisher's Foreword

I have tried to pin down the moment when I had the inspiration to have a history of Jewish Milwaukee written. It was more than two years before the publication of this book. The idea seemed simply to be an extension of the thinking and planning that I had been doing for several years with the great people who put together the Jewish Museum Milwaukee.

As soon as I mentioned the idea to my husband, Shel, he agreed whole-heartedly. From then on, it was a team effort. We had both seen the television presentation of John Gurda's history of Milwaukee, which included many Jewish references, and we decided that John was the one to write about Jewish Milwaukee.

The next step was convincing John to do it. He had many other plans, and we were very pleased when he told us he found the project so interesting that he would commit the time to us. We met many times during the process of his research and his writing of *One People, Many Paths*. For Shel and me, this was an extraordinary learning experience, mainly about Jewish Milwaukee but also about book-writing and publishing.

We hope that this book will illustrate the continuing dynamism of the Jewish community in Milwaukee and will help its readers to understand how many ways there are to express one's Judaism.

Marianne and Sheldon Lubar

One People, Many Paths
A History of Jewish Milwaukee

Contents

...AND I SHALL DWELL IN THE HOUSE
OF THE LORD FOREVER. PSALM 23

FRANSISCA HEIMAN 1862
IDA HEIMANN 1869
HIRSH HEINE 1862
ROSA HEINE 1866
A. HORWITZ
FLORA JACOBS
J. JACOBS 1850
JONKER FAMILY
FREDERICA KUSEL 1854
BERTHA LAWBER 1864
BELLA M. LEVY 1874
ISAAC LEVY 1868
JACOB LEWIT 1875
LITT FAMILY

EMMA LOB 1881
AMALIAM LOWENBACK 1869
ALEXANDER MACK 1862
BABETTE MANN
M. MANN
MICHAEL MARCUS 1884
ELLA MARKWELL
LEWIS MARKWELL 1860
EMIL MARQUE 1852
EDWARD MAY 1862
MATHILDA MAY 1861
DINA MORAWETZ 1868
CONRAD MUESEL

*A single stone identifies
the Jewish pioneers
buried in the Hopkins
St. cemetery.*

Chapter 1
Planting a Community, *1844-1882*

As graveyards go, the Hopkins Street cemetery is quieter than most. A rusting chain-link fence surrounds the solitary acre of land, and the flotsam of twenty-first-century America has drifted deep into its corners. The grass is still mowed, after a fashion, but most of the property has long since been claimed by box elder and buckthorn trees. The individual monuments are gone. In their place, flanked by a pair of overgrown yews, stands a single stone of more recent vintage and more generous dimensions. It is inscribed with the names of everyone buried on the premises: 124 names in all, including whole families, with the dates they were interred, none earlier than 1849 and none later than 1884. More than a century has passed since the last "resident" was laid to rest.

Here, in this forgotten, nearly forsaken acre of ground on Milwaukee's North Side, lie the pioneers. Here, near the corner of Sixteenth and Hopkins Streets, is all that remains of Milwaukee's earliest Jewish residents, a group that included Adlers and Friends, Neustadtls and Rindskopfs, Macks and Litts. When their graves were new, the cemetery was safely in the country. Today it lies, somewhat less safely, in the heart of the inner city, a beleaguered landmark in a neighborhood that has also known better days. Although it is anything but a tourist attraction, the cemetery plays a special role in the history of Milwaukee's Jewish community, for here are the last and most lasting traces of the first arrivals.

A Home in the New World

They came in the mid-1800s, part of the same exodus that brought thousands of other Europeans to Milwaukee. Like most of their contemporaries, the Jewish immigrants came west without a Moses, responding to the same forces of push and pull that emptied countless Old World villages. But the Jews had traveled a more circuitous route, and one infinitely better-chronicled, than their Christian counterparts. From bondage in Egypt to a homeland in Israel and then to a series of exiles imposed by the Assyrians, the Babylonians, and the Romans, Jews had been on the move for nearly 4,000 years. Remarkably, their sense of peoplehood remained intact through every change

in locale. While the fractious tribes of pre-Christian Europe were working out the rudiments of a civilization, the Jews shared a cohesive culture whose story was told in a single sacred text and whose faith was rooted in a single deity.

These wandering monotheists spread, over the centuries, to all quarters of the known world, settling throughout Asia Minor, northern Africa, Europe, and even India and China. They were occasionally welcomed, more often persecuted, and regularly expelled, but Jews found a place in the interstices of their host societies, working most often as merchants or traders at points of exchange. They frequently settled in port cities, which became points of

1

Neville Public Museum of Brown County

*Fur trader
John Lawe of
Green Bay was one
of Wisconsin's first
Jewish residents.*

Franks went into business for himself, trading throughout what is now the upper Midwest. He built some of the first mills in Wisconsin and was even present by proxy in Milwaukee, when the state's future metropolis was at best a minor trading post. Augustin Grignon, one of Franks' Green Bay contemporaries, described his dealings in an 1857 account:

> *About 1804 or '05, Laurent Fily was sent with a supply of goods, by Jacob Franks, of Green Bay, to carry on a summer trade at Milwaukee, buying deer skins in the red. With Mash-e-took and other troublesome Indians, he came near getting into difficulty, but was befriended and protected by Match-e-se-be, or* Bad River, *a brother of the chief O-nau-ge-sa.*

Although he was making money—or at least deerskins—Franks retreated to Montreal when the War of 1812 made life insecure for British subjects living on American soil. His nephew, John Lawe, stayed behind in Green Bay. After a lengthy period of adjustment to the American regime, Lawe emerged as one of the settlement's leading citizens, expanding his uncle's business and even serving as a county judge.

They may have planted the flag, but neither Jacob Franks nor John Lawe could be considered the founder of a permanent Jewish settlement in Wisconsin. (There is also considerable doubt as to how Jewish Lawe, at least, could be considered: although he was born to a Jewish mother, Lawe served on the governing board of Green Bay's first Episcopal church in the 1820s.) A genuine community would come to life not in Green Bay but in Milwaukee, and it would reflect a completely different demographic pattern. In the 1830s, when

departure as well. When Columbus sailed to America in 1492, there were Jews on board. When the Dutch colonized the isle of Manhattan, there were Jews in the neighborhood. And when the French and English opened a fur trade with the tribes of the North American interior, there were Jews among them—even in the wilds of Wisconsin. There is no better illustration of the Jewish Diaspora's breathtaking scale than the fact that Jewish traders were in Wisconsin at a time when Indians vastly outnumbered whites and animal skins were the preferred medium of exchange.

Jacob Franks was the first. In the early 1790s, when the region was nominally under American control, this English-born Jew found his way to Green Bay, a French-speaking sub-capital of the fur trade. After clerking for others, the fur trade was fading as fast as the beaver that supported it, Wisconsin was taking on a new identity as part of America's breadbasket. The territory attracted thousands of Yankees who were searching for new fields to replace the tired soils of the settled East, and Milwaukee, with the best natural harbor on Lake Michigan's western shore, was the region's leading urban opportunity. The pioneers established not one but three settlements near the mouth of the Milwaukee River and proceeded to make their fledgling community the commercial capital of Wisconsin.

Years before those three settlements coalesced to form one city in 1846, the first European immigrants started to arrive. They were resoundingly, overwhelmingly German. Wisconsin opened to settlement at the very beginning of mass emigration from the German states, with predictable results. The trickle of the 1830s quickly became a flood, and by 1860 German families made up a majority of Milwaukee's population. They were Catholic, they were Lutheran, they were Christian Reformed, and they were Jewish. In 1850, when the city's population topped 20,000, roughly 70 families and perhaps 350 individuals were German Jews—hardly a multitude, but a significant beachhead.

When the first Germans sailed for Milwaukee, their homeland, strictly speaking, did not exist. The future Germany was a loose-knit confederation of principalities, free cities, and minor kingdoms until 1871, when Prussia forced a unification "through blood and iron." The Jewish experience in the various German states had been, more often than not, difficult. Jews were not allowed to marry each other without permission in some districts, and they were forced to pay a head tax

A bird's-eye view of Milwaukee in 1858, when the city was receiving immigrants by the thousands

Milwaukee Public Library

3

every time they entered a town in others. The Enlightenment marked a turn for the better, at least temporarily. In the 1700s, as science created a new way of knowing, a surge of rationalism entered the intellectual currents of western Europe, ultimately finding its way into the culture of the continent, including the German states. The result was a new regard for reason that tended to discourage blind prejudice.

One of the giants of the Enlightenment—sharing the limelight with such figures as Descartes, Voltaire, and Locke—was Moses Mendelssohn, a philosopher who managed to be both German and Jewish at the same time. In Mendelssohn's view, Judaism was less a way of life than a way of belief—"one historical manifestation," he wrote, of "the universal religion of reason." Hoping to broaden the common ground shared by German Christians and German Jews, Mendelssohn translated the Bible into German and stressed the underlying principles common to both faiths, including the unity of God and the immortality of the soul. As his fellow Jews experienced their own Enlightenment, or *Haskala*, they increasingly saw themselves, and were increasingly seen by others, as one denomination among many within the larger German fold. There were still vivid lines of demarcation, but the trend was clearly toward greater integration; when Jewish immigrants reached America in

Beer gardens multiplied as Milwaukee became America's most German city, and German Jews were an integral part of the immigrant community.

4

the mid-1800s, it was German they spoke, not the Yiddish of their ancestors.

The first Jewish Milwaukeeans, according to tradition, were the Shoyer brothers. Their names and even their number vary from one account to the next, but it is certain that Gabriel Shoyer entered the United States in 1844 and that his family was in Milwaukee no later than 1845— one year before the city was chartered. The Shoyers were not penniless newcomers like the Irish who were pouring into the New World or the eastern Europeans who would arrive later. They left Europe not because they had to but because they wanted to, and their activities in Milwaukee had a decidedly modern ring. Charles Shoyer was the city's first Jewish physician, some of his brothers were active in the fledgling community's first synagogues, and several Shoyers—Gabriel, Emanuel, William, Samuel, and Mayer— managed a successful family business. In all these particulars—their occupational choices, their religious activism, and their economic circumstances—the Shoyer family provided a template for much of what followed in Jewish Milwaukee.

Even the business they started fit a broader pattern. In part because other handcrafts were the exclusive province of Gentiles, European Jews had been plying the needle trades for generations, and that tradition survived the Atlantic crossing. In 1844 or 1845, Emanuel Shoyer went into business as a "merchant tailor" on N. Water Street, the frontier community's main commercial thoroughfare. He was not an instant success. When an 1845 fire destroyed two square blocks of businesses on Water

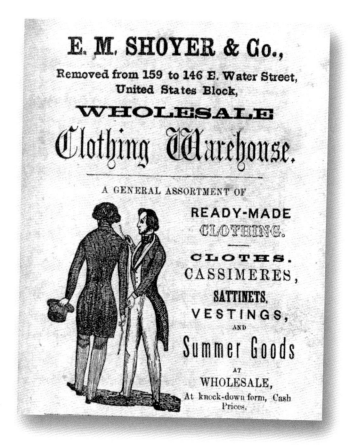

Street, including Shoyer's, his total loss was only $150. But the enterprise grew, providing a living for Emanuel and an opportunity for several of his brothers. In the 1854-1855 city directory, E.M. Shoyer & Co. advertised "A General Assortment of Ready-Made Clothing," as well as "all varieties of Hosiery, Gloves, Cravats, Stocks, Ties, Suspenders, Collars, Oiled Silks, Patent Shirts, [and] Ready-made Drawers." Some of those items were purchased from outside vendors and others produced by Shoyer's own work force, which numbered seventy people as early as 1850. Within a decade, Emanuel owned a fine home on the city's East Side and employed two

Emanuel Shoyer, a member of Milwaukee's first Jewish family, advertised his wares in the 1854-55 city directory.

Jewish Museum Milwaukee

David Adler & Sons
.....CLOTHING
.....COMPANY.
East Water and Huron Streets.
+ + MILWAUKEE.

Clothing magnate David Adler was the undisputed patriarch of the local Jewish community in its first generation.

Irish servants. Other Shoyers were doing just as well, and one of them was a walking advertisement for his family's products. Pioneer historian James Buck sketched a colorful portrait of Samuel Shoyer:

This well-remembered clothier and merchant tailor was noted for his sharpness in trade as well as his fine physique. He was a nobby boy. He generally wore a blue coat of the "claw-hammer" pattern, ornamented with the regulation brass buttons, a striped vest, drab pants, and in summer white ones, and a white fur hat. He was, in fact, the dude of the town.

The Shoyers may have been Milwaukee's first (and most fashionable) Jewish tailors, but they were not the largest for

long. Emigration from the German states accelerated through the 1840s and '50s, fed in part by a failed revolt against royal rule in 1848. The famed Forty-Eighters, many of them well-educated and all of them decidedly liberal, suffered exile for their assault on the established order, and Milwaukee became one of their American strongholds. Although few Jews had fought on the barricades in Baden or Berlin, many were openly sympathetic to the Forty-Eighters, and the general turbulence of the post-revolt years prompted others to leave. The seventy Jewish families who had settled in Milwaukee by 1850 swelled to perhaps 200 in the next decade. They included natives of Austria and Bohemia as well as the Teutonic states, but German was their common tongue.

The newcomers included the Adler and Friend families, both of whom established a Milwaukee presence before 1850. Like the Shoyers, they were bands of brothers seeking opportunity in the New World and, like the Shoyers, they instinctively sought it in the needle trades. Both would become, in time, the equivalent of royalty in the local Jewish community. David Adler, who had learned the baker's trade in Europe, crossed the Atlantic at the age of twenty-five and opened his own bakery in New York City. It was a success, but Adler soon developed, as one biographer put it, "a belief in the coming greatness of the west." In about 1851, he moved to Milwaukee, where his brother Solomon had settled a few years earlier. With $1,200 in profits from his bakery—roughly $35,000 in current dollars—David Adler rented a storefront on Water Street and began to sell men's clothing to the

general public. He expanded into the wholesale side a few years later and finally added manufacturing. In partnership with a shifting cast of brothers, sons, and a son-in-law, David Adler headed one of the largest clothing firms in the Midwest. During the Civil War (1861-1865), an order for 12,000 blue Union Army uniforms pushed annual sales to $600,000. David Adler himself was a ubiquitous figure in the city's Jewish community, serving as president of no fewer than three pioneer synagogues.

The Friend brothers—Henry, Elias, Meyer, Isaac, and Emanuel—followed much the same path. Their father had been a member of the king of Bavaria's bodyguard, but the brothers found a future in retail. After a sojourn in Montgomery, Alabama, Henry and Elias moved to Milwaukee in 1847 and opened yet another men's clothing store on Water Street. As more Friends joined the firm, they began to manufacture their own clothes in a

larger building on Broadway and Michigan Street. The brothers were the first in Milwaukee to use steam cutting machines, an innovation no doubt appreciated by their scissors-wielding employees. Those employees numbered 300 by 1870, when sales reached $175,000—the beginning of a growth spurt that would make the Friend family's enterprise even larger than the Adlers'.

Brothers Elias, Henry, and Isaac Friend (l. to r.) oversaw another clothing empire from a landmark building near the center of town.

FANCY DRY GOODS.

YANKEE NOTIONS & FURNISHING GOODS

369 H. S. MACK & COMPANY 371

Jewish Museum Milwaukee

*Herman Mack was
a prominent dry
goods merchant …*

In a city better known for beer and machinery, the clothing industry has traditionally been overlooked, but it was Milwaukee's second- or third-largest (by value added) in the mid-1800s—well ahead of brewing until 1880 and surpassed only by flour-milling and iron goods in previous census years. Although German Jews dominated the field, not every clothing manufacturer was Jewish, and not every Jew was a clothing manufacturer. The dry goods business—textile products and notions— attracted several newcomers, including the Mack brothers (Herman, Max, Lewis, and Hugo), the Landauers (Max and Adolph), and Henry Stern, who formed a rather unusual partnership with Julius Goll, a German-born Gentile. Other Jewish immigrants gravitated to a pair of frontier staples: tobacco and alcohol. Bernard Leidersdorf processed and sold both smoking and chewing tobacco, and Louis Rindskopf and his sons were distillers as well as importers of various liquors. (Rindskopf also attracted notice for his distinctively named daughters: Bella, Della, and Stella.) Some new arrivals practiced trades they had mastered in Europe, including optician Julius Lando, whose "scientific education," he claimed, ensured that his "Eye-Patients will … be served intelligently" with "large assortments of phylosophical and mathematical instruments." Others gained their expertise on American soil. Nathan Pereles, who had once clerked in a Prague seed store, launched a Milwaukee grocery business in 1847, became the city's first Jewish lawyer in 1857, and ended up as a leading private banker. The sheer variety of occupations prompted one *Milwaukee Sentinel* correspondent (December 28,

1874) to comment on the breadth of the local Jewish economy: "In this city, besides the few rich wholesale dealers in clothing, tobacco, dry goods and liquors, the majority of them are mechanics and hard-laboring men ... perhaps tailors, shoemakers, tinsmiths, soapmakers, butchers, blacksmiths and jewelers."

Diversity may have been the rule, but Jews showed an unmistakable preference for independent business. In a sample of eighteen immigrants who came to Milwaukee between 1845 and 1850 and lived in the city for at least five years, all eighteen were operating their own businesses in 1855, selling groceries, clothing, dry goods, liquor, tinware, and even ice, often in association with relatives. This intense focus on mercantile trade would cause some concern in later years. When the Jewish Alliance of America opened a Milwaukee branch in 1891, its leaders declared their intention to steer new immigrants away from "the more common pursuits of the Jewish people," i.e., business and commerce, and to "induce them to enter farming and industrial occupations." The pattern also fed an old (and evergreen) stereotype. In 1893, Sigmund Hecht, one of Milwaukee's leading nineteenth-century rabbis, blasted the prevailing prejudice that "every Jewish babe was born with a pair of scales in its hand and with a brain which, even in infancy, could reckon the interest tables."

The Jewish predisposition to business was the product not of genetics but of history. After experiencing the capriciousness and often the viciousness of their host societies for hundreds of years—the Spanish Inquisition and the English and French expulsion decrees come to mind—Europe's

Julius Lando, Optician,
436 EAST WATER STREET.
[KIRBY HOUSE BLOCK.]

Having had the benefit of a scientific education, he is enabled, to carry on his business himself and Eye-Patients will therefore be served intelligently. He has always large assortments of physiological and mathematical instruments. Eyeglasses of every description, Telescopes etc. on hand, constructs new instruments and makes changes and improvements in instruments to order. He inserts Artificial Eyes and does repairing at very low rates. By observation of strict and solid business principles this firm is enjoying a well deserved reputation throughout our city and its vicinity. Correspondence solicited.

...Julius Lando helped his patients read the fine print...

Milwaukee County Historical Society

... and Nathan Pereles was a prominent figure in both law and banking.

Jewish Museum Milwaukee

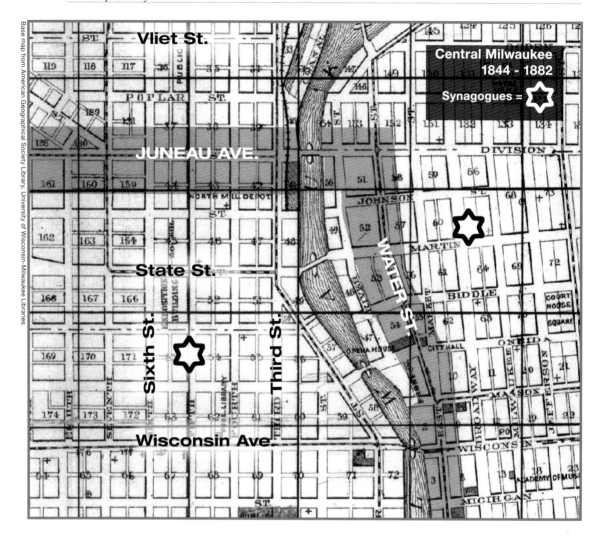

Base map from American Geographical Society Library, University of Wisconsin-Milwaukee Libraries

Jewish families were interspersed among Gentiles on both sides of the Milwaukee River, and their shops dotted the Juneau Ave. and Water St. business districts.

Jews had learned self-reliance the hard way. Some governments may have been paragons of tolerance and some neighbors the picture of kindness, but never for very long. There was always the threat of confiscatory taxes, irrational edicts, and even death. The Jews of Christian Europe could, in the end, trust no one but themselves. Small wonder, then, that so many started businesses of their own, often on a shoestring. In fields like the garment industry, start-up costs were low, demand was constant, and even the younger children in a family could contribute their labor. And if the business grew, who better to trust for additional help than brothers and sisters, daughters and sons? In a world that offered a bare minimum of opportunity, going into business offered maximum control, maximum independence, and the chance to take maximum advantage of the close family ties that have always been a cornerstone of Jewish life.

And so the descendants of the farmers and shepherds who populate the Bible became shopkeepers and tradesmen in Europe—a pattern that swelled to gigantic proportions in the United States. America was like a hothouse, and in that hothouse—free, for the first time, from blight and depredation—the transplanted Jewish families blossomed with astounding vigor. Newcomers who had scraped by as peddlers in the Old World rose to the leadership of large dry goods houses, and siblings who had stitched clothing together by lamplight in their own homes eventually ran entire garment factories. From small to large, from darkness to light, the pattern would be repeated again and again through the nineteenth century and well beyond.

The pattern found specific geographic expression in Milwaukee. In the mid-1800s, the city's principal business districts were located along Water Street east of the Milwaukee River and, on a somewhat smaller scale, along Juneau Avenue on the West Side. The city's Jewish businesses were split almost evenly between east and west, as were Jewish residences. The east-west split would become problematic in later years, but it signaled an early and egalitarian mixing of German Jews with German Christians and, to a lesser extent, with Yankee Protestants.

The pioneers had indeed planted well. No less a figure than Isaac Mayer Wise, the guiding light of Reform Judaism in America, declared that Milwaukee's Jews were off to a most promising start, particularly in economic terms. Based in Cincinnati, Wise traveled the country to build support for the Reform movement, and his newspaper, *The Israelite* (August 22, 1856), published a glowing account of the rabbi's first trip to Milwaukee:

Milwaukee Public Library

The condition of our Jewish brethren is so far a happy one, that none of them is actually poor or subsisting on charity, many of them do an extensive business in real estate, grain, cattle, provision, dry goods, clothing, groceries, &c. &c., and there is no small number of wealthy men among the two hundred families of Israelites living there.... Almost every one owns some real estate and therefore they contribute largely to the rise of the city. This is universally acknowledged, and the Jews are respected as industrious, peaceful and law abiding citizens.

Water Street was the heart of Milwaukee's downtown.

"The Israelitish Congregations"

Even before they were established in business, the industrious German Jews of Milwaukee had established a foundation for their faith. In 1847, according to legend, twelve adult males (two more than the minyan, or prayer quorum, of ten) met to observe Yom Kippur—the highest of the High Holy Days—in Isaac Neustadtl's grocery store on Fourth and Juneau. Neustadtl would soon become one of the community's leading liberals, supporting the refugees of 1848, serving as an alderman, and helping to found both the German-English Academy and the Milwaukee Musical Society. When Yom Kippur rolled around the next year, the gathering was hosted by merchant tailor Henry Newhouse, presumably at his new house on Jefferson Street, east of the river. True to a pattern that held the world over, the immigrants' first communal institution was a burial ground; in 1848 a cemetery association headed by pioneer Emanuel Shoyer purchased the now-neglected acre of land on Hopkins Street. This postage stamp of green space was not a major investment (and it lay more than a mile beyond the northern edge of settlement), but its purchase was Jewish Milwaukee's earliest collective act. Yom Kippur moved back to the West Side in 1849, when Nathan Pereles, not yet a lawyer, welcomed guests to his grocery store on Juneau Avenue. After three years of informal worship, the group was finally ready to organize, and in 1850 the congregation of Imanu-Al came into existence. The name itself—"God is with us"—was a confident statement of arrival in the New World and a new city.

From that time forward, the story of Milwaukee Judaism was a tale of devotion and division. The immigrants were serious about their faith—so serious that disagreements regarding rite and ritual soon splintered the original congregation. In 1854, Ahabath Emuno ("Love of Faith") broke off from Imanu-Al, and one year later Anshe Emeth ("Men of Truth") broke off from Ahabath Emuno. There were now three congregations of German Jews, none with a rabbi and only one (Imanu-Al) with even a modest synagogue, serving a community of just 200 families—hardly a model of cooperation or efficiency.

Isaac Mayer Wise, the Reform leader, was appalled. Milwaukee's Jews may have been thriving economically, but they had fallen apart religiously, and Wise resolved to bring them back together. In a second dispatch to *The Israelite* (August 29, 1856), the renowned rabbi described the forceful message he delivered from the pulpit of Imanu-Al:

Isaac Mayer Wise, the prime mover of Reform Judaism in America, had a formative influence on Milwaukee's pioneer congregations.

Jewish Museum Milwaukee

"I turned my face into a rock," and argued without fear against the existing evils which require immediate remedy from the hands of our brothers. As severely as I attacked the impertinence and wickedness of atheism, I also rebuked the benumbed and senseless conservatism which not only gives birth to atheism, but also tears into fractions the house of Israel, so that they can not oppose their foes either by words or actions.

I.M. Wise was an unusually persuasive figure—so persuasive, in fact, that he became the Moses of Milwaukee Judaism. Wise practically shamed two of the congregations into a reconciliation, and in October 1856—just in time for the Day of Atonement (Yom Kippur)—Imanu-Al and Ahabath Emuno joined forces as B'ne Jeshurun ("Sons of the Upright"). The "new" group, seventy families strong, worshiped in Imanu-Al's little temple on Fourth and State.

The mainstream press, which regularly printed news of "the Israelitish congregations," had been paying attention. Without commenting on the recent divisions, the *Milwaukee Sentinel* (October 9, 1856) published a surprisingly perceptive, and surprisingly sympathetic, story in connection with B'ne Jeshurun's inaugural Yom Kippur:

> *To-day the Hebrew population of this city, and of all other cities and places, will close their shops and their stores; prayer and supplication will take the place of traffic and trade; their places of business will be deserted....*
>
> *While many of the holidays of the Hebrews may be forgotten or neglected—the New Year, the Passover, the Weekly Sabbath, the Feast of the Tabernacle and others—a neglect of the day of Atonement is never thought of. It has been truly said, that the most unbelieving Jew—he whose faith has waxed faint amid the strife of worldly passion, and whose conscience is hushed and stilled by the war of traffic—yet remembers for a time that he belongs to the chosen people, when the season of penitence, of fasting and of prayer rolls around.*
>
> *And to-day, as we notice through our city, the closed stores of the Hebrew population of Milwaukee, let no jeer or slur curl the lips, but in harmony with the Christian Religion itself, knowing that one is founded on the other, and that each is teaching to the human race the great lesson of universal charity, let us not forget from what race sprang the people who fill their synagogues this day, but remember what they once were, how they once trod the earth, the chosen people of God.*
>
> *When the Declaration of Independence was launched, bigotry sank in its wake....*

The remnant of the chosen who made up B'ne Jeshurun turned next to the selection of a rabbi, and in April 1857 Isidor Kalisch took the pulpit. Kalisch, a German-trained scholar of some reputation, had been recruited through the pages of *The Israelite,* and he reflected Isaac Mayer Wise's brand of Reform Judaism. Although relatively moderate by later standards, the rabbi was decidedly more liberal than his congregation—a pattern that would be repeated time and again in the synagogues of America. Isidor Kalisch introduced such novelties as weekly sermons, confirmation classes,

Jewish Museum Milwaukee

*Isidor Kalisch,
Milwaukee's first rabbi,
led Congregation B'ne
Jeshurun in its new
home on Fifth St.*

Jewish Museum Milwaukee

THE OLD TEMPLE BNE JUSHURUN.

a choir, and mixed-gender seating. Each prompted its share of grumbling, but all were ultimately accepted. Unity, in fact, was the prevailing standard for long enough to bring Anshe Emeth into the fold. In 1859, during pioneer Gabriel Shoyer's tenure as president, Anshe Emeth merged into B'ne Jeshurun. Milwaukee now had one congregation with a membership of 115 families—a substantial majority of the 200 who resided in the city.

It was perhaps no accident that the merger occurred just as B'ne Jeshurun was starting construction of a new synagogue. It stood on Fifth Street between Kilbourn and Wells—barely a block from the group's old home on Fourth and State. The wisdom of one temple for everyone was compelling, and any lingering tensions seemed to have dissipated by the time the 400-seat synagogue was dedicated in September 1859. Rabbi Kalisch spoke for over an hour in German, and Isaac Mayer Wise followed in English. The Cincinnati sage wrote later that the new temple was a powerful instrument of unification:

> *The few hyper-orthodox who are dissatisfied take too much pride in the new temple which is free of debt, and feel too profoundly the benefit of union, that they should think of separation. Their number is too small to form a congregation, and so they will submit.*

Although unity prevailed, prosperity did not. The Panic of 1857—a deep recession in modern parlance—had ushered in a period of general belt-tightening, and a full-time rabbi began to seem like an extravagance. When Isidor Kalisch's three-year contract expired in 1860, it was not renewed. A *Sentinel* correspondent (May 10, 1860) offered a parting wish for Milwaukee's first rabbi: "May another city, in better pecuniary circumstances, acknowledge our loss by giving him a support, and afford him a greater sphere of action, so that he many never be in trouble as to his earning a living."

B'ne Jeshurun was without a regular rabbi for the next three years. Congregational officers and a part-time cantor led worship until 1863, when Samson Falk left a post in Albany, New York, to take charge of the Milwaukee flock. He represented the "modern phase" of American Judaism through the trying years of the Civil War—a conflict that transcended all religious divisions. Following Abraham Lincoln's assassination in 1865, Falk preached what the *Milwaukee Sentinel* called "an able sermon … upon the life and labors of our late President." Although he was offered a new contract, Samson Falk left the city in 1866, starting

another interregnum that lasted until Elias Eppstein was hired in 1869.

Unity was maintained through B'ne Jeshurun's first decade, but fault lines had been developing beneath the surface. As the local economy matured, there was a widening gap between the richest Milwaukeeans and their less-affluent neighbors. The East Side attracted an increasing share of the city's wealth, and the pattern held true for Jews and Gentiles alike; it seemed natural for the Adlers and the Friends, for instance, to live east of the river. The economic and geographic fault lines were increasingly obvious, but they were probably less conspicuous than a religious split. From its very first days as a congregation, B'ne Jeshurun had been a somewhat uneasy alliance of Jews who aggressively favored liturgical reform—the faster the better—and those who maintained a fondness for the older forms of worship. The upwardly mobile East Siders were in the vanguard of reform,

Jewish Museum Milwaukee

Jewish Museum Milwaukee

Rabbis Samson Falk (l.) and Elias Eppstein followed Kalisch in B'ne Jeshurun's pulpit.

Jewish Museum Milwaukee

B'ne Jeshurun's most liberal (and most affluent) members left in 1869 to form Temple Emanu-El. Their new home on Broadway was one of Milwaukee's architectural showplaces.

and their West Side brethren favored the more traditional path.

In the end, a divorce was the only solution to the quandary, and no words from Rabbi Wise could prevent it. On August 22, 1869, B'ne Jeshurun voted to split in two. The West Siders retained the name and the temple, and the East Siders received $4,250 for their share of the property. David Adler, who had been the first president of pioneer congregation Imanu-Al, was president of B'ne Jeshurun at the time of the split, and he was the obvious choice to lead the thirty-five families who broke away. They called

themselves Emanu-El. The choice echoed the affirmation implicit in the name of the city's first temple, but it could also have been read as a somewhat defiant assertion. "God is with us," the departing members declared, and not, by implication, with the Jews across the river. Emanu-El's leaders saw themselves as the bearers of a new Judaism firmly planted in the New World. From the very beginning, all temple business was conducted exclusively in English.

And so matters would stand for the next fifty-eight years: two congregations, one east of the river and one west, both dominated by

16

German Jews but different enough to remain determinedly separate. The division was soon expressed in bricks and mortar. Emanu-El worshiped in a rented hall at first, but in 1870 the congregation bought a lot on the northeast corner of Broadway and State Street. On June 15, 1871, hundreds of Milwaukeeans, including the city's leading Masons, gathered to lay the cornerstone for a new temple on the site. Rabbi Max Lilienthal, a Reform leader from Cincinnati, was the orator of the day. Lilienthal made it perfectly clear that Emanu-El's new home would represent a new stage in the evolution of Judaism:

> *It will not be an old synagogue, with its obsolete ceremonies and antiquated customs. It will be a temple in the sense and spirit of modern and reformed Judaism. It will be an edifice in which the common Fatherhood of God and the common Brotherhood of man will be taught and preached....*
>
> *Judaism has broken the old rusty shackles; it has cheerfully surrendered all antiquated ideas; it considers it to be its supreme duty, to reconcile religion with the progressive ideas of our age, and to bring it in full harmony with the demands made either by science or the modern state.*

Lilienthal closed his address with a stout declaration of Jewish patriotism and a somewhat gratuitous slap at the nation's proto-Zionists:

> *Oh, how we Israelites love this country, as our home and the sweet home of our children! How we revere that star-spangled banner as the Heaven-born emblem of human happiness and liberty! Thankfully and cheerfully we have given up all ideas of ever returning to Palestine; we say with the Psalmist: "This is our resting place; here we shall reside, for we love it dearly and sincerely." Thankfully have we given up all sectarian education; we send our children to our free schools, the pride of our country, the bulwarks of our common liberties; for we wish them to be first Americans and then Israelites....*

After fourteen months of construction activity, Temple Emanu-El was formally dedicated on August 30, 1872. Milwaukee had never seen anything quite like it. Designed by local architect Matthew Sheard, the new synagogue was built of Milwaukee brick—a pale yellow variety that gave the Cream City its nickname. The exterior featured a gracefully gabled roofline and a full complement of stained-glass windows, while the interior was a study in black walnut and white oak, illuminated by a hundred gaslights. The center of attention was, of course, the gilded and painted ark that enshrined the Torah scroll. "Inside and out," wrote the *Evening Wisconsin* (August 31, 1872), "it is considered the most tasteful church structure in the city." Emanu-El also added a new element to Milwaukee's religious mix. The temple's back-lot neighbor was a Welsh Congregational church, and German Catholic, German Lutheran, and Yankee Protestant congregations all stood within a few blocks.

Temple Emanu-El was consecrated on August 30, 1872.

Jewish Museum Milwaukee

B'ne Jeshurun was forced to rebuild its temple in 1872, but the only photographs of the building date from its later use as a sheet metal shop.

The members of B'ne Jeshurun, in the meantime, were building a new synagogue of their own. The choice, however, was not entirely theirs. The original temple on Fifth Street was "not as substantially constructed as it should have been," in the understated words of the *Milwaukee Sentinel* (July 20, 1872), "and recently its walls gave evidences of an impending crash." Rather than risk being buried in rubble, the faithful moved to rented quarters and proceeded to erect a new temple on the site of the old. Designed by the local firm of Koch and Hess, it was "plain but pleasing," according to the *Sentinel*, with an arched ceiling and a central stained-glass window. B'ne Jeshurun's new

home was dedicated on September 19, 1872, just three weeks after Emanu-El occupied its Broadway temple.

With two sparkling new synagogues on opposite sides of the river, chances of a reconciliation between B'ne Jeshurun and Emanu-El were more distant than ever. The schism was cast in concrete, and the new temples spoke volumes about their respective congregations. B'ne Jeshurun's edifice cost $18,000 and seated 400, while Emanu-El's was built for $60,000—more than $1 million in current dollars—and provided room for 800. Although the Jews of the West Side were hardly impoverished, it was Emanu-El's members who were typically described as "the most influential Israelites of the city" and "one of the richest societies in the Northwest."

Emanu-El's affluence reflected the rapid expansion of the local economy after the Civil War. Enterprises launched in the 1840s and '50s reached new heights of prosperity in the postwar period, and even the Panic of 1873 couldn't slow them down for long. The Friends and the Adlers, who practically took turns in the president's chair at Emanu-El, were Milwaukee's first- and second-largest manufacturers of men's clothing by 1880. As the prejudice against ready-made garments faded, the Friend Brothers Clothing Company watched its sales soar to $800,000 in 1880—more than $16 million in current dollars—and its employment reach the 600 mark. The comparable benchmarks for David Adler & Sons were $675,000 in sales and a work force of 500. The Landauer brothers, Max and Adolph, parlayed their pre-war dry goods success into an enterprise that grossed $875,000 in 1881. There were newcomers like Adolph W. Rich, who opened a dry goods store in 1867, branched out into the manufacture of corsets and hoop skirts, and soon became a force in women's clothing and finally in footwear. Other entrepreneurs entered fields the first generation hadn't even considered. Henry Benjamin became the city's leading coal dealer in the 1870s, Philip Carpeles ran a successful traveling trunk factory, Benjamin Weil was a major figure in local real estate, and the Leopold family made waves in Great Lakes shipping circles. Each and every one of these business leaders belonged to Emanu-El, and the Jewish community's weight shifted steadily from West Side to East.

Shortly after the 1869 split, B'ne Jeshurun had a membership of 80 families and Emanu-El counted only 40. By 1875, the rolls stood at 72 for the West Siders and 75 for their brethren east of the river.

The distinctions extended even to the grave. When the congregation divided in 1869, B'ne Jeshurun must have retained the Hopkins Street burial ground, for in 1873 members of Emanu-El established a second Jewish cemetery: Greenwood, on the outer limits of Milwaukee's South Side. A committee led by the ever-present David Adler purchased ten acres of wooded land across the road from Forest Home Cemetery. The choice of locations was revealing.

Emanu-El attracted the city's most prominent Jews, including dry goods magnate Max Landauer and the entire Adler family.

19

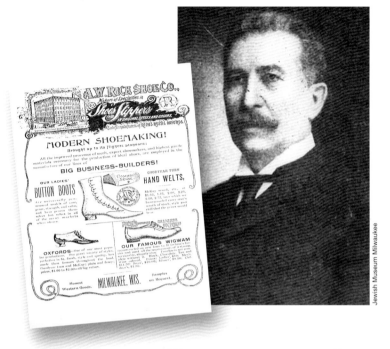

Adolph Rich (top) in shoes and Benjamin Weil in real estate were two more Emanu-El members who rose to civic prominence.

Established in 1850 by St. Paul's Episcopal Church, Forest Home was Milwaukee's most prestigious burial ground, and it would become the final address of more brewers, bankers, industrialists, and political leaders than any other cemetery in the state. Just as Emanu-El had built its temple a few blocks west of the city's elite neighborhood—Yankee Hill—its leaders placed Greenwood Cemetery next to the city's elite graveyard. Henry Friend, the senior brother in Friend Brothers Clothing Company, was one of Greenwood's founders. In 1875, when the steamship *Schiller* went down off the coast of England, he tragically became one of Greenwood's first burials. The bodies of Friend and his wife, Franziska, were recovered and laid to rest in the new graveyard. Across the road in Forest Home Cemetery stood an even larger monument to another victim of the *Schiller* tragedy: brewer Joseph Schlitz.

Although their economic differences were obvious, B'ne Jeshurun and Emanu-El were hardly armed camps. In matters of ritual, in fact, the distinctions between them were less a matter of kind than of degree. Rabbis Elias Eppstein, who served the West Side temple from 1869 to 1880, and Moritz Spitz, who held the East Side pulpit from 1872 to 1879, both preached alternately in English and German, generally using the first language at 7:30 on Friday evening and the second at 10:00 on Saturday morning. Both congregations offered full Sunday school programs. (Jeshurun adopted a schoolbook on Biblical history authored by Rabbi Eppstein himself.) Both favored mixed-gender seating, high-caliber choirs accompanied by organs, and a certain level of decorum. Although worship was their main reason for being, both temples were also centers of social life, often in conjunction with fund-raising efforts for Jewish charities. Emanu-El showed a preference for higher-brow entertainment, like the 1878 benefit featuring a Shakespearean "elocutionist" who performed—on the same evening—the witches' scene from *Macbeth*, the graveyard soliloquy from *Hamlet*, and King Henry's lamentation from *Richard III*, with organ interludes. B'ne Jeshurun was widely known for its Purim masquerade ball, a spectacle held every year at the West Side Turner Hall, with coveted prizes for the best costumes.

Rabbi Eppstein of B'ne Jeshurun stressed the underlying unity of Milwaukee's two congregations in an 1877 sermon: "Within Judaism no differences of opinion can arise, because in itself it is only an essence—an idea, for he who believes in one God—who adheres to the monotheistic idea—is an Israelite whether he belongs to the reformed or the orthodox camp." But there were differences nonetheless. The West Siders celebrated Rosh Hashanah for two days, and their New Year services lasted for three hours. The East Siders limited themselves to one day and a single ninety-minute service. The West Siders adopted Isaac Mayer Wise's *Minhag America* as their prayer book, while the East Siders used the less traditional version developed by Temple Emanu-El of New York. The West Side temple required male worshipers to wear their yarmulkes (skullcaps) long after its counterpart across the river had banned the practice in 1870. Emanu-El outlawed the tallit, or prayer shawl, three years later—even for its presiding rabbi.

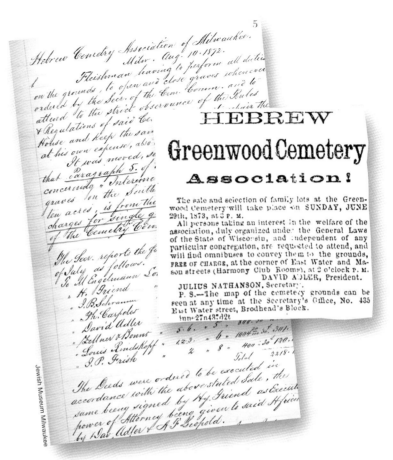

Jewish Museum Milwaukee

Greenwood Cemetery became the final home of Milwaukee's Jewish elite.

If there had been such a movement in the 1870s, B'ne Jeshurun might well have been in the Conservative camp. Emanu-El, by contrast, was clearly in the vanguard of Reform Judaism. Rabbi Moritz Spitz blasted the "insipidness" and "antique dullness" of inherited Jewish tradition in 1875, insisting that the ancient religion had turned over a new leaf in the New World:

We have adopted the American way of thinking. We have Americanized ourselves in our families, in our social circles, in our congregations. The shadow of medieval ages has vanished

Jewish Museum Milwaukee

Rabbi Moritz Spitz
with an Emanu-El
confirmation class
in the 1870s

from our midst. Servility is not rec-
ognizable in us any more, and
timidity has disappeared to be one
of the prominent characteristics of
our race. Even our temples are no
more dark, repulsive, small and
insignificant structures, but beauti-
ful, grand and imposing edifices.
The barrier that had separated the
Israelite from society no longer
exists. We are amalgamated with
the great American people of which
we are justly proud.

Although he was proud to be an American, Spitz was just as proud to be a Jew;
assimilation, in his view, did not mean
abandoning tradition. In an 1875 sermon, the rabbi drew a pointed distinction between the major figure of his faith
and the founder of Christianity:

All efforts of Moses tend toward con-
version of men into good men, while Jesus
aims at making of angels. Moses would
bring down the blessings of heaven to us,
to Jesus it seemed far better to lift this
earth to heaven. According to Moses, this
life is to become more and more beautiful,
because it is of God. With Jesus it is a
curse softened only by the expectation of
the future world.

Let us be what Moses has been—let
Christians be what Christ has been.

What Rabbi Spitz and the people of
Emanu-El sought was a blend of cultural
assimilation and religious continuity that
may have been possible only in America.
Reform-minded synagogues elsewhere in
the country were moving in the same direction. In 1873, under the guidance of the
ubiquitous Isaac Mayer Wise, they all came

together in the Union of American Hebrew Congregations. Emanu-El was prominent enough in the Union to bring the group's 1878 national convention to Milwaukee. The gathering was the first at which East Coast congregations joined forces with the Midwesterners and Southerners who had started the organization. Hailed as "the first real united council of American Israelites," the meeting reached its high point at a sumptuous Plankinton House banquet. As guests feasted on broiled young grouse with currant jelly and glazed calves' sweetbreads a la Macedoine, speaker after speaker extolled the virtues of unity. Emanu-El's leaders were highly visible as hosts; B'ne Jeshurun's were conspicuous by their absence.

"United upon the Rock of Charity"

There were, by actual count, 2,068 Jewish Milwaukeeans in 1875. Elias Eppstein, in addition to his rabbinical duties at B'ne Jeshurun, had undertaken a complete census of the city's Jews, and he unearthed some interesting facts. The average family size was 4.8 people in 1875, 514 children were old enough to attend school, and there was not a single Milwaukee Jew in the poorhouse. The largest number of citizens—864—had been born in the United States, but most of them were undoubtedly children of German-speaking immigrants.

Perhaps the most interesting conclusion of the survey was one Eppstein didn't draw. The combined membership of Milwaukee's two congregations in 1875 was just under 150 families, or approximately 720 individuals—only 35 percent of the total Jewish population. Belonging to a synagogue, in other words, was a minority practice in Milwaukee. That didn't mean that the other 65 percent of Milwaukee's Jews had abandoned their faith. Both temples were often filled to overflowing during the High Holy Days, and one local baker sold three tons of matzos—the unleavened bread associated with the ancient Jews' hasty departure from Egypt—during the 1871 Passover season. Although many remained observant (at least twice a year), there were definite obstacles to formal synagogue membership. High pew rents kept some people away. Both B'ne Jeshurun and Emanu-El supported their temples with a three-tiered system of annual dues, and the largest contributors always had their pick of the pews. The top of the scale at Emanu-El was $160 in 1876—more than $3,000 in current dollars and enough to cast a definite chill on lukewarm believers.

Other Jews avoided the synagogue on principle. The liberal Forty-Eighter strain in Milwaukee's German culture found expression in any number of schools, cultural groups, Turner societies, and freethinker congregations. The movement's leaders espoused the rationalism, the religious universalism, and sometimes even the atheism of their various Enlightenment heroes. A small but influential number of German Jews were active in the movement, among them Isaac Neustadtl, the pioneer grocer who had hosted Milwaukee's inaugural Yom Kippur in 1847. Neustadtl traded his ancestral Judaism for what he considered a more progressive view of the world.

The conflicting currents met in a memorable 1876 debate at the Academy of Music. The disputants were Solomon Sonnenschein, a Reform rabbi visiting from St. Louis, and Fritz Schuetz, speaker of the local Freie Gemeinde, or freethinker assembly. Sonnenschein, who

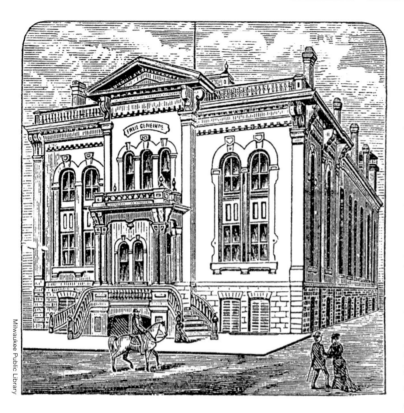

Freethinkers' Hall was a center of resistance to all forms of organized religion.

up the evening neatly: "The discussion, never very cheerful, became painfully dreary after 11 o'clock."

Milwaukee's Jewish residents had a much broader range of organizational choices than the synagogue and the freethinker hall. Whether they were formally religious, formerly religious, or somewhere in between, Jews with a joining instinct had an impressive number of options. Some organizations were charitable and others strictly fraternal, but all transcended the major religious differences and expressed another dimension of Jewishness. Charity came first. The ancient injunction to care for the poor was heard early in Milwaukee, and it was women, in typical fashion, who answered the call. Soon after Congregation Anshe Emeth was established in 1855, the women of the temple formed the Deborah Ladies' Hebrew Benevolent Society. The more broadly based Benevolent Association of True Sisters followed within a year or two; in 1858 the group sponsored a winter masquerade ball to raise funds for its projects. Both organizations showed particular concern for widows, orphans, and other "deserving poor." Not every Milwaukee Jew was an Adler or a Friend. In the absence of adequate public welfare programs, families could be reduced to poverty practically overnight if their breadwinners were killed or injured. The demand for private charity was always greatest in winter, when donations of food, fuel, and rent money could mean the difference between life and death. But the ladies did not limit their compassion to fellow Jews. When the excursion steamer *Lady Elgin* went down in 1860 with a loss of nearly 300 lives, many of them Irish residents of Milwaukee's Third Ward, the True Sisters donated $25 "for the relief of the sufferers."

had come north to preach at Emanu-El, tried to establish his own rationalist credentials early in the discussion. He believed in the Bible, the rabbi said, but not literally: "There is in the Bible both diamonds and glass, and reason decides between them." Schuetz rejected any hint of a connection between the divine word and reason. Every human being, he declared, was "a mere speck on the ocean of time" who had evolved from matter and would return to matter. "It is," Schuetz said, "a glorious view to see this evolution and follow it up from the human being to human thought." Both men quoted liberally from German savants, particularly Goethe, before a largely German audience. After several hours of intellectual tennis, however, the volleys began to lose force. The *Milwaukee Sentinel* (February 8, 1876) summed

When yellow fever ravaged Memphis, Tennessee, in 1873, the group sent $100 south to aid relief efforts.

In his groundbreaking 1875 survey, Rabbi Elias Eppstein counted eight "benevolent associations" in the Jewish community, both charitable and fraternal, and men were just as involved as women. The largest charity was the Hebrew Relief Society, which embodied a proud tradition of self-help. When its leaders, Aaron Leopold and David Adler, appealed for support in 1878, they stressed the all-Jewish nature of the effort:

> It has been characteristic of our race, and we have received the applause of the community at large for our disinterested acts of charity, and more especially for always caring for our poor and indigent. It is desirable that we should keep on in this good labor, and show by our deeds that while we may differ in our opinions as to dogmas, be they orthodox or reformed, we do stand united upon the rock of charity and benevolence.

Its size and influence made the Hebrew Relief Society the only group in town that could bring some order to the scatter-shot approach of Jewish charities. In 1880, the society proposed new policies that indicated some unhappy experiences with the not-so-deserving poor:

> All application for relief shall be made to one source where charity will be dispensed with uniformity according to the condition and character of the applicant, and not bestow the most upon the one that understands begging the best, as is now frequently the case; to discriminate against the so-called professional beggars, who are too indolent and too lazy to care for their own support, and who prefer to trust to Providence, and to their benevolent co-religionists than to use their own energies for the purpose of elevating themselves to a higher sphere of life than perpetual pauperism, and who make it a point to always get all they can wherever they can.

Organizational politics prevented a truly coordinated effort, but the Hebrew Relief Society made certain, in the meantime, that the Jewish poor were "relieved from immediate destitution, and aided, if possible, to improve their condition in life."

Although freeloading may have been an occasional problem, "professional beggars" were vastly outnumbered by Jews who believed devoutly in self-help and in helping each other. Long before health insurance and Social Security appeared on the horizon, most American immigrant groups formed mutual benefit societies to provide assistance their government did not, and Jews were active in the movement. In 1868, for instance, a group of West Siders established the Bikur Cholim ("Visiting the Sick") society "to afford relief to their members in sickness or distress, to contribute the expenses for burying their dead, and to furnish aid to their widows and orphans." Mutual benefit societies like Bikur Cholim were, in effect, alliances of the self-insured; their members pooled individual resources to prevent catastrophe from overwhelming any one of them.

Established to aid the indigent, the Hebrew Relief Society became Milwaukee's leading Jewish charity.

Milwaukee Sentinel, Nov. 15, 1880

The B'nai B'rith fraternal order stood for "Benevolence, Brotherly Love, and Harmony."

mutual benefit societies or direct aid, Jewish welfare efforts embodied a belief in mutual support and mutual obligation that outsiders came to recognize as one of the community's hallmarks.

A larger class of organizations combined good works with good times. The grandfather of the bunch was B'nai B'rith ("Sons of the Covenant"). Founded by the German Jews of New York City in 1843, B'nai B'rith reached Milwaukee in 1861, when Gilead Lodge held its organizational meeting. Three more lodges followed: Isaac in 1866, Milwaukee in 1870, and Excelsior in 1872. All were part of a grand fraternal organization modeled after the Masons, with high-flown rhetoric and complex secret rituals. B'nai B'rith saw itself as a full-service institution, a sort of "secular synagogue" whose creed stressed "Benevolence, Brotherly Love, and Harmony" without once mentioning God or the Torah. There were tangible advantages to membership in B'nai B'rith. Not only did the order provide burial benefits, but it even provided a burial ground. In 1876, Gilead Lodge opened Spring Hill Cemetery just beyond the city's western limits, sandwiched between Calvary (the last stop for most Milwaukee Catholics) and the graveyard for Union veterans at the National Soldiers Home. By 1884, after only eight years of operation, Spring Hill had a total of 180 burials, compared with 225 at Greenwood and 400 in the old Hopkins Street cemetery.

B'nai B'rith buried the dead, but it was much more interested in serving the living. The order's Midwestern lodges focused their philanthropic energies on a single pet

Even those without resources to pool trusted in group solidarity. Although the city provided its poor with modest supplies of firewood and food, Jewish indigents were reluctant to accept even those. Aaron Leopold described an attitude his Hebrew Relief Society volunteers encountered on a daily basis: "Their experience has been that Israelites as a class held conscientious scruples against applying for aid from the poor department. They preferred the kind consideration of their brethren in the faith." Whether they took the form of project: the Hebrew Orphan Asylum in Cleveland. Established in 1868, the orphanage ultimately housed 500 children, not all of them Jewish. Milwaukee usually had orphans at the home, and the city's Jews provided both officers (including David Adler) and funds. With essential help from the women in their families, members of B'nai B'rith organized a continuing round of Orphan Asylum benefits. The *Milwaukee Sentinel* (July 23, 1868) described one "Grand Fair" that practically took over City Hall for four days running:

> *The hall where our city fathers are wont to discuss the important questions of street-cleaning, dog-poisoning and contract-making, is now metamorphosed into a beautiful and brilliant temple of the aesthetic, horticultural and culinary arts. Seldom, if ever, have we seen at a like occasion such a profusion of the very choicest flowers, embroideries, lace and white goods, furniture and all kinds of wearing apparel, as meet the eyes of the lucky visitor wherever he may look. And how many are the chances to procure for a comparatively small sum of money a "nice piece of honey soap," a "bottle of cologne," a "sweet cake," all offered by the very handsomest of handsome young ladies.*

Although benevolence and burial benefits were part of its program, the heartbeat of B'nai B'rith was lodge night. Once a week, regardless of the weather, members of every lodge gathered for an evening of ritual and recreation. Lodge nights became, in time, weekly reunions of old and cherished friends. In 1874, after years

in makeshift quarters, the four Milwaukee lodges combined their funds and opened Covenant Hall in downtown Milwaukee as a common home. The dedication ceremony featured speeches in both English and German, followed by a picnic and dance at the Milwaukee Garden. Covenant Hall's location signified B'nai B'rith's status in the community. It stood on the corner of Water Street and Wisconsin Avenue—the epicenter of Milwaukee's business district. The four lodges had a combined membership of 300 in 1874, which was twice the number of adult males who paid dues to the city's two synagogues.

B'nai B'rith tended to attract the more mature members of the Jewish community. Another national organization with a local presence appealed to its youthful residents: the Young Men's Hebrew Association. Organized as a Jewish counterpart of the Young Men's Christian Association, the YMHA established a Milwaukee beachhead in 1883. Organizational meetings at Progress Hall drew up to 150 people, but unanimity did not prevail. One bylaws discussion consumed an entire evening without resolution. "Hunger and darkness finally brought the gentlemen to a realization of existing circumstances," reported the *Milwaukee Sentinel* (December 3, 1883), "and an adjournment was taken." The group finally adopted a rather lofty statement of purpose—"to develop, foster and promote the elevation of the moral,

Milwaukee Sentinel, July 21, 1868

One of the order's favorite causes was the Hebrew Orphan Asylum in Cleveland.

social, religious and intellectual position of the Israelites of the city of Milwaukee"—but there was still disagreement about the YMHA's priorities. When the rabbis in attendance suggested that religious work come first, the idea, wrote the *Sentinel*, "was quickly resented by the prime movers in the matter, who affirmed that religious matters were to be a secondary consideration with the association"—the same position taken by B'nai B'rith.

Steering well clear of the issues that already divided the community, the charter members considered any number of cultural and philanthropic proposals: a reading room and library, a home for the indigent, an employment bureau, and even a hospital. Those ideas came to nothing, but the YMHA did sponsor a series of well-attended lectures, musical programs, and dances. Nearly 500 people turned out for a "grand musical and literary entertainment" in 1884. The program's highlights included Liszt's *Hungarian Rhapsody,* an aria from Wagner's *Tannhauser*, an essay read by Emanu-El's rabbi, and a "comic recitation" contributed by theater impresario Leo Wachsner. Within a few months of its founding, the local chapter of the YMHA had nearly 100 members.

In the roster of organizations that rose from Jewish Milwaukee, there were some, finally, that made absolutely no pretense to civic benevolence, intellectual improvement, or higher social goals of any kind. As their fortunes grew, wealthier members of the community had more leisure to enjoy, and they preferred to enjoy it in each other's company. The Harmony Club was founded in 1866 as a haven for the Jewish elite. Its members outfitted rooms on N. Water Street that included a stage for

musical entertainment, a billiard room, a bar, and a well-appointed reception room. Reorganized more than once, the club remained faithful to the social mission of its well-to-do founders. The Progress Club, formed in 1877, drew from a similar stratum of West Siders, adding one more choice to the community's organizational menu. From the posh to the pedestrian and the sacred to the profane, Milwaukee's Jews had an abundance of activities that expressed their unity as well as their diversity.

German Jews or Jewish Germans?

It was hardly surprising that local Jews would develop their own social clubs, fraternal organizations, and private charities. Throughout American history, every ethnic group has established cultural institutions that reflected its specific outlook and interests. What is remarkable about the Milwaukee experience is that Jews participated fully in mainstream German organizations as well as their own. The fact that Milwaukee was the most German city in America had a formative impact on the fledgling metropolis, determining everything from its favorite beverage to its particular brand of politics. But beer and Socialism were not the only expressions of Milwaukee's Germanism. The preponderance of Teutonic names and faces provided an extra measure of security for other European groups, enabling them, within certain limits, to maintain strong and cohesive cultures. Yankees—those Americans of British stock who had migrated from the East—may have held political sway in the early decades, but they were a minority group; Milwaukee's English-speakers had

*From singing societies to
Turner gymnastic clubs,
German Milwaukee was
filled with organizational
choices, and German Jews
were full participants in
virtually all of them.*

to adjust to life in one of the most "foreign" cities in the country. Willard Glazier, author of *The Peculiarities of American Cities,* a popular Victorian travel guide, recorded his impressions of Milwaukee in 1884, when the German community was already nearly fifty years old:

> *No one who visits Milwaukee can fail to be struck with the semi-foreign appearance of the city. Breweries are multiplied throughout its streets, lager beer saloons abound, beer gardens, with their flowers and music and tree or arbor-shaded tables, attract the tired and thirsty in various quarters. German music halls, gasthausen, and restaurants are found everywhere, and German signs are manifest over many doors. One hears German spoken upon the streets quite as often as English, and Teuton influence upon the political and social life of the city is everywhere seen and felt.*

The most obvious quality of this colorful ethnic community was its diversity. Milwaukee's Germans were already divided among Catholics, Lutherans, Reformed Christians, and freethinkers—as well as the devoutly unchurched. In some respects, Jews were simply one more element in the broader Teutonic mix. But the liberal strain in Milwaukee's German population had special relevance for Jewish residents. Although the famed Forty-Eighters were relatively few in number, their pervasive cultural influence fostered an atmosphere of tolerance and intellectual openness. Passionately committed to equality, they helped to hold in check the anti-Semitism codified in the old German laws and presumably carried to America by less-enlightened newcomers. Just as Socialism would find fertile soil among the Germans, so did Judaism.

The evidence was everywhere. Jews tumbled with the Turners and sang in the Liedertafel and Liederkranz men's choruses. Jewish families sent their children to the German-English Academy. "News in German Circles," a regular *Milwaukee Sentinel* column, included coverage of Jewish social doings. The Stadt Theater, one of America's leading German stages, was managed for decades by Leon Wachsner, a German-born Jew. When David Adler, probably the city's most best-known Jew, lost his wife in 1880, the *Sentinel* eulogized her not as a prominent Jewish resident but as "an exemplary German mother." Adler himself was

B'ne Jeshurun's congregational minutes were written in German until 1906.

Jewish Museum Milwaukee

one of many Jews who belonged to mainstream fraternal orders as well as groups like B'nai B'rith. The clothing magnate served as treasurer of the Odd Fellows grand lodge in Wisconsin for decades, and scores of other Jews spent lodge night with the Masons, the Elks, and the Sons of Hermann—all of them German-speaking. In 1874, the Sons of Hermann sponsored a parade and picnic that attracted nearly 800 members of Milwaukee's Germanic fraternals, including the Odd Fellows, the Knights of Pythias, the Druids and, significantly, B'nai B'rith. The orator of the day was Rabbi Elias Eppstein of B'ne Jeshurun. Addressing a throng that represented a broad range of religious denominations, including his own, the rabbi gave an especially robust declaration of German, and German-American, cultural unity:

We are Germans by tongue; Germans by the will of reasoning our way onwards; Germans by the avowed determination to develop our mental faculties; Germans by the desire to seek knowledge and wisdom, and foster them; Germans by uniting in social life; and Germans by assisting each other in times of need…. [But] we wish not to express the idea to our fellow-citizens that we will remain Germans bound by the state. We are members of this great republic, and such we will remain; hundreds of our ranks have fallen upon the battlefield of the South, in order to support the government, and no doubt hundreds of

The Stadt (later Pabst) Theater was a national center of the German stage, and Leon Wachsner, a German-born Jew, managed the theater for decades.

Milwaukee County Historical Society

Distiller Samuel Rindskopf was a prominent politician as well as a leading businessman.

Palmer, a prominent Yankee attorney who would spend most of his career as president of Northwestern Mutual Life. When the synagogue was dedicated in 1872, one of the principal speakers was Rev. John Dudley, whose Plymouth Congregational Church was a bastion of Yankee Protestantism. "The Israelites were liberal enough to invite him," wrote the *Milwaukee Sentinel* (August 31, 1872), "and he was liberal enough to accept their invitation."

Jews also took an active part in the community's political life, particularly after the Civil War. Coal dealer Henry Benjamin, a popular West Side alderman, was elected Common Council president by his peers in 1874; Benjamin even served as acting mayor for several months when Harrison Ludington left the office to become Wisconsin's governor. Distiller Samuel Rindskopf contended seriously for a congressional seat in 1874. On the state level, real estate mogul Benjamin Weil, investor Jacob Friend, and grain merchant Moritz Becker all served in the Wisconsin Assembly. Although Milwaukee's Jews were never numerous enough to constitute a "Jewish vote," politicians were always quick to seek their favor. In 1880, when Emanu-El held a fair to eliminate the last $8,000 of its capital debt, Mayor Thomas Brown opened the festivities by showering praise on the synagogue:

> *At the corner of Broadway and Martin [State] streets stands a handsome edifice, a building of architectural beauty—a monument of masonry more substantial possibly than the temple of King Solomon—an ornament and glory to the city of Milwaukee.*

our ranks would this very day offer life and health to our adopted fatherland would it be necessary. We are Americans, but German Americans, who are willing to amalgamate the good which we have brought from Europe with the good which we found here.

The Sons of Hermann gathering demonstrated a high level of Jewish integration within the German community, and the same acceptance was apparent among the Yankees, who had learned early the value of getting along with their German fellow citizens, whether Gentiles or Jews. When Emanu-El laid the cornerstone of its new temple in 1871, the ceremony was performed by a contingent of Masons led by Henry

Another revealing sign of Jewish integration was the attitude of the English-language press. The *Milwaukee Sentinel*, the city's leading daily in the nineteenth century, provided generous and continuing coverage of events in the Jewish community. The full round of holidays, from Rosh Hashanah and Yom Kippur to Passover, was dutifully reported, often with Biblical citations, and sermons supplied by Milwaukee's rabbis were sometimes printed verbatim. (Emanu-El and B'ne Jeshurun generally received equal space.) Jewish balls, fairs, and other entertainments were previewed alongside those of the Caledonian Club, the Scandinavian Benevolent Society, and the full range of other ethnic organizations. Reporters who actually attended the events sometimes had surprising reactions. The *Sentinel* writer who covered a "Hebrew festival" at Turner Hall in 1865 seemed to have fallen in love: "Without at all disparaging our fair Christian readers, we can say that a more brilliant galaxy of female beauty has not shone in the Milwaukee firmament than was to be seen on this occasion."

Other stories read like dispatches from a foreign country, as reporters discovered the exotic in their own backyards. On April 6, 1884, for instance, and just in time for Passover, the *Sentinel* published a lengthy feature article about "a veritable matzos manufactory" on Walnut Street run by "a robust Hebrew" named Julius Kohn. Kohn turned out 25,000 pounds of the cracker-like matzo in a typical year, enough to supply Milwaukee and several adjoining states. The heart of the operation was a brick oven that finished the sheets in just two minutes:

A glance into the oven shows scores of the matzos, some just placed there, some beginning to harden and some whose slightly browned surfaces show they have been subjected to the heat long enough. Quickly two of them slide upon the empty shovel and are brought out crackling from their fiery sojourn. There is no time wasted by the perspiring workman; in and out, in and out go the long shovels and tirelessly the man watches his baking bread.

The finished sheets were carried to an upstairs room for storage:

And what a sight! Piled high to the ceiling, the room is two-thirds full of unleavened bread, and a workman is still further increasing the amount by basketful after basketful, just hot from the oven, which crackles sharply on being subjected to the cool atmosphere.

A decorative Seder Schussel *from the 1800s, used to hold matzos for the Passover meal*

Jewish Museum Milwaukee

There were occasional howlers in the mainstream press coverage. As reporters used phonetics to render unfamiliar terms, Yom Kippur became "Tom Kipoohr," and Rosh Hashanah appeared alternately as "Rosch Haschonoh" or "Roash Hashona." The Torah was likewise mangled to become the "Thora," and Bar Mitzvah appeared at least once as "armitsba." It was also common to confuse the Jewish Passover with the Christian Easter, yielding "the Jewish Easter." Misunderstandings aside, the coverage of the local Yankee press was uniformly positive. When both Milwaukee congregations built new synagogues in 1872, the *Sentinel* (July 20, 1872) used the occasion to congratulate its Jewish neighbors:

> *The Israelites of Milwaukee are numbered among our most respected and progressive citizens, and not without cause. Not a business enterprise, scheme for the amelioration of mankind, or movement for the social advancement of our people is without their support and influence. The city is, in fact, largely indebted to them for the proud position she holds to-day. With innate tact and discrimination they have rarely failed to accomplish their aims and large business houses, magnificent stocks, steamboat lines and elegant residences suggest themselves in proof of their indomitable spirit of enterprise.*

As welcome as such praise might have been, it did not prevent anti-Semitism from raising its ugly head on occasion. Milwaukee was, after all, part of Western society. A crass remark in a courtroom, a nasty letter to the editor, even a casual newspaper reference to "dark-eyed Rebeccas and hook-nosed Josephs" showed that the old prejudices had not perished. In nearly every case, Milwaukee's Jews moved quickly to parry the perceived insults and serve notice that America demanded a higher standard. In 1859, for instance, trial lawyer J.B. Cottrill, apparently seeking to discredit the testimony of a Jewish defendant, stated that "all Jews have been branded as thieves, liars and swindlers, by all civilized nations." A band of outraged Jews promptly gathered at Treat's Hall to "express their indignation" at the "grievous offences" of lawyer Cottrill. The group unanimously declared that "the Jews of Milwaukee will use all their efforts and influence against every one who may attempt to depreciate their rights, on account of their Religious faith, and that they will use all legal means to maintain their rights as citizens of this glorious Republic."

Perhaps the most novel anti-defamation case began with the gift of a book. In 1858, Rabbi Isidor Kalisch of B'ne Jeshurun sent an English copy of his Biblical commentary to President James Buchanan, who promptly acknowledged the present. Not long after, Buchanan referred to "all the nations of Christendom" in a message to Queen Victoria—an exclusionary remark that moved Rabbi Kalisch to write a letter of protest to his new-found correspondent. Remarkably, even in those long-gone days before press secretaries and media handlers, the president responded with a personal letter, suggesting that the good rabbi was being "somewhat hypercritical." Kalisch had Buchanan's full reply printed in the *Milwaukee Sentinel* (September 22, 1858):

Both as President of the United States and as an individual, I have ever been the advocate of Religious liberty and the perfect freedom of conscience. For many of your persuasion I entertain the highest personal regard, and I would be the last man in the world, either in an official document, or a private letter, to use any expression derogatory to their character, or calculated to wound their feelings.

The fact that a humble Midwestern rabbi could criticize the leader of his country and receive a thoughtful personal reply was convincing evidence that America's Jews had picked the right destination. The United States was a glorious place for nearly everyone who crossed the ocean voluntarily, but it was especially so for Jewish immigrants. "In no other country but America," wrote the *Milwaukee Sentinel* (June 6, 1871) "does the Jew step forth in the fullness of political, civil and religious rights—in the United States alone does he at once attain to the full equality of his fellowmen." Religious freedom in post-colonial America was a blanket privilege, available to everyone by the sheer fact of citizenship, not by special dispensation.

That was a refreshing change for the German-speaking Jews, but if the United States was a good place to settle, Milwaukee was even better. The city's overwhelmingly "foreign" character and its obvious Germanism not only eased the transition to new surroundings but completed a process that had commenced in Europe. Ever since the Enlightenment, Jews had been moving from the edges of German society to a place in the mainstream. That slow

Library of Congress

President James Buchanan sent a personal reply to a Milwaukee rabbi who accused him of insensitivity in 1858.

process of integration reached its climax, ironically, in the New World, and the results were nowhere more obvious than in Milwaukee. A complex nesting occurred on the shores of Lake Michigan. The city's German immigrants created a parallel society in their new hometown, establishing institutions that mirrored those of the Yankee community—separate but equal, and in many cases superior. Jews did precisely the same thing within the German community. They could, without surrendering their own traditions, become full members of German-speaking society, not simply "passing" but weaving themselves into the fabric of Teutonic Milwaukee. As a result, they were distinctively German and distinctively Jewish: neither one nor the other, but both. This dual identity was not destined to last, but Milwaukee, for a time, gave Jews the best of two worlds, and no one looked back across the ocean with regret. Preaching on the feast of Purim in 1876, Rabbi Moritz Spitz of Emanu-El spoke with feeling of the Promised Land his people had found in America, and more particularly in Milwaukee:

> *We are not persecuted any more for having different customs and usages from those of other people. We are no more oppressed because we are scattered among the nations and therefore unable to defend ourselves. Times have changed…. We, too, have changed. We are no more a lamenting and mourning people, forced by a sad, miserable present to look back into the past for comfort. We have cause to say: "Let us be joyful at least on Purim to compensate for the mournful days of a whole year—because our days pass by quietly and peacefully in the midst of our fellow-men."*

The German Jews had indeed found a congenial home in Milwaukee. As the nineteenth century entered its final decades, however, they were not alone.

Chapter 2

Here Come the Russians, *1882-1914*

On June 27, 1882, local relief officials received some rather startling news: a trainload of 350 refugees, all of them Russian Jews, was already on its way from Montreal to Milwaukee—the group's first and final destination in the United States. The telegram struck "like a thunderbolt from a clear sky," recalled Bernhard Gross, a Hungarian-born soapmaker who was active in Jewish relief circles, and its effect was electric. A mass meeting was called, a mayoral proclamation was issued and, with only hours to spare, stockpiles of food and clothing were hastily thrown together. When the train finally arrived, there were 218 refugees on board, not the 350 anticipated, but they were as sorry a lot of humanity as the city had ever seen: some of them sick, all of them hungry, dirty, travel-weary, and still t r a u m a t i z e d by the violence they had experienced in their homeland.

The newcomers had not been invited, but they were taken in just the same. The group was whisked away to shelter in a number of underused industrial buildings near the heart of town, where a small army of volunteers sprang into action. "Many carts full of eatables and clothing," wrote Bernhard Gross, "were unloaded at the temporary quarters and disappeared as if by magic." At the Blascow dye works, idle vats were pressed into service as impromptu bathtubs. At the vacant Leedom building, one woman gave birth within two days of her arrival, and a second delivered soon after. (The babies were named, appropriately, Washington and Garfield.) The men of the party, all of them sporting the forelocks and full beards of tradition, were surprised to find that their appearance did not pass muster with their Jewish hosts. The *Milwaukee Sentinel* (July 3, 1882) described the group's first lesson in New World tonsorial styles:

The 1882 arrival of refugees from the Russian Empire made headlines in the local press.

> *When their ablutions had been concluded, the chief committee thought it well to call barbers into requisition to relieve the male refugees of their barbarous superfluity of hair. Most of the men yielded a very tardy assent to the application of the razor to their chins, and [one] was so demonstrative in opposition to the process that it was necessary to invoke the presence of a policemen to reduce him to order.*

Within three days, boasted Gross, "the trainload of dilapidated humanity had the appearance of a lot of American citizens in caucus assembled."

Milwaukee Sentinel, June 30, 1882

THE REPUBLICAN-SENTINEL:

RUSSIAN REFUGEES.

Arrival of Three Hundred Destitute Polish Exiles in Milwaukee.

The Men, Women and Children Huddled Together in Narrow Quarters.

Meeting of the Local Relief Association —The Mayor's Proclamation.

Arrangements Perfected for a Mass Meeting at the Academy To-Day.

On Tuesday last Mr. Louis B. Schram, secretary of the Milwaukee Emigrant Relief Society, received from the executive committee of the New York Relief Association the following dispatch, bearing date of Monday evening :

Montreal Committee telegraphs Mr. Yates that 250 refugees from England pass through there to night booked for Milwaukee.

Mr. Schram lost no time in submitting the dispatch to the board of directors of his society, who at once set about the work of verifying the startling intelligence which

For the immigrants of 1882, both the newborn and the newly shorn, Milwaukee was the last stop in one journey and the first step in another, much longer odyssey. Although the June arrivals were the largest single group to reach the shores of Lake Michigan, other eastern European Jews had preceded them, and thousands more would follow. In a movement that lasted for more than thirty years—from the first Russian pogroms of 1881 to the opening shots of World War I in 1914—the refugees would eventually outnumber their German-Jewish hosts. They transformed Milwaukee's Jewish community and were in the process transformed themselves. For older residents—the Adlers, Friends, Landauers, and Macks who had long constituted the Jewish establishment—the changes were not altogether welcome. They watched in wonder as the city, and the world, changed before their very eyes.

From Shtetl to New World

The eastern European Jews were, to all appearances, different from their German-born counterparts in everything but religious faith. Appearances, however, concealed a not-so-distant shared past. The newcomers were, in some important respects, simply German Jews once removed. Both groups were Ashkenazic, one of two great branches of Diaspora Jews that had emerged in Europe by the Middle Ages. The Ashkenazim were concentrated in the central part of the continent, particularly in Germany and France, while the Sephardim—the second major branch—lived in Spain and Portugal. (Indeed, "Ashkenazic" and "Sephardic" are derived from the Hebrew words for Germany and Spain.) Each group developed a distinct culture, with its own religious rites, its own secular literature, and its own dialects; the Ashkenazim spoke Yiddish among themselves, and the Sephardim conversed in a nearly forgotten tongue called Ladino.

Neither group put down permanent roots. The Sephardim were expelled from Spain in 1492, forcing them to renew a wandering that would lead to northern Africa, Italy, Turkey, and elsewhere in the Mediterranean world. The Ashkenazim, in the meantime, were doing some wandering of their own. Many stayed in Germany where, after generations of struggle, they began to find widespread acceptance during the Age of Enlightenment. Other, less-fortunate Ashkenazim moved east and south, settling in what are now Russia, Poland, Lithuania, Belarus, Ukraine, Romania, and Hungary. Much of this sprawling territory was under the control of the Russian tsars, a geographic circumstance that would lead later American observers to lump all the eastern Europeans together as "Russian." Their German relatives called them *Ostjuden*—"eastern Jews." Although some prospered for a time in their new homes, the more general experience was poverty and persecution.

The divergent fortunes of the two Ashkenazic groups provide a telling case study of the power of cultural evolution. After a century or two of separation, the former peers could barely recognize each other. By the mid-1800s—the beginning of mass emigration from Europe—the German Jews spoke German, lived in cities, worshiped in Reform temples, and participated fully in the life of the society around them. Not so the eastern Europeans. They still spoke Yiddish, a robust amalgam of Hebrew and medieval German (or, in comedian Billy

Crystal's formulation, "Hebrew, German, and phlegm"). Although a sizable professional class had developed in the cities and on the estates, most of the Russian Empire's Jews lived in shtetls, small settlements separated physically and socially from the surrounding societies. The eastern Ashkenazim also worshiped in shuls, the Yiddish term for both synagogues and schools, where the dress, the rituals, and the furnishings were all strictly orthodox—a word that no one felt the need to capitalize at the time. The eastern European faithful did not consider themselves part of a distinct religious movement. There was only Judaism, and the only kind the shtetl-dwellers knew had survived virtually unchanged for generations. The Reform rite was a recent German mutation, and the Conservative variant was decades in the future.

Two conflicting views of life in the shtetl have come down through the decades. One features idealized versions of Tevye the milkman, his long-suffering wife Golde, and their high-spirited daughters—typical residents of a place where the music of a rooftop fiddler drifts out over a landscape enriched by human drama and ennobled by human effort. The opposing view pictures the shtetl as a place of unrelenting misery, where the light of civilization never penetrates, the next meal is never certain, and the oppressor is always near. There are probably elements of truth in both views, but the darker side eventually prevailed. In a painful reprise of past experience, Jews became convenient scapegoats for the economic and political dislocations of the late nineteenth century. Following the assassination of Tsar Alexander II in 1881, a wave

For all their human warmth, conditions in the shtetls of eastern Europe—congested, isolated, and impoverished—gave residents ample reason to leave.

Pogroms soon made flight the only alternative. A particularly violent outbreak in Odessa left hundreds dead and thousands homeless.

of anti-Jewish violence roiled the Russian Empire. Reports of murder, rape, and pillage on a massive scale reached the West, and still the pogroms continued. The infamous May laws followed, further limiting the mobility and the opportunities of a group that was already living on the margins of Russian society. Paroxysms of violence would recur with distressing frequency until the overthrow of the last tsar in 1917 and even beyond.

It was 218 individual victims of that mass hysteria who reached Milwaukee's North Western train depot on June 29, 1882. The "thunderbolt" described by Bernhard Gross had been gathering for well over a year. Although the Jewish communities of western Europe had done much to help the exiles, America was an obvious destination for people without a home in the late 1800s. Baron Maurice de Hirsch, a German-Jewish capitalist, funded a network of resettlement agencies that funneled the flow of refugees to the New World, and every community with even a modest Jewish population was expected to absorb its share. Milwaukee received its first newcomers in October 1881, most of them fleeing pogroms in Kiev and Odessa, but they numbered only two or three dozen. Their numbers swelled to hundreds in 1882 and would soon grow to thousands.

When the German Jews of Milwaukee met their eastern European counterparts at the train depot in June, the event marked, on one level, a reunification of two peoples who had been separated for centuries. It did not, however, feel remotely like a family reunion. A gulf had opened between the two Ashkenazic communities in Europe, and it had grown significantly wider on the

American side of the Atlantic. The eastern European refugees looked, behaved, and even smelled different from the German Jews who greeted them, and their economic circumstances could hardly have been more dissimilar. The Germans hadn't been hounded out of their homes, nor had they watched their loved ones fall beneath the hooves of Cossack horses. The vast majority had come to America voluntarily, seeking new opportunities and, more often than not, finding them in abundance. Although Milwaukee's resident Jews sympathized with the refugees, they were acutely aware of the gap that separated them from their distant relatives. "If the ancestors of the Russian Jews had remained in Germany, they would be quite different by now," concluded *Der Zeitgeist*, a German-Jewish journal published in Milwaukee. Instead, the editors wrote, they had become "half barbarians."

Helping the poor was one of the Torah's central commandments, and Milwaukee's Jews had been taking care of their own for decades—including the relative handful of eastern Europeans who had found their way to the city before 1881. But it was hardly surprising that many German Jews would approach the task of refugee relief with some reluctance. These newest newcomers were, after all, markedly different from the ones who had arrived earlier, and there were so *many* of them. For a Jewish community that numbered fewer than 2,500 people in 1882, even 281 refugees represented a major proportional increase, and there was no telling when the movement might end.

Although the relief effort presented both financial and psychological challenges, Milwaukee's Jews rose to the occasion, and they

Jewish Museum Milwaukee

carried the rest of the community with them. When the overwhelming scale of the exodus became apparent in the summer of 1882, the venerable David Adler, president of the Russian Relief Association, took the "unusual course" of asking non-Jews for monetary help, assuring them that the funds would be well-spent:

> The well-known probity of those Israelites, already in your midst, their honesty of purpose, cannot but be guarantee to the public that means so contributed will be expended only upon subjects worthy of such charitable consideration.

Civic titan David Adler spearheaded efforts to help the newcomers in 1882, acting as much out of duty as desire.

41

Milwaukee Public Library

Mayor John Stowell urged his fellow citizens to provide "sustenance and shelter" to the refugees.

Adler's humanitarian appeal won an eloquent endorsement from the city's mayor, John Stowell, who issued this proclamation on June 29:

> These people have been driven from a despotic government by the most cruel atrocities known in the history of man. They are in God's image and entitled to room and life on God's earth. We must temporarily afford them sustenance and shelter until they can help themselves. The little band of noble workers who have been furnishing succor to the comparatively few that have arrived hitherto, are utterly unable to provide for such a number as are at our doors. I called upon all who are in any degree able to be ready to respond to the appeal which must, in some form, be made to their charity immediately upon their arrival…. I earnestly hope that our national holiday may be a glad day to these poor people.

It was a mark of the Jewish community's stature that the mayor would take such an active interest in their relief effort, to the point of chairing the fund-raising committee himself. What made the campaign all the more remarkable was the fact that Milwaukee was receiving thousands of other immigrants just as the eastern Ashkenazim were arriving. The city's population soared from 115,587 to 204,468 between 1880 and 1890—a gain of 77 percent in just ten years—and newcomers from Poland, in particular, but also from Italy, Greece, Slovakia, Serbia, Croatia, and Hungary were adding a cosmopolitan flavor to the formerly German stronghold. Although none had experienced the same persecution as the Jews, poverty was an all-too-common condition for the newcomers. By 1890, immigrants and their children made up 86.4 percent of Milwaukee's population—the highest proportion in urban America. The Jews of the Russian Empire found themselves in one of the world's most European cities outside Europe.

The fact that Milwaukee could pay particular attention to one group when so many others were pouring in was certainly a mark of the Jewish community's standing, but it also provided a measure of the city's capacity for kindness. The plight of the refugees quickly became a common cause, and the response to Mayor Stowell's appeal extended far beyond the Yankee and German elites. The Irish residents of the Third Ward, for example, who were no strangers to poverty themselves, held their own mass meeting for refugee relief. "A quite liberal collection was taken up," reported the *Milwaukee Sentinel* (July 3, 1882), "and the meeting resolved itself into a committee of the whole to collect funds and render all the assistance in their power."

But charity had its limits—even, surprisingly, among the native Jews who directed the effort. Anxious, perhaps, to avoid the perception that their brethren were being dumped on the city, relief leaders tried desperately to stem the tide of refugees. Only hours after the trainload of 218 arrived, local officials drafted an angry telegram to resettlement authorities in London: "Sending refugees without notice is an outrage upon humanity. All citizens without distinction denounce the act. No more will be allowed to land." David Adler went even further in a telegram to the New York resettlement office: "We are done and refuse to countenance England's shameful abuse of America's generous charity toward Europe's paupers. Our connection with you and the alliance is severed and our society dissolved." The message from Milwaukee's resident Jews was decidedly mixed: We're glad to help those who got here, but don't you dare send any more.

Their obvious ambivalence did not prevent relief officials from providing genuine assistance to the refugees. In addition to food, shelter, and clothing, the newcomers received a great deal of help in finding jobs—some in local factories (including the Adler and Friend garment plants), others on farms and in lumber camps and quarries across the Midwest. But even here the message was mixed. The employment program underscored just how assimilated the German Jews had become. They were quite happy with their American identities, and they were determined to mold the newcomers in their own New World image. Shaving off beards was the least of it. Many Jewish leaders, both local and national, believed that assimilation could

be accomplished only by scattering the exiles across the country. Concerned about the fearful overcrowding in New York City and sensitive to the stereotype of the urban-dwelling, business-loving Jew, some actively promoted the idea of Jewish agricultural settlements. They were trying, in other words, to turn the refugees into something they were not and never had been. When Moritz Ellinger, a New Yorker who represented the Russian Immigrant Relief Society, made a fund-raising visit to Milwaukee in 1881, he left no doubt as to his group's intentions:

> *We propose to make these Jewish immigrants citizens of which the country will be proud. Those that have trades, as many of them do, will be furnished employment, and the others are to be made into farmers.... It is not our purpose to either start a large Jewish colony in this country or innumerable small ones. We want these people to become Americanized, and for this reason we shall remove all opportunity for clannishness by scattering them broadcast over the land.*

This rather aggressive experiment in social engineering (whose backers included Milwaukee's own Elias Friend) was doomed to failure from the start. America, it turned out, was a free country after all. The spirited objections of their hosts couldn't keep eastern European Jews from coming to Milwaukee, and the best efforts of the agricultural advocates couldn't keep their charges from ending up in the city. In Milwaukee, as in so many other urban centers, the refugees found security, they found sustenance, and they found each

Milwaukee Public Library

The Chicago, Milwaukee & St. Paul Railroad depot was the gateway to Milwaukee for thousands of Jewish immigrants from eastern Europe.

other. Despite the attempts of some influential citizens to bar the door, at least 400 eastern European Jews had settled in Milwaukee before 1882 was out—nearly twice the number who had stepped off the train in June.

The events of 1882 foreshadowed developments in the Jewish community that would continue for the next thirty years. Savage pogroms and official repression recurred in the Russian Empire, rising to peaks of intensity in 1890-1891 and 1903-1906. An 1891 crackdown prompted relief leader Bernhard Gross to label Russia "a living tomb" whose Jewish residents faced two choices: flight or death. The horror stories could still stir Milwaukeeans to sympathetic action. A wave of particularly brutal massacres in 1905 sparked a fund-raising campaign that involved such mainstream community leaders as Charles Pfister, Frederick Vogel, and Patrick Cudahy. Milwaukee alone raised $10,000 "for the relief of the Jewish survivors," exceeding the goal set for the entire state of Wisconsin. After every surge of violence and every downturn in the Russian economy, resettlement programs geared up to manage the inevitable influx of refugees. The programs were administered with the same blend of altruism and ambivalence that had characterized the efforts of 1882—and, on occasion, with the same lack of communication. In 1892, Milwaukee's relief office was asked to help a refugee family of five who had been stranded without means in Waterloo, Wisconsin. It appeared that Chicago officials had misread their papers: the family's real destination was Waterloo, Iowa.

Although the long-term trends were constant, significant change did occur during the period. Subsequent waves of immigrants attracted far less attention than the influx of 1882. "The coming of these stragglers," reported the *Milwaukee Sentinel* (January 31, 1892), "was hardly noticed by the community." There were no more mass meetings and no more mayoral proclamations. In the time-honored tradition of "chain migration," many of the newcomers were simply joining relatives or friends already established in Milwaukee, which eliminated the need for industrial dormitories and dye-vat bathtubs. Jewish refugees joined the general flood of Europeans who were swelling Milwaukee's population and transforming the city's civic life. Their plight still drew a sympathetic response from local German Jews, but later relief efforts tended to be more sensitive and less coercive than those of 1882. (Perhaps the most surprising fruit of those efforts would be a world-famous cookbook.) All the while the tide of refugees kept rising. There were roughly 5,000 eastern Ashkenazim in Milwaukee by 1900—a clear majority of the city's Jewish population—and their numbers probably doubled by 1914. Eastern European Jews became a significant factor in the life of the city—and this time they were allowed to keep their beards.

At Home on the Haymarket

Once they had established even a tentative foothold, the eastern Europeans began to develop a life of their own in Milwaukee, one separate from but parallel to the German-Jewish community's. Although the newcomers benefited enormously from their native brethren's help, daily contact between the two groups was almost nonexistent, particularly as each wave of refugees outgrew its need for relief. The separation was most visibly expressed in the urban landscape. German Jews generally occupied the better sections of the East and West Sides, while the eastern Europeans, like so many other new immigrants, settled near the center of town, typically in houses handed down from earlier groups. The refugees' first neighborhood was on the east side of the Milwaukee River, a few blocks north of City Hall. One of their earliest synagogues, Anshe Jacob ("Men of Jacob"), was established as early as 1884 on Market Street near Knapp, on a site now occupied by the Milwaukee School of Engineering's athletic facility. Water Street became the neighborhood's commercial center, particularly near its intersection with Juneau Avenue. Three kosher butcher shops were in business on Water by 1888, and the scene reminded one *Milwaukee Sentinel* reporter (March 26, 1888) of the Jewish immigrant quarter in Manhattan:

> *East Water street, in the vicinity of the market hall, is honeycombed with the little shops and stores of these people, that are but little better than those of Baxter street, New York. There are several notion stores on the street, which will transfer the visitor to lower New York in an instant.*

The riverside settlement was a typically crowded "receiver neighborhood" that would soon house Greeks, Italians, and Hungarians as well as Jews. As immigration continued, there was almost no room to expand. The area upstream was dominated by Poles who showed little inclination to move, and the houses to the east, toward Lake Michigan, were miles beyond the means of the typical refugee family. The Jewish community's center of gravity shifted steadily to the area west of the river, particularly to the blocks around the haymarket at Fifth and Vliet Streets. The haymarket—a sort of fuel depot for hungry urban horses—was the principal landmark in one of the oldest and most randomly built neighborhoods in the city. Situated squarely between the Schlitz brewery to the east and the Pabst complex to the west, the Haymarket area was a hodgepodge of small frame homes, assorted commercial buildings, worn-out mansions, and factories that made caskets, corks, church furniture, barrels, boots and shoes, horse collars, and ice cream. The yeasty smell of the nearby breweries and the din of industrial machinery were day-and-night presences for everyone who lived in the area.

The neighborhood had been part of Milwaukee's original German settlement, which included a generous sprinkling of Dutch and Czech families as well. All of them were moving out by the late 1800s. Pulled by the prospect of better housing and pushed by the incursion of Jewish newcomers, the older groups were migrating steadily to the north and west. They left behind only their churches, and former residents came back each Sunday to worship at St. John's Lutheran (German), St. John de Nepomuc (Czech), First Reformed (Dutch), and a number of other congregations. During the rest of the week, eastern European Jews held sway, and their numbers continued to grow. By 1900, the Haymarket neighborhood had eclipsed the original refugee settlement east of the river. The eastern Ashkenazim dominated a small but densely settled area bordered roughly by Third and Eighth Streets between Juneau Avenue and Walnut Street—an area of twenty-five square blocks that housed perhaps 5,000 people. It was from this base that the

Milwaukee Public Library

of hands. Relief official Bernhard Gross surveyed the eastern European employment scene in 1892:

> *There are more tailors than any-thing else. A great many are in tanneries. There are many carpenters, blacksmiths and locksmiths, many employed in the planing-mills and the foundries. Many make a good living from buying rags—perhaps twenty-five families get their support from this industry. In this way part of the dry goods trade has its beginning and its end amongst these refugees. On one end the fabric is sold at wholesale and at the other end it is bought back again after it has run its course.*

Because the Yiddish they spoke was relatively close to German—Milwaukee's second (and in some areas first) language—the refugees were quite capable of finding jobs themselves, but they took full advantage of employment programs established by movers and shakers in the German-Jewish community. Continued overcrowding in New York City and elsewhere on the East Coast led to a new round of resettlement efforts, the most ambitious of which was the Industrial Removal Office. Established in 1901 with funds supplied by Baron de Hirsch, the IRO worked with local officials and private employers to spread refugees across the country. The program's most enthusiastic Milwaukee backer was probably Adolph W. Rich, the business leader who served multiple terms as president of Temple Emanu-El. Rich personally found work for at least 600 immigrants in the early 1900s, some as laborers, others as skilled tradesman like tanners, machinists, carpenters, and tinsmiths.

The haymarket on Fifth and Vliet was the focal point of Milwaukee's emerging Jewish quarter.

community would expand to the north and west for the next two generations.

As soon as they had found even rudimentary shelter, the immigrants devoted their energies to finding work. For anyone who had learned a skill in the Old World—or was willing to acquire one in the New—the task was relatively simple. Despite periodic recessions, Milwaukee's economy was growing with the nation's, and there was nearly always room for one more pair

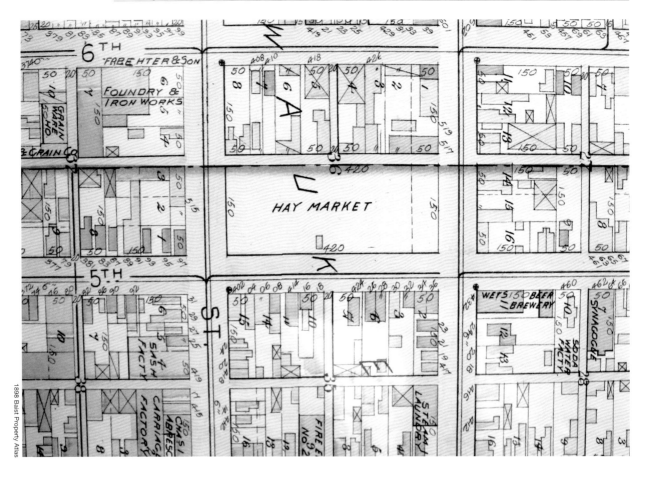

The blocks surrounding the haymarket featured a motley blend of shops, industries, and houses, none of them palatial.

Working in a tannery or a machine shop had its rewards, but there were drawbacks as well. For shtetl-dwellers who had observed the Sabbath all their lives, working on Saturday—the prevailing pattern in American industry—created a crisis of conscience. Some bowed to economic necessity, like many of the German Jews who preceded them, but others solved the problem—and satisfied their craving for independence—by going into business for themselves. Scores of small shops cropped up in the Haymarket neighborhood, most of them operated on a shoestring by newcomers who sold groceries, milk,

meat, clothes, and other necessities to their neighbors. An even larger number of entrepreneurs went into the street trades, pushing their carts or driving their wagons throughout the city. Most of them dealt in rags, scrap iron, or fruit and vegetables, always hoping to buy low and sell high. Business in general and peddling in particular became pillars of the Haymarket economy. A survey published by the federal Dillingham Commission in 1911 found that fully 55 percent of the neighborhood's Russian-Jewish breadwinners were in business, and nearly half that number were peddlers.

Although they were ubiquitous, peddlers were not always welcome on the city's streets. Periodic attempts to raise license fees drew literally hundreds of itinerant produce merchants to hearings at City Hall, where they squared off with retail grocers who wanted to keep the trade to themselves. During an especially heated debate in 1897, one retailer conceded that Jewish peddlers were "a necessary evil" because they bought fruit and vegetables no one else wanted: "The regular grocers would not buy the stock after more than a day old. The peddlers, therefore, picked them up every afternoon in summer and disposed of them the same afternoon." A Haymarket peddler argued that the real beneficiaries were poor families, who could buy a peck of apples from him for fifteen cents instead of paying a quarter at the grocery store.

The proceeds from a day's work—whether factory wages, till receipts, or the change in a fruit peddler's pocket—were typically meager, particularly in the first generation. The Haymarket neighborhood, in fact, was among the poorest in the city. But a lack of funds did not mean a lack of places to worship. As the neighborhood became more Jewish, an assortment of synagogues, known invariably as shuls, joined peddler's wagons and Yiddish shop signs as the community's earmarks. Nearly a dozen synagogues came to life in the Haymarket area between 1882 and 1914, including several that survived into the twenty-first century (either intact or through mergers) as Beth Israel, Anshe Sfard, Agudas Achim, Anshai Lebowitz, and Temple Menorah.

Within that cluster, the congregation that became Beth Israel was the largest and, in its early years, the most contentious. In

The street trades, from umbrella-mending (left) *to rag-recycling* (below), *were mainstays of the neighborhood economy.*

Milwaukee Sentinel, May 25, 1893

Beth Hamedrosh Hagodol & GUS. H. LEIPOLD & CO. ARCHITECTS

Beth Hamedrosh Hagodol on Fifth St., later Beth Israel, was the largest and most influential of the Haymarket area's many congregations.

1886, a group of refugees, most of them from Lithuania, opened a small synagogue near Fourth and Vliet and named it for Moses Montefiore, an affluent British Jew who had become a folk hero for his efforts to help his struggling brethren in Europe and Palestine. The Montefiore group was at least loosely affiliated with Anshe Jacob, the refugee synagogue on the east side of the river. "Both congregations were composed of the working classes," reported the *Milwaukee Sentinel* (May 25, 1893). "There were few among the members who could afford to contribute to the church and their numbers were so small that they were threatened with extinction." Desperate for funds, the congregations imposed a joint tax on kosher meat in 1888—without consulting the butchers who prepared that meat. At least one, Jacob Weinfeld, refused to pay the levy, which prompted a boycott by synagogue members. Weinfeld sued them,

claiming that the boycotters were denying him a livelihood. The case finally went to trial, and the *Sentinel* (April 27, 1888) treated it as a "roaring farce":

> *Long-tailed Hebrew guttural rustled through the still air of Judge Mallory's court room yesterday, blunt pointed Jewish slaughtering knives were brandished, attorneys wrangled over the meaning of Talmudic rules, long bearded Russian witnesses clacked their tongues like flutter mills and interpreters disputed as to their meaning.*

According to butcher Weinfeld ("a little, quiet man, with a long beard and a worried aspect"), the boycotters threatened to declare his meat *treyf*, or ritually unclean, if he didn't pay the half-cent-a-pound assessment. Joseph Glueck, a butcher who regularly led services at Anshe Jacob, was likewise threatened. "Mr. Glueck," reported the *Sentinel*, "has a beard that grows in seventeen different directions, talks with the speed of an electric dynamo, and is given to frantic gestures, to jumping out of his chair and dancing about the floor." The dispute was finally resolved, but not before the immigrants had received far more publicity than they had bargained for.

Financial pressures continued to drive Anshe Jacob and Moses Montefiore together, and the two congregations finally merged in 1892 under a new name: Beth Hamedrosh Hagodol ("Great House of Study"). As if to confirm the refugee community's shift from the east side of the river to the west, the Anshe Jacob group sold its building on Market Street and moved into the Moses Montefiore shul on Vliet. It was instantly overcrowded. An aggressive building campaign began at once, and in September 1893, Beth Hamedrosh Hagodol dedicated a new synagogue on Fifth Street between Vliet and Cherry. Its immediate neighbors included a weiss beer brewery and a cooper shop. Although its surroundings were anything but glamorous, the shul was an imposing brick structure built "in the Oriental style," with seating for over 500 worshipers. "The new synagogue will be conducted on strictly orthodox principles," reported the *Milwaukee Journal* (September 2, 1893), but that proved to be an overstatement. A difference of opinion regarding ritual led to open conflict between Rabbi Solomon Israelson and Solomon Fein, a Water Street merchant who was Beth Hamedrosh Hagodol's president and leading financial supporter. Fein favored a liturgy closer to the Reform movement's, and Israelson stood foursquare for tradition. The schism ended when both principals moved on: Israelson resigned in 1897, and Fein ultimately transferred his membership to Temple Emanu-El, the city's most prominent Reform congregation.

Orthodoxy prevailed for the time being, but the drama was not over yet. The budget for Beth Hamedrosh Hagodol's new synagogue had ballooned from $12,500 to $20,000 during construction, and the congregation was perennially behind in its mortgage payments. Bankruptcy proved to be the only alternative; the shul went on the block in a 1901 sheriff's sale. The winning bidder was Benjamin Weil, a German-Jewish real estate mogul who was acting on the congregation's behalf. The synagogue ended up back in its original owners' hands, but only after the congregation had been legally reconstituted. In 1901,

Jewish Museum Milwaukee

Beth Hamedrosh Hagodol became Beth Israel ("House of Israel"), and so it has been known ever since. Beth Israel was generally regarded as the most important of the immigrant synagogues. With a membership of at least 150 families in 1901, it was significantly larger than Emanu-El and roughly the same size as B'ne Jeshurun— Milwaukee's two German-Jewish temples.

Other eastern European congregations had far less tumultuous early histories. In about 1887, a group of Hungarian Jews began to worship in a rented house near the haymarket. They organized formally as B'nai Israel ("Sons of Israel") in 1889 and added an important modifier in the next decade:

B'nai Israel provided a spiritual home for the neighborhood's Hungarian Jews.

Jewish Museum Milwaukee

Anshe Sfard was a Sixth St. landmark built by Russians who favored the Sephardic style of worship.

the congregation sponsored a ball to raise money for a two-story brick synagogue projected to cost between $5,000 and $7,000. Seven years would pass before there was enough cash on hand to start the project. In 1905, finally, B'nai Israel Anshe Ungarn took proud possession of a small shul on Tenth Street near Walnut.

A smaller number of Haymarket residents were Russian by birth and Sephardic by liturgical style. In about 1889, they came together as Anshe Sfard ("Sephardic Men") and began to meet for prayer in rented quarters on Cherry Street. They, too, longed for a home of their own. In 1898, several years before the Hungarians, the Russians had raised enough money to build a $7,000 synagogue on Sixth Street near Cherry. "The Temple Ansche S'Phard is not an imposing structure," reported the *Milwaukee Sentinel* (April 2, 1899). "It is a rather small, oblong building with a steep pointed roof and two flights of steps leading to the sanctuary." The congregation's rabbi was none other than Solomon Israelson, who had just left Beth Hamedrosh Hagodol (Beth Israel) after his spat with that shul's president. Anshe Sfard prospered in its new home; the synagogue was remodeled in 1908 to accommodate 456 male worshipers on the main floor and 285 women in the balcony.

Other religious groups, notably Catholics and Lutherans, were known to build their churches close together, each serving a particular ethnic group or synodical body, but none could begin to match the Jewish tendency to cluster. In the early 1900s, an observer standing on the roof of the Schlitz brewery at Third Street could look out over a row of three synagogues that practically touched each other: B'nai Israel Anshe Ungarn on

Anshe Ungarn ("Men of Hungary"). Although their converted residence on Fourth Street had enough room on an ordinary Sabbath, the spike in attendance during the High Holy Days forced the group to rent Liederkranz Hall or the West Side Turner Hall several times each year. The members of B'nai Israel Anshe Ungarn desperately wanted a genuine shul of their own, and fund-raising efforts were nearly continuous. In 1898, for instance, the women of

Fourth, Beth Israel on Fifth, and Anshe Sfard on Sixth, all between Cherry and Vliet. And these were by no means the only synagogues in the Haymarket neighborhood. In about 1902, a handful of Polish Jews bought a little house on Cherry Street near Sixth and started Agudas Achim Anshe Polen ("Association of Brothers, Men of Poland"). The floors were dirt, the women's section was the former kitchen, and the rooms were so hot in summer that candles melted to blocks of wax in their boxes, but Agudas Achim had at least made a start. Romanian Jews followed in 1904, launching Anshe Roumania in rented quarters on Vliet near Fifth. By 1912, Anshe Roumania was prosperous enough to take over a former Methodist church on Eleventh and Vine, which was promptly remodeled for use as a synagogue with room for 600 faithful. In about 1906, a group of immigrants from the vicinity of Lubavitch in eastern Russia established Anshe Lebowitz, taking over a storefront on Vliet Street and then graduating to a larger building on Eighth and Walnut in 1911. Breakaways, mergers, and aborted start-ups were all too common in the Haymarket's synagogue circles, and each development added one more layer to a religious landscape that was already perhaps the most complex in Milwaukee.

Why such an abundance of synagogues? Although many Milwaukeeans, including their German brethren, lumped the newcomers together as "Russian" Jews, they were in fact quite different from each other, particularly in the early years. Despite the fact that Yiddish was their common tongue and Judaism their common faith, Jews from Russia, Poland, Lithuania, Hungary, Ukraine, and Romania could easily tell each other apart by nuances of dialect, diet, dress, and

Jewish Museum Milwaukee

other cultural giveaways. They formed their religious congregations accordingly. Anshe Sfard was known to one and all as "the Rushishe shul," Agudas Achim as "the Poilishe shul," Beth Hamedrosh Hagodol (Beth Israel) as "the Litvishe shul," B'nai Israel as "the Ungarishe shul," and so on down the line. There were also differences in ritual, not all of them subtle. Ever since the mid-1700s, when a charismatic figure known as

Anshe Roumania began in 1904 as one of the smallest Haymarket shuls.

Jewish Museum Milwaukee

Rabbi Solomon Scheinfeld was the acknowledged spiritual leader of the eastern European Jewish community. The breadth of his knowledge and the depth of his compassion made Scheinfeld a unique figure in the history of Jewish Milwaukee.

the Baal Shem Tov sparked a revival of mystical Judaism in eastern Russia, the Chasidic movement had been gaining adherents throughout eastern Europe. Preaching a message of joyful prayer and personal devotion within the framework of Mosaic law, Chasidic holy men established centers throughout the region, including the little town of Lubavitch. Milwaukee's own Anshe Lebowitz included numerous followers of the Lubavitcher rebbe, and Chasidism in

one form or another has remained a vital element in Milwaukee Judaism ever since.

Many of the Haymarket synagogues, probably most of them, functioned without full-time rabbis. The typical congregation could hardly maintain a building, much less pay a rabbi's salary. Services were often led by members with a little more education than their peers, and some doubled as kosher slaughterers (*shokhets*) and ritual circumcisers (*mohels*). Although they couldn't afford individual rabbis, the various congregations did have a rabbinical leader: Solomon Scheinfeld. Born in Lithuania in 1860, Scheinfeld immigrated to the United States in 1891, shortly after his ordination. He made Milwaukee his permanent home in 1902, taking the pulpit at Beth Israel and staying until his death in 1943. Although nominally employed by one synagogue, Scheinfeld functioned by common consent as chief rabbi for practically all the Haymarket congregations, even those with ordained leaders of their own. Widely read, fervently spiritual, and deeply intellectual, he was a singular figure in the history of Milwaukee Judaism. Even though he was a careful student of the Talmud, Scheinfeld did not preach punctilious observance of its every jot and tittle. The rabbi could, in fact, be openly critical of tradition. In 1912, he dismissed some popular prayers as "vestiges of ancient times, when man conceived of his deity as a sheik who would become angry and exact vengeance, and could be soothed by pleas and gifts." Scheinfeld was so deeply authentic that even non-religious Jews turned to him to settle disputes, and his word was regarded as law.

Rabbi Scheinfeld was one unifying force in the Haymarket neighborhood, and the

Jewish calendar was another. They may have worshiped behind separate closed doors on most Sabbaths, but certain festivals brought the Jewish faithful out into the open. Rosh Hashanah—the Jewish New Year—provided one opportunity for the community to come together, particularly during the Tashlikh ("throwing") ceremony. Following an ancient custom long abandoned by Reform Jews, the people of the Haymarket gathered at the nearby Milwaukee River on the first day of Rosh Hashanah to cast their sins into the water—symbolically, of course. "The celebration is a very quiet one," reported the *Evening Wisconsin* (September 3, 1903), but the sight of Old World Jews in their prayer shawls and black hats, gesturing toward the river in the shadow of the Schlitz brewery, must have stopped some Gentiles in their tracks. Sukkot, or the Feast of Tabernacles, was even more picturesque. The holiday was observed only symbolically in Reform temples, but the eastern Ashkenazim took it literally. Commemorating the forty years their ancestors had spent wandering in the desert, the Haymarket's Jews erected shelters each harvest season that served as temporary living spaces. The *Milwaukee Sentinel* (September 20, 1899) noted that the structures dressed up an otherwise drab neighborhood:

> *In many of the forlorn yards, opening on to the squalid and bad smelling alleys, real tabernacles had been built in remembrance and in the fulfillment of the old Mosaic law…. As a rule they were built box-shape of rough boards, against the wall of the house or perhaps under or adjoining an outside staircase.*

Sheets were stretched across the doorways of each shelter, the roofs were covered with straw or branches, and the walls were hung with cranberries and grapes. For eight days, at least, the neighborhood proclaimed its Jewishness as well as its poverty.

The rhythms of religious life kept a sort of time for the neighborhood, but not everyone followed the same clock. A substantial number of eastern Europeans were, like many of their German brethren, unaffiliated, entering a synagogue only during the High Holy Days or for life-cycle events like weddings and funerals. The ranks of the irreligious multiplied as the years passed. Although the Haymarket community was insular, it was not insulated; young people, in particular, absorbed the pulse of American society every time they stepped outside the neighborhood. Meyer Boruszak, who served as Agudas Achim's rabbi from 1902 to 1917, offered a wistful prayer at the birth of his son: "May the Lord will that I should raise him to Torah, Chuppah and good deeds which is very, very difficult in this country."

Some of the newcomers, particularly the young, found a religion of sorts in political activity. The climate of oppression in the Russian Empire had created, over the years, a stratum of intellectuals, many of them Jewish, who developed some radical ideas for the reordering of society. Leon Trotsky, a leading light of the 1917 revolution, was Jewish by ancestry, and he drew his inspiration from the writings of a rabbi's grandson named Karl Marx. But the impulse to change the world spawned more than one movement. Many Milwaukee Jews came of age in the revolutionary ferment that preceded the fall of the tsars in 1917,

Jewish Museum Milwaukee

Victor Berger, the Austrian immigrant and non-observant Jew who guided the remarkable development of Milwaukee Socialism

card-carrying Socialists. Their leader was Victor Berger, a secular Jew who had emigrated from Austria-Hungary in 1878. Under Berger's guidance, the Socialists forged an alliance with the city's labor unions and began to field candidates for elective office in 1898. Their first victories came in the German working-class wards north and west of the Haymarket neighborhood. Once in power, the Socialists proved themselves capable, creative, and absolutely incorruptible. Voters soon learned to trust the reformers, and in 1910 they virtually handed them the reins of government. Emil Seidel, a patternmaker by trade, became mayor; a Socialist majority took over the Common Council; and Victor Berger himself went to Congress. Milwaukee would choose Socialist mayors for most of the next fifty years.

No other major American city followed suit. Just as the early German Jews had happily found themselves in the most German city in the country, the eastern European radicals found themselves in the nation's capital of municipal Socialism. They quickly made themselves at home, joining the Jewish branch of Victor Berger's party, translating the Socialist message into Yiddish, and thoroughly canvassing their neighborhood at election time. Some went even further. In 1907, eastern European immigrants established the first Milwaukee branch of the Arbeiter Ring, or Worker's Circle. Drawing its support from the great mass of wage workers, the Ring worked to graft class-consciousness onto secular Jewish culture, developing a self-contained, self-conscious movement that was distinctly Jewish and distinctly Socialist at the same time. Its activities ranged from lecture series on Socialist topics—in

and they crossed the ocean as committed Bolsheviks, Mensheviks, Bundists, anarchists, and—within a purely Jewish context—Zionists. These assorted radicals were a minority, but they were a highly vocal minority, and their reputations preceded them. The *Milwaukee Sentinel* (September 11, 1893) described "the anarchistic spirit" that seemed to pervade New York City's Jewish population and reassured its readers that they had nothing to fear: "In this city we have a considerable body of Russian Jewish immigrants. Thus far they have given no cause for complaint on the ground of seditious tendencies."

The left-leaning newcomers were probably flabbergasted by what they found in Milwaukee. After enduring years of corruption on all levels, local voters were rallying behind a reform movement led by a group of well-spoken, highly disciplined,

The Grand Gate of the Order Knights of Zion

קומי אורי כי בא אורך

Yiddish—to sick and death benefits not unlike those of B'nai B'rith and other mainstream fraternals.

At the other end of the political spectrum were the Zionists, whose radicalism lay in their solution to "the Jewish problem." Zionists believed that the Jews of the world would have no rest until they had a homeland of their own, preferably in the original Promised Land: Palestine. The idea of a national home had enormous appeal to immigrants who had seen far too much persecution and poverty in their countries of origin. In 1899, just two years after the inaugural Zionist Congress in Switzerland, Milwaukeeans organized the first of three local "gates" of the Knights of Zion, a group that was particularly strong in the Midwest. Milwaukee emerged as a regional stronghold of the movement; in 1910, the city hosted 500 Knights of Zion convention delegates who dined, deliberated, and donated funds "to recover Palestine from the Turks by purchase."

Rabbi Solomon Scheinfeld served on both the local and the national councils of the Knights, signifying the Zionist movement's deep support within the eastern European religious community.

The Arbeiter Ring and the Knights of Zion each had hundreds of members, but their rosters were mutually exclusive. The Socialists of the Ring dismissed dreams of a Palestinian homeland as a sentimental distraction from the larger task of liberating the working class. The Zionists considered dreams of the "cooperative commonwealth" a utopian fantasy that diverted attention from the need of the Jewish people for a national identity. A third group fell between the first two: the labor Zionists, whose goal was to combine the national aspirations of the Jewish people with the political aspirations of the working class. Their organizational vehicle for achieving those ends was Poale Zion ("Workers of Zion"), which established its

The fervent desire for a Jewish homeland made Milwaukee a Zionist stronghold, and membership in the Knights of Zion soared.

Jewish Museum Milwaukee

*Poale Zion members
gathered for a Fourth
of July picnic in 1917.*

first Milwaukee branch in 1906. Poale Zion members were zealots on behalf of a Jewish homeland, even going from door to door to raise funds for the small worker colonies that had sprouted in Palestine. They believed just as fervently that workers should own both the land and the means of production when that homeland was finally secured. What made the labor Zionists so distinctive was their blend of religious secularism and what might be termed cultural pietism. In preparation for that great day when a national homeland would finally be theirs, Poale Zionists labored to build a strong "national spirit" among the Jewish people. They sponsored debates, opened a library, and established a variety of educational

programs, including a folk school that offered its first classes in 1911. The folk school gave the children of the Haymarket a chance to explore firsthand the riches of the Hebrew and Yiddish languages, Jewish literature, and Jewish history.

There were plenty of other political and quasi-political organizations in the neighborhood, from reading circles to civic councils, but the Arbeiter Ring, the Knights of Zion, and Poale Zion were the largest and most influential. They cooperated when they could, bickered when they couldn't, and generally kept the pot boiling. The abundance of political activities added one more layer of energy to a neighborhood that seemed to grow livelier by the year.

58

Urban Village or Urban Slum?

The Haymarket neighborhood offered something for everyone. There was a full complement of synagogues for the assorted eastern European faithful. There were nearly as many outlets, especially political outlets, for the irreligious and even the anti-religious. Homegrown charitable organizations abounded, including a residence for the indigent elderly (Beth Moshav Zekanim), a shelter for transients (Hachnosath Orchim), and a free loan society for aspiring businesspeople (Gemiluth Chesed), all of which were in operation by 1905. Locally owned shops supplied the necessities of life, from basics like milk and bread to specialties like matzo and Sabbath candles, all within easy walking distance.

Even though they had plenty to worry about in the present, the people of the Haymarket were also looking to the future. Despite their poverty, the eastern Ashkenazim believed devoutly in the power of education. In about 1905, they established a Talmud Torah, or Hebrew free school, that held its first classes in the basement of Beth Israel's synagogue. Several private Hebrew schools (*chederim*) cropped up in the area, most of them tiny and ill-equipped, and a roving band of self-employed tutors (*melamdim*) helped boys prepare for their Bar Mitzvah ceremonies. As a counterpoint to these religious efforts, both Poale Zion and the Arbeiter Ring stressed secular Jewish culture in their after-school classes. The public schools themselves were crammed with students. The Dillingham Commission study published in 1911 found that 91 percent of the Haymarket area's Jewish boys were enrolled in public schools—the highest proportion of any ethnic group in Milwaukee. Even the adults, as overworked as they typically were, found time for cultural pursuits. In 1894, the Milwaukee Operatic and Dramatic Club mounted a production of *The Witch*, "a Jewish melodrama." The *Milwaukee Sentinel* (January 19, 1894)

The Talmud Torah free school demonstrated the community's commitment to education.

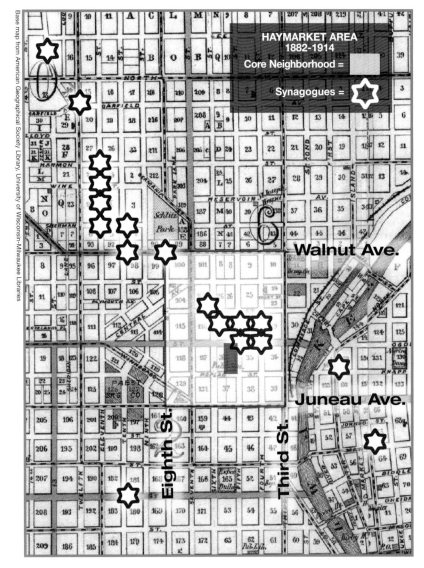

HAYMARKET AREA
1882-1914
Core Neighborhood =

Synagogues =

Walnut Ave.

Juneau Ave.

Eighth St.

Third St.

The densely built Haymarket area struggled economically, but it was unusually rich in human terms.

its population, the neighborhood expanded naturally to the north and west. By 1910, the community was pushing beyond Walnut Street toward North Avenue and past Eighth Street to Sixteenth. Jewish shops, synagogues, and households moved in just as fast as the original Germans moved out, cloning the cultural landscape of the blocks behind them. Even as it grew, the Haymarket settlement remained one of the most compact and cohesive in the city. Few Milwaukee neighborhoods have ever developed such a powerful sense of place.

For outside observers, especially journalists, the Jewish quarter served as a sort of Rorschach inkblot test. Just as two divergent views of the European shtetl had emerged—as a place of unusual human warmth or unusual human suffering—the same dichotomy applied to the neighborhoods the shtetl-dwellers created in America. Walking the same blocks in Milwaukee's Haymarket, some outsiders saw an urban village and others beheld only an urban slum; the district was either a specimen of the picturesque or an object of pity. The *Milwaukee Sentinel* (March 11, 1889) saw nothing but the village in this account of Fannie Rosenberg's wedding to Meyer Bank:

> *The scenes … yesterday afternoon involuntarily reminded one of a Polish village one hundred years ago. The village was in a state of excitement. Long-coated and bushy-bearded Jews, gaily dressed women and girls, boys with long ear-locks, ran from all directions. Music was heard in the distance, and behind the music there marched a long procession. The daughter of the popular village inn-keeper was to marry a young*

reported that the group was "composed entirely of Jewish amateurs" who donated their ticket revenue to agencies serving the poor. The 1894 production marked the emergence of what would become a thriving Yiddish theater scene.

All this activity took place in an area that originally covered only twenty-five square blocks. As new immigrants swelled *man famed as being fully versed in all the accomplishments of his time, and the whole village turned out to be present at the ceremony.*

"Everything," the *Sentinel* concluded, "belonged to another age and to a foreign country."

A *Milwaukee Journal* reporter (January 2, 1906) saw the same neighborhood in a much different light, as a community enduring hardships that were all too present:

> *Up crazy, creaking tenement stairs. Stumbling down into damp, reeking basements. Trying to hold my breath long enough to avoid the stenches that even the frosty December air did not serve to dispel…. For just two and one-half hours I saw sights so appalling, some of them as to make any description unprintable.*
>
> *Milwaukee need not read Jacob Riis to find out how the other half lives. Just catch an Eighth-st. car that will take you down near Fifth-st. Just see for yourself those alleys, the unspeakable filth, the hovels, the horror of it all. When you lie down to sleep in your own big, clean room at night, with the air blowing fresh and clear through its windows, you'll offer up an extra little prayer of thankfulness. I am sure that I did….*

Whether they saw it as a village or a slum, outsiders reported their own impressions of the neighborhood inkblot. They generally looked past the people who actually lived in the community, and those residents left scant evidence of their feelings. The most complete recollection, in fact, comes from the neighborhood's most famous product: Golda Meir. Known in childhood as Goldie Mabowehz,

University of Wisconsin-Milwaukee Library Archives

she arrived from Pinsk, in present-day Belarus, with her mother and older sister in 1906. Nothing in her European experience had prepared the eight-year-old for what she found in Milwaukee. A visit to Schuster's Department Store on nearby Third Street left her spellbound:

> *I was delighted by my pretty new clothes, by the soda pop and ice cream and by the excitement of being in a real skyscraper, the first five-story building I had ever seen. In general, I thought*

Goldie Mabowehz, the future prime minister of Israel, came to Milwaukee at the age of eight and stayed into adulthood.

Jewish Museum Milwaukee

Goldie (extreme right) *was the valedictorian of her class at Fourth Street School.*

Milwaukee was wonderful. Everything looked so colorful and fresh, as though it had just been created, and I stood for hours staring at the traffic and the people.... It was all completely strange and unlike anything I had ever seen or known before, and I spent the first days in Milwaukee in a kind of trance.

Goldie's father, Moshe, had settled in Milwaukee two or three years earlier and found intermittent work as a carpenter in the Milwaukee Road shops. His first reaction to his wife and daughters spoke volumes about America's impact on immigrant aspirations: "Refusing to listen to any arguments, on the morning after our arrival he determinedly marched all of us downtown on a shopping expedition. He was horrified, he said, by our appearance. We looked so dowdy and 'Old World'...." Although Moshe Mabowehz had enough money for new outfits, he couldn't afford to house his family in anything more

than a two-room apartment on Sixth and Walnut—a place his daughter would later realize was a hovel. "But in 1906," Meir wrote in her autobiography, "the clapboard houses with their pretty porches looked like palaces to me. I even thought that our flat (which had no electricity and no bathroom) was the height of luxury." Not everyone saw such splendor in the slum, but the wretched conditions they had known in the shtetls of Europe enabled the immigrants to tolerate and even appreciate life in the ghettos of the New World.

Public health and housing officials thought differently. Study after study portrayed the Haymarket neighborhood as one of Milwaukee's worst, rivaled only by the Italian Third Ward and the Polish Fourteenth. Hoping to rouse public sentiment and spur public action, government reformers emphasized the horror stories. *Socialists and Slums*, a 1910 report prepared by Carl Thompson, the Socialist city clerk, was entirely typical:

In the Ghetto, in one building live seventy-one people, representing seventeen families. The toilets in the yard freeze in winter and are clogged in summer. The overcrowding here is fearful and the filth defies description.

Within the same block are crowded a number of tenements three and four stories high with basement dwellings. One of these is used as a Jewish synagogue. Above and beneath and to the rear this building is crowded with tenement dwellers. The stairways are rickety, the rooms filthy, and all are overcrowded. The toilets for the whole population are in the cellar adjoining some dwelling rooms, reached by a short stairway. At the time of our visit the floors of this toilet, both inside and outside, were covered with human excrement and refuse to a depth of eight to twelve inches. Into this den of horrors all the population, male and female, had to go.

Local residents, with something approaching humor, had dubbed the seventeen-family tenement "Castle Garden," after the New York City depot where immigrants were processed before Ellis Island opened in 1892. The decrepit synagogue was Anshe Roumania's first home.

The Housing Problem in Wisconsin, a state-sponsored 1906 study, covered similar territory. After decrying the area's housing conditions, the authors observed that the line separating home from work was indefinite at best in the Haymarket:

Seventeen families crowded into a Haymarket tenement known locally as Castle Garden.

from "Socialists and Slums" in *The Survey,* Dec. 3, 1910

"Socialists and Slums"

"Socialists and Slums"

Housing conditions were so wretched that Progressive-Era reformers used the neighborhood as a case study of urban blight. The hovels at right were on Cherry St. near Sixth.

Milwaukee Public Library

"Socialists and Slums"

In an apartment in one of the tene-ment houses lives a cobbler with his family. The rear rooms are used as living rooms. The front room is used as the cob-bler's work-shop where he sits at his bench near the window. Back of him against one corner of the room, and reaching half way to the ceiling, lies a pile of old shoes, twist-ed and brown, or green and mildewed, gathered from alleys, refuse heaps and rag peddlers' stores.

These shoes are eventually soaked, scraped, repaired, blackened and sold, all in the room opening into the living rooms of this family. The offensive odor permeating the whole apartment testi-fies to the insanitary condition pre-vailing there.

It was clear to the reformers that some-thing had to be done. The immigrants, who in truth had never known anything better, might have been satisfied with conditions in "the Ghetto," but the prevailing squalor was unacceptable to Americans with a loftier conception of the common good. Although public housing was on the hori-zon (Milwaukee's first project would open in 1923), public slum clearance and social welfare programs were not. That left pri-vate charities to address the neighborhood's problems, and it was at this point that the city's German Jews re-entered the picture. Since the first flurry of relief activities in 1881-1882, they had not been entirely absent. The Hebrew Relief Association helped the neediest immigrants with fuel, food, and rent money. The Widows and Orphans Soci-ety supported families who had lost their breadwinners. The Ladies' Relief Sewing Society made clothes—4,000 items in 1893 alone—and distributed shoes, bedding, and other household goods. Members of the Sis-terhood of Personal Service, traveling in pairs, made home visits in the Haymarket and worked to "improve the physical con-dition of the poor." All four organizations relied heavily on Milwaukee's German-Jew-ish women, many of them pillars of Emanu-El and B'ne Jeshurun congregations. Although

Lacking a playground, a Haymarket youngster scooped manure from the alley behind his home into a toy wagon.

65

Jewish Museum Milwaukee

The farming colony near Arpin, Wisconsin, was born of a desire to remove Jewish families from the blighting influence of the city.

a good deal of their time was spent organizing balls and bazaars to benefit their charities, these women were not afraid to get their hands dirty, as later events would demonstrate. In 1893, the four organizations joined forces as the United Hebrew Charities, bringing much-needed coordination to the provision of direct material aid. In 1902, they united with others to form an even broader umbrella group: the Federated Jewish Charities, whose goals included "checking pauperism among the Jewish poor." It was this organization that would ultimately become the Milwaukee Jewish Federation.

There were still some who wanted to "broadcast" the newcomers across the land, and the farther the better. Adolph Rich, the mainstay of the Industrial Removal Office

effort in Milwaukee, found work for hundreds of refugees in the city, but he was just as determined to plant agricultural colonies. Although he presided over a dry goods empire, Rich had once been a farmer in Michigan, and he still believed, with Thomas Jefferson, that the sturdy, self-reliant tiller of the soil represented the best hope for America's future. In 1904, he arranged for the purchase of 720 acres of land near Arpin, a small town west of Stevens Point in central Wisconsin, and divided it among five families of Jewish refugees. The Arpin colony peaked at perhaps eighty people on the eve of World War I. In 1915, they established Wood County's first and only synagogue, with a Torah scroll donated by Adolph Rich himself. The group's fortunes plummeted soon thereafter—the result of back-breaking labor, cultural isolation, and fear of intermarriage. By the 1920s, many of the Arpinites had become Milwaukeeans.

Although social experimentation continued and direct relief remained important, attitudes in the philanthropic community started to change in the 1890s. Americanization was still their overriding goal, but some activists began to look at the immigrants in a new and more realistic light: as urbanites who were likely to stay for the rest of their lives, and who needed help in making the necessary adjustments. The focus of private charity shifted accordingly, from basic material support—food, shelter, employment—to social and educational development. One of the first concrete signs of the shift was an evening school that opened in 1891, during a steep rise in the flow of eastern European refugees to Milwaukee. Sponsored by the local branch of the Jewish Alliance and housed in a second-floor hall on Water Street, the school offered instruction in the English language and American civics—both prerequisites to citizenship. "Youth and frosty age alike will be welcome," reported the *Milwaukee Journal* (October 19, 1891), and the school soon enrolled nearly 100 students between the ages of six and forty-eight. "Their progress," wrote the *Journal* on December 5, "is phenomenal." The evening school was a relatively modest and ultimately short-lived effort, but it represented a new way of addressing immigrant poverty.

Then came Elizabeth Black Kander. There was an obvious chasm between the local German-Jewish establishment and the eastern European newcomers, and no one bridged that gap more enthusiastically—or more effectively—than Lizzie Kander. Her credentials

Jewish Museum Milwaukee

were impeccable. The daughter of a South Side dry goods merchant, she was a staunch member of Temple Emanu-El and a cousin of Nathan Pereles, one of the Jewish community's founding members. Her husband, Simon Kander, was a prominent figure in real estate, mining, and political circles, serving on the Milwaukee School Board and in the Wisconsin legislature. Like many women of her time and station, Lizzie Kander was a dedicated community volunteer. She joined the Ladies' Relief Sewing Society as a young woman and took part in city-wide efforts to improve the public school system. An offhand remark

Lizzie Kander evolved from a conventional do-gooder to an inspired reformer during her long career of community service.

Milwaukee Sentinel, June 13, 1897

Kander's efforts began with a children's program in the vestry of B'ne Jeshurun ...

and vice." Kander wanted to help, but she concluded that material relief was not enough. "I am almost sure," the reformer wrote, "that this <u>giving</u> for nothing is doing them more harm than good." She began to consider programs that would help every poor immigrant become "a bread winner instead of an alms receiver."

Kander started with the children. In 1895, she and a group of volunteers, many of them Sewing Society stalwarts, launched the Keep Clean Mission in the vestry rooms of Temple B'ne Jeshurun. The Mission hosted immigrant children once a week for games, craft lessons, and "entertainments" that included songs and recitations, all of them somehow related to "the Gospel of order and cleanliness." Well-scrubbed hands and faces were a prerequisite, reported the *Milwaukee Journal* (January 6, 1897), since Kander and company considered "the use of soap and water as a preliminary to the higher branches of a practical education." Attendance soared to 100 within weeks, and after the inaugural year, wrote the founder, "we were such a dignified body, we changed our name to 'The Milwaukee Jewish Mission.'"

The Mission's programs soon broadened to include "manual training" for boys (woodcarving, clay modeling, and painting) and sewing and embroidery for girls. Cooking classes were added in 1898, but B'ne Jeshurun's facilities were already taxed to the limit; the girls did their mixing and measuring in the basement of Temple Emanu-El's synagogue hall on the other side of the river. Although the programs taught useful skills, Kander considered them just as essential for building "moral character," because they encouraged "to a

at a school meeting may have launched her real career. A North Side socialite—a Gentile—complained that the schools in her district were so crowded with "untidy" Jewish kids that "they were driving out the better class of children." Lizzie Kander saw red. "I was very much aroused," she recalled, "and made up my mind, that if we Jews cared for ourselves, for the respect of our fellow citizens, we would have to do more than feed, clothe and shelter our unfortunate brethren."

Her chance to change things came when she was elected president of the Ladies' Relief Sewing Society in 1895. Repeated visits to Haymarket homes had already put Kander on intimate terms with the lives of the immigrants. She came to see their plight as an "unwritten living Drama" filled with "heros and heroines, who are struggling against poverty and prejudice, against ignorance great extent, a sense of neatness and exactness, and cultivating patience and perseverance." The Jewish Mission also promoted a proud Americanism in its young charges. The *Milwaukee Sentinel* (June 13, 1897) described the end of the day at B'ne Jeshurun: "At the mission when the sewing lesson is over and the bags are gathered up, the children sing and to Mrs. Kander's surprise the favorite song, the one most often asked for, is 'America.'"

Success built on success. As the Mission gained the confidence of its young participants, there was corresponding growth in the confidence of the women who ran it. In 1900, they made the enormous leap from the safe confines of their synagogues to the very heart of the neighborhood, leasing an old house on Fifth Street just south of Galena—one block north of Beth Hamedrosh Hagodol. They called their new venture, with elegant simplicity, The Settlement. The move enabled the women to consolidate their existing programs and to add a host of new ones, including programs for the community's adults. The Settlement was busy from 9 A.M. to 11 P.M. nearly every day of the week, with a roster of activities that included the original manual training and sewing classes, an expanded cooking school, debating societies, literary clubs, a penny savings bank, a public library branch, a night school for more than 200 students, and a reading room well-stocked with Yiddish newspapers. Nearly every Haymarket resident could find something to do at The Settlement, and it quickly became a community hub much like Chicago's famed Hull House, which Jane Addams had established in 1889. One of The Settlement's early head residents, in fact, was Stella Loeb, who had spent eight years at Hull House.

Jewish Museum Milwaukee

University of Wisconsin-Milwaukee Library Archives

If the programs were extensive, they were also expensive. Lizzie Kander was a superb fund-raiser, but she saw the need for a sustaining source of revenue that did not depend entirely on the kindness of others. In 1901, she decided to bind the recipes developed for her cooking school or contributed by its supporters in a single book, with user-friendly instructions and a variety of helpful hints. When her board declined to spend the eighteen dollars necessary to print the volume, she turned to underwriters and advertisers. The result was *The Settlement Cookbook.* Published in 1901, it was an instant success, selling out its first edition within a year (at fifty cents a copy) and generating $500 in profits for the organization. Not all the recipes were heart-healthy by

... and blossomed into The Settlement, a bustling community center in the heart of the Haymarket neighborhood.

69

The way to a man's heart

The Way To a Man's Heart

"The Settlement" Cook Book.

Milwaukee, WIS.

Mrs. Simon Kander

University of Wisconsin-Milwaukee Library Archives

modern standards (clotted cream, goose fat, and egg yolks were common ingredients), but *The Settlement Cookbook* offered an appealing range of comfort foods like pot roast, fried chicken, and macaroni and cheese alongside more exotic fare like frog legs a la Newburg and fig and pieplant dessert—all accompanied by directions simple enough for a child to follow. Although The Settlement's cooking classes were kosher, *The Settlement Cookbook* was not; it contained recipes for such *treyf* foods as pork chops and shellfish. Her culinary forays may have led far beyond the borders of tradition, but the inclusion of favorites like chicken soup, beef brisket, matzo dumplings, creplech, and kugel endeared the guide to Jewish cooks as well as non-Jews who appreciated good food. *The Settlement Cookbook* became an American standard, selling well over a million copies in multiple editions during its first fifty years. One appreciative male sent Lizzie Kander a letter of thanks, suggesting that she deserved "a Carnegie medal

The wildly successful Settlement Cookbook *debuted in 1901 as a source of revenue for Settlement programs.*

for life-saving, as I am sure that many a young husband owes the fact that he is still alive to your Settlement Cookbook."

With a promising source of revenue and growing demand for its programs, The Settlement moved to larger quarters in 1904—four doors south of its original home on Fifth Street. Lizzie Kander described the new facility as a "beautiful and substantial home," with "pleasant and commodious class and club rooms, and [a] spacious and artistic room for entertainments and social gatherings." One of the building's chief advantages was its location next to the Jung brewery. The Jung operation used copious quantities of scalding hot water to wash its beer bottles, and the owners generously piped some of it next door to The Settlement. The result was a battery of four bathtubs and six showers that were an overnight sensation. Before the High Holy Days each autumn, as many as 400 Haymarket residents used them on a daily basis. Years after the Keep Clean Mission closed, its successor was achieving Lizzie Kander's original goal on a much broader scale. But the baths were only one of many reasons to visit The Settlement. Ann Waligorski, a Kander biographer, described some of the center's programs in her master's thesis, *Social Action and Women*:

> By 1906 The Settlement was running a circulating library, 13 graded sewing classes, 5 classes in English, 2 dancing classes, 7 afternoon girls' clubs, 1 Saturday night drilling club, 11 evening clubs, game night and entertainment every Sunday, afternoon as well as evening parties and a public bath house (3¢ for adults, 1¢ for children) where 23,582 baths were taken during 1906.

There was one more move on the horizon. Although The Settlement's second home was "substantial" in Kander's estimation, it was not big enough to keep pace with demand for all the programs offered there. In October 1911, with a significant financial boost from cookbook sales, the organization moved into a brand-new and much more substantial brick building on Ninth and Vine, just north of the Walnut Street shopping district. (Elm Creative Arts, a Milwaukee public specialty school, now occupies its approximate site.) Although Lizzie Kander's board wanted to name the new facility for her, she insisted that the honor go to an American she considered even more worthy of emulation: Abraham Lincoln, who had risen from dire poverty to great heights. Lincoln House was The Settlement squared; it offered an abundance of new programs and more space for existing programs, whether classes or clubs, entertainments or lecture series. The cooking school doubled its allotment of stoves, the showers multiplied in number, and the central hall became the venue for everything from formal dances to boxing matches. Lizzie Kander was clear about the new facility's mission. Although she had begun her career as a society matron who wanted to "uplift the downtrodden," Kander's 1912 dedication speech showed how much she had grown:

> We want it distinctly understood that this is not a charitable organization. We do not claim to uplift people, neither do we seek to reform them. All we ask is justice toward every one. Our problem is that of the normal human being, to work with him and for him that he may remain normal.

Continued growth led to the building of Abraham Lincoln House, a much larger and more elaborate center, in 1911.

Jewish Museum Milwaukee

Jewish Museum Milwaukee

*Mount Sinai Hospital began in a former home for "fallen women" (top)
and graduated to a state-of-the-art facility on Twelfth St. in 1914.*

"Normal," in Kander's view, meant "American," and Lincoln House served as an important mediator, a key point of transition, between Jewish culture and mainstream society. Its programs helped the immigrants become full participants in American life, but they also honored the diversity, even the divisions, of the Jewish community. Lincoln House was aggressively open to everyone, from the most devout rabbi to the most secular laborite. The center offered Sabbath classes each week and a community Seder meal each Passover, but it also hosted Poale Zion events, Arbeiter Ring meetings, and Socialist reading circles. Lincoln House, in Kander's eyes, served all neighborhood residents as "a mother house, a community home, where people come with their joys and sorrows," regardless of their religious affiliations or political views. It was, in other words, a genuine Jewish community center.

Abraham Lincoln House and its predecessor, The Settlement, were, in fact, the direct ancestors of today's Jewish Community Center. They began as small-scale programs established by German Jews for the eastern Europeans of the Haymarket ghetto, and they evolved, over the years, into a metropolitan agency that serves not only Milwaukee's Jews but many of its non-Jewish residents as well. Two other organizations followed the same path: Mount Sinai Hospital and the Children's Outing Society. All three institutions embody both the depth and the durability of the Jewish commitment to charity and social justice.

For the vast majority of immigrant families, health care varied from scarce to nonexistent. When the Federated Jewish Charities became the umbrella group for

Jewish nonprofits in 1902, one of its highest priorities was a hospital for the community. In 1903, a group led by Max Landauer, a German-Jewish dry goods tycoon, leased a building on Fourth and Walnut—near the heart of the immigrant quarter—and opened Mount Sinai Hospital, naming it for the summit on which Moses received the Ten Commandments. The building had already served as the "German branch" of the YMCA and then the House of Refuge, a facility for "fallen women"—a group defined in those days as recovering prostitutes and unwed mothers. Remodeled for hospital purposes, Mount Sinai had a total of fifteen beds, and they were open to Gentiles as well as Jews. Rabbi Victor Caro of B'ne Jeshurun, a driving force in the hospital campaign, made that point clear in his 1903 dedication speech:

> *This occasion demonstrates an era in Judaism, not in the country or in this commonwealth, but in the city of Milwaukee. On a foundation wide in scope we have builded a house wherein shall be nursed the sick and distressed of all races and of all creeds. Today we dedicate this house, where all alike, rich and poor, Jew or Gentile, will be welcomed ….*

The philanthropic impulse was genuine, but there was another, generally unspoken reason for the establishment of a Jewish hospital. Anti-Semitism had never been entirely absent in Milwaukee, and it intensified as the Jewish community grew in numbers and influence. Well-educated professionals often felt the chill most directly. As their ranks swelled, the city's Jewish physicians frequently found the doors of other hospitals closed to them; Mount Sinai enabled them to practice their professions without fear of discrimination or outright rejection.

Popular from the start, the new hospital was perennially overcrowded, even after a twenty-six-bed addition was completed in 1909. Mount Sinai's board decided to build a new facility, and they received major assistance from Abraham Slimmer, an Iowa entrepreneur who had made a fortune in cattle, land, and lumber. Slimmer, a non-observant Jew and confirmed bachelor, developed a second career as a philanthropist, giving away millions to hospitals and homes for the elderly across the Midwest, with a particular fondness for institutions run by Catholic nuns and Jewish businessmen. Slimmer offered a $50,000 challenge grant to Mount Sinai's directors, and a community-wide campaign brought in the necessary matching funds. The resulting hospital, dedicated on November 15, 1914, was a state-of-the-art facility at Twelfth and Kilbourn, with four stories, 100 beds, and perhaps the best maternity ward in the city. Although it was only a few blocks removed from the heart of the immigrant quarter, most of the patients Mount Sinai served were non-Jews, and most of them paid nothing for their care. The Twelfth Street facility, many times enlarged, is still very much in operation as Aurora Sinai Medical Center.

If Mount Sinai Hospital aimed to cure its patients, the Children's Outing Society emphasized prevention. In 1906, convinced that the polluted air and "insanitary" conditions of the Haymarket area were harming neighborhood children, the Sisterhood of Personal Service began to take them out into the country. Their first venture was a "tent colony" near Whitewater, southwest of Milwaukee, but within three years, the women had named

The Children's Outing Society took Haymarket youngsters out to the country for "fresh air and wholesome food."

their effort the Children's Outing Society and purchased a sylvan four-acre parcel on the Milwaukee River outside Thiensville, a small town north of the city. The property's centerpiece was a home described in the 1912 annual report as "a large, airy old frame homestead in an apple and cherry orchard." Here, in two-week sessions that lasted through the summer months, the women of the Society hosted those Haymarket children "whose need for rest and change is most urgent." Activities included swimming, reading, rowing, baseball, and hayrides provided by a kindly local farmer. The children were weighed when they arrived and again after two weeks of "fresh air and wholesome food." The Society's hope was always to send them home a few pounds heavier, and with significantly lighter hearts.

Lincoln House, Mount Sinai Hospital, and the Children's Outing Society had a paradoxical impact on the Haymarket neighborhood.

Few Milwaukeeans would have called it anything but a slum; the area's income levels and housing conditions were among the worst in the city, and that is precisely why reformers like Lizzie Kander lavished so much attention on the community. But the Haymarket was also the home of synagogues, self-help societies, businesses and, above all, family networks that reflected a far more positive reality. The reformers built on that native wealth, listening to local residents and changing their programs as circumstances dictated. The Settlement and later Lincoln House thus became the single most important institutions in the neighborhood, reaching virtually every resident on every block, and Mount Sinai and the Children's Outing Society cut across the internal lines just as effectively. As a result, institutions rooted in a concern for poverty helped to make the Haymarket one of the city's richest human communities—an urban village like few others in Milwaukee's history.

The German Jews: Affluence and Assimilation

There is no doubt that the coming of the eastern Europeans and their multiple adjustments to American life were the defining events of the 1882-1914 period in Milwaukee's Jewish history. The immigrants were new, they were numerous, and they were unmistakably different. But the Jews who preceded them—the German-speakers who had established their foothold in pioneer days—still constituted a sizable and influential community in their own right, one whose members, despite the inspired outreach of figures like Lizzie Kander, generally kept a careful, even wary, distance from the newcomers. The world of the German Jews changed just as much as the eastern European community's after 1882, but it evolved in different directions. The major trends of the early years continued and even intensified: affluence, assimilation, and an increasingly attenuated Judaism.

The story of the German Jews is most clearly told through their Reform synagogues. B'ne Jeshurun, Milwaukee's pioneer congregation, and Emanu-El, its more opulent daughter, were probably the best-known Jewish institutions in the city—at least until Mount Sinai Hospital emerged as a leading health-care facility. The downtown synagogues were joined by a third and much smaller Reform synagogue whose presence has been all but forgotten: Temple Sinai. Although Milwaukee's Jews were concentrated on the East and West Sides, there had long been a minor settlement on the city's South Side. Many of the families there, including Lizzie Kander's, crossed the Menomonee Valley to worship at Emanu-El or B'ne Jeshurun each Sabbath—until 1900, when a group of South Siders decided to form a congregation of their own. They worshiped in a rented school building at first, but in 1905, after the usual round of fund-raising activities,

The short-lived Temple Sinai was the first and only Jewish institution on Milwaukee's South Side.

Jewish Museum Milwaukee

Dedicated in 1887, B'ne Jeshurun's new synagogue was a concrete expression of the congregation's growing affluence.

the faithful dedicated Temple Sinai on the corner of S. Ninth and Mineral Streets—near the heart of today's Walker's Point neighborhood. The congregation was prosperous enough to employ its own rabbi for a time, but Temple Sinai never emerged from the shadow of its larger Reform sisters. Rabbi Bennett Grad, himself a West Sider, looked on the bright side in a 1913 newsletter: "The interest and loyalty of its members more than counterbalance the paucity of numbers and the smallness of place." Grad's enthusiasm was apparently not shared by everyone in the congregation. Temple Sinai disbanded in 1915, and its site was eventually cleared for the construction of Interstate 94.

B'ne Jeshurun and Emanu-El experienced no such vicissitudes. Stable memberships

and steady pew rents enabled both to upgrade their facilities continuously after 1882. For B'ne Jeshurun, that meant practically starting over. Industrial development was fast overtaking its Fifth Street neighborhood, and in 1885 the congregation sold its temple to a manufacturer who converted it to a galvanized iron works. After worshiping in a rented hall on Wisconsin Avenue for nearly two years, B'ne Jeshurun dedicated a new synagogue on the southeast corner of Kilbourn Avenue and Tenth Street—five blocks west of its old home. The site was not far from the impoverished Haymarket neighborhood but close enough to the mansion district of Wisconsin (then Grand) Avenue to absorb some of its cachet. B'ne Jeshurun's new home was "of the modern Moorish or Romanesque style," reported the *Milwaukee*

Milwaukee County Historical Society

Journal, and "imposing in the extreme," with an ornate brick façade and room for 700 worshipers. The 1887 structure became even more imposing in 1906, when the sanctuary was enlarged and stained-glass windows were installed to mark the congregation's fiftieth anniversary.

The people of Emanu-El were content to remodel rather than rebuild. Their landmark building on Broadway was selectively updated—central heating was installed in 1881 and electric lights flickered on in 1896—but the major improvement was a building next door. Concerned about their lack of social and educational facilities, the women of the temple organized a "monster fair" in 1892 that netted $12,000 for the cause. Emanu-El Hall, built on the lot immediately north of the synagogue, was dedicated in 1893. It provided parlors and a dining room for social events, classrooms for the congregation's Sunday school, and space for a variety of other programs during the week, including the Seventh Ward kindergarten and Lizzie Kander's cooking classes. Although the temple and hall were more than adequate for a community of 100 families, Emanu-El's location was not. What had been a largely residential district when the synagogue was built in 1872 had become part of Milwaukee's downtown, and encroaching commercial development convinced the temple's leaders to start looking for a less lively address.

Ever since the congregations divorced in 1869, there were periodic rumors (and even newspaper reports) that Emanu-El and B'ne Jeshurun were on the verge of a

Emanu-El Hall (highlighted) closed the gap between Milwaukee's most prestigious synagogue and the German-English Academy next door.

77

reconciliation that would create a single large Reform body in Milwaukee. Major investments in new buildings made that prospect increasingly remote, but the synagogues grew closer in other respects. Although B'ne Jeshurun remained the more conservative of the two temples, the rabbis on both sides of the river shared a commitment to classical Reform Judaism. Emanuel Gerechter, a soft-spoken immigrant from the German partition of Poland, held B'ne Jeshurun's pulpit from 1880 to 1892. His successor was Victor Caro, a theological liberal and community activist who stayed until his death in 1912. Caro was instrumental in the establishment of Mount Sinai Hospital, among other institutions. Emanu-El's religious leaders tended to be somewhat more colorful and certainly less orthodox than B'ne Jeshurun's. Isaac Moses, who served Emanu-El from 1879 to 1887, was a genuine radical who earned national attention—and widespread criticism—for presiding over the marriage of a Jewish man and a Christian woman in 1880. When the rabbi's own daughter eloped with a Gentile bookkeeper fifteen years later—over his vehement objections— one disaffected Emanu-El member declared that Moses was getting "a dose of his own medicine." (Others took a more philosophical view of intermarriage, accepting the union of a Jew and a Christian as nothing more than "the Old and New Testament bound together.") Sigmund Hecht, another liberal and a fervent ecumenist, followed Moses at Emanu-El. Hecht served from 1888 to 1899, when he left to take a pulpit in Los Angeles. His successors were Julius Meyer from 1900 to 1904 and then Samuel Hirshberg, a Harvard alumnus who stayed until 1947—one of the longest rabbinical tenures in Milwaukee's history. Although none of the Reform rabbis rose to the stature that Solomon Scheinfeld enjoyed in the eastern European community, Samuel Hirshberg came the closest. For more than forty years, he was the leading voice of Reform Judaism in Milwaukee.

Rabbis Emanuel Gerechter (left) and Victor Caro (right, with confirmands) led B'ne Jeshurun from 1880 to 1912.

Although they varied widely in outlook and temperament, Milwaukee's Reform rabbis often worked in tandem. Emanu-El and B'ne Jeshurun alternated Sabbath services during the summer months in the 1890s, preferring to see rows of empty pews in one temple rather than two. The congregations jointly hosted regional Reform conventions—meetings that B'ne Jeshurun would have shunned a decade or two earlier—and regularly held joint Thanksgiving services. The rabbis also participated in each other's celebrations as well as those of the eastern European community. When Emanu-El marked its silver anniversary with a lavish banquet in 1894, Rabbi Caro of B'ne Jeshurun offered a toast to "the two congregations—mother and daughter." One year earlier, when Beth Hamedrosh Hagodol (Beth Israel) dedicated its new shul on Fifth Street, Rabbis Caro and Hecht were among the officiants.

Worship was another point of convergence. Members of both Emanu-El and B'ne Jeshurun had grown accustomed over the years to dignified services, erudite sermons, and fine music

each Sabbath. Professional choirs added a high gloss to the ancient melodies, and a professional organist kept them in tune. (Both temples employed the same organist in the 1890s: Rafael Baez, who may have been Milwaukee's first Mexican immigrant.) The same emphasis on decorum applied to social and cultural events. In 1891, Rabbi Hecht of Emanu-El issued a call to "the entire progressive Jewish community of Milwaukee," urging the development of programs for "the promotion of social and intellectual improvement." The result was the Literary and Social Life Society. Some of its activities were the epitome of high culture, including "An Evening with Longfellow" in 1893, which featured a recitation of the unabridged *Hiawatha*, complete with "living pictures." Others were quite the opposite, including an 1894 program that was utterly scandalous by modern standards. Hoping to raise money for charity, the Literary and Social Life Society staged a "women's minstrel entertainment" at Emanu-El Hall. "A number of leading Jewish society women will blacken their pretty faces and entertain the audience," wrote the *Milwaukee Sentinel*

Three rabbis dominated the 1879-1947 period at Emanu-El (l. to r.): Isaac Moses, Sigmund Hecht, and Samuel Hirshberg. Hirshberg held Emanu-El's pulpit for forty-three years.

Jewish Museum Milwaukee

Jewish entrepreneurs made Milwaukee a national capital of the knitwear industry. Phoenix (top left), Holeproof (above), and National Knitting (top right) were among the local giants.

(March 31, 1894). Their production featured racist chestnuts like *Mammie's Little Boy* and *Dem Chiming Bells*.

For all they had in common, and despite the occasional lapses in taste, there were important differences between Milwaukee's two leading Reform congregations. The people of Emanu-El took a predictably liberal approach to the issues of the day. In 1898, the East Siders, who had long worshiped exclusively in English, began to consider Sunday services—a radical departure from the traditional Sabbath—while their West Side counterparts were still offering prayers on Friday evening and Saturday morning in the old-fashioned German—a practice that would persist until the early years of World War I. Rabbi Hecht of Emanu-El was generally the only

Jew at local interfaith worship services. In 1891, he became the first rabbi ever to attend a gathering of the Milwaukee Ministers' Association, which opened with the singing of *All Hail, the Power of Jesus' Name*. Hecht presumably remained silent.

Although powerful forces were pushing them closer together, the two congregations were also different demographically. Simply put, B'ne Jeshurun was larger and Emanu-El was richer. In 1895, the West Side temple had 150 families on its membership rolls and Emanu-El only 95—a ratio that would hold relatively constant for the next twenty years. Attendance at B'ne Jeshurun sometimes topped 1,000 during the High Holy Days. If dollars alone were counted, however, the scales tilted to the East Side. In 1890, not long after B'ne Jeshurun completed its "imposing" new building, the West Side temple was assessed at $32,000; the corresponding figure for Emanu-El was $80,000. The *Milwaukee Sentinel* (August 10, 1890) confidently declared that the aggregate wealth of Emanu-El's membership totaled $9 million. There was plenty of money on both sides of the river, but the lawns, and the pocketbooks, were generally greener on the East Side.

For the affluent families who supported Milwaukee's major Reform congregations, or at least attended their services on High Holy Days, business had never been better. Fortunes created in the mid-1800s grew larger with time, and often in the same industries. Milwaukee's garment trade employed 3,500 people in 1899, most of them making men's and boy's clothing for the western market, and Jewish firms were absolutely dominant. The Friends and Adlers were still the undisputed kings, but there were also promising newcomers like National Knitting, Holeproof Hosiery, and Phoenix Knitting Works. Dry goods remained another Jewish stronghold, with the Landauer, Mack, and Rich families leading the way. Adolph Rich broadened his reach from wholesale and retail trade to manufacturing, turning out 2,500 pairs of shoes every day in two Milwaukee plants.

Other entrepreneurs found new opportunities in retail. The itinerant army of Jewish peddlers who had been scouring the countryside for decades finally produced a few generals who took command of Milwaukee's department store scene. Edward Schuster opened his first store in 1884 with partner Albert Friedman and eventually became the largest general retailer in Wisconsin. It was a Schuster's department store on Third Street that entranced Golda Meir during her first days in Milwaukee. Boston Store was another contender. Founded by Julius Simon in 1897 and acquired by Nat Stone

Footwear was another Jewish stronghold, largely due to the efforts of Adolph Rich, whose factories turned out 2,500 pairs of shoes a day.

81

Milwaukee Public Library

Milwaukee from their family's first commercial foothold in Vincennes, Indiana. The new store was so successful that various brothers left town to start similar establishments up and down the East Coast. Jewish retailers served the city's neighborhoods as well, and one business—Goldmann's department store—became a South Side legend. With its wooden floors, vast array of "plus" sizes, and old-fashioned lunch counter, Goldmann's was a fixture on Mitchell Street from 1898 until its closing in 2007.

Still other aspiring business leaders made forays into fields not typically associated with Jewish enterprise, particularly heavy industry. In 1890, Jacob Friend, a lawyer by training, put some of the capital from his family's garment business into a fledgling factory started by Bruno Nordberg, a Finnish-born engineer and inventor. Nordberg's first device, a steam engine governor, was an instant success, and other products followed in rapid

Schuster's (above) *and Gimbel's department stores were two more Jewish contributions to local commerce.*

and Carl Herzfeld in 1906, it followed the "Boston plan" of multiple departments under a single roof. The main Boston Store on Fourth and Wisconsin, completed in 1900, remains a prominent downtown landmark well over a century later. America's first full-fledged Gimbels department store opened a few blocks east in 1887, when six of the seven Gimbel brothers moved to

Milwaukee Public Library

succession. In 1895, Jacob Friend became president of the Nordberg Manufacturing Company, a firm that rose to a position of world leadership in steam engines, marine diesels, and mining equipment. The Friend family would supply Nordberg with executive talent and financial backing for the next seventy-five years.

Success in the business world was always welcome, but it also entailed a few cultural adjustments. Working on the Sabbath and even on the High Holy Days was a given, and constant contact with mainstream society tended to dilute purely Jewish associations. That was just fine with most of the community's entrepreneurs. Grateful for their opportunities and pleased with their success, the newly affluent businessmen embraced their American identities, whatever the collateral damage to their ancestral ties. Nathan Pereles, a community founder and first president of B'ne Jeshurun, was probably an extreme case. As his assets multiplied, the lawyer and financier left no doubt as to his primary allegiance, naming his three sons Benjamin Franklin Pereles, James Madison Pereles, and Thomas Jefferson Pereles.

There were no cautionary tales from the community's rabbis. Even the most ardent assimilationists heard nothing but affirmative echoes from the pulpits of their synagogues. Reform leaders tended to view Judaism as one strand among many in the American tapestry and, although they insisted on their religious particularity, the rabbis were just as insistent on asserting their place in the larger society. They had been good Germans in Germany, and they were intent on being good Americans in America.

Milwaukee Public Library

Metso Minerals

Metso Minerals

There were also forays into manufacturing. Jacob Friend was president of the Nordberg Company, whose Bay View plant made some of the largest diesel engines in the world.

The Milwaukee Sentinel *(Jan. 1, 1893) illustrated three Jewish holiday customs: lighting the menorah at Chanukah, blowing the shofar at Rosh Hashanah, and playing with the dreidel at Chanukah.*

Victor Caro made the point emphatically in his 1899 Thanksgiving Day sermon:

> *With the only exception of separate channels in which our religious life may flow, we refuse all imputations to lead a separate life from Christian fellow citizens.... We do not want separate parochial schools, we abhor the idea of a separate Jewish ballot box, we renounce allegiance to a Hebrew trades union—in short we loathe anything and everything which may seem as an entering wedge between us and American institutions.*

There was the ever-present danger that the baby would be thrown out with the bathwater. Milwaukee's German Jews and their religious leaders were attempting a difficult balancing act: to become loyal Americans and to remain faithful Jews at the same time. That has been a challenge in every age, including our own, and there were clear indications that Reform Judaism was losing ground at the turn of the twentieth century. As more Jews took a greater interest in the majority culture, their minority faith was typically one of the first things to go. That did not necessarily imply a conversion to Christianity. Few converted, in fact, but many deserted. In Milwaukee and elsewhere, members of the second and even the first generation decided that their ties to Judaism were more cultural than spiritual, and that material concerns were quite enough to occupy their time. As a result, the ranks of the formerly faithful swelled. Nathan Pereles, for instance, became a self-described freethinker later in life, and his sons,

although they held positions of influence in the public school and public library systems, were absent from the leadership rolls of the synagogues. Many of the community's most successful German Jews became just as secular as the poorest and most radical revolutionaries in the Haymarket neighborhood, although for different reasons. For the radicals, traditional Judaism was too freighted with superstition and irrationality to take seriously. For the affluent and even for the merely comfortable, traditional Judaism was frequently seen as a worn-out relic of the buried past. Without bothering to change their names, in most cases, or to submit formal letters of resignation to their rabbis, they simply left the fold.

The rising tide of secularism was apparent even among those who continued to rent pews. Emanu-El and B'ne Jeshurun had a combined membership of perhaps 250 families in 1900, or roughly 1,250 individuals. That was a minority of the Jews in Milwaukee—even the German Jews—and within that select group, only a minority could be described as devout. Those who maintained their memberships were often lukewarm at best—a cause of endless rabbinical hand-wringing. "There is no truth, no kindness, no knowledge of God in this congregation as a congregation," Sigmund Hecht thundered to the people of Emanu-El in 1890. "There is more levity, more sacrilege, more blasphemy to the square inch here than can be found in any other community in the land." Harsh words, but Victor Caro came to the same conclusion at B'ne Jeshurun in 1898:

American Jews are undoubtedly alive and active, but we cannot truthfully say that they are spiritually strong or healthy. In most cases the form is upheld, while the substance is sacrificed or virtually left out of consideration.... Prayer is as good as gone, and to make a long story short, we are Jews in name, not reality.

The rabbis were tired of looking out Sabbath after Sabbath on a sea of empty pews. In 1898, shortly before his departure for what he hoped would be the greener pastures of Los Angeles, Sigmund Hecht described the prevailing tenor of worship at Emanu-El: "I would say that the most regular in attendance at the weekly services were the Rabbi and the Choir; next to them may be mentioned the presidents and the vice-presidents, and a few, very few, of our men and some of our good ladies." One of Hecht's successors, Samuel Hirshberg, found conditions virtually unchanged six years later. Soon after taking Emanu-El's pulpit in 1904, Hirshberg grumbled that his flock contained "a great many people who are unbelievers, skeptics and doubters, people who ... take delight in boasting that they are as little Jew as it is possible to be." The rabbis had no difficulty naming the culprit: it was the materialism that pervaded American society and waylaid even the most devout. "An age has been reached," Sigmund Hecht lamented in 1898, "when everyone foolishly, unreasonably struggles for one position—to be rich." The inevitable result was religious apathy, an even greater calamity than religious strife. "Nothing," said Hecht, "is so fatal to the prosperity of a cause than apathy."

One City, Two Worlds

The sagging fortunes of the Reform temples underscored the differences that had developed between Milwaukee's German Jews and their eastern European brethren. The newcomers were not immune to the pressures of American society, but there is no doubt that religion was a more integral part of their lives than it was for the native community. The *Milwaukee Sentinel* (April 15, 1900) described the transformation that came over the Haymarket area each Sabbath:

On Friday nights and Saturday mornings, the neighborhood puts on new aspects. The shawls disappear and the women blossom out in gay headgear. Those who can afford black satin gowns flaunt their insignia of aristocracy in the faces of their less fortunate neighbors. The children are dragged in from the streets and are scrubbed about those portions of their anatomy that their best clothes will not conceal, and into these best clothes they are ruthlessly thrust with many injunctions to beware of rents and dirt....

Then everyone goes to church. The synagogues are filled with worshippers who carry great Bibles printed in large Hebrew text, and the men bring with them besides their "taliths," rolled up carefully in calico bags.... It is the Jewish Sabbath and the Haymarket district observes it with a fervor that many a rabbi of a more fashionable congregation would give much to have repeated in quality if not in kind.

Jewish Museum Milwaukee

Abraham Forman posed with tallit, tefillin,
and prayer book for his Bar Mitzvah
ceremony, probably at Anshe Sfard. Such
strict fidelity to tradition was unheard-
of at Milwaukee's Reform synagogues.

Reform rabbis may have envied the fervor of the Haymarket shuls, but they wanted no part of their rituals. Although they visited the neighborhood on special occasions and accorded Rabbi Solomon Scheinfeld the respect he was due, Reform leaders rarely hesitated to criticize the Old World ways of the eastern Europeans. Isaac Moses of Emanu-El lampooned the "meaningless forms and old unintelligible ceremonies and foreign costumes that had their origin in superstition and fear." The immigrants' opinion of their longer-tenured neighbors was just as unflattering. They viewed the Germans as nothing less than apostates, whose religious rites, dress, and manners seemed Jewish only in the most generous sense of the term. One outcome of the continuing stand-off was a capitalization. There had been no distinctly "orthodox" worship in the shtetls of eastern Europe. In America, however, the traditional forms were finally subsumed under the heading of Orthodox to distinguish them from Reform practice.

Of all the issues that separated Orthodoxy from Reform, there was none more divisive than Zionism. Steeped in suffering, the eastern Europeans embraced the idea of a Jewish homeland with messianic fervor; they looked to Palestine as a spiritual and emotional anchor for themselves and a place of deliverance for all those Jews who had not been fortunate enough to reach America's shores. The Reform movement in general and Milwaukee's Reform leaders in particular wanted nothing to do with the national aspirations of the newcomers. Judaism was their faith, but America was their home, and fantasies of a far-off utopia seemed pointless in the extreme. Sigmund Hecht said as much in an 1899 sermon:

The Jewish nationality was ended some 1800 years ago. Since then Israel's mission is purely spiritual. The Jew does not today stand for race or nationality; his is the religious mission of peace and good will, his it is to verify the prophetic vision of the Messianic time.

If to suffer be the lot of the Jew today, let him still continue to do his duty. Instead of dreaming day-dreams that cannot and ought not be fulfilled, let him work and hope.

Hecht blasted Zionism as "economically impossible, as anti-religious and as historically inadmissible," and the rabbi went even further in an 1890 letter to the *Milwaukee Sentinel*: "I would venture the assertion that if every Jew here [in America] were offered a free pass first-class to Palestine he would not accept it unless it were a round-trip ticket."

Zionism was a particularly potent example of the issues that separated German Jews from their eastern European counterparts, but much of the distance between the two groups was simply cultural. To German-speakers whose families had been in Milwaukee since the mid-1800s, the newcomers were unfamiliar, uncouth, and frequently unwashed. They were, in short, an embarrassment. Victor Caro complained in 1897 that the immigrants were not particularly gracious recipients of German-Jewish charity, calling them "insolent and imperative in their demands, freely criticizing and even cursing the almoner when their wishes were not acceded to." Sigmund Hecht was even more appalled by their willingness to form Hebrew political clubs:

Our dear Russian brethren, who have done much to cast a stigma on the Jewish name, are now adding this new sin to their long list of offenses which we are asked to stand responsible for. What we combat with zeal, they introduce, and what we seek to dispel as unworthy, they approve and establish.

If the German-Jewish rabbis expressed such sentiments in public forums, we are left to wonder what they might have said in the privacy of their inner circles. Even Lizzie Kander, in the early stages of her career, described charity work as a question of Jewish self-defense:

We must uplift our downtrodden and shiftless poor, not alone for their own sake and for that of humanity, but for the reputation of our own nationality. Their misdeeds reflect directly on us and every one of us, individually, ought to do all in his power to help lay the foundation of good citizenship in them.

It should be emphasized that the German Jews never shirked what they considered their moral obligation to help the newcomers, and there were some marvelous examples of human interaction at The Settlement, Lincoln House, and other community institutions. But the atmosphere of mutual distrust and thinly veiled dislike that characterized relations between the two dominant Jewish groups is hard to mistake.

Precisely what the eastern Europeans thought of their German-Jewish neighbors is difficult to say—there are apparently no surviving accounts—but we can at least surmise. The gap between affluence and poverty is always more visible to the poor than

Milwaukee Public Library

The aristocratic Henry Benjamin used the profits from his coal business to build an imposing mansion on Prospect Ave.

Milwaukee Public Library

to the rich. The immigrants could not have failed to notice the opulence of the Reform synagogues, particularly in contrast to the shabbiness of their own first attempts, or the scale of the Jewish businesses in which many of them found employment. The German Jews were indeed ensconced in the upper strata of Milwaukee society. There was a cluster of Adlers on the lower end of fashionable Prospect Avenue and a sprinkling of Friends in the posh Yankee Hill neighborhood to the west. Coal dealer Henry Benjamin's home on Prospect was lavish enough to merit inclusion in the standard Milwaukee viewbooks of the day. The Phoenix Club, established in 1885, was a playhouse for the cream of German-Jewish society. Its stone mansion on Jefferson Street, acquired for $50,000 and remodeled in 1899 for another $18,000, was described by the *Milwaukee Sentinel* (November 18, 1899) as "one of the handsomest and most commodious club houses in the west," with features that included a bowling alley, a gymnasium, card rooms, a wine cellar, a "gentleman's sitting room," a library, ladies' parlors, a billiard hall, a ballroom, and a dining room for 200 that was connected to a servants' room "where twenty-five waiters can be marshaled." For residents of the Haymarket neighborhood, such luxury must have seemed as distant as Mars.

There were roughly 15,000 Jews in Milwaukee by 1914. Although their community made up less than 0.5 percent of the city's population, Jews demonstrated more internal diversity than groups many times their size. Two worlds developed within one city; two paths emerged for one people. The eastern Europeans probably outnumbered the German Jews by a margin of two

Jewish Museum Milwaukee

The Phoenix Club on Jefferson St. was another symbol of German-Jewish affluence.

or three to one, but the Germans had just as disproportionate a share of the economic power. What emerged from within the confines of a single small community was a split between the bourgeoisie and the proletariat. The immigrants were often employees on the lower rungs of the economic ladder, and the native Jews were frequently employers at the very top. Conflict, in the charged labor climate of the time, was probably inevitable. One entrepreneur earned widespread censure for firing an observant worker during the High Holy Days of 1889. Rabbi Sigmund Hecht thought the end of the world was at hand: "When finally Jewish business men can find it in them to discharge their Jewish employees who will not work on Yom Kippur … it is no wonder that all grows dark and gloomy around."

Even more troubling was the garment workers' strike of 1910. The Adler clan was famously philanthropic and intensely committed to Reform Judaism, but its members were just as earnestly opposed to labor unions. By December 7, 1910, nearly 2,200 garment workers were on strike, and David Adler & Sons was their primary target. Haymarket residents were well-represented on the picket lines. One of the largest Adler plants was on the eastern edge of their neighborhood, and the strike meetings were held at Bohemian Turn Hall on its western border. The garment industry's polyglot work force presented special challenges for labor organizers,

The 1910 Adler Clothing strike exposed a gulf between the old German-Jewish establishment and working-class Jewish newcomers.

who had to address the crowd in Yiddish, Russian, Bohemian, German, and English. The dispute was finally settled on December 10. Adler agreed to reduce the standard workweek to fifty-four hours and to pay time-and-a-half for overtime—without accepting a closed shop—but the firm's labor troubles were far from over.

There must have been times when the gap between the well-established German Jews and the still-struggling eastern Europeans seemed all but unbridgeable. One group had size but the other had influence and, despite some highly effective philanthropic efforts, they disagreed on matters of religion, politics, and even labor conditions. But the gap was not destined to last forever. Although no one noticed at the time, the ground was shifting beneath the feet of both groups. As the world prepared to go to war in 1914, the natives and the newcomers were inching toward a cultural confluence that neither of them could have begun to predict.

Chapter 3
Into the Whirlwind, *1914-1945*

Few periods in American history have brought so much change on so many levels in such a short time. The years between 1914 and 1945 began with one global conflict and ended with another, and between those traumatic bookends came a breathtaking economic rise in the 1920s and an equally vertiginous collapse in the 1930s. Any of those events would have been epoch-making in its own right, but together they constituted a whirlwind that blew without pause for more than three decades. Not since the Civil War had the nation experienced such palpable stress. Not since the beginning of mass emigration from Europe had there been such a trans-formation of its social landscape. And never had the United States played such a pivotal role on the world stage. The whirlwind blew from the start of the 1914-1945 period to its close, col-lapsing the established order and shattering ancient expectations.

The whirlwind touched everyone, but Milwaukee's Jews experienced it more directly than some of their neighbors. For German Jews, as for all German Milwaukeeans, the cultural foothold that had taken them generations to secure seemed to crumble practically overnight. For eastern Euro-pean Jews and their German neighbors alike, purely local concerns were overshadowed by events taking place on the far side of the ocean. The previous decades had been eventful for both groups, but the changes of the pre-World War I era seem measured and inevitable in comparison with the tumult that followed. As the whirlwind carried the nation from war to boom, from boom to bust, and from bust to war again, the Jewish community tumbled along with it, absorbing the shocks and adjusting as it could. By the time the period ended, the whirlwind was slowing down to reveal America—and Milwaukee's Jewish community—in their modern forms.

The Great War

The outbreak of the European war in August 1914 was greeted with enormous trepidation in Milwaukee. Although the United States was offi-cially neutral—a stance it would maintain until April 1917—the city's German majority viewed their government's tacit support of the Allied cause with growing unease. They may have lived on American soil for generations, but German Milwaukeeans, whether Gentile or Jewish, retained a sentimental attachment to the Fatherland, and Kaiser Wilhelm's portrait had a place of honor in many homes. Eastern European Jews were just as worried but for different reasons, most of them based on Old World attachments that transcended mere sentiment. Although their community had been planted in the early 1880s, most of the immigrants were significantly more recent arrivals. The Dillingham Commission study published in 1911 found that 49 percent of the Haymarket area's Russian Jews had been in the country for fewer than five years and 68.5 percent for fewer than ten. It is likely that a sub-stantial majority still had parents, siblings, or even spouses and children in Europe. Some of those relatives were living under the Cen-tral Powers—Germany and Austria-Hun-gary—and a greater number were marooned in tsarist Russia, which fought on the side of England, France, and ultimately the United States. When the shooting started in 1914, thousands of Milwaukeeans had family members trapped behind the lines on both sides of the eastern front. Emigration was an impossibility, and the telegraph brought horrific reports of shtetls being overrun, houses burned, and people displaced by the millions. The embryonic Jewish community in Palestine—85,000 settlers strong in 1914—was also in harm's way. The crumbling Ottoman Empire, whose holdings included Palestine, sided with Germany, and its religious minorities, Christians as well as Jews, suffered privation and persecution throughout the war years.

Although they were thousands of miles from the action, Milwaukee's eastern European Jews felt neither helpless nor hopeless. A handful actually joined a British detachment fighting in Palestine, but the vast majority channeled their energies and anxieties into a massive relief effort. In

The Ezra Betzar campaign brought crucial help to Jews trapped behind the lines during World War I.

September 1914, only weeks after the first shots were fired, a movement called Ezra Betzar ("Help in Distress") began in Milwaukee's eastern European community. Part of a national initiative, it brought together an unprecedented array of organizations— forty-three in all, from Socialist circles to Orthodox synagogues—who put aside their differences to raise money for the relief of Jewish "war sufferers." The campaign, chaired by Rabbi Solomon Scheinfeld, was absolutely relentless. Two-person teams made a house-to-house sweep of the entire Haymarket neighborhood every Sunday morning, and collectors were much in evidence at weddings, circumcisions, picnics, dances, High Holy Day services, and anywhere else two or more Jews might gather. Banquets and rallies featured speakers who brought tales of suffering from the Russian front and made eloquent appeals for support. Dr. Judah Magnes, a prominent Reform leader who visited in 1917, pronounced Ezra Betzar a moral imperative:

> *This is not a charity, not a philanthropy, nor a dole which you are asked to give. It is a tax you are asked to pay in fulfillment of a sacred duty. We demand that you give what you can, your conscience to dictate the amount, that you may retain your self-respect, and that the lives and dignity of the Jewish people across the sea may be preserved.*

Although their neighborhood was still one of the poorest in Milwaukee, Haymarket residents were constantly reminded of the "comfort and luxury" they enjoyed in comparison with the suffering of their brethren in the war zone. The theme of the 1916 Ezra Betzar drive was "A life blessed for a

Jewish Museum Milwaukee

life blighted." The eastern European Jews were intensely conscious of their good fortune as Americans, but the group's Old World roots kept showing through. The *Milwaukee Journal* (March 26, 1916) described a popular attraction at a Haymarket relief bazaar: "In one corner were five antique Russian samovars from which hot tea was served. The visitors drank from glasses, an old country custom." The bazaars and the banquets, the Sunday drives and the pulpit pleas had their desired effect. By the time Ezra Betzar folded its tent in 1922, the group had raised $127,889.36 for the relief of fellow Jews reduced to want by war—nearly $1.8 million in current dollars.

Milwaukee's German Jews were generally supportive of the relief effort, but they had far less at stake than the eastern Europeans; the natives viewed Ezra Betzar as a response to human need, not a lifeline to starving relatives. Their perspective began to change on April 6, 1917, when the United States entered the war on the Allied side. Nearly two million Americans ended up "over there," including perhaps 700 Milwaukee Jews. Emanu-El, the leading Reform congregation, had sixty sons and daughters directly involved in the war effort. The conflict suddenly took on a personal dimension for the community's parents, and American citizenship outweighed German ancestry for nearly everyone. The faithful of Emanu-El were just as busy with bond drives and bandage-wrapping as their Orthodox counterparts across the river.

The "Great War" became a communal preoccupation, but it was not the only one for Milwaukee's Jews. As the fighting continued, they took part in an extraordinary experiment in communal democracy. In

Milwaukee Public Library

1915, even before the United States entered the war, American Jewish leaders began to look beyond the armed conflict to the new order that was bound to emerge in peacetime. The fruit of their efforts was the American Jewish Congress (AJC), an advocacy group whose primary goals were the protection of Jewish rights in postwar Europe and, after some discussion, the creation of a Jewish state in Palestine. The success of Ezra Betzar had demonstrated that Milwaukee's Jews could work together across religious and ideological lines. The American Jewish Congress hoped to develop the same unity on the national level. The most novel feature of the AJC was its insistence on representative democracy. Every Jewish organization in the country—every synagogue, fraternal lodge, political group, ladies' auxiliary, mutual aid society, even youth camp—was considered an "election precinct" whose members could vote for their

When the United States entered the fray in 1917, nearly 700 Jewish soldiers were among the Milwaukeeans who marched off to war.

In the spring of 1917, while the rest of the city was buzzing with war news, Milwaukee's Jewish community was in the midst of a red-hot election contest. Corner rallies, pulpit talks, and newspaper ads touted the virtues of several candidates, each with a somewhat different view of the American Jewish Congress's proper role. One of the Zionist slate's most effective campaigners was none other than Goldie Mabowehz. At nineteen, she was already a seasoned organizer with a well-developed sympathy for the underdog. In 1908, when she was only ten, Goldie had founded the American Young Sisters' Society, a group of Haymarket youngsters who, without adult prompting or supervision, contributed three cents a week to buy schoolbooks for children too poor to afford them. The young woman had blossomed into a fierce Zionist and a fearless public speaker. In 1917, the future Golda Meir stood on a soapbox outside Beth Israel on Fifth Street and made a passionate plea for the Zionist ticket—"not without some panic," she recalled in *My Life*. Her father, a Zionist but clearly not a feminist, had made it apparent that he disapproved of her public appearances, and Moshe Mabowehz threatened to "come after me and publicly pull me home by my braid" if she insisted on speaking at Beth Israel. As it turned out, Goldie had nothing to fear:

When I finally got home, I found my mother waiting up for me in the kitchen. Father was already asleep, she told me, but he had been at the street corner meeting and had heard me speak. "I don't know where she gets it from," he said to her wonderingly. He had been so

Goldie Mabowehz—the future Golda Meir—in 1917, when she was already one of Milwaukee's most ardent Zionists

district's delegates to a national convention. Poale Zion, the voice of labor Zionism in Milwaukee, got the ball rolling, but virtually every Jewish organization in town was involved in the campaign, even German-Jewish groups whose leaders had been skeptical at first.

completely carried away listening to me perched on my soapbox that he had completely forgotten his threat! Neither of us referred to the incident again but I consider that to have been the most successful speech I ever made.

The result of all the electioneering was a split ticket. The first nominating convention for AJC delegates was held at the North Side Auditorium on May 20, 1917—less than two months after the United States declared war on Germany. The *Milwaukee Journal* billed it as "the most important gathering in the history of Milwaukee Jewry" and predicted that "every Jewish organization will be represented." The newspaper wasn't far off the mark. Members of sixty-four organizations cast their ballots, narrowing the field to four candidates: two eastern European Zionists and two German-Jewish leaders who were less convinced of the need for a national homeland. The final election, held on June 10, brought out 4,123 voters who paid a poll tax of ten cents each to cast a ballot for their favorites. In a community of roughly 17,000, including infants and children, that was a rather remarkable turnout. The winners again represented a split decision: Ephraim Lisitzky, a Hebrew teacher and ardent Zionist, and Charles Friend, a leading lawyer and Emanu-El stalwart who headed the Hebrew Relief Association.

The inaugural session of the American Jewish Congress was finally called to order in Philadelphia on December 15, 1918, with Milwaukee's delegates duly seated. Although its high hopes for a Jewish state in Palestine and minority rights in Europe were not realized—at least not in 1918—the AJC was a singular achievement for America's

Jews. It was a shining demonstration of their overarching sense of peoplehood and an equally clear sign of their extraordinary penchant for organization. By insisting on grassroots participation, the Congress enhanced both of those qualities—in Milwaukee and throughout the nation.

By the time the inaugural session began, World War I was over. The stirring sound of the shofar—the ram's horn traditionally blown on Rosh Hashanah—was heard all over the Haymarket neighborhood when the Armistice was declared on November 11, 1918. For Milwaukee's Jews—and for American Jews generally—the war would be viewed, with time, as a watershed experience. It turned many of them, particularly the eastern Europeans, into staunch internationalists and, at the same time, stronger Americans. The plight of their brethren across the sea made the immigrants look beyond the confines of their ghetto to a larger world. Many had come to the United States as recipients of resettlement aid; now *they* were providing the aid. Haymarket residents developed a sharper awareness of their identities as American citizens, called to help Diaspora Jews who were forced to live in less fortunate locales, which was to say virtually everywhere but the United States. That blended perspective—at home in the New World but engaged overseas—would prove to be a permanent addition to the American Jewish consciousness.

World War I also swelled the ranks of the Zionist movement. Europe was patently no place of safety for the Jews, and Palestine emerged as the best hope for a permanent homeland. In 1915, when settlers there were facing starvation, Milwaukee's Orthodox synagogues served as collection points

Jewish Museum Milwaukee

Neighborhood grocers like Philip Srulowitz, who owned a store on Sixth and Juneau, sent tons of food to starving Palestinian settlers in 1915.

for 8 tons of flour, 1,400 pounds of rice, and 1,600 pounds of beans—much of it donated by neighborhood grocers and all of it delivered to Palestine courtesy of the U.S. Navy. A more strategic lifeline was extended in November 1917, when England, the dominant European power in the Middle East, issued the Balfour Declaration. Great Britain stated unequivocally that it "views with favor the establishment of a Jewish National Home in Palestine," and promised to "use its best endeavors" to make that home a reality. The Balfour Declaration was intended to broaden the base of Allied military support, but it also gave Zionism a legitimacy that had been lacking before the war. The German-Jewish

community took notice. Reform Jews had long viewed the Zionist movement with feelings that ranged from deep suspicion to outright hostility; many of them dismissed it as a nationalist fantasy that had nothing to do with true Judaism. Wartime suffering and the Balfour Declaration changed their minds. Lizzie Kander, who lived at Lincoln House for several months in 1917, found her Reform assumptions melting away. Her conversion, described in a 1919 paper, was probably typical:

> *I saw men and women old and young flocking almost daily to the different Zionist meetings.... I became interested, and though somewhat skeptical, made up my mind that some day I*

96

would look more deeply into the subject. I am indebted to this club today for this opportunity, for now I am more than convinced that the Zionist movement is a most powerful force for good and must be recognized and heartily supported. That today it represents the strongest, largest grouping of Jewish people in the whole world, and in every separate civilized country of the world.

A spurt of organizing activity followed the war. The Zionist Organization of America (which absorbed the earlier Knights of Zion) and Poale Zion both gained members, and a wide range of new groups emerged, most of them local branches of national associations. The largest was probably Hadassah, a women's group organized locally in 1920. Its members promoted Zionist ideals in Milwaukee and supported Jewish institutions in Palestine, with a particular interest in health care. There was so much activity in town that the *Jewish Community Blue Book of Milwaukee and Wisconsin,* a compendium of Jewish life published in 1924, proclaimed Milwaukee "one of the strongest Zionist communities in the country." Some residents, in fact, felt so strongly that they moved to Palestine. The most notable was the former Goldie Mabowehz, a pillar of the local movement. She married Morris Meyerson in 1917 (with Rabbi Solomon Scheinfeld officiating) and departed for her ultimate homeland in 1921, when she was twenty-three. "It didn't make sense to me," the future prime minister recalled years later, "to be a Zionist and not to come."

As support for the Jewish homeland snowballed, new groups emerged to advance the cause, including the Zionist Organization of America and Hadassah (lower), whose local membership reached nearly 1,500.

Jewish Museum Milwaukee

Jewish Museum Milwaukee

A Zionist pageant in 1919 featured Goldie Mabowehz as the menorah-bearer.

Milwaukee's delegation to a Young Poale Zion convention in 1928

The labor Zionists staged a Chasidim masquerade ball in 1925, complete with fake beards and side curls. Their more devout neighbors were presumably not amused.

Internationalism and Zionism were two unexpected beneficiaries of World War I, but there were also some major casualties that had nothing to do with the carnage on the battlefield. In the local context, the most important was Milwaukee's deep-seated Germanism. For decades the city had proclaimed itself the "German Athens" of America, a stronghold of German music, art, culture, and cuisine without equal in the country. When the United States entered the war in April 1917, an anti-German propaganda campaign quickly approached the level of mass hysteria. Once-proud Germans found themselves unable to speak their native tongue in public without risking ridicule. Sauerkraut became "liberty cabbage," hamburger became "Salisbury steak," and the German-English Academy, which had educated many of the German-Jewish elite, became Milwaukee University School.

German Jews felt the same lash as their Gentile compatriots. From the very beginning, they had been full participants in the life of the larger German community, joining its fraternals, singing in its choruses, going to its schools, and living in its neighborhoods. But they had also maintained a separate ethnic and religious identity, expressed in specifically Jewish organizations like B'nai B'rith, the Young Men's Hebrew Association, the Phoenix Club and, of course, the Reform synagogues. The German Jews, briefly stated, were *in* but not completely *of* the larger German community. With the explosion of anti-Teutonic sentiment during World War I, they underwent a painful molting process. As Old World associations became politically incorrect, they were forced to shed their self-conscious Germanness, a shift in identity that brought their underlying Jewishness to the fore. That shift, in turn, led their neighbors to lump them together with Milwaukee's "other Jews"—the eastern Europeans, whom many German-speakers had long regarded, at least in their more candid moments, as unwashed and practically uncivilized. In 1915, for example, Rabbi Charles Levi of B'ne Jeshurun blasted the eastern Europeans' campaign to add Yiddish to the public school curriculum. "The Yiddish language," he wrote, "is of no earthly good and might as well be abolished. It has no grammatical sense and interferes with Americanism more than anything else." That was before the native community felt its own cultural foundations coming under attack.

By the end of the war, Milwaukee's German Jews found themselves occupying a most uncomfortable middle ground. Too Jewish to identify with the fading German Americans but still too German (and too American) to identify with the rising eastern Europeans, the city's first families muddled along, hoping to find a psychological safe haven. An untold number simply dropped out. Many families still tell stories of uncles who became Episcopalians and aunts who married Lutherans and stopped going to temple. For the majority who remained faithful, Judaism trumped Germanism, and emphatically. Like the eastern Europeans but for different reasons, they were casting off their ties to the Old World. Slowly but inevitably, the Germans were becoming more Jewish, the eastern Europeans were becoming more American, and the two groups were coming closer together as American Jews.

Goodbye to the Ghetto

The melding of Milwaukee's two dominant Jewish communities was accelerated by another round of changes in American society. Most observers had assumed that, with the end of hostilities, the country would soon return to its pre-1914 state—an era of general prosperity and massive immigration. They were wrong on both counts, at least initially. Visions of a postwar boom were marred by a short but sharp recession and a round of double-digit inflation. The cost of living jumped 17.4 percent in 1917 alone and stayed above the 14-percent mark through 1920. The spike of 1917 prompted an unusual alliance between women of the Haymarket neighborhood and the South Side Polish Housewives' League. The two groups, Jewish and Catholic, agreed to boycott certain foods they deemed overpriced and to buy sugar, coffee, and other staples in wholesale quantities. Some items were of exclusive interest to the North Siders. The price of matzo flour, for instance, rose nearly 50 percent in one year—a definite irritant to homemakers planning their Passover meals.

The Twenties would eventually begin to roar, but the same could not be said of immigration. After reaching an all-time high of 1,285,349 in 1907, the number of new Americans had plummeted to 326,700 in 1915—the first full year of World War I—and kept on dropping to 110,618 in 1918. There was a brief rebound after the Armistice, fueled largely by newcomers joining their relatives in America, but then, in 1921, the doors began to close. For all the high-flown rhetoric that accompanied the war effort—America's crusade to make the world

"safe for democracy"—the realities of modern warfare had had a distinctly chilling effect on the American public. Poison gas, submarine warfare, and machine guns caused destruction beyond anyone's imagining, and civilians suffered as much as soldiers. There had been a strong isolationist undercurrent in the discussions that led to America's declaration of war. When the shooting stopped, it gained considerable momentum. The desire to avoid foreign entanglements derailed President Woodrow Wilson's plans for the League of Nations and quickly evolved into a desire to avoid foreigners altogether, particularly the "wretched refuse" of southern and eastern Europe. Not only were they a perceived economic threat to native-born workers, but the "new" immigrants were also viewed as likely carriers of the revolutionary virus that had brought down tsarist Russia in 1917. Fear of strangers, especially subversive strangers, led Congress to pass a pair of quota laws—the first in 1921 and the second, more restrictive measure in 1924—that had the effect of cutting off emigration from Russia, Poland, Ukraine, Yugoslavia, Italy, Greece, and a host of other countries that had together sent millions across the Atlantic before World War I.

Eastern European Jews knew they were among those being targeted, and their Milwaukee representatives spoke out forcefully. On February 19, 1924, the local ethnic groups most affected—Poles, Italians, and Jews—organized a mass protest meeting at a downtown hall. Joseph Padway, an attorney prominent in the eastern European Jewish community, took the quota laws personally:

I resent the insult, inferences and imputations to the people of my faith and those of the Catholic faith contained in this un-American bill. It seeks to brand us as inferiors to the English and the Germans, the latter whom we so bitterly fought against to save the world for democracy.

Father Waclaw Kruszka, the city's leading Polish cleric, agreed wholeheartedly: "This is not the country of any one nationality from across the seas. It is not an Anglo-Saxon country. It is God's country and as such belongs to us all."

The protests were to no avail. Quotas became the law of the land, and the flow of new arrivals dropped from 706,896 in 1924 to 294,314 one year later. Newcomers already in America faced the sobering realization that they were here for good, and that they were likely the last of their groups to have lived and breathed their ancestral cultures on their native soil. Just as the Germans were "cleansed" of their Old World associations, the eastern Europeans felt their ties to ancient homelands

growing weaker by the year and their American identities gaining strength. The process of assimilation, already well under way, developed a new intensity.

Jewish Americans felt an additional pressure that affected no other ethnic group in the country: anti-Semitism. The same xenophobes who had worked to pull up the nation's welcome mat mounted a campaign of hate against groups that didn't conform to their exceedingly narrow definition of "American." The Ku Klux Klan made a comeback in the urban North in the 1920s, providing a new platform for malice toward African Americans, Catholics, and Jews. Henry Ford filled the pages of his *Dearborn Independent* with diatribes against the "international Jewish conspiracy." Anti-Semitism even entered the sacrosanct confines of America's Ivy League colleges, which had long been considered strongholds of civility. In 1922, Harvard University announced that it was considering a cap on Jewish enrollment. When a Milwaukee alumnus, Alfred Benesch, sent an angry letter of protest, President A. Lawrence Lowell replied with a masterpiece of flawed logic:

Milwaukee Klansmen represented anti-Semitism at its most virulent.

Milwaukee County Historical Society

Area resorts made their "Gentiles only" policy crystal-clear.

Jewish Museum Milwaukee

MAPLE BEACH LODGE

PELICAN LAKE, WISCONSIN

Where Nature Smiles for Miles and Miles Along with the Host and Hostess

Main Lodges and Cottages are ideally situated for comfort and scenic beauty. Cottages and rooms are equipped with comfortable and absolutely clean beds. Bathrooms in main lodge. Maple Beach Lodge serves the best food — ... kets ... dens ... pe- ... led

Numerous Lakes and Streams which abound with game fish—Muskellunge, Pike, Bass, Pickerel and Brook Trout — are within easy access of the resort. Pelican Lake is one of the best lakes for Muskellunge of any in this wonderful region. Try the months of June, September and October for the "big fellows."

...DER—GENTILES ONLY

PELICAN LAKE, WIS.

One of the Finest Sand Beaches in All Wisconsin at

LA BELLE VILLA
ON BEAUTIFUL LAC LA BELLE

La Belle Villa is ideally situated, and is open the year 'round. All conveniences. Parties solicited. Rates, $25 per week. Gentiles only.
MRS. THERESA M. SMITH, Prop.
OCONOMOWOC, WIS.

Jewish Museum Milwaukee

The anti-Semitic feeling among the students is increasing, and it grows in proportion to the increase in the number of Jews. If their number should become forty per cent of the student body, the race feeling would become intense. When, on the other hand, the number of Jews was small, the race antagonism was small also. Any such race feeling among the students tends to

prevent the personal intimacies on which we must rely to soften anti-Semitic feeling. If every college in the country would take a limited proportion of Jews, I suspect we should go a long way towards eliminating race feeling among the students; and, as these students passed out into the world, eliminating it in the community.

Carrying Lowell's premise to its logical conclusion, Alfred Benesch suggested that perhaps the most effective way to eliminate anti-Semitism would be to eliminate Jewish students entirely.

Milwaukee experienced some of the postwar backlash that was sharpening ethnic tensions elsewhere in the country. A number of area resorts advertised "Gentiles only" guest policies, private clubs generally selected members from among "our own kind," and Jewish students at Marquette University, a Catholic institution, started their own fraternity, Sigma Alpha, when the school's other Greek bodies refused to accept them. Such incidents were, however, exceptions to the general pattern. The world has probably never seen the Jew who has not felt the sting of anti-Semitism, but Milwaukee, relatively speaking, was an oasis of tolerance. Golda Meir described the social atmosphere of her youth:

I myself never once encountered any anti-Semitism in Milwaukee. Although I lived in a Jewish district and mingled almost entirely with Jews, both in school and out of it, I had non-Jewish friends, of course—as I was to have all my life. But even though they were never quite as close to me as were the Jews, I felt entirely free and at home with them.

Even the Marquette University situation was resolved happily. When the Pan-Hellenic Council balked at admitting Sigma Alpha to full membership, Father Herbert Noonan, Marquette's president, stepped in personally, declaring that the Jewish fraternity would indeed be given a seat. Five years later, a Jewish student was the council's vice-president.

Why did Milwaukee escape the most virulent anti-Semitism of the postwar years? Part of the answer may lie in the city's official intolerance of intolerance. Daniel Hoan, a Socialist who served as mayor from 1916 to 1940, lampooned the Ku Klux Klan as the "hoods and nighties set" and advised them to steer clear of his city: "Milwaukee will become the hottest place this side of hell for the Ku Klux Klan if any of the Klan pounce upon one of our citizens, whether he be black or white, red or yellow, Jew or Gentile, Catholic or Protestant." More important, perhaps, was the fact that Milwaukee's largest ethnic group was suffering a purge of its own. The anti-German hysteria of the late war years continued without pause after the Armistice. Germans were kept constantly on the defensive, and they were such a huge target that they may have absorbed or at least diverted some of the animosity that was elsewhere directed toward Jews. As a result, the foolishness of the Ku Klux Klan and the fulminations of Henry Ford had relatively little impact on the people of Milwaukee.

Although the level of anti-Semitism varied widely by locality, American society as a whole was demonstrably different after World War I than it had been before the conflict: less welcoming, more suspicious, and generally less sure of itself. But that was by no means the whole story. America was also growing more affluent—remarkably more affluent. As immigration tapered off and group dynamics shifted, something far less complicated was going on in the country: prosperity. After sputtering early in the 1920s, the American economy shifted into overdrive, bringing in a prosperity broader and deeper than any the nation had ever known. The roar was audible, and it reached even the immigrant quarter of Milwaukee's Jewish community. On July 10, 1898, the *Milwaukee Sentinel* had described the residents of the Haymarket ghetto in terms that proved to be prophetic:

Milwaukee County Historical Society

Mayor Daniel Hoan was an outspoken champion of equal rights for all Milwaukeeans.

These people do not look like desirable acquisitions when they first arrive, but it is safe to say that the younger generation of them will turn out some valued citizens, however unpicturesque their parents may continue to look. The racial desire for self-betterment is not snuffed out by the filthy environment into which their poverty forces them....

It was in the 1920s that the prophecy began to come true. The immigrants' children came of age under a cloudless sky, relatively speaking. They spoke English at least as well as Yiddish. They were educated to standards unheard of in the shtetls of Europe, nearly all graduating from high school (typically from North Division) and many going on to college. The prosperity of the 1920s made their upward mobility close to automatic. Quietly but practically en masse, members of the second generation entered the middle class, taking jobs in the professions and the business world that were cleaner and better-compensated than anything their parents had known.

As they moved up, they invariably moved out. The German families who first settled the Haymarket neighborhood had migrated to the north and west when Jewish immigrants began to arrive. In a classic process known to geographers as residential succession, eastern European Jews followed precisely the same corridor when their turn came to leave. They didn't travel far at first, generally resettling within a mile of their first homes. Even at that short distance, they took their institutions with them. In the early 1900s, the Haymarket's "synagogue row" had been a short stretch of Cherry Street between Fourth and Sixth, where B'nai Israel Anshe Ungarn, Beth Israel, and Anshe Sfard—the Hungarian, Lithuanian, and Russian shuls—were practically next-door neighbors. In the 1920s, Eleventh Street emerged as the Orthodox community's new "synagogue row," particularly the section between Vine and Brown Streets, where Agudas Achim, Anshe Lebowitz, and Anshe Roumania were less than a block apart. The second

The American vogue for mandolin orchestras did not bypass Milwaukee's Jewish community. The Hasomir Society posed for a photograph in 1925.

row was barely a mile from the first, but its synagogues were newer and generally nicer than the buildings they succeeded. One by one, the other Orthodox congregations followed suit, until only Anshe Sfard remained in the original Haymarket neighborhood. It, too, sold its building in 1925 and announced plans to move "in a northwestern direction that will conform with the expansion of the Jewish community." As it turned out, the move covered all of a dozen blocks; Anshe Sfard dedicated a new temple on Twelfth and Garfield in 1926. Two years later, the congregation hired a dynamic new spiritual leader: Rabbi Jacob Twerski. The scion of a Chasidic dynasty with deep roots in eastern Europe, Twerski was the first local representative of a family that has exerted a strong influence on Milwaukee Judaism ever since.

Beth Israel, Milwaukee's leading Orthodox synagogue, made the longest move (by a few blocks) and the grandest architectural statement. In 1925, the congregation held its first services in an imposing new temple on Teutonia Avenue near Thirteenth Street—just over a mile from its old home on Fifth and Cherry. Built for $250,000—a formidable sum in 1925—the tan brick synagogue featured matching towers, ornate stained-glass windows, and a worship space as impressive as either of the local Reform temples'. Beth Israel's new home quickly earned praise as one of the finest in Orthodox America, but the building was much more than a place of worship. I.J. Rosenberg, the congregation's president, articulated a broader vision at the 1925 groundbreaking ceremony:

Jewish Museum Milwaukee

As their circumstances improved, the Orthodox faithful built larger, more lavish synagogues just outside the old Haymarket neighborhood. The new shuls included (from top) *Anshe Lebowitz, Anshe Roumania, and Anshe Sfard.*

Jewish Museum Milwaukee

Rabbi Jacob Twerski was the guiding light of Anshe Sfard and the founder of a Milwaukee rabbinic dynasty.

Milwaukee Public Library

*Completed in 1925,
Beth Israel's Teutonia
Ave. synagogue was the
showplace of Orthodox
Judaism in Milwaukee.*

Jewish Museum Milwaukee

Jewish Museum Milwaukee

We are building an institutional synagogue in which we shall install every modern facility for the use and education and enjoyment of our younger elements. We shall equip one of the finest gymnasiums in the state. We shall provide facilities for theatrical productions and for entertainments and dancing. We shall not attempt to curb the effervescent spirit of modern youth, but rather to give it a setting in a Jewish atmosphere that should inspire the youth to forever hold fast to his Jewish heritage.

In addition to the gym and auditorium, Beth Israel's new building included a full kitchen, a chapel and and, at Rabbi Solomon Scheinfeld's insistence, a ten-room annex that housed the congregation's Talmud Torah—a school founded on Orthodox principles and offering instruction in the Jewish faith and traditions.

As they occupied more modern buildings, the Orthodox congregations often adopted more modern modes of worship as well. The 1920s were not an especially congenial decade for fervent traditionalists. Younger members expected, even demanded, forms of religious observance that were more in keeping with the times, and many temples, rather than risk losing the second generation, decided to accommodate them. When Beth Israel began to make plans for its new building, Rabbi Scheinfeld, ever the realist, said, "It cannot be as it was until now. We must make it Orthodox, but modern so that it will be appealing to everyone." Soon after relocating to Teutonia Avenue, his congregation introduced mixed-gender seating, a choir, services at a fixed hour each Friday night (supplementing the

traditional sunset liturgy), English sermons, and at least some English prayers.

Other congregations followed Beth Israel's lead, but by no means all. Milwaukee's Orthodox religious scene had always been diverse, and it became even more so in the unsettled conditions of the 1920s. The abundance of shuls and the general lack of order exasperated some observers. The *Wisconsin Jewish Chronicle*, which began its distinguished editorial career in 1921, quickly became the most reliable and most widely read source of information on the local scene. This "Weekly Paper for the Jewish Home" registered a familiar complaint on July 1, 1927:

There are too many Orthodox congregations in every large city. It is pathetic to watch these institutions struggling madly to meet their expenses in maintaining separate buildings and competing with other congregations to attract the very same elements. This competition leads to economic waste, confusion, and the ultimate defeat of the very aims of the synagogue.

Launched in 1921, the Wisconsin Jewish Chronicle *quickly became an indispensable source of news about Jewish Milwaukee.*

We know that it is well nigh impossible to impress upon small Orthodox congregations the value of consolidation. There are more divisions among Orthodox Jews than there are among Protestant Christians. These divisions are not based on ritual however. All Orthodox congregations worship in essentially the very same form. They differ only in the "national" origins of their memberships....

These Orthodox congregations are beginning to be faced with grave problems. The stoppage of immigration has reduced the possibilities for recruiting new memberships and the growing generation of native-born American sons and daughters do not share the old world loyalties and prejudices of their parents. The American generation is willing to adhere to the Orthodox faith but it wants the synagogue to mean much more to it than a meeting place of the "landsleute." It wants the institutional synagogue with its educational, entertainment and athletic facilities. The American youth doesn't care a snap of his fingers whether the President of a congregation came from Pinsk or Minsk so long as he can derive something of benefit from the synagogue. And if the synagogue will not supply that benefit he will have no interest in it whatever.

There was some movement in the direction suggested by the *Chronicle*. In 1924, B'nai Israel Anshe Ungarn dropped the Hungarian ethnic modifier from its name and was known thereafter as simply B'nai Israel. The congregation also adopted "family" seating, introduced English prayers, and even flirted (briefly) with a change in affiliation from Orthodox to Conservative. In 1919, after fifteen years as the Romanian subgroup's home, Anshe Roumania added "Degel Israel" ("Banner of Israel") to its name in another effort to downplay the old ethnic ties. Traditionalists were less than pleased. The various liberalizations fed a backlash that led to the formation of the "strictly Orthodox" B'nai Jacob ("Sons of Jacob"), Beth Hamidrosh Hagadol (the city's second "Great House of Study"), and Anshe Brith Sholem ("Men of the Covenant of Peace"), all of which were chartered in the 1920s. Instead of fewer synagogues in Milwaukee, there were suddenly more, and all put down roots in the familiar expansion zone just northwest of the old Haymarket neighborhood.

Hundreds of Jewish families moved miles beyond the growing cluster of synagogues. They generally followed the well-worn German path leading north and west from the Haymarket area, seldom straying far outside the six-block corridor defined by Lloyd and Center Streets. The Jewish newcomers bought or rented second-hand homes at first, but once they had crossed the railroad corridor at Thirty-first Street, they entered a brand-new neighborhood: Sherman Park. Sprawling from Thirty-First to Sixtieth Streets and from North Avenue to Capitol Drive—an area of nearly four square miles—Sherman Park developed in the Teens and Twenties as a suburban-style community that extended to the city's western limits. Massive duplexes and sturdy bungalows were its dominant house types, and many backyards contained structures that the previous generation would not have recognized: garages. Established during the automobile era, Sherman Park

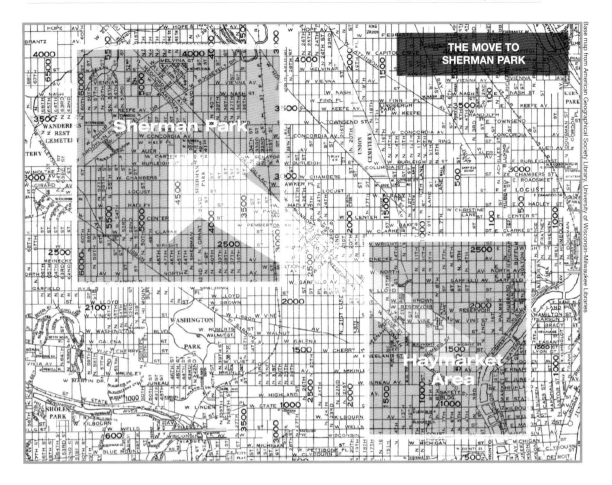

came to maturity as a community of middle-class commuters who traveled to jobs closer to the heart of town. Although they settled in all sections of the neighborhood, Jewish families were concentrated in the vicinity of Fifty-first and Center Streets. Before the Twenties were out, the following establishments had opened within two or three blocks of the intersection: Guten & Son's grocery store, the Sanitary Kosher Market, the New Method Hebrew School, Abraham Morris's tailor shop, the Yiddish Folk School, Leon Cohen's bakery, Gindlin's fruit market, and delicatessens run by the Lipkin and Tischer families.

Curiously, there was not a single synagogue in Sherman Park—not in the 1920s, at least. The sole religious institution on the far West Side was located just south of Sherman Park, in what is currently known as the Washington Heights neighborhood. In 1921, a group of West Siders organized the Oer Chodosh ("New Light") Society and began to meet in members' homes for "social, religious and educational purposes." Within a few weeks, the group had coalesced into a congregation, but its members had little interest in transplanting the religion they had learned in the Haymarket shuls of their childhoods. They wanted

The exodus from the Haymarket area to Sherman Park gathered speed through the 1920s.

109

Beth El was Milwaukee's first Conservative congregation and for many years the only synagogue west of 13th St. Its programs included a well-attended Sunday school.

Jewish Museum Milwaukee

Jewish Museum Milwaukee

a community, as one put it, "more liberal than the Orthodox synagogues and yet not reaching as far in the realm of liberalism as the Reformed temples." The result was Beth El ("House of God"), Milwaukee's first Conservative congregation. After rejecting one small lot at Forty-Eighth and Center—near the heart of Sherman Park—Beth El purchased a larger parcel at Forty-ninth and Garfield and erected a pleasant Mediterranean-styled synagogue for $50,000. The first service was held on Rosh Hashanah in September 1923.

Conservatism required some explanation in the Twenties. Eugene Kohn, Beth El's first rabbi, described the movement as the authentic centerline of the Jewish faith:

If Orthodoxy errs in its assumption that Judaism can be summed up finally and for all time in the precepts of a specific code, Reform Judaism errs in assuming that the whole rich content of Judaism can be summed up in a single creed and in a rather platitudinous creed at that.

110

The Conservative movement, by contrast, viewed Judaism as "the cumulative spiritual inheritance of a historic people," an inheritance that was both constant and constantly evolving, rooted in the ancient world but relevant to the modern world. That dynamic faith, Rabbi Kohn insisted, "represents the movement of Judaism as a whole with reference to which both Orthodoxy and Reform are but temporary aberrations."

Beth El's temple on Forty-ninth was the first and for many years the only Milwaukee synagogue west of Thirteenth Street. Its Conservative affiliation was no surprise. The farther west they traveled, the less traditional the eastern European Jews seemed to become; moving away from the Haymarket area in the 1920s meant moving away from the accumulated weight of the past. "Live Where All Is New," urged a 1919 ad for one Sherman Park subdivision. The neighborhood was filled with new houses, new cars and, in many cases, new families. It was perhaps inevitable that they would seek new forms of religious expression as well.

The generational dynamics were obvious, but there was another, almost-subliminal reason to embrace practices that lay closer to the American mainstream: Jews were a minority group in their new neighborhood. In the Haymarket area, they had lived largely in their own company. The Dillingham Commission survey published in 1911 found that Jewish families made up 89 percent of the households in a densely populated two-block stretch of Sixth Street near Vliet. With every step those families took to the north and west, the Jewish presence was diluted. Immigration quotas had

stopped the eastern European community's population growth. In the 1920s, the same number of people—12,000, by one count—were spread more thinly over a much larger area. When Rabbi Solomon Scheinfeld—the guiding light of Orthodox Judaism in Milwaukee—moved to 2563 N. Twelfth Street in about 1920, he settled into a comfortably middle-class section of the German North Side. Although his home was close to the new site of Beth Israel (on Teutonia Avenue, of all streets), there were two Adolphs, two Gustavs, and a Diedrich on

With its generous setbacks and substantial homes, Grant Boulevard was one of Sherman Park's most desirable addresses. The bungalow (lower) was the house type of choice for a larger number of residents.

Milwaukee County Historical Society

Washington High School was the pride of Sherman Park and widely considered the best public high school in the city.

the rabbi's block; Scheinfeld was the sole Solomon. The same pattern was even more pronounced in Sherman Park. Along Fifty-first Street—the closest approximation to a Jewish main street in the neighborhood—the residents of 1929 included Joseph Lubar, Israel Goldberg, Louis Cohen, Joseph Rosen, Libby Rubin, Louis Podell, and Max Lebowsky, but Jewish names in the city directory were far outnumbered by listings for residents like Alfons Fischer, Emil Schroeder, Eberhard Mees, Anton Tiefling, Carl Andressohn, Daniel McTavish, John Mahoney, and Henry McMahon. At Fifty-first and Center Streets—generally acknowledged as the epicenter of Sherman Park's Jewish community—the dominant landmark was, and still is, St. Catherine's Catholic Church. Although they were a substantial presence in practically every block, Sherman Park's Jewish transplants were a Semitic minority in a Christian matrix.

Sharing the streets, sidewalks, and shops with a variety of other groups encouraged a certain relativism among all residents of Sherman Park, whether Jewish or Gentile, but public schools were probably the main engines of assimilation. Young residents of the Haymarket district had grown accustomed to multi-ethnic student bodies at Fourth Street and Ninth Street Elementary Schools and at North Division High School, but they enjoyed considerable safety in numbers within the confines of their old neighborhood. A study done for Abraham Lincoln House in 1922 claimed that 96 percent of the students at Ninth Street School were Jewish. There was nothing approaching that concentration in the public schools of Sherman Park, which included Sherman Elementary, Steuben Junior High, and Washington High School; Jews were a distinct minority in every class. They did, however, develop loyalties that transcended ethnic divisions, and Washington exerted the strongest pull. The English Tudor landmark on Sherman Boulevard opened in 1915 and quickly earned a reputation as the city's finest public high school, especially under George Balzer, a principal so demanding that he was known to pupils and faculty alike as "the Kaiser." Jewish students were a vital part of Washington High School's success, and they took a vital interest in the life of the institution. No less than the German, Irish, and Scandinavian kids with whom they both cooperated and competed, Purgolders of Jewish ancestry wanted to shine in the Alphanea Literary Society, star in Washington Players productions, and earn Coach Lisle Blackbourn's respect on the football field. Like adolescents of every generation, they wanted to fit in. The sons and daughters of immigrants learned to slick back or perm their hair just like the movie stars and to arrange their bows and collars in the most up-to-date styles. They watched the latest films, read the latest magazines, and listened spellbound to the same radio programs as their Gentile peers. As America became ever more a mass consumer society in the 1920s, the pressures to conform were almost overpowering.

Public education and popular culture tended to pull young people out of their Jewish orbits, but there were countervailing pressures. The West Side's more traditional families could choose from any number of Jewish schools for their children. Beth Israel and Beth El both had extensive educational programs, the latter housed in a spacious school built behind the Forty-ninth Street temple in 1928. There were at least a dozen private schools and perhaps fifteen private tutors whose specialty was preparing boys for their Bar Mitzvah ceremonies. Poale Zion and the Workmen's Circle (Arbeiter Ring) continued to offer culturally based programs with strong Socialist orientations and liberal helpings of Yiddish. A community-wide Talmud Torah (not to be confused with Beth Israel's school of the same name) was organized in 1913. Housed in a converted residence at Seventh and Galena, it provided one hour of instruction each afternoon after public school classes had ended. In 1922, the Talmud Torah broke ground for a new building on Eleventh and Vine, along the West Side's new "synagogue row." In a retrospective slap at traditional Jewish religious training, the campaign's leaders stressed that their institution would also break new ground educationally:

> It is not a "Cheder" or old type of school visioned by the average Jew when he hears a Jewish school mentioned. The old "Cheder" has given way to the modern Talmud Torah just as the horse and buggy has been superceded by the automobile. Instead of the badly furnished, ill-smelling, dark and insanitary room in which the old time "Rebbe" forced Jewish learning into the minds of his pupils with the aid of a powerful voice

A communal Talmud Torah served the minority of young people who wanted to continue their Jewish educations, including these graduates of 1928.

University of Wisconsin-Milwaukee Library Archives

ANNUAL REPORT
of the
Milwaukee
Talmud Torah
FOR 1917

יעהרליכער רעפאָרט פון דער
הינער

תלמוד תורה

דין וחשבון שנתי
מבית התלמוד תורה דמילוואקי
לשנת תרע״ז

Jewish Museum Milwaukee

and stinging rod, the Hebrew school of today, known as the Talmud Torah, is housed in buildings equipped and constructed in as clean and beautiful a fashion as the most modern public school erected in the city.

That vision proved to be wishful thinking. The fund drive failed, and Milwaukee's Talmud Torah was forced to move into Abraham Lincoln House. There was simply not enough community interest to sustain the effort. A 1922 study found that fewer than one-fourth of the city's Jewish children received any form of religious instruction. Six years later, Haim Margalith, the Talmud Torah's superintendent, complained that Jewish education "has now come to be either totally forgotten or relegated to a remote corner in our consciousness." Barney Padway,

one of the school's supporters, had even harsher words: "There is no term of condemnation strong enough to apply to local Jewry for the inertia which it displays towards the religious training of the Jewish child." In the struggle between Jewish tradition and American secularism, secular society seemed to be winning.

By 1929, Milwaukee's eastern European Orthodox community had moved materially from its base. The old Haymarket ghetto had not disappeared, but it was fading fast. The *Wisconsin Jewish Chronicle* (July 18, 1924) printed a bittersweet obituary when the end was in sight:

It is conceded that the Ghetto with all its evils of physical congestion and advantages of mental intensity is doomed to virtual extinction.

Jewish businesses like Zilberbrand's grocery store continued to serve the Haymarket neighborhood even as it began to change racially.

Jewish Museum Milwaukee

Without the intimate contact of fresh recruits from abroad the Ghetto will lose its charm of distinctiveness in speech and manner, for those who now people the Ghetto will in a few short years have become Americanized to the extent that they will of their own volition leave the districts marked by a foreign and alien atmosphere....

To those who have lived in the Ghetto and who understand its hardships, its struggles, its pathos, its sympathies, its loyalties, its hopes, and everything that made it human, its passing will bring a sigh of regret, a regret more inspired by reminiscence than actual sorrow, for whatever can be said in its favor, the Ghetto as an institution is not desirable in American life from a broad viewpoint.

What was replacing the ghetto was a broader but shallower band of settlement that stretched from the heart of the Haymarket all the way west to Sixtieth Street in Sherman Park. It was a place where the Jewish presence was always apparent but never dominant, a zone in which some families remained devout and others gladly shed their Jewish associations. More than one Chaim became a Herman and more than one Yetta a Henrietta as the children of the Haymarket moved west. What they left behind was their poverty—every step out was a step up—but a sizable number were also putting distance between themselves and their inherited traditions. In that respect, the eastern European Jews were coming more and more to resemble their German brethren on the other side of the river.

The Reform Temples: From Two to One

As the West Side Jewish community grew more attenuated and its residents more assimilated, history was repeating itself. Decades earlier—during the first years of settlement, in fact—the city's German Jews had willingly aligned their cultural expectations with those of other German immigrants and then with those of their "American" neighbors. They saw themselves as Jewish Milwaukeeans rather than Milwaukee Jews. In the years following World War I, the eastern Europeans were headed in much the same direction. The German Jews, however, had not yet completed their cultural evolution. There was still abundant room for movement—both geographic and religious—and the currents of the 1920s took the community's first families in some rather surprising directions.

Geography, first of all. Even in pioneer days, there had been no single concentration of German Jews that corresponded to the Haymarket area for Milwaukee's eastern Europeans. The first arrivals had settled on both sides of the river, and their synagogues—B'ne Jeshurun and Emanu-El—reflected the prevailing split. Emanu-El had always been the more affluent of the pair, drawing its members from Yankee Hill, Prospect Avenue, and other elite sections of the East Side. In the post-World War I years, those members continued to move north along the lake bluff, settling in the North Point and Prospect Hill neighborhoods bordering Lake Park and then crossing into Shorewood, a leafy suburb incorporated (as East Milwaukee) in 1900. Emanu-El's center of gravity was shifting steadily to the northeast, but there was also a push from behind. The area surrounding the temple on Broadway and State became increasingly commercial in the early 1900s, creating an atmosphere distinctly at odds with quiet worship. In 1905, not even a year after taking the pulpit, Rabbi Samuel

Milwaukee County Historical Society

As its Broadway synagogue neared a date with the wrecking ball, Emanu-El laid the cornerstone for a new home on Milwaukee's upper East Side.

Hirshberg expressed his desire for "a new and more commodious temple" at some remove from State Street. That desire would become a central theme of Hirshberg's early rabbinate. By 1915, the congregation had made a definite decision to move. "A new temple," reported the *Milwaukee Journal* (May 3, 1915), "will be built on the upper East Side as soon as the present one is sold."

Emanu-El's initial choice was a row of lots on Hackett Avenue near Park Place, within a block of the Downer Avenue commercial district. After deciding to leave one noisy location, members began to worry that they had just acquired another. In 1917, Edward Freschl, chairman of the building committee, identified a problem that no one had anticipated: "the existence of dance music which goes on almost nightly either on one side or the other of our location, namely: at the Kenwood [Masonic] Lodge

Jewish Museum Milwaukee

or at the St. Mark's Church Annex." The good Episcopalians of St. Mark's might have been surprised to learn that anyone considered them noisy, but the problem, wrote Freschl, was "absolutely insurmountable." In 1919, after taking a break for World War I, Emanu-El found a larger and much quieter property even farther north, on Kenwood Boulevard west of Downer Avenue. In his Rosh Hashanah sermon, Rabbi Hirshberg issued a battle cry: "The New Temple in the New Year!" Fund-raising took somewhat longer than Hirshberg had anticipated, but the congregation finally broke ground for its new home on January 2, 1922. The Broadway synagogue's days were numbered. "Yes, the old building is passing," Hirshberg told a reporter in 1923. "It was indeed an old landmark, and beloved by us all. But as the center of Jewish population moved from its location, a new temple was necessary for us and is soon to be ours."

The structure that rose on Kenwood Boulevard was unlike any other synagogue in the city: a massive limestone edifice with Ionic columns and carved scrollwork trim that seemed both classical and modern at the same time. The interior was divided into an elegantly understated sanctuary with space for 1,450 worshipers and an auditorium and "community house" with a capacity of 600. The new synagogue, which cost a hefty $500,000, was formally dedicated in the first week of November 1923. The *Wisconsin Jewish Chronicle* praised it as "one of the most modern and well equipped buildings of its kind in America." Samuel Hirshberg, a fervent ecumenist, made sure that one of the

The result was a towering statement of restrained classicism that cemented Emanu-El's position as the flagship of Reform Judaism in Milwaukee.

Jewish Museum Milwaukee

inaugural events was an interfaith service with sermons by a full line-up of Methodist, Congregational, Unitarian, Presbyterian, Episcopalian, and Baptist ministers.

Hirshberg's own leadership skills had helped swell Emanu-El's rolls to nearly 350 families by 1923, and the move to Kenwood attracted many more. By 1926, membership approached the 500 mark, and Emanu-El was larger than B'ne Jeshurun for the first time in either congregation's history. It was soon apparent that the flock was simply too large for even the most dynamic rabbi to manage alone. In 1926, Emanu-El hired its first associate, Joseph Baron, who had previously served in Davenport, Iowa. The two rabbis functioned effectively as a team. Hirshberg was a roving ambassador for Judaism, addressing Gentile audiences as often as once a week, while Baron was of a more scholarly turn of mind, widely read and eager to share his passion for Jewish learning and culture with the congregation.

B'ne Jeshurun, in the meantime, was considering a move of its own. Charles Levi, an Englishman who had served as Isaac Mayer Wise's associate in Cincinnati, became the congregation's rabbi in 1913. Within two years, he had persuaded his members to adopt the standard Reform prayer book and to drop the German-language sermon. The liturgical differences between B'ne Jeshurun and Emanu-El, mother and daughter, shrank to insignificance, becoming so slight that the two congregations began to seem practically interchangeable. They were soon to get even closer. Planning for a civic center on the west side of Milwaukee's downtown had been under way since 1909, and the favored site for a new courthouse included B'ne Jeshurun's synagogue at Tenth and Kilbourn. Political discord delayed a final decision for more than a decade, but "some very grave problems" were aired at the 1922 annual meeting; the congregation's leaders reported that Milwaukee County, after years of foot-dragging, seemed intent on "securing our Temple site for their new court-house."

With the handwriting so clearly on the wall, B'ne Jeshurun weighed its options. A merger with Emanu-El was one possibility, but it was not universally popular; some members feared a loss of identity, and Rabbi Levi feared the loss of his job. In 1923, the congregation decided to build a new temple instead. Its planned location would have shocked B'ne Jeshurun's founders, but the choice spoke volumes about German-Jewish mobility patterns. There had once been

Charles Levi was the last rabbi to serve B'ne Jeshurun as an independent congregation.

Jewish Museum Milwaukee

a hard-and-fast geographic division between Milwaukee's two Reform congregations; West Siders worshiped on the West Side and East Siders on the East Side. That border became more and more permeable with time, and the prevailing movement was to the east. As the East Side became Milwaukee's most prestigious neighborhood, a significant number of B'ne Jeshurun's more affluent members joined their daughter congregation; in 1898, 27 percent of Emanu-El's families lived west of the river. Their next logical step was to move bodily to the East Side, and many B'ne Jeshurun members did just that—so many, in fact, that in October 1925 the congregation voted to build a $300,000 temple east of the river. In a bow to the minority who wanted to stay in the old neighborhood, the building committee promised to find a site "easily accessible to members living on the West Side," preferably near North and Prospect Avenues.

An East Side temple made demographic sense, but some members began to question the wisdom of building an expensive new synagogue only a mile away from Emanu-El's expensive new synagogue. The merger option gained new momentum, and it was aided immeasurably by Rabbi Charles Levi's decision to step down. In March 1927, with that last impediment removed, B'ne Jeshurun voted, by a margin of 154 to 22, to unite with Emanu-El. (Rabbi Levi was awarded a sabbatical year at full salary, after which he retired.) The *Wisconsin Jewish Chronicle* called the merger "the most important event in congregational history in the Jewish community of Milwaukee." Arthur Polacheck, B'ne Jeshurun's last president, characterized it less dramatically as "a logical development":

The fact that B'ne Jeshurun and Emanu-El had the same form of ritual, the fact that the old divisions between west side and east side had been wiped out by the removal of many of our members to the east side, and the fact that it was obvious that Milwaukee Jewry did not require two major Reform congregations within a short distance from each other, made it logical and practical that we should join forces....

On September 23, 1927, B'ne Jeshurun's Torah scroll was installed in the ark of the Kenwood Boulevard temple, and Congregation Emanu-El B'ne Jeshurun formally came into existence. Rabbi Samuel Hirshberg described the ceremony as a wedding. "The two congregations," he said, "have combined their resources—material, mental and spiritual—to foster the cause of the Jew." The merger was, more accurately, a reunion. After fifty-eight years apart, Milwaukee's pioneer congregations were finally functioning as a single organism again.

B'ne Jeshurun and Emanu-El—mother and daughter—finally merged in 1927, putting decades of rumors to rest.

With roughly 800 families, an ample treasury, and an energetic rabbinical team, Emanu-El B'ne Jeshurun was a new and noteworthy force in American Reform Judaism. The congregation came into being with great expectations, but it also faced an old problem: the indifference of its own members. The "season of revival" so earnestly sought by Milwaukee's rabbis since the 1800s had never come to pass. Charles Levi used his 1923 Rosh Hashanah sermon—one of his last—to blast the entire community's lack of fervor:

> *Our Jewish constituents of Milwaukee have no Sabbath that they keep holy; no synagogue or temple where they frequently worship; no religious educational institutions that they consider as of permanent value for life. Not ten per cent of our Jewish people are regular temple worshippers in our synagogues, Orthodox or Reform; not five percent of our boys and girls receive any religious instruction after the Bar Mitzvah and Confirmation age. Fifty percent of our people never contribute as regular year-in-year-out members to any Jewish congregation or Religious school....*

Mrs. Emanuel Friend, whose family had belonged to Emanu-El from the beginning, voiced a similar complaint when the Broadway temple fell to the wrecking ball in 1923. Recalling a time when the only excuses for missing a Sabbath service were "absence from the city or illness," Mrs. Friend offered a plaintive prayer: "Could we not say 'Backward! Turn backward oh time in thy flight!' and allow our indifference to religion to crumble with the ruins of this synagogue."

Emanu-El B'ne Jeshurun's leaders had every reason to hope that the union of two old stalwarts would generate a fresh perspective and abundant new energy. In May 1928, less than a year after the merger became final, Rabbi Samuel Hirshberg was forced to admit "with acute regret and disappointment" that his dream of better attendance "has not been realized." In fact, Emanu-El alone had drawn more worshipers before the merger than Emanu-El B'ne Jeshurun did after. There were continuing efforts to fill the pews, including a Sunday service introduced in 1927. Although the service was described as "merely supplementary," the senior rabbi preached on Sunday morning rather than Friday evening. And yet attendance continued to sag.

It occurred to some members that the answer might lie not in endless innovation but in a more careful cultivation of tradition. Addressing the 1930 annual meeting, Abraham L. Saltzstein, the congregation's president, suggested that the currents of liberalism had caused too much erosion:

> *To my way of thinking, we have gone to extremes in our reform. Reform Judaism has been woefully bereft of emotional appeal. The rabbinical orators, scholars, and philosophers all have tried to attract crowds. Some of them appeal to our intellect but still leave our emotions unmoved. Such religious instincts as we have are permitted to slumber.*
>
> *Fundamentally, all religion is an appeal to emotion.... It is true that in our attempt to rationalize religion; to analyze it in a sort of scientific manner, to appeal to our logic, we have*

lost the appeal to the emotion. We have over-emphasized the rational element. In so doing we have forgotten one of the fundamental objects of religion: the stimulation of our sentimental feelings….

In our reformed ritual, we have done away with practically all forms of ceremonialism. We have removed much of the color and beauty and left but little to appeal to our hearts.

Saltzstein's remarks must have struck a nerve, because the people of Emanu-El B'ne Jeshurun approved a host of changes that would have been unthinkable in any previous generation. They voted by a margin of two to one to hire a cantor—a position Emanu-El had never authorized and B'ne Jeshurun had abandoned years before. They agreed to form a congregational choir to supplement the work of their paid professionals. They abandoned the "undemocratic" practice of annual pew rentals in favor of open seating. And they installed stained-glass windows to create the "proper religious atmosphere." The windows, imported from Munich and embodying Jewish themes, filled the Kenwood Boulevard sanctuary with a warm glow, but their most novel feature may have been their lack of naming rights. Saltzstein had insisted that all donors remain anonymous. "Let us make our house of worship a place of joy," he urged, "instead of a perpetual monument or a constant reminder of our dear departed."

A bank of stained-glass windows flooded the sanctuary of Emanu-El B'ne Jeshurun with warm light.

John Gurda

121

The congregation's attempts to reform Reform Judaism were part of a national return to tradition that ran counter to the rampant secularism of the 1920s and early '30s. "We have tried everything else in the Reform Synagog," said Abraham Saltzstein in a memorable quote. "Let us try religion only." The results were mixed—Emanu-El B'ne Jeshurun eventually went back to reserved seating and a paid choir—but the various experiments demonstrated the membership's determination to remain relevant. They also marked the emergence of trends that continue to shape the Reform movement in the twenty-first century.

Although Emanu-El B'ne Jeshurun remained a work in progress, the "new" congregation reflected and reinforced a sea change in what might be termed the ecology of Milwaukee's Jewish community. Since the late 1800s, there had been a sharp separation, even a schism, between different elements of Jewish Milwaukee: German and eastern European, native and immigrant, helper and helped, Reform and Orthodox, affluent and struggling, liberal and conservative. By 1930, the old lines of demarcation had blurred significantly. The eastern European community had become less monolithic, less traditional, and more affluent; its members were leaving the ghetto and entering the American mainstream. During the same years, as a result of the anti-"Hun" witch hunt during World War I, the German Jews had become far less German and significantly more Jewish. They were returning to tradition, doubling back in the direction of the assimilating eastern Europeans. Again, the two groups were moving by degrees toward a common middle.

Even as one set of differences faded, another was emerging. Once divided by ethnicity and tradition, Milwaukee's Jews were increasingly separated by geography and, to some extent, by class. The new schism was expressed in a strengthening of the old distinction between East Side and West Side. B'ne Jeshurun's move across the river cemented the East Side's image as the stronghold of Reform Judaism and affluent Jews, including eastern Europeans who were climbing the social ladder. The West Side was rising as well, but its residents were still relatively less prosperous than their East Side counterparts. The breach between East and West—often amicable, sometimes not—was different from but potentially just as divisive as the earlier rivalries. It would also prove remarkably durable, lingering, if only in memory, to the present day.

remained the single busiest place in the Jewish community:

> *If you are a real Jew and are quite pessimistic about the future of Judaism and the Jewish youth and if you'd like to experience a real thrill, just jump into your auto some evening and drive to the corner of Ninth and Sherman [Vine] Sts. You will be greeted at this point by the sight of a trim little building with every window glowing with light. You will discern many little heads bobbing behind these windows upstairs and downstairs. Your ears will detect the busy hum of activity, the strains of a piano or violin, the words of a budding orator. This busy hive is the Abraham Lincoln House, a real community center, for which Milwaukee Jewry ought to be very proud.*

Abraham Lincoln House remained a beehive of activity, but its days in the old neighborhood were numbered.

"All Phases of Social Uplift"

There had always been a handful of institutions that cut across the various lines of demarcation in Milwaukee's Jewish community. They rarely brought the disparate groups together on an equal footing, but at least they brought them together. By far the most important was Abraham Lincoln House, established as The Settlement in 1900. Lincoln House began as a German-Jewish charity for eastern European Jews, but that one-dimensional relationship became more complex after World War I. Not only did Lizzie Kander and her intrepid band of do-gooders learn to see the immigrants on their own terms, but the line dividing helper from helped became far less distinct—like so much else in the Twenties.

The *Wisconsin Jewish Chronicle* (September 15, 1922) reported that Lincoln House

All the traditional activities continued after World War I: cooking classes, literary and debating societies, an orchestra, Americanization classes (with free child care), boxing sessions, music lessons, and a remarkable profusion of clubs. There were nearly fifty in operation by 1922, with something for everyone. The Mothers Club met for support and instruction provided by Lizzie Kander herself. Science Club members explored wireless telegraphy. The Nature Study Club organized birding expeditions to Milwaukee County parks. The Writers Club provided "a source of mutual inspiration for embryonic writers." The Young Helpers served as junior social workers. The Tiny Theatre, despite its name, performed "only heavier drama," choosing its plays from the English canon. The Young Literary and Dramatic Society, organized in 1921, staged its productions in Yiddish and blossomed into one of the most durable Yiddish companies in America. And there were purely social clubs, including Ve Toiv Lev—a name that meant "Happy Hearts" in Hebrew but was translated by its young participants as "Very Talented Lovers." One new activity reflected the creeping secularism of the Twenties: Friday night dances. The very thought of social dancing on the Sabbath must have horrified the community's older members, but Kurt Peiser, the Lincoln House director, explained it as a defensive measure. The neighborhood's teens flocked each weekend to downtown dance halls and movie theaters, he said, "where the environment was not always the best." Lincoln House sponsored dances as a wholesome alternative: "simple neighborhood social gatherings" that most parents agreed "would not alienate their children's respect for home teachings, as would the public amusement places."

The smorgasbord of activities drew an average of 12,000 participants to Abraham Lincoln House every month in 1922, and the programs kept multiplying: a public library branch, the Talmud Torah school, and a "milk station" that served a half-pint bottle of milk (with graham crackers) to neighborhood children every morning. Attendance climbed to a new peak of 19,000 in 1924. Space was becoming an issue, particularly for athletic activities, but there was another problem that could not be solved with bricks and mortar: the surrounding neighborhood. As more and more Jewish families moved to the north and west, they created a vacuum in the Haymarket district that was quickly filled by non-Jewish newcomers. Slovaks established St. Stephen's Catholic Church on Fifth and Walnut in 1907. St. Mark African Methodist Church moved from its original downtown site to Fourth near Cherry in 1914.

Lincoln House activities ranged from a thriving Yiddish theater program ...

124

Ten years later, Beth Israel sold its old Fifth Street synagogue to Saints Constantine and Helen Greek Orthodox Church, whose members presumably appreciated the structure's Byzantine design. The old Haymarket neighborhood was no less poor than before, but it was becoming much more diverse, and Lincoln House officials were worried. John Landesco, the center's director in 1924, demonstrated that Jews, so often the victims of unthinking prejudice themselves, were not above some prejudices of their own:

> *From Third street to Eighth street we have a vast mixture of twenty different retarded nationalities, four thousand negroes, many Greeks, Slavs and Italians. At the Fourth Street school, one-third of the school population moved out and was replaced by another set during the last school year. In other words, we have a*

great mixture of retarded people with a great transient population. No Parent-Teachers' association can be organized because there is no neighborhood spirit and no leadership. In other words, a typical slum is growing up.... Even the most enthusiastic assimilationist would not wish that our Jewish children should form their characters in such association. Any impartial sociologist knows that in such areas demoralization and delinquency grow up.

Saddled with an undersized facility and stuck in a service area being overrun by strangers, Abraham Lincoln House decided to move. As early as 1922, center officials began to beat the drum for a new building elsewhere. Kurt Peiser described the Ninth Street facility, built only a decade earlier, as "woefully inadequate" and outlined the requirements for a new one:

3ʳᵈ ANNUAL BOYS BANQUET Given by BOY'S COUNCIL ABRAHAM LINCOLN HOUSE FEB. 23, 1928

... to social and leadership clubs like the Boy's Council.

Nat Stone was a tireless fund-raiser for community causes—both Jewish and non-Jewish—in addition to running Boston Store.

What we are in need of now more than ever before is a new Jewish community center whose facilities will include a gymnasium, swimming pool, showers, club and class rooms, auditorium dance hall and various other rooms necessary to carry out the purposes of a community center.

Lizzie Kander signed on to the effort, promising to set aside all revenues from her *Settlement Cookbook* "in anticipation of the drive for a half million dollar Jewish Community Center."

The ensuing campaign marked a subtle turning point in the Jewish community's evolution. Abraham Lincoln House and The Settlement before it had begun as products of a missionary impulse to "uplift our downtrodden and shiftless poor." They were organized by German Jews for the benefit of eastern European Jews. In the 1920s, as the first group shed its Germanness and the second outgrew its poverty, they found themselves sharing a broader common ground. The idea of charity dispensed by affluent families to what Kander had once called "our unfortunate brethren" was no longer relevant, and it yielded by degrees to a more expansive notion of community. The center's focus shifted accordingly, from ghetto-based social work to a more general program incorporating the latest middle-class amenities. An institution established by one segment of Jewish Milwaukee for another was about to become a facility for everyone.

Given the prevailing geographic realities, there was only one possible location for a new center: downtown. In 1929, the community purchased a spacious four-story building on Milwaukee Street just north of State. It had housed the high school department of Milwaukee University School (the former German-English Academy), which had just moved to a posh new home on the upper East Side—not far, ironically, from Emanu-El B'ne Jeshurun's new synagogue. (In a double irony, the new center was in the same block as Emanu-El's old temple, which had been replaced by an automobile showroom.) Nat Stone, president of the Federated Jewish Charities, outlined the rationale for the purchase:

The Jewish people do not herd themselves in one section any more. They live in every section of the city, and in Milwaukee the only possible location equally accessible to the West, Northwest and East sides all generously populated by Jewish people, is some place downtown, and Milwaukee street between East State and East Highland is as logical as any other. This place may be reached easily by auto, street car, and motor bus from every section of the city.

Fund-raising was not a major challenge, particularly with Nat Stone in charge. Born in Germany and raised in St. Louis, Stone had settled in Milwaukee in 1906 and promptly risen to a position of leadership in the community. As president of Boston Store, he was one of the city's most powerful merchants, but his role as a civic figure was even more prominent. Stone's pet projects ranged from the Boy Scouts to the Civic Opera to Marquette University, and his fondness for Jewish causes was legendary. As president of the Federated Jewish Charities for more than a decade, from 1918 to 1929, Nat Stone was generally the largest and always the most enthusiastic giver to every drive. Samuel Hirshberg, his rabbi at Emanu-El B'ne Jeshurun, called Stone "the chief cornerstone upon which Jewish philanthropy was built."

The combination of Nat Stone's leadership, the prosperity of the times, and $75,000 in *Settlement Cookbook* revenue enabled the community to pay cash for the Milwaukee Street building and then remodel it from top to bottom for $150,000. The volunteers in charge decided early on to call it the Jewish Center rather than the Jewish Community Center, solely to avoid conflict with the "community centers" maintained by congregations

like Beth El and Beth Israel. Five times larger than Lincoln House (which was sold, pianos and all, to the Milwaukee Urban League for $15,000), the Jewish Center was finally dedicated on March 21, 1931. The *Wisconsin Jewish Chronicle* printed an enthusiastic inventory of its amenities:

> ... the delightful coffee shop, the elegant lounge, the spacious lobby, the commodious library, the auditorium with its complete stage, the gymnasium, the swimming pool, the handball courts, said to be the best built in this section of the country, the locker rooms and showers for men and women, the completely equipped kitchen with its separate units for the preparation of various foods, the sewing and work rooms, the class rooms for art, music, and education of every

Dedicated in 1931, the Jewish Center on Milwaukee St. replaced Abraham Lincoln House as the institutional heart of the Jewish community.

A 1922 addition made Mount Sinai the second-largest hospital in Milwaukee.

The Jewish Orphan Home
on McKinley Ave. served the
community's neediest young people...

sort, the club and meeting rooms, large and small, and all the details so painstakingly planned and worked out by the administration.

The Jewish Center offered more activities for more people than either of its predecessors. It was undoubtedly the Jewish community's major institutional achievement of the Twenties, but other local mainstays, rising on the same tide of prosperity, experienced comparable growth. A $350,000 addition increased the number of beds at Mount Sinai Hospital from 100 to 150 in 1922, tying it for second place (after St. Mary's) among Milwaukee's eleven private hospitals. A free outpatient dispensary followed in 1925, offering "medical and surgical service of every type to all needy persons who apply." Housed two doors north of the hospital on Twelfth Street, the clinic drew heavily from the fading North Side Jewish quarter. Nearly 75 percent of the patients in the hospital itself were Gentiles, many of them taking advantage of one of the finest obstetrical departments in the city. Mount Sinai did not even serve kosher meals, a reflection of its aggressive non-denominational policy.

Another local stalwart focused on programs for Jewish youngsters. In 1928, after nearly twenty years on the Milwaukee River near Thiensville, the Children's Outing Society purchased a larger, more attractive property in Waukesha County's lake district. Located on Upper Nemahbin Lake, the new fresh-air camp had been a Cudahy family estate, and it came complete with buildings, tennis courts, and a six-car garage that was quickly converted to a manual arts facility. Sophie Cohen made the purchase possible with a $25,000 grant in memory of her husband. The *Wisconsin*

Jewish Chronicle called her donation "the largest gift made by any individual in Milwaukee Jewish history," and the facility, which opened in the summer of 1929, was known ever after as Camp Sidney Cohen.

Two West Side institutions moved to more spacious quarters in the same decade. The Jewish Orphan Home, established by a group of Orthodox women in 1919, took over a large residence on Twenty-first and McKinley in 1922 and put up a three-story addition six years later. At the other end of the age spectrum, elderly Jews with no other means of support had been housed in a converted residence on Seventh and Galena since 1906. The Jewish Home for the Aged did not age particularly well. By 1922, the facility was "utterly unfit to care for any type of inmates," according to a study of Jewish welfare agencies released that year. The study's authors didn't stop there. "Its equipment and management are below any criticism," they declared, "and the lack of physical care and medical supervision render it positively dangerous to its so called beneficiaries." In 1929, a conscience-stricken community built a new Jewish Home for the Aged on Fiftieth Street near Meinecke. Its location reflected the continuing westerly drift of Jewish families from the Haymarket area to Sherman Park. At the formal dedication ceremony on January 26, 1930, board chairman Nat Stone called the facility "all that a modern up-to-date home for aged people should be."

Dependent older adults and disadvantaged children were constants even during the sky-high prosperity of the 1920s, and the number of poor families seemed irreducible regardless of economic conditions. The Hebrew Relief Association, a Milwaukee mainstay since the Civil War era, had always provided material aid to the poor. In 1921, the Relief Association took a new name that reflected a quiet revolution in social work practice: the Jewish Social Service Association (JSSA). The agency's priorities shifted from the provision of food and fuel to a casework approach; professional social workers helped roughly 150 families every month deal with medical, housing, educational, and behavioral problems. The same approach guided the actions of the Federated Jewish Charities, which had been coordinating the community's charitable activities since 1902. Simon Peiser, the Federation's director in 1922, noted that the "mere alms giving society" of 1902 had evolved into "an organization deeply interested in all phases of social uplift and, therefore, ready not only to alleviate suffering and want but also to serve wherever advice and counsel are needed to prevent men, women and children from slipping their moorings." The Federation

... while the Jewish Home for the Aged on Fiftieth provided a safe haven for its oldest members.

Jewish Museum Milwaukee

Milwaukee County Historical Society

functioned as a sort of Jewish United Way, raising funds and distributing them to member organizations that included the Jewish Social Service Association, Abraham Lincoln House, the Children's Outing Society, the community Talmud Torah, the venerable Ladies' Relief Sewing Society, and national charities ranging from an orphanage in Cleveland to a tuberculosis hospital in Denver.

Woodmont (top) *and then Brynwood Country Clubs gave Jewish golfers a place to play when they were not welcome to join other private clubs.*

The 1920s were indeed a decade of growth and prosperity for Milwaukee's Jewish institutions. The *Wisconsin Jewish Chronicle* estimated that $4 million was raised for religious, medical, and social welfare activities during the decade—nearly $50 million in current dollars. From Reform synagogues to Socialist labor groups, most of the community's institutions moved into new and improved quarters. Benjamin Glassberg, director of the Federated Jewish Charities, described 1929 alone as "the year when there came into being what had been hopes and dreams for many years," including Camp Sidney Cohen, the new Jewish Home for the Aged, a Board of Jewish Education, and the definitive groundwork for the Milwaukee Jewish Center.

While some institutions devoted themselves to good works, others concentrated on good times. The 1920s witnessed an epidemic of joining in America; new clubs of all kinds were formed, and old ones experienced surges in membership. Milwaukee's first Jewish golf club, Woodmont, had been organized in 1907 by the Adlers, Gimbels, Landauers, and other first families—with a ceiling of ninety, according to the bylaws. Woodmont Country Club maintained a nine-hole course just west of the Milwaukee County line at Lincoln Avenue, in what is now the City of New Berlin. (Expanded to eighteen holes, it is still in operation as New Berlin Hills.) In 1926, some of Milwaukee's younger Jews, not all of them German by background, formed Brynwood Country Club as a more up-to-date alternative. They purchased a 160-acre farm on Good Hope Road, in the northern reaches of Milwaukee County, and began to play golf in 1929. In contrast to its older sister,

4th ANNUAL MEETING
SHOLOM ALEICHEM CIRCLE
WISCONSIN HOTEL MILWAUKEE APR 5 1924

Jewish Museum Milwaukee

Brynwood developed a full eighteen holes in its first year and capped its roster at 200 families. Both Woodmont and Brynwood reflected the community's penchant for organization, but they were given extra impetus by the fact that, with few exceptions, Jews were simply not welcome at other private clubs.

One of the more interesting in-town groups of the 1920s was the purely Jewish Sholom Aleichem Circle, a group of 120 business and professional men who met for lunch every weekday in a private room at the Wisconsin Hotel. In the spirit of the decade, members of Sholom Aleichem ("Peace be with you") declared that their reason for being was "to meet just for the joy of meeting, without reason or excuse." The club became a sort of community forum, airing the issues of the day—often with the help

of prominent speakers who happened to be in town—and lending material and moral support to any activity for the common good. The group's de facto chairman for many years was Jacob Bitker, a well-known clothing retailer who had emigrated from Russia in his teens.

The largest Jewish social organization of the 1920s was also the oldest: B'nai B'rith, a national fraternal order that had been a fixture on the local scene since 1861. Gilead Lodge, the sole survivor of the nineteenth-century branches, grew from 350 members in 1913 to 600 in 1919 and 916 in 1927. Lodge night was still its main activity, and in 1926 Gilead Lodge acquired a spacious hall at Twelfth and North. (It is now the home of the Prince Hall Masons, an African-American fraternal group.) Although social activities were paramount,

The Sholom Aleichem Circle was both a social club and an important community forum.

131

B'nai B'rith also launched some singularly important community initiatives. A network of Hillel centers, devoted to "enhancing the value of Jewish communal life" on America's college campuses, began to take shape in the 1920s. The first Hillel center opened at the University of Illinois in 1923 and the second at the University of Wisconsin one year later. The Anti-Defamation League was another of B'nai B'rith's offspring. Organized nationally in 1913, ADL eventually spread to every lodge in the country. The Milwaukee branch of the League campaigned to ban *The Merchant of Venice* from public schools (for Shakespeare's unflattering portrait of Shylock) and to delete the most egregiously anti-Semitic scenes from *The King of Kings*, Cecil B. DeMille's film biography of Jesus.

If any ethnic or religious group could ever be described as hyper-organized, it was Milwaukee's Jewish community in the 1920s.

The 1924 Blue Book *was a comprehensive digest of Jewish Milwaukee's organizational life.*

The *Blue Book* compiled in 1924 listed 102 Jewish organizations—religious, charitable, social, educational, and political—in a city with only 22,000 Jews, barely 4 percent of the total population. The abundance of outlets, offering something for every taste and tradition, expressed a buoyancy that matched the national mood perfectly. Americans were living large in the 1920s, and there seemed to be no limit on the upward mobility of the individual or the economic potential of the country as a whole. Soon enough, however, in Milwaukee and elsewhere, those sky-high expectations would come crashing to the ground.

Depression and War

By 1929, the underlying dynamics of Milwaukee's Jewish community had reached a point of at least provisional clarity. The Orthodox congregations were becoming more liberal, and the Reform communities were becoming more traditional. Everyone, or nearly everyone, had entered the middle class. The old ethnic divisions—German vs. eastern European—had softened, and the geographic divisions—East Side vs. West Side—had hardened. As the flow of newcomers slowed to a halt, Milwaukee's Jews felt a growing sense of commonality, despite the geographic divide, and their underlying unity was expressed in a thriving charitable scene and a robust organizational life.

What followed was fifteen years of very rough weather. The stock market crash of October 24, 1929, marked the beginning of a downturn that would plunge the nation into economic darkness for nearly a decade. The Depression was followed immediately by a second global conflict significantly more destructive than the first, a conflict that held particular horrors for the world's Jews. The twin cataclysms of depression and war submerged local concerns for the duration; America's focus shifted to individual survival in the 1930s and the free world's survival in the 1940s. As traumatic as the events of the period were, however, they did not disrupt the underlying dynamics of the Jewish community. The long-term trends in place before 1929 continued to work beneath the surface, and Milwaukee's Jews—chastened, perhaps, but not fundamentally changed—left the period at approximately the same point they had entered it.

Milwaukee felt the impact of the Depression somewhat later than its peers in urban America. It was not until 1932 that the hardest of the hard times descended on the city, but they descended with a vengeance, pushing the local unemployment rate to 40 percent and ultimately forcing nearly half the county's population onto the relief rolls. Milwaukee's Jews suffered with everyone else. As their members experienced layoffs or pay cuts, some of the smaller congregations faced bankruptcy. In 1931, Degel Israel (Anshe Roumania) implored other Jews to attend a benefit its leaders had organized to raise mortgage funds: "The present depression has made it difficult for many of our members to respond in the usual generous fashion to the need of the congregation and we are forced to extend our appeal to the entire community." Even Emanu-El B'ne Jeshurun, the wealthiest congregation in the entire state, was forced to slash its payroll. Rabbi Samuel Hirshberg's salary dropped from $10,000 in 1930 to $6,000 in 1933, and Joseph Baron's fell accordingly. The Gilead Lodge of B'nai Brith watched its membership plummet from 916 in 1927 to a mere 269 in 1933. Brynwood Country Club went bankrupt and was forced to operate as a public course under its long-time golf pro, Joe Frank, as receiver. (Season tickets sold for $50, and a single round cost as little as forty cents.) Mount Sinai Hospital, still committed to serving the neediest patients, operated at such a deficit that the theme of its 1934 fund-raising campaign was "Keep the Doors Open." For those with money to spend, the Thirties created some real bargains—Beth Israel offered "greatly reduced" pew rents during the 1933 High Holy Days, and the price of corned beef at Guten's Deli

fell from $1.10 a pound in 1931 to 79 cents a year later—but fewer and fewer Milwaukeeans could take advantage of the decade's deflation.

The Depression created special problems for one stereotypical group of Jewish businessmen. As housewives kept more of their recyclable materials and as charities absorbed the balance, the city's junk collectors found their sources of supply drying up. In 1931, they formed the Progressive Junk Peddlers Association and opened an office at Eleventh and Walnut. The group's members appealed to their fellow Milwaukeeans to bring in "clothing, furniture, rags, metals, paper and everything else known as 'junk' that they wish carted away." Professing themselves to be at "the point of desperation," they promised to pay prevailing rates for all household refuse. The collective's members also persuaded local wholesalers to buy exclusively from them, arguing that they had "already done much to raise the standard of junk collecting."

As the gloom deepened, Jewish charities were simply overwhelmed. Not since the 1880s, when the eastern European exiles began to arrive, had there been such a surge of poverty in the Jewish community. The Jewish Social Service Association's caseload doubled between 1929 and 1931, and rising needs were met with dwindling resources. Fund drive after fund drive fell short of its goal. Community leaders decided that their only feasible alternative was to

The Depression forced price cuts in everything from a round of golf to a pound of corned beef.

Benjamin Glassberg (top) *ran Milwaukee County's entire relief effort, while Aaron Scheinfeld headed the Federated Jewish Charities.*

abandon, for at least the time being, their commitment to "taking care of our own." Benjamin Glassberg, director of the Federated Jewish Charities, had questioned the self-help model as early as 1929, even before the Depression hit:

> *We as practical men, and as realists, must make our policy fit the facts of the American scene of the present day. We American Jews are tax-payers to the same extent as the non-Jews, and are, therefore, equally entitled to draw upon public resources along with all other groups.*

In 1931, with community needs nearing the critical point, the Jewish Social Service Association began to accept public funds. One year later, Benjamin Glassberg himself was named head of Milwaukee County's entire relief program—a tribute to his abilities as well as to the stellar record of the Jewish charitable establishment. Glassberg supervised a staff of 300 social workers and administered a budget of $10 million, some of which was channeled through the JSSA to needy Jewish families.

The Federated Jewish Charities, his former agency, continued to operate, but in 1933 the Federation combined its annual campaign with that of the Milwaukee Community Fund—the predecessor of United Way. If the problems were indeed community-wide, Federation officials reasoned, it made sense to work toward community-wide solutions. Although Jewish charities still provided kosher meat and Passover supplies to indigent households, most fund-raising was done through a "Jewish unit" of the larger Community Fund.

As difficult as conditions were, the long-term trends affecting Jewish Milwaukee had developed a life of their own; changes first evident in the 1920s persisted into the 1930s. Although geographic mobility slowed considerably, West Siders continued to move to the northwest and East Siders kept migrating to the northeast. Sherman Park was one of the few Milwaukee neighborhoods where home-builders could still find customers during the Depression, and the collapse in demand for construction materials enabled even moderate-income families to build with brick and Lannon stone. The low-density Jewish community west of Thirty-first Street kept growing at the expense of the crowded Haymarket neighborhood.

The gap between German and eastern European Jews continued to narrow. An important line was crossed in 1934, when Bert Broude, a native of Russia, was elected president of Emanu-El B'ne Jeshurun. The very idea of a "new" immigrant joining the former flagship of German Reform Judaism, much less leading it, would have been inconceivable a generation or two earlier. Another barrier fell in 1935, when the Federated Jewish Charities—long identified as a German institution—made Aaron Scheinfeld its president. Scheinfeld was a rising young attorney who happened to be the son of Rabbi Solomon Scheinfeld, the leading voice of Orthodoxy in Milwaukee. The younger

Scheinfeld championed a more central role for the Federation, calling it the greatest single force for "keeping the fires of Jewish conscience alive and burning." B'nai B'rith, yet another German-Jewish mainstay, recruited aggressively within the eastern European community during and after the Depression. West Siders organized the Washington Park Lodge in 1941 and four years later formed the Sholom Aleichem Lodge, described as "the only Yiddish-speaking B'nai B'rith lodge in the United States."

The Milwaukee Jewish Center opened just in time to address the problems of "New Deal leisure." From the day the Milwaukee Street facility was dedicated in 1931, its programs helped ensure that, in director George Peizer's words, "this leisure can be harnessed and directed into constructive fields." Sports enjoyed a new prominence, including gym classes for "senior men"—defined as anyone over twenty-five—and basketball leagues that pitted the West Side Buicks against the Lubotsky Tires. Debate, dramatics, and discussion groups attracted less-athletic members of the community. The Food Exchange sold noodles, herring, strudel, kuchen, "and other palatable products of an old-fashioned kitchen" made by Jewish women who were struggling to get by. Although the needy and unemployed remained a priority, the Jewish Center was no longer a charity. Many of its programs reflected, even in the Thirties, the typically middle-class concerns of a group entering the American mainstream.

Family ties remained strong even as the economy crumbled. The Becker clan gathered for their Passover Seder in 1935.

Jewish Museum Milwaukee

The Jewish Center met the challenge of "New Deal leisure" with programs that ranged from athletics to folk dancing.

The Round Table of Jewish Problems relied on "a free interchange of ideas" to develop "a positive, non-cringing attitude toward Judaism." A lecture series covered topics like "Sex in Civilization," "How Not to Raise Children," and, tellingly, "The Middle Classes at the Crossroads." Even more revealing was a 1931 announcement that the center's coffee shop would be open for dinner on Thursday evenings—"the maid's night off."

Another theme that carried over from the 1920s was secularism. The community's more devout members fervently hoped that the hard times would spark a revival of interest in religion. In 1934, an ad hoc committee of Reform, Conservative, and Orthodox rabbis issued a call for more regular Sabbath attendance:

Cognizant of the social distress and bewilderment which engulf our people today, we feel all the more keenly the importance of a genuine popular return to this age-old fountain-head of Jewish inspiration. The Jew needs at the present time a mighty faith, a serene and unconquerable soul, a deep-rooted loyalty to his prophetic idealism. Where can he find these but in the sanctuary of his religion?

There was some movement toward greater observance. Orthodox congregations reported larger numbers in the pews on Friday evenings, and a new Reform temple opened just west of the city. Rabbi Joseph Baron of Emanu-El B'ne Jeshurun was planting the seeds of Reform Judaism in his travels across the state, and the result was a bumper crop of new synagogues. One of the healthiest seedlings was Congregation Emanu-El in nearby Waukesha. Organized in 1939, Emanu-El moved into a converted residence on Arcadian Avenue two years later, sharing the space with Waukesha County's B'nai B'rith lodge and a fledgling Jewish community center.

There may have been a revival in some quarters, but the overall picture continued to be discouraging. At Emanu-El B'ne Jeshurun's annual meeting in 1936, Bert Broude, the congregation's president, engaged in some revisionist thinking about the previous decade:

Surveys and symposiums delineated in the [Reform] bulletin reveal the well known saga of that golden decade—1919 to 1929—of that era when spiritual values were not the paramount quests, but rather the construction of bigger and better Temples, and beautiful edifices were the order of those days. Suddenly it seems an unwelcome miracle was wrought—a visitation came upon us, and found us spiritually insolvent. I stress this fact by indicating to you that in our own Congregation we slumped from a sensible and creatively possible budget of about $64,000 to half that amount. The first symptom of economic panic struck at our haven of spiritual inspiration. Our great and wise and beneficent Jehovah, our prophets, sages and Psalms singers, our noble traditions, our much vaunted heritage, the reverence we are supposed to bear for the passionate faith of our Fathers and our Mothers, withered away with the very first breeze of the depression. It was like

a withering fever, this fear that overtook us. Resignations poured in, we were literally inundated with a flood of requests for reductions of dues. The Temple was the first line of attack—not of shelter.

Although most Jews did not turn reflexively to religion, some still sought an explanation for the country's manifest problems and a plausible alternative to the existing order. Lulled to sleep during the prosperous Twenties, radicalism was reawakened. The Socialist Party attracted new adherents, and Communism gained ground as well, with disastrous results for at least one Jewish family. Lebia Magarschak, the sexton of Congregation Anshe Lebowitz. was a Russian immigrant who had fled the October revolution of 1917. His teenaged daughter, Haia, became a Communist in Milwaukee, changed her name to Sonia Mason, and went to jail for her part in a 1930 riot at the Vliet Street haymarket. The elder Magarschak was called to the witness stand during her trial. "Have you a daughter?," asked the district attorney. "I had a daughter," he replied weakly.

A sharp rise in anti-Semitism was another by-product of the Depression. Some high-profile commentators blamed Jews for the nation's prolonged collapse—a familiar tactic in times of economic stress. Father Charles Coughlin used his syndicated radio program of the 1930s as a platform for anti-Jewish invective so extreme that his superiors eventually silenced him. But the real threat came from overseas, particularly after Adolf Hitler rose to power in Germany in 1933. There was little apparent reason for concern at first. Addressing a forum at the Jewish Center, Rabbi Charles Rubenstein of Beth Israel said, "Jewry has nothing to fear from Adolf Hitler, German chancellor, who is destined for a short ride." Those were words that Rubenstein would soon have reason to regret. As Hitler strengthened his grip, he made scapegoating a cornerstone of state policy. The tragic result was that World War II began six years earlier for the Jews of Germany than it did for the general population. One outrageous edict after another made the Third Reich a distinctly inhospitable society and, despite strict quota limits, a steady stream of Jewish refugees reached America's shores. Roughly 400 made it to Milwaukee between 1933 and 1941, many of them affluent exiles whose property had been confiscated by the Nazis. One business executive found work as a butler, and a society matron supported herself as a cook. The Jewish Vocational Service, established in 1938 "to aid Jewish youth to find a place in industry," broadened its mission to help the refugees find work—no easy task in the Depression—while the Jewish Center beefed up its

Americanization classes and offered the newcomers one year's free dues.

Hitler had his supporters in Milwaukee. A local chapter of the Friends of New Germany, commonly known as "the Bund," was organized in 1933, drawing its members largely from the ranks of post-World War I immigrants who had never gotten over their homeland's humiliation in the Treaty of Versailles. Bund leaders parroted the anti-Jewish rhetoric of Der Führer and even copied his uniforms. Far more obvious, however, was the breadth and depth of anti-Hitler sentiment in Milwaukee. A 1933 rally drew 4,000 people, both Jews and Gentiles, to the Auditorium for an evening of speeches, resolutions, and general indignation. Hitler's anti-Jewish policies, the assembly agreed, were "repugnant to the moral instincts of civilized mankind and inconsistent with the high reputation which the German people has won for itself by its achievements and sacrifices." Mayor Daniel Hoan, who called the Bund a "rotten, scandalous, reactionary group," sounded like

Adolf Hitler's anti-Jewish policies stirred a reaction in Milwaukee as early as 1933.

Wisconsin Jewish Chronicle, Mar. 31, 1933

The communique by the Nazi Party, announcing the boycott, enumerates eleven points.

Action committees are to be set up in all towns and villages in order to caution clients against entering Jewish shops. These committees are to operate also against Jewish lawyers and physicians, whose clients are to be warned against patronizing them. Under the auspices of these committees, tens of thousands of meetings are to be held throughout the length and breadth of Germany in order to popularize the boycott movement and to evoke a demand for the introduction of a numerus clausus in the schools, the universities, and in the professions, calling for the limitation of Jewish participation in the cultural and economic life of Germany, proportionate only to their numbers; that is, eight-tenths of one per cent. Under the official slogan of "No German Buys from Jews," to be posted everywhere, the drive is to be made as thorough as possible, embracing even newspapers that might be considered to manifest insufficient enthusiasm in pushing the boycott. Such newspapers are to be denied adver-

occasions of this sort.

The Chronicle will be glad to publish letters from responsible members of the community on this very important subject. The letters should be reasonably brief and signed with the name and address of the writer.

PROTEST HITLER ANTI-SEMITISM AT BIG MEETING HERE

Christians and Jews Join in the Milwaukee Auditorium Gathering, Wed. Eve.

GOVERNOR, MAYOR, AND CIVIC LEADERS SPEAK

Christians and Jews of Milwaukee joined the world-wide protest against persecution of the Jews in Germany in a huge mass meeting held in the

Governor Smith told a cheering audience of more than 20,000 Jews assembled in Madison Square Garden Monday night to protest against Hitler's treatment of the Jews in Germany.

An overflow crowd estimated at 6,000 heard the speeches on the street through an amplifying system. The meeting was broadcast on a national radio hook-up and short-wave throughout the world.

Mr. Smith brought the audience to its feet as he denounced racial and religious bigotry and suppression of civil liberties and appealed to the German people to remember the principles of human love and brotherhood. He absolved the German people of any wrongdoing or sympathy with anti-Semitism but laid these at the door of those whom he denounced as demagogues and enemies of the German people.

Mr. Smith was one of a group of leaders of Jewry and the Christian world who joined in protest. Others who spoke included Senator Robert Wagner, Bishop William T. Manning, Bishop Francis T. McConnell, H. Tuttle, Mayor O'Brien a war hawk: "If they take away liberty in Germany today, they'll wipe out liberty in America tomorrow, unless we fight." The *Milwaukee Journal* (March 30, 1933) summarized the tone of the rally: "A political caucus could boast no greater enthusiasm, a lecture classroom no greater attention to speakers and a church no higher ideals."

Even more convincing was the patriotism of the mainstream German community. The Federation of German-American Societies, representing seventy-three groups, banned Nazi sympathizers from its annual German Day celebration and took pains to distance itself from the pro-Hitler lunatic fringe. The *Wisconsin Jewish Chronicle* (March 18, 1938) published an appreciative report of one German Federation meeting and printed verbatim the resolution adopted by its members:

> *We ... most vehemently condemn the activities of the pro-Nazi Volksbund, as it seriously disturbs harmonious co-operation among racial groups throughout the United States....*

> *Our sincere aim is to foster the spiritual unity of our nation—undivided by racial prejudice of any kind—so that we and our descendants may enjoy the blessings of a free America forever.*

> *Therefore, let it be said here and now, that it is not true that the average German-American is a Nazi, but in fact is strongly opposed to Nazi doctrine of hate. Our disposition in this matter of intolerance is ample proof of the common sense that prevails within our group in distinct contrast with the German-American Volksbund. America, please take notice!*

Although Milwaukee offered poor soil for Nazism—or indeed for any of the more aggressive forms of anti-Semitism—local Jewish leaders weren't taking any chances. In 1938, they organized the Milwaukee Jewish Council "as a clearing house for local action and leadership" on issues of Jewish rights. The Council favored cooperation rather than confrontation in its efforts to stamp out anti-Semitism. Its organizers believed that the best defense against hatred was a fully functioning free society, one committed to pluralism and tolerant of its internal differences. Working with a broad range of religious and ethnic groups, the Milwaukee Jewish Council, like its counterparts across the country, labored to make America live up to its highest ideals.

If American principles shone more brightly against the dark specter of Nazism, Zionism fared even better. The palpable suffering of Germany's Jews dissolved the last vestiges of opposition to a Jewish national home, even among the Reform diehards. In 1935, Milwaukee Jews organized a bazaar to benefit the Jewish National Fund, a global initiative to buy land in Palestine. Meyer Lubotsky, the bazaar's chairman, noted a sea change in community sentiment:

> *Even two years ago it would have been impossible to arouse the enthusiasm that is being shown in the present campaign. But the sad events in Germany and the ever present danger of persecution of our people in other countries has shown all of us that Palestine is the only land in the world that can offer a haven of refuge to our suffering people.*

That Palestinian haven required major infusions of cash, of course—to purchase land, build settlements, and develop world-wide support. It seemed that every Jewish home in Milwaukee had at least one blue-and-white coin box for donations to the National Fund. Twice a year during "box clearance week," tons of small change went into bags for the Zionist cause. One of the movement's most effective fund-raisers was a familiar figure: Goldie Mabowehz Meyerson, a rising star in Palestine's Labor Party. Golda—her name in adulthood—returned to her old home every year or two, invariably seeking financial and political support. "Milwaukee will welcome home one of its best known daughters," reported the *Wisconsin Jewish Chronicle* (January 7, 1938) during one sojourn, and she never went away empty-handed.

The blue-and-white coin box of the Jewish National Fund was a fixture in thousands of homes. The proceeds were used to buy land in Palestine.

Golda's visits came to an end after September 1, 1939, when the German invasion of Poland touched off World War II. The attack made headlines, naturally, but for Jewish residents of Milwaukee and other American cities, the news was ever so slightly anti-climactic. Hitler's war on the Jews had begun several years earlier—a fact made painfully apparent in the European dispatches that filled the *Jewish Chronicle* every week. But a conflict specific to one group broadened to include everyone. First as a supporter of the Allies in 1939 and then as a major combatant after the 1941 bombing of Pearl Harbor, the United States shifted completely to a war footing.

Just as they had shared in the trauma of the Depression, American Jews took full part in the trials and triumphs of World War II. In 1941, just three weeks after Pearl Harbor, Rabbi Joseph Baron of Emanu-El B'ne Jeshurun noted with pride "the Maccabean spirit" in his congregation. "The young people … and their elders," said Baron, "are anxious to fulfill each patriotic duty," much like the Jewish rebels who had taken on their Syrian tormentors more than 2,000 years before. The roster of Milwaukee Jews who served in World War II ultimately approached 2,500, and many risked their lives on the front lines. (The tally was kept, reported the *Jewish Chronicle*, "to scotch the ugly little rumors you hear about the 'desk men' and 'soft jobs' among the Jews in service.") Nearly 200 earned decorations, and sixty-four never came home.

For those on the home front, the war was a never-ending, day-and-night presence. The Jewish Vocational Service provided "pre-induction orientation" for young men entering the military and placed those

staying at home in defense jobs. The local Hillel center sponsored dances and discussion groups for soldiers spending their leave time in Milwaukee, and the Jewish Center provided cots and free breakfasts for those who couldn't find rooms in the city's hotels. There was an endless procession of campaigns to sell war bonds and war stamps, some of them highly creative. When the Jewish Center staged its Purim pageant in 1944, children who bought war stamps earned the right to nominate candidates for the roles of Queen Esther and King Ahasuerus. The Jewish Welfare Fund, organized in 1938 to raise money for Jewish agencies that provided services outside the scope of the Community Fund, sent Chanukah gifts, Rosh Hashanah cards, Passover supplies, and mezuzahs (small boxes containing prayer scrolls) to local Jews in the military. The *Jewish Chronicle* published a weekly column filled with reports from "Our Boys in Service." Captain Ralph Goldman, "living in the jungles" in 1943, wrote that "he is now wearing our Mezzuzah with the family Mogen David, and that the other Jewish men in his battalion are envious of it." Sergeant

Goldie Meyerson. shown addressing a Labor Party caucus in 1935, was a rising star in Palestinian politics.

141

Jewish Museum Milwaukee

When the attack on Pearl Harbor drew the United States into World War II, bond rallies became a fixture of life in Milwaukee.

Sol Weinberg, stationed "somewhere overseas," noted that his 1943 Purim celebration included hamentashen (three-cornered pastries filled with fruit) made for the occasion by Army bakers. Private Joe Kupferberg, serving in Hawaii, reported that "his mouth is watering for a good corned beef sandwich and a dill pickle, which is something no amount of money can buy there." Milwaukee also entertained visitors from the front, among them Rabbi Martin Weitz, an Army chaplain who showed off a portable ark created for Sabbath services behind the front lines. Its candleholders were crafted from 105-millimeter artillery shells, its Torah cover was sewn by "a sergeant in a salvage unit," and the Ten Commandments were rendered in Japanese aluminum "against a background of Japanese flare silk."

Support for the war effort was virtually unanimous, but the conflict had special relevance for the nation's Jews, whether they were serving in or out of uniform. Long before the last bomb fell, Americans knew, in detail, what was going on behind the barbed wire at Dachau and Buchenwald. The *Wisconsin Jewish Chronicle*, relaying reports from the underground, described the "laboratories of hatred" at those two camps as early as 1939, and the accounts of "mass annihilation" and "extermination facilities" thereafter were nearly continuous. Although Hitler's obsession with Aryan purity led to the wholesale liquidation of Gypsies (Roma), homosexuals,

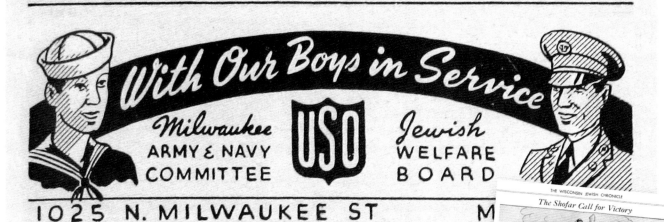

April 2, 1943

With Our Boys in Service

Milwaukee ARMY & NAVY COMMITTEE

USO

Jewish WELFARE BOARD

1025 N. MILWAUKEE ST

THE WISCONSIN JEWISH CHRONICLE

The Shofar Call for Victory

Poles, and other Slavs, it was Jews who bore the brunt of his diabolical campaign. Reading the press dispatches was horrific enough; actually seeing the camps was another matter entirely. Private Jerome Rogatz of North Fifty-second Street provided a graphic account of his visit to a German death camp in a 1945 letter home:

In this camp I saw human beings stacked like cord wood who had died of starvation, and thousands of other people who would soon die. It was very difficult to distinguish because they looked so much alike. From boys twelve years old up to old men of 70 years—they all looked alike, nothing but a skeleton with a haggard, wan, and sorrowful face. In this camp I visited the crematorium where the Nazis burned the victims. In the furnaces were still the charred skulls and bones of many victims. The ashes of hundreds of victims were readily seen....

I wish all Americans could see what I have seen and they would realize why this war of right against wrong had to be fought and won if civilization was to continue.

The war was indeed fought and won. The declaration of victory over Japan on August 14, 1945, ended a conflict that had lasted four years for the United States, six for Europe, and twelve for the Jews of Germany. Very few of those Jews were left to savor the victory. Elation over the Allied triumph was tempered by the awful knowledge that an entire continent's Jewish population had been wiped out. Europe, the homeland to which most American Jews still looked back, was now a desert, and beneath the revelry and relief that marked the war's end was a deep pool of sorrow for the six million lives that were, with all their memories and all their potential, gone forever.

As the war lengthened, the Jewish Chronicle *ran a weekly column of news from Milwaukee Jews in military service as well as cartoons promoting a fervent patriotism.*

143

◇◇◇◇◇◇◇◇◇◇◇◇◇◇◇◇◇◇◇◇◇◇◇◇◇◇◇◇◇◇◇◇◇◇◇◇◇◇◇

V-J Day capped one of the most extraordinary periods in the nation's history. For more than thirty years, Americans were constantly off balance, whipsawed from one crisis to the next: two wars, a depression, and in between a wave of prosperity that many would later come to consider corrosive. There was no rhythm to the period, no room to breathe, but it was momentous nonetheless. For the Jews of Milwaukee, the 1914-1945 years were a time of both outer and inner transformation. By 1945, the cramped Haymarket ghetto had been all but emptied of its Jewish residents, and the community's center of gravity had shifted to the clean middle-class enclave of Sherman Park. A large, and largely affluent, secondary settlement had emerged on the East Side and in the adjacent suburbs of Shorewood and Whitefish Bay. More important but far less visible was a generational shift in perspective. With the end of mass immigration, Old World associations lost their intensity, and strictly American concerns came to the fore—modified, always, by an attachment to the Palestinian homeland that would prove to be permanent. By 1945, in Milwaukee and elsewhere, the old divisions and ancient schisms were fading in the light of an emergent national Jewish identity. As the American people groped toward a new equilibrium in peacetime, Milwaukee's Jews, like their counterparts elsewhere in the country, knew that their situation had materially changed. Leaving the whirlwind, they looked ahead with a sobering awareness that the future of world Judaism was in their hands.

Chapter 4

Triumph Out of Tragedy, 1945-1967

There must have been Jews in the throng that jammed the streets of downtown Milwaukee on V-J Day. Jewish residents, after all, no less than their Gentile neighbors, had bent their energies to the war effort, and they felt the same jubilation, the same sense of sweet deliverance, when it ended in victory. For America's Jews, however, the spirit of celebration was qualified, even compromised, by the awareness of a catastrophe that had befallen no other group on the same scale. When the cheering and horn-blowing finally ended in the wee hours of August 15, 1945, Jews returned to the knowledge that a systematic frontal assault had been waged on their very existence as a people, one that dwarfed any previous act of hatred in a chronicle of persecution that stretched back well over 2,000 years. The Holocaust left six million dead—many, probably most, with relatives in America—and the sorry aftermath was written in the emaciated faces of hundreds of thousands of survivors.

With the return of peacetime, Milwaukee's Jews faced the same central task that occupied their neighbors all across America—remaking lives interrupted by fifteen years of depression and war. Accomplishing that task, in Milwaukee and elsewhere, would produce a staggering number of new homes, new neighborhoods, and new synagogues, but American Jews, following dictates as old as Moses, assumed the responsibility to remake other lives as well: among the tattered remnants of Europe's Jewish population and on the bold new frontier of Israel. By the time the 1945-1967 period ended, the results of their efforts, both at home and abroad, had far surpassed their most extravagant expectations.

"One Destiny Binds the House of Israel"

Israel was a foregone conclusion after the Holocaust. It may not have seemed so at the time, but an idea that had been gathering steam for centuries developed an irresistible momentum in the wake of World War II. With the survivors huddled in European camps and the Allies unwilling to absorb more than a relative handful of families, Israel was their only viable alternative in the entire world. America's Jews, faithful to a spirit of peoplehood that had endured for millennia, knew that the creation of Israel and the resettlement of the refugees would not take place without their help. Milwaukee's response to the crisis was

entirely typical. On January 17, 1946, the Jewish Welfare Fund met to establish the goal for its first postwar campaign. The city's major Jewish umbrella group had never tried to raise more than $400,000, but 1946 was different, said president Bert Broude. He called the assembly "the most critical meeting in the history of this community" and described its task as "unprecedented." Broude knew what was at stake. "Upon our efforts," he said, "together with those of the Jews of the United States, hang the lives of hundreds of thousands of our brethren overseas and in Palestine." The Welfare Fund promptly set a goal of

Jewish Museum Milwaukee

With the stark reality of the Holocaust looming in the background, the 1946 Jewish Welfare Fund campaign was the most successful on record.

The campaign that followed surpassed all others for energy and efficiency. It also set a new standard for directness. One Welfare Fund ad spoke pointedly to the providence shared by American Jews:

> Some years ago you were lucky enough to have a father (or a grandfather) fortunate enough to leave the Old Country with its hates and fears, and come to America where a Jew never has to hide in the cellar after eight o'clock at night.
>
> Because your father came here, you are alive. And prospering.
>
> If he hadn't you'd probably be dead. And so would your children.

$1 million, more than double its previous best effort, and pledged to "subordinate all other activities" to "European Jewish relief and Palestinian upbuilding." The assembled delegates adopted a resolution that eloquently expressed the rationale for their decision:

> We mourn the millions of Jews who were slain because they were Jews. Six million of our brethren have perished and their blood stains the soil of Europe. Their fate is a solemn warning to all living Jews that one destiny binds the House of Israel.
>
> The year 1946 is crucial in the struggle for the survival of the remnant of European Jewry. A decimated remnant of a people lacking adequate food and shelter, home and hope, these Jews must be given the assurance that their fellow-Jews want them to live; that they are desperately eager to make their life secure, tolerable and hopeful. That task must be undertaken and performed primarily by the Jews of America.

Appealing as it did to such powerful emotions—compassion, gratitude, survivor's guilt—the 1946 fund-raising effort was a rousing success. Pledges reached the million-dollar mark in June, concluding what the *Wisconsin Jewish Chronicle* called "the most successful fund raising event in community history." Fully 83 percent of the dollars raised went overseas, some to improve conditions in refugee camps and the balance to buy land and support Jewish settlers in Palestine. Buoyed by the campaign's success, the Jewish Welfare Fund's leaders raised their sights to $1.7 million for 1947.

The vigor of the Milwaukee effort, multiplied by hundreds of campaigns elsewhere in the country, offered some measure of the American response to the postwar emergency. The United States was by far the leading source of both material and moral support for the pioneers building a Jewish national home and for the legions of refugees who wanted to settle there. All the striving, all the struggle were finally rewarded on November

29, 1947, when the United Nations voted to divide Palestine into two states, one for Arabs and the other for Jews. Arab leaders objected strenuously, but Israel was rising to the dignity of statehood again for the first time in nearly 2,000 years.

The news was greeted with unadulterated joy in Jewish America. Here was V-J Day without the mixed emotions. What gave the birth of Israel such power—and such poignancy—was the fact that it came so close on the heels of the Holocaust. The homeland materialized too late for the six million victims of Hitler, but it was ready to welcome their survivors and all who might follow. Some Milwaukeeans celebrated at Congregation Beth Israel, a Zionist stronghold from the very beginning. Thousands sang, listened to speeches, and danced the hora in the vestry, eventually spilling out onto Teutonia Avenue. The UN vote came close to the beginning of Chanukah—the festival of lights—and speaker after speaker noted that a new day was dawning for the world's Jews. Other celebrations took place in private homes, including Ann Agulnick's. She recalled the scene in her East Side residence just after the vote was announced:

Everybody rushed to their telephones and began calling each other. At that particular point, I was president of Hadassah, and so my phone began to ring. Everybody wanted to know, "What are we going to do? What are we going to do?" And I kept saying, "Well, come over." Before everybody came, we ran over to Plotkin's delicatessen and we just emptied their shelves of all the bakery we could lay our hands on, and everybody came to the house bringing everything they had.

And then the people came. There must have been 300 people in our house. There was hugging and kissing and feeling as though it was all happening to us. We didn't have to be in Israel to feel part of the yeshuv [settlement].... It was a real party. The doors were open to the basement, to the bedrooms, to the outside. It was November, but a mild day, so people were just stuffed inside the house and out onto the sidewalk.

Israel's new day did not dawn without violence. Fighting broke out within hours of the UN announcement and entered a broader stage after May 14, 1948, when Israel formally declared its independence. Incited by the Grand Mufti of Jerusalem, the surrounding Arab states attacked one day after the declaration; Israel entered statehood in a state of war. Once again American Jews were asked to help. Golda Meyerson, a key member of Prime Minister David Ben-Gurion's team, had emerged as the fledgling nation's chief fund-raiser. On a whirlwind tour of the United States in February 1948, she visited her old hometown and challenged Milwaukee's Jews to join the struggle:

After so much death in World War II, the birth of Israel marked a new beginning and a dream come true.

ℬℍℯ Wisconsin Jewish Chronicle
A Weekly Paper for the Jewish ℬime

Goldie Meyerson Speaks Here Monday Noon

Community Invited to Reception for Former Milwaukeean Who Is Now Head of the Security and Political Department of Jewish Agency

The entire community is invited to hear Milwaukee's own Mrs. Goldie Meyerson when she speaks at a public meeting this Monday afternoon, February 16, at 12:45 at the Pfister hotel.

In the interest of saving time, there will be no dinner served at the occasion. Mrs. Meyerson's heavy schedule does not permit her to stay in Milwaukee for more than a few hours and she has asked that the meeting be concluded as quickly as possible. It is expected that the meeting will be over by about 2 o'clock.

was a member of the Histadruth executive.

She has been a director of Histadruth's air-minded Aviron company since 1930. In addition, she was chairman of the supervisory board of the Jewish Workers' Sick Fund, which provides medical services for nearly 40 per cent of the Jewish population of Palestine.

During the war she was a member of the Government's War Economic Advisory Council. She was on the Vaad Leumi (National Council of Palestine Jewry), as well as on the Inner Council of the World Zionist Organization.

Following the riots in 1936, she appeared before the Peel Royal Commission. She was the only woman to address that body. She also presented the Jewish case before the Anglo-American Commission in 1947.

Mrs. Meyerson was one of the group of Jewish leaders in Pales-

Golda, or Goldie, Meyerson returned to her old home regularly on behalf of the new state.

You cannot decide whether we will fight or not. We will. No white flag in Palestine will be raised for the Mufti. That decision has been taken. You can only decide one thing: whether we will be victorious or whether the Mufti will.

That decision, American Jews can make.

Four months later, with independence declared and a full-blown war under way, Golda returned to Milwaukee with an even more urgent appeal:

I am going to tell you what we need in the next two months. Not at the end of the two months, but during the next two months. We must have in cash during the next two months at least $75,000,000—at least…. I am telling you I don't care how you get the money.

I know that some of you have taken loans; many communities have taken loans. You have done it beautifully. I have gone home and I have told my people that never did I do a job that brought me so much joy and so much satisfaction as during those few weeks that I spent with you a few months ago.

The Milwaukee Jewish Welfare Fund did in fact borrow money to help Israel—a total of $500,000, using future pledges as collateral—and then shifted its fund-raising machinery into overdrive. Leaders hailed 1948 as "the year of destiny," when "true liberation" finally came to the Jewish people. Irving Rhodes, publisher of the *Jewish Chronicle* and general chairman of the 1948 drive, called it "more a crusade than a campaign." Dozens of businessmen put their careers on hold to raise funds. The community's young people turned over their Bar Mitzvah and confirmation gifts. Agudas Achim, Milwaukee's smallest congregation, added $1,225 to the fund by raffling off a gold watch lovingly carried from Romania fifty years earlier. When the results were tallied in June 1948, Milwaukee had raised $1,750,766—more than $15 million in current dollars. The Welfare Fund had set its goal at $2.5 million, but the group's leaders were more than satisfied with the results; the $1,750,766 contributed in 1948 was a record that would stand for the next two decades. In the United States as a whole, gifts to the United Jewish Appeal totaled $200 million. As if to reward America's generosity, Israel turned the tide in its war with the Arabs during the summer of 1948. By year's end, the new nation had won a decisive victory, adding thousands of square miles of territory and forcing a tense truce that would last until 1956.

Jewish Museum Milwaukee

MILWAUKEE JEWISH WELFARE FUND
$2,500,000 **CAMPAIGN**
CAMPAIGN HEADQUARTERS...817 BRUMDER BUILDING...MARQUETTE 3907

April 22, 1948

Dear Friend:

A meeting of all Captains and Workers on the Welfare Fund teams under my direction will take place on TUESDAY EVENING, APRIL 27, 8:00 P.M. IN PARLOR B OF THE SCHROEDER HOTEL.

This meeting will help us to prepare for work in the great $2,500,000.00 campaign. It will provide us with an opportunity to obtain campaign facts and figures and to discuss methods of reaching our goal. One goal is a tremendous one but we can achieve it if we are determined to do our job.

It is urgent that everyone attend this meeting and I shall look forward to seeing you on Monday evening.

Sincerely yours,

Gerald Glauninger, Marshall
Men's Division

For Europe, Palestine, Refugees, National and Local Needs

With its existence assured—for the time being—Israel turned to the task that had been its destiny from the start: welcoming home wandering Jews from all over the world. The United Nations surveyed German refugee camps in 1946 and found that 96 percent of their residents wanted to go to Palestine; all hope for a revival of Jewish life in Europe had been abandoned. By early 1949, Israel was absorbing more than 25,000 immigrants every month, with no end in sight. "We take in the sick, lame, blind," said Golda Meyerson. "We take them all. We may break our neck, but we are willing to risk our neck. That is why Israel was created."

Milwaukee's Jews, like their peers across the United States, offered crucial assistance to refugees still waiting in European camps. In 1946, the community sponsored a Supplies for Overseas Survivors (SOS) drive that shipped eight tons of canned food, soap, shoes, baby clothes, and "comfort items" across the ocean. One year later, Milwaukeeans took part in a national campaign that delivered five million pounds of Passover essentials to the refugees, including 3.3 million pounds of matzos, 200,000 bottles of sacramental wine, 20,000 Haggadas (Passover Seder service books), and 53,000 prayer shawls.

Determined to make the Israeli experiment a success, Milwaukee's Jews set another fundraising record in 1948.

149

Local Jews also provided more permanent help, resettling roughly 500 displaced persons in Milwaukee between 1945 and 1950. "We are back in the relief business," said Rebecca Tenenbaum, the director of Jewish Family and Children's Service. Immigrants were nearly half of her agency's caseload by 1951, and they added a distinctively European flavor to a community that had been growing more American by the year.

Milwaukee's 500 refugees were a small fraction of the approximately 80,000 displaced Jews who settled in the United States after World War II, and those 80,000 were only a fraction of the hundreds of thousands who made their way to the Jewish homeland. Israel was the primary destination. Its population soared from 800,000 in 1948 to nearly 2,000,000 in 1958, and immigrants accounted for nearly all the increase. Most came from Europe, but many were fleeing the Arab backlash in Iraq, Yemen, Morocco, Algeria, and other countries of the Middle East and northern Africa. The open-door policy was expensive to maintain—Golda Meyerson estimated that it cost Israel $2,500 to resettle a single refugee—and the weight of immigration threatened to sink a nation whose economy was still in its infancy. Once again, Israel turned to America's Jews for aid. It proved difficult, however, to maintain a sense of urgency. Concerned as they were, Americans couldn't keep up a crisis mentality forever. In Milwaukee, for instance, contributions to the Jewish Welfare Fund dropped to $726,311 in 1955—less than half their 1948 peak—and it took another war to rekindle the flame. When Israel went head-to-head with the

Arabs for the second time in 1956—and was for the second time victorious—Milwaukee's giving shot up to $926,747 and passed the million-dollar mark a year later.

Fortunately, a more dependable source of support was already producing income, one that didn't require a constant state of emergency. In 1951, as signs of giving fatigue began to surface, the new state introduced Israel Bonds. Instead of asking its supporters to simply donate money, Israel invited them to invest it as well—in coupon bonds paying 3.5 percent annually or in savings bonds that matured at 150 percent of their purchase price after twelve years. The money was earmarked for a broad portfolio of development projects: watering the Negev Desert, building port facilities at Haifa, constructing roads and houses, and expanding both agriculture and industry throughout the country. Golda Meyerson once again stumped the United States to raise interest in Israel Bonds. "Trust us," she implored a Milwaukee banquet audience in May 1951. "Trust us to repay you every cent you loan us.... Be with us not only when we come to you and speak of tragedy and sorrow but also be with us when we of Israel come to you and speak of building the bright future." Golda found the community as receptive as usual. Milwaukeeans bought more than $250,000 in bonds on the evening of her speech, and the total rose to $4.5 million in the next decade. Door-to-door canvassing on BIG (Bonds of the Israel Government) Day helped, but the most effective salesmen proved to be Milwaukee's religious leaders. Local rabbis and their congregational presidents used the power of the pulpit to promote Israel

Jewish Museum Milwaukee

Bonds on the High Holy Days every year—a practice followed across the country. In 1951 and for several Yom Kippurs thereafter, Milwaukee's synagogues led the nation in per-capita bond sales.

All this "bonding" activity, combined with nonstop fund drives and the beginnings of mass tourism, reflected an attachment to Israel so intense that some commentators worried about the "divided loyalties" of American Jews. The new state was, without exaggerating in the least, a dream come true. Zionism had once been viewed as a quixotic, hopelessly utopian movement, and the issues it raised—particularly nationalism vs. religion—divided Jew from Jew in the United States for decades. When Israel became a tangible reality in 1948, so soon after the Holocaust, pride overflowed in all quarters of the Jewish community. Once a sticking point, the Zionist cause became part of the glue that held America's Jews together, from the most ardently Orthodox to the most avowedly secular. The new nation's military success erased any lingering doubts about the lack of Jewish resistance in World War II, but Israel was much more than a vindication. Here, at long last, was a touchstone of identity for all Jews, an ancient and indivisible motherland to which they had returned after an exile that had lasted 2,000 years. Other American ethnic groups, of course, looked back to homelands across the sea, but the typical Jew's attachment to Israel was markedly different from an Irishman's feelings for the Auld Sod or a Norwegian's fondness for the fjords of

Introduced in 1951, Israel Bonds represented an investment in the Jewish homeland's future.

151

David Ben-Gurion, born David Green in Poland, was the dominant figure in early Israeli politics, serving as prime minister for thirteen years.

Abba Eban, one of Israel's most erudite and most eloquent leaders, was guest of honor at a Milwaukee banquet in 1950.

ancestral memory. For Jews in the United States and elsewhere, ties to Israel were not sentimental but instrumental. The new nation resolved a sense of loss and longing that had been part of the Jewish experience for ages. Diaspora Jews saw Israel as the one sure place they could call their own, a second home even for those who never intended to visit.

Israel responded in kind. The country's leaders viewed their work as a magnificent mitzvah—a commandment they had fulfilled on behalf of all Jews everywhere. Israel, in their eyes, was not simply the one sure place; it was the only true home for the wandering tribes of the Diaspora, the single authentic wellspring of Jewish civilization. When they came to America in search of funds, therefore, they came not as supplicants, hats humbly in hand, but as brothers and sisters who had every right to expect help from their siblings across the sea. Support for Israel, they believed, was not a matter of charity; it was simple justice. David Ben-Gurion, the irascible but unstoppable figure who dominated early Israeli politics, felt that Americans owed a particular debt of gratitude. For them, he said in a 1958 speech, Israel was nothing less than a spiritual lifeline:

> *Never was such a great Jewish community in such danger of gentle extinction as American Jewry today. If this great historic miracle had not taken place in our time and the State of Israel had not risen, the great majority of the Jews of the United States would have been left without any bond of Judaism.*

Golda Meyerson was just as blunt. Following Ben-Gurion's orders, the former Milwaukeean Hebraized her surname to Meir in 1956, when she became Israel's foreign minister. Golda Meir searched in vain for signs of comparable devotion in Israel's "long-distance friends" across the Atlantic. "Jewish youth sing-songing about the Negev in New York and Boston will not build up our wastelands," she complained in 1957. Meir wanted young Americans to settle in those wastelands, just as she had in 1921. "We cannot become reconciled," she admitted, "to the idea that only a small minority of world Jewry will live in Israel." American Jews were just as unwilling to concede that they were exiles, or that life in the Diaspora was somehow inferior to residence in Israel. The differences of opinion were sharply felt, but they did not compromise the pride that Jews everywhere felt in the sheer, shining fact of Israel, nor did they dim the remarkable accomplishments of those who had brought the nation into being. Abba Eban, Israel's leading diplomat for decades, took the long view when he addressed a 1954 fund-raising banquet in Milwaukee:

> *The history of this generation will forever be dominated by this most fantastic transition from the depths of paralyzing weakness to the heights to which we suddenly rose. This is at once the most fearful and the most sublime decade in all the Jewish epochs. It has seen us at the lowest depths of our despair, and also at the highest moment of our salvation. It has seen the vindication of the eternal and triumphant tenacity of the Jewish spirit.*

"A Temple in a Proper Neighborhood"

As the rest of the world recovered from the devastation of global warfare, Milwaukee's Jews led what might be termed a bicoastal existence. They were spellbound by events taking place on the eastern shore of the Mediterranean, and they followed, often through the pages of the weekly *Wisconsin Jewish Chronicle,* the saga of "triumphant tenacity" that led to the creation of Israel—from the plight of the refugees on Cyprus to the actions of Haganah soldiers, from the pronouncements of conflicted British authorities to the pressures exerted by Harry Truman. But they were just as absorbed by events taking place on the western shore of Lake Michigan. Like their Gentile neighbors, Milwaukee's Jews were caught up in the welcome and intensely local preoccupations of peacetime. Whether they were resuming old lives or building new ones, they had to establish themselves in the frameworks of family, work, worship, and community, and they did so, for the first time in fifteen years, without the clouds of an economic collapse or a military emergency over their heads.

The Depression and World War II were, in some respects, an interruption—a prolonged and painful gap in an otherwise steady chronicle of material progress for most Americans. With the return of peace and prosperity after V-J Day, the trends of the 1920s resumed with their original intensity. For Milwaukee's Jews, the most important of those trends was residential mobility. Ever since the First World War and even before, the Haymarket ghetto had been steadily emptying out. Some eastern

Milwaukee Public Library

Center Street was Sherman Park's major commercial corridor. The view is west from 47th St. in 1950.

Jewish Museum Milwaukee

The neighborhood was filled with kids, including these kindergarteners at Sherman School. Herb Kohl, future U.S. senator, is seated front and center.

European families had moved to the east side of the Milwaukee River, joining old-line families, most of them Reform by practice, who were already migrating up the lakeshore to suburban addresses. A far greater number of Haymarket residents had dispersed to the north and west, settling first in formerly German sections of the North Side and then in the brand-new Sherman Park neighborhood. The exodus from the Haymarket area was virtually complete in the first decade after World War II, and Sherman Park became the center of gravity for Milwaukee's Jewish population. The children of junk dealers and petty merchants settled into a solidly middle-class neighborhood of bungalows and duplexes, with broad lawns, generous setbacks, and plenty of trees. Some blocks, particularly on Grant, Sherman, and Fifty-first Boulevards, rose to the architectural dignity of the leafier sections of Wauwatosa and Whitefish Bay.

The geographic trends were revealed most clearly in the movement of Milwaukee's synagogues. Since 1923, there had been a single Jewish house of worship west of Thirteenth Street: Beth El, a Conservative congregation on Forty-ninth and Garfield. In the postwar years, one North Side synagogue after another moved to Sherman Park until all but one—Beth Israel—had either moved west or disbanded. All were following their congregations; none put down new roots until its members had prepared the soil.

The first to move, and ultimately the only one to stay, was Beth Jehudah ("House of Judah"). Rabbi Jacob Twerski had come to Milwaukee in 1928 as the spiritual leader of Anshe Sfard, but he soon developed an independent following that met for daily worship on the first floor of his home at Eleventh and Garfield. It was this group that constituted itself as Beth Jehudah in about 1939, with Twerski at the helm. Not since Solomon Scheinfeld's day had a Milwaukee rabbi demonstrated such spiritual depth, Talmudic scholarship, and personal magnetism. "They came there like thirsty people looking for water," said Twerski's wife, Leah, of the Sabbath gatherings at her family's residence. Beth Jehudah lacked a proper home until after World War II, when its members were moving northwest in droves. In 1949, the congregation broke ground for a new shul at Fifty-fourth and Center Streets, near the heart of Sherman Park. Harry Bass, the building committee chairman, predicted that the new synagogue would meet needs that went well beyond Beth Jehudah's immediate circle:

> *There are hundreds of orthodox Jews on the West side who do not have a House of Worship in their vicinity. For many this has meant moving in with relatives for the high holiday season in order to be within walking distance of a Shul. For many others this has meant missing the Sabbath services week after week. With the erection of the new synagogue on 54th and Center streets, there will be very few of our West side brethren who live out of walking distance.*

Jacob Twerski spoke more personally at the groundbreaking. "The Jewish people of Milwaukee have become a part of me," said the rabbi. "They have felt with me in my pains, and their sorrows were mine…. Such a tie is a lifelong one. It can never be broken." Beth Jehudah's new home, a simple $80,000 structure with a seating capacity of 325, was formally dedicated on December 24, 1950.

Anshai (formerly Anshe) Lebowitz, founded by Russian immigrants in the early 1900s, was next to pull up stakes. The congregation paid off its mortgage in 1944 and almost immediately found itself in trouble. After the war, wrote the author of a 1954 history, "Our congregation and other orthodox congregations felt the loss of active and virile leaders and members." Younger families, in particular, were moving northwest, and Anshai Lebowitz had little choice but to follow. In 1952, the congregation bought a lot on Fifty-second and Burleigh and began to raise funds for a $200,000 stone synagogue that could seat 700 worshipers. When it was dedicated on August 30, 1953, the faithful of Anshai Lebowitz walked behind their Torah scrolls from the old shul on Eleventh and Reservoir to the new building on Burleigh—a distance of nearly four miles. Rabbi Solomon Schulson, who led the procession, called the new synagogue "a structure whose magnificence far surpasses our fondest dreams."

Agudas Achim made the same move a year later. Established by Polish immigrants in about 1902, the congregation had once again become a haven for refugees, largely because of Rabbi Israel Feldman, a Holocaust survivor from Poland. Agudas Achim sponsored Feldman's move to Milwaukee in 1949 and promptly signed him to a five-year contract. Other refugees gathered around Rabbi Feldman, who led what the *Jewish Chronicle* called "a revival of orthodox ritual and of Jewish learning." That revival, the congregation decided, would have to take place at a new address. In 1954, after selling their old home on Eleventh Street, Agudas Achim moved into a $75,000 synagogue on Fifty-eighth and Burleigh. The structure could accommodate 350 people—as many as Beth Jehudah—but it had one feature that

True to the spirit of the
1950s (and the realities of
congregational budgets),
the Orthodox shuls of
Sherman Park followed
the same utilitarian design
template. They included
(top to bottom) Beth
Jehudah, Anshai Lebowitz,
and Agudas Achim.

was still novel on the West Side: a mik-vah, or ritual bath, built for the women of the community.

Anshe Sfard, which had been the last of the Haymarket synagogues to leave the original neighborhood, was nearly as slow to move to Sherman Park. In 1948, the congregation installed a new spiritual leader: David Shapiro, a rabbi's son and an accomplished scholar who had published extensively in Hebrew, Yiddish, and English. A financial crisis delayed the inevitable move, but in 1956, Anshe Sfard sold its shul on Twelfth and Garfield to the YMCA, which tore it down to erect a state-of-the-art community center. Suddenly $58,500 richer, the congregation bought a lot on Fifty-first and Keefe and proceeded to build a new synagogue. Although finishing touches delayed its formal dedication until 1960, the $175,000 structure was occupied in September 1958. Echoing virtually every other Sherman Park rabbi, David Shapiro expressed the hope that "the congregation might now serve former members who for geographical reasons were obliged to leave."

For the people of Beth Jehudah, Anshai Lebowitz, Agudas Achim, and Anshe Sfard, moving to Sherman Park was a fairly straightforward process: members moved, and their shuls followed. Not all relocations were so simple. One, in fact, was aborted in rather public fashion, creating a good deal of embarrassment for everyone involved. Like most large American cities, Milwaukee had long had a surplus of small Orthodox synagogues divided by national origin—a pattern that made little sense decades after mass immigration had ended. Two of those tiny synagogues took a step toward consolidation in 1945.

Only weeks after V-J Day, Degel Israel and B'nai Israel—founded by immigrants from Romania and Hungary, respectively—joined forces as the United Synagogue. The merged congregation was soon making plans for "a temple in a proper neighborhood," by which its leaders could mean only Sherman Park. In 1948, even before Beth Jehudah began construction of its new home, the United Synagogue broke ground for a $200,000 building on Fifth-fifth and Burleigh. Max Stein, the congregation's president, declared that it would break new ground religiously as well:

The United Synagogue promises to its congregation and to the public that this will not be the expensive "luxury type" of religion. This will be religion for the common man who does not find it possible to spend large sums for memberships, seats for the high holidays, and other costs in some congregations. At no time will the financial aspect be thrust on the congregation….

The object will be to provide enough dignity to blend with the religious meaning yet enough warmth and informality to create a feeling of ease and sociability….

Recreational, athletic, social and education portions of the building will be larger than the worship halls or chapels. The most modern conception of communal activities will be the goal.

Their respective rabbis were (top to bottom)*: Jacob Twerski, Solomon Schulson, and Israel Feldman (shown with wife Sara).*

Jewish Museum Milwaukee

Under Rabbi David Shapiro's leadership, Anshe Sfard became one of Sherman Park's larger Orthodox congregations ...

Jewish Museum Milwaukee

Building this temple "for the common man" proved far more difficult than Stein and his colleagues had anticipated, in part because Israel was absorbing such a large share of the community's available funds. Plans for the new building were scaled back significantly, and still the money failed to materialize. The United Synagogue was forced to give up its Burleigh Street project in 1951, with only the foundation completed.

The congregation's saga was not over yet. After retreating from Burleigh in some disarray, United moved into an old church on Forty-seventh and Garfield—only two blocks from Congregation Beth El—and changed its name to B'nai Sholom ("Sons of Peace"). In 1957, apparently unable to go it alone, B'nai Sholom merged into Beth Hamedrosh Hagodol, one of the splinter congregations that had emerged from the ferment of the 1920s. Originally located at Eleventh and Lloyd, Hamedrosh Hagodol had joined the parade to Sherman Park in 1953, building a simple shul

on Fiftieth and Center. After the 1957 merger, the congregation was known, rather formidably, as Beth Hamedrosh Hagodol B'nai Sholom. There matters stood until 1964, when Isaac Lerer became the synagogue's rabbi. A native of Jerusalem with years of experience in outstate Wisconsin, Lerer found it ironic that one of Milwaukee's smallest congregations had the longest name. In 1964, his new charge became simply Temple Menorah. So it has remained ever since, with Isaac Lerer presiding until his death in 2009—a rabbinate that spanned forty-five years.

And what happened to the United Synagogue's hole in the ground at Fifty-fifth and Burleigh? It did not stay empty for long. Milwaukee's labor Zionists remained a vital force after Israel was created in 1948, but their focus shifted from promoting the dream to supporting the reality. In 1949, the city's leading labor Zionist organizations—Poale Zion, the Pioneer Women, the Farband fraternal society, and the Habonim youth group—decided to build a home for "all sections of the

... while Temple Menorah was one of the smallest. Isaac Lerer began his long rabbinate in 1964.

movement" at Fifty-sixth and Burleigh. They had barely started when a more promising option emerged only one block east: the aborted United Synagogue project. In 1951, the Zionists bought the unfinished building for $20,000—an obvious bargain—and completed it to their own specifications. The coalition's Beth Am Center was dedicated in 1952 as a home for all member organizations, but the building was much more than that. It became a popular venue for Sherman Park's weddings, Bar Mitzvah celebrations, lectures, and social events, and it also served West Siders as a sort of secular synagogue. Although labor Zionism's focus was largely political, members of the Beth Am Center lit Chanukah candles, organized a choir that performed religious standards, and sponsored High Holy Day services (in both Hebrew and English) for Jews without formal synagogue affiliations. The name itself set the center apart from its Orthodox and Conservative neighbors. In contrast to nearby synagogue Beth El—"House of God"—the Zionists called their center Beth Am—"House of the People."

By the late 1950s, the Jewish exodus from the old North Side neighborhoods was practically complete, with only a handful of businesses lingering as evidence of the former order. The original haymarket went out of business, blocks of worn-out homes and shops were razed for the Hillside housing project, and the Near North Side became the heart of Milwaukee's African-American community. Between 1940 and 1960, black residents grew from 46 percent of the old Jewish quarter's population to 85 percent. Nearly all the old synagogues that

159

Beth Am

Dedication

Souvenir Program

1 9 5 2

✡

BETH AM BUILDING

Milwaukee's labor Zionists built their Beth Am Center on the foundation of an aborted synagogue.

survived the wrecking ball were purchased by African-American congregations whose members worshiped the same God in the same sanctuaries as their predecessors.

As the North Side's Jewish identity faded, Sherman Park's shone all the more brightly; the new neighborhood played the same role for the postwar generation that the old one had for their parents and grandparents. Sherman Park was liberally sprinkled (but hardly saturated) with Jewish homes, businesses, and institutions from end to end, and Burleigh Street emerged as the most Jewish thoroughfare in Milwaukee. In the early 1900s, the city's "synagogue row" had been Cherry Street between Fourth and Sixth. In the 1920s, it was Eleventh Street between Vine and Brown. By the late 1950s, it was Burleigh Street between Sherman Boulevard (Forty-Third) and Sixtieth Street. Although Center Street had anchors like Congregation Beth Jehudah and Temple Menorah, Burleigh could claim the greatest critical mass of Jewish institutions: Congregation

Anshai Lebowitz, Congregation Agudas Achim, the Beth Am Center, the Goodman-Bensman Funeral Home, and a row of businesses that included Kohl's flagship grocery store, Sherman's Deli, Bubrick's Food Market, the Kosher Meat Club, and Miller's Bakery, whose rye bread had earned a devoted following far beyond Milwaukee. For the Jewish families of Sherman Park, trips to Burleigh were a daily necessity.

Although their presence was well-established, Jews were hardly the only group in the neighborhood, or even the largest. In the Burleigh Street district, in fact, the dominant landmark was (and still is) St. Joseph's Hospital, a Catholic institution that had moved from the same section of the North Side as its Jewish neighbors. Nor were the community's new buildings architectural standouts. The synagogues tended to be ecclesiastical boxes—single-story structures of brick or stone with flat roofs and little exterior ornament. They were purely functional, but the shuls accurately reflected the tastes of their time. When the United Synagogue launched its ill-fated building project in 1945, the group's leaders promised a synagogue "along modern classic lines" that would definitely depart from "the now outmoded type of oriental architecture." Although their vogue proved to be short-lived, the utilitarian buildings of Sherman Park satisfied a desire for the new and a critical need for more space.

The sole exception to Sherman Park's pattern of architectural mediocrity was Congregation Beth El, the first and by far the largest synagogue in the district. Shortly after World War II, Rabbi Louis Swichkow and his members began to dream of one big congregation that would take in every Jew on the West Side. They felt that Judaism in the old neighborhood was too fragmented and its practices too old-fashioned to survive the move to the city's edge. Why not, they argued, leave the disordered past behind and come together as one body in the new neighborhood? In December 1945, Beth El spearheaded the formation of the Milwaukee Greater Temple Association, whose goal, naturally enough, was "the building of a greater temple, which will satisfy the present and future religious, educational, cultural and recreational needs of the west side." The *Jewish Chronicle* described the endeavor as "the greatest Jewish consolidated religious effort in the past 25 years." Although the association's slant was definitely Conservative, plans for the new temple included a chapel for Orthodox services, a Little Theatre for "Jewish and Hebrew drama," "a comprehensive youth program," spacious playgrounds, and a large auditorium—something for everyone, with plenty of free parking.

It soon became clear that visions of a "Greater Temple" were premature, to say the least. Although there was some

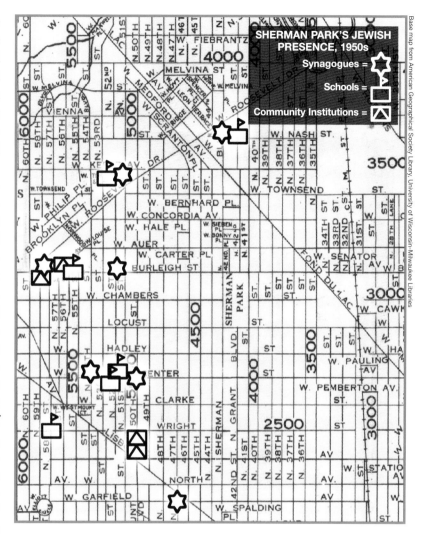

movement toward consolidation—as the unhappy experience of the United Synagogue demonstrated—most of the little congregations preferred to stay little, and to stay independent. The fragmentation of the North Side passed nearly intact to Sherman Park. That left Beth El to pursue its own course, but the congregation was attracting enough former North Siders to merit a new name and a new building. In 1949, the former Beth El was elevated to Beth El Ner Tamid—"House of God, Eternal Light."

Sherman Park was far more diverse than the Haymarket area, but the Jewish imprint on the neighborhood was unmistakable, particularly in the blocks west of Sherman Blvd.

Jewish Museum Milwaukee

Jewish Museum Milwaukee

Inside and out, Beth El Ner Tamid was the largest and most elaborate of Sherman Park's synagogues.

Rabbi Swichkow expressed boundless optimism in announcing the change:

> *I hope that this congregation will serve as a beacon of light to the members of our community and will help lead it towards the realization of the magnificent ideals which are part of the Judaic faith and of the democratic American traditions.*

Beth El Ner Tamid's members had outgrown their old synagogue on Forty-ninth and Garfield as well as their name, and a

new temple was soon under construction on the triangle bordered by Sherman Boulevard, Fond du Lac Avenue, and Roosevelt Drive—one of the most visible locations in Sherman Park. The congregation was dreaming no little dreams. Their synagogue, dedicated in 1951, featured a sanctuary with 1,300 seats (all of the "theater type" and "upholstered in a rich cardinal red"); an auditorium, said to be the largest in the Midwest, that accommodated 1,000 for meetings and 700 for banquets; a 220-seat chapel for daily worship; a kosher kitchen; a fully equipped school; and the usual offices and meeting rooms. The exterior was clad in buff-colored limestone and embellished with the names of the prophets above each window and oversized tablets of the Ten Commandments at each entrance. Beth El Ner Tamid's new home cost $800,000, and its square footage probably exceeded the combined area of every synagogue that had ever stood in the old Haymarket neighborhood. Under Louis Swichkow, the temple was a beehive of activity. The congregation

162

exploded from roughly 300 families in 1945 to 900 in 1956. Beth El Ner Tamid had nearly as many members as Emanu-El B'ne Jeshurun—Milwaukee's leading synagogue—and it was, in Swichkow's considered opinion, on "practically the same level" socially.

The runaway growth of Beth El Ner Tamid was part of a larger renaissance in American Judaism. For at least a century, the nation's rabbis had been lamenting the irregular attendance and tepid religiosity of their flocks; the true Jew, in their judgment, was a rapidly vanishing species in the United States. Such carping was heard far less often in the first decades after World War II. Americans as a whole were turning, or perhaps returning, to religion, and none did so with more alacrity than Jewish Americans. The horrors of the Holocaust, the triumphant rise of Israel, and the enlarged responsibilities of the American community encouraged every Jew to become more Jewish. The prevailing trend was noted by the *Wisconsin Jewish Chronicle* (April 14, 1950):

> *The wail and despair of parents of twenty and thirty years ago that their children were becoming assimilated in the maw of apathy towards religion in America seems to have come to naught. Synagogue membership is probably at a record level.*

Although the depth of their attachment was open to question—joining became an American obsession in the 1950s—there is no doubt that Jews were returning to temple. They were not, however, returning to the same old religion practiced by their mothers and fathers. The postwar generation found the strictures of Orthodoxy, in its most orthodox forms, confining in the extreme; they were quite ready

to abandon Biblical prohibitions and prescriptions they deemed out of place in twentieth-century America. More than one set of Pesach dishes—reserved specifically for use during the Passover season—did not survive the move to Sherman Park. Nor did Orthodoxy itself, at least in its pre-World War II form. By the time the synagogues on Burleigh and Center Streets were dedicated, at least half had adopted mixed-gender seating, English-language prayers and sermons, Friday night services, and a variety of other modern adaptations. Even these were not sufficient to breathe new life into the congregations for more than a decade or two. Rabbi Louis Swichkow described postwar Orthodoxy as "a very tenuous affair," a dying religion dominated by the elderly and the foreign-born. Swichkow was familiar with Milwaukee's religious scene as both a participant and an observer. He was the spiritual leader of Beth El Ner Tamid, the city's Conservative mainstay, but he somehow found time to write *The History of the Jews of Milwaukee,* a comprehensive chronicle published (with co-author Lloyd Gartner) in 1963.

Louis Swichkow was both Beth El Ner Tamid's rabbi and the author of a scholarly history of Milwaukee's Jewish community.

Jewish Museum Milwaukee

Jewish Museum Milwaukee

Beth Israel sold its landmark synagogue on the North Side ...

"By 1950," Swichkow noted wryly in his account, "there were very few orthodox Jews left in the city, even among the membership of the orthodox congregations." Jacob Twerski, David Shapiro, and Israel Feldman kept the light of tradition burning in their respective shuls, but each presided over a dwindling circle of aging congregants. In a comprehensive 1955-1956 survey of Milwaukee's Orthodox Jews, Howard Polsky found a movement in steep decline. Fully 67 percent of the community's grandfathers observed the Sabbath every week, but the number dropped to 12 percent for their sons and only 2 percent for their married grandsons. "There is little doubt," Polsky concluded, "that Jewish Orthodoxy is an aging group which is not reproducing itself."

As Orthodoxy waned, Conservatism flourished. Swichkow's own congregation swelled at the expense of its more traditional neighbors, and for obvious reasons. Conservatism attempted to strike a balance between the demands of tradition and the dictates of modern life; its faithful-but-flexible approach attracted legions of adherents in Milwaukee and across the country. In 1945, Beth El had been the sole outpost of Conservatism in the city, with approximately 300 families on its rolls—well under 10 percent of Milwaukee's affiliated Jews. When a community census was taken twenty years later, 49 percent of Milwaukee's Jewish family heads described themselves as Conservative, outpacing Reform at 24 percent, Orthodox at 22 percent, and "other" at 5 percent. The greatest number of those Conservatives belonged to Beth El Ner Tamid, whose roster grew to 1,038 families in 1966. Temple Menorah, which represented the melding of three formerly Orthodox synagogues, switched its affiliation in 1959, opening a second Conservative front in Sherman Park, and other congregations at least toyed with the idea.

The most celebrated switch—and the most acrimonious—took place at Beth Israel. Under Rabbi Solomon Scheinfeld, Beth Israel had been the citadel of Orthodox Judaism in Milwaukee for generations, but the congregation went into a tailspin after Scheinfeld's death in 1943. By the mid-1950s, its membership had plummeted from a peak of nearly 1,000 families to about 400, and relatively few were active. The magnificent synagogue on Teutonia Avenue—once the pride of the North Side Jewish community—became a fading landmark in a racially changing neighborhood; it was practically empty Sabbath after Sabbath, attended only by the aged and the infirm. Beth Israel was in some ways a victim of its own members' success. The congregation had always attracted the North Side's most prosperous families, and those families tended to move northeast rather than northwest as their circumstances improved. Instead of settling in Sherman Park, they bought homes in affluent North Shore suburbs like Shorewood, Whitefish Bay, Glendale, and Fox Point—foreshadowing a movement that would become general in the 1970s and '80s. If it wished to survive, the congregation had only one choice: to follow. In 1956, Beth Israel bought a four-acre lot in Fox Point (on Santa Monica Boulevard at Green Tree Road) and began to interview architects. While they were at it, a majority of members voted to change their affiliation from Orthodox to Conservative, a decision made in late 1957.

The switch touched off a minor civil war. Rabbi Harold Baumrind, who had ably served Beth Israel since 1939, refused to accept the new affiliation, and a committed minority of members sided with him. In October 1957, they sued the congregation's board, charging that the trustees had "physically and forcefully removed" Baumrind from his pulpit during a September service. The two factions came to

a parting of the ways in the next month. Harold Baumrind and his followers left to form Anshe Emeth ("Men of Truth") and ultimately built an Orthodox synagogue of their own at 8057 Appleton Avenue, on Milwaukee's far Northwest Side. Baumrind's departure left Beth Israel without a rabbi and, to make matters worse, Fox Point refused to rezone the congregation's lot for institutional use. Membership sank to a record low of fifty families, but that faithful remnant refused to give up. In 1957, they purchased fifteen acres on Green Bay Avenue in Glendale and announced plans for a $450,000 complex that would include a school, a social hall, and a sanctuary. The Teutonia Avenue synagogue was sold in 1959 to Greater Galilee Baptist Church, a pillar of Milwaukee's African-American community since 1920. Beth Israel worshiped in rented quarters in Shorewood until 1962, when the first phase of its Glendale complex was ready for occupancy. By the time the second phase was completed in 1966, membership had rebounded nicely to 300 families, most of them North Shore residents.

... and built a new home in suburban Glendale, switching its affiliation from Orthodox to Conservative in the process. Rabbi Harold Baumrind (above) did not make either move.

Reform and Tradition

The Reform contingent was already there, of course. Milwaukee's old-line Jewish families, German by ancestry and Reform by practice, had been edging north and east along the lakeshore for decades. The suburban migration accelerated after World War II, and by 1960 most of the former East Siders—or their descendants—lived

Emanu-El B'ne Jeshurun remained the grandest of Milwaukee's synagogues.

in Shorewood, Whitefish Bay, Fox Point, Bayside, Glendale, and River Hills. There they were joined by a larger group of former North Siders, eastern European by ancestry and Orthodox from birth, who had crossed the river to the greener pastures of the North Shore. By the 1960s, Nicolet High School in Glendale was fast replacing Washington High School in Sherman Park as the educational institution most strongly identified with Milwaukee's Jewish community. As the North Siders left their old neighborhood, they moved away from their childhood faith as well. Although Beth Israel offered the suburbanites a Conservative option, most of the North Shore's affiliated Jews, whether old-line German stalwarts or eastern European "converts," worshiped at Reform temples. The greater West Side, in brief, was an Orthodox stronghold moving rapidly to Conservatism, while the greater East Side was Reform territory with a significant Conservative minority.

The North Shore's Reform Jews commuted back to Emanu-El B'ne Jeshurun on Kenwood Boulevard at first. The temple was still Milwaukee's silk-stocking synagogue, and its membership swelled from 807 families in 1946 to 1,076 in 1950. Emanu-El's growth rate accelerated after 1951, when Herbert Friedman succeeded Joseph Baron as rabbi. A passionate Zionist, Friedman had spent the immediate postwar years as an Army chaplain in Europe, helping resettle Jewish refugees and, in an unofficial capacity, directing arms to the Israeli underground. After returning to civilian life, the rabbi led a large temple in Denver before accepting the Milwaukee post. The strength of Friedman's personality and the eloquence of his sermons boosted Sabbath attendance from a few dozen to an average of 400 by 1954, and that number included the typically slow summer season. Milwaukeeans knew they had caught a rising star—an impression confirmed in autumn of 1954, when Herbert Friedman moved to New York as head of the entire United Jewish Appeal. He quickly became a legend in the world of Jewish philanthropy and remained so until his death in 2008.

Friedman's successor at Emanu-El B'ne Jeshurun was Dudley Weinberg, a scholarly St. Louis native who had previously served a temple in Boston. Weinberg, who inherited a congregation of nearly 1,300 families, declared himself proud to be part of "the thrilling renaissance of interest in Judaism which has been occurring throughout the West." Emanu-El was growing, but the congregation was also feeling pressure from the University of Wisconsin-Milwaukee, which opened literally across the street in 1956 and created instant parking problems. In 1957,

the temple's trustees bought twenty acres on Port Washington and Bradley Roads in Fox Point. "Prudence dictates," they wrote, that the congregation act "to meet the needs in the long-range future." That future seemed to lie beyond the confines of the upper East Side. A membership analysis done in 1960 showed that 74 percent of Emanu-El's households lived in North Shore suburbs and only 25 percent in the city proper.

Emanu-El B'ne Jeshurun remained the largest congregation, but it was no longer the only choice for North Shore residents with Reform leanings. The Kenwood Boulevard temple was too big for some and too distant for others; a significant minority of the membership also felt that their rabbis were too conservative theologically. The result was a division of Milwaukee's Reform Jews into two more congregations: Sinai and Shalom. In 1951, a nucleus of twenty-eight people constituted themselves the North Shore Temple. The *Jewish Chronicle* (June 15, 1951) explained the group's reason for being:

Rabbis Herbert Friedman (top) and Dudley Weinberg led the East Side congregation in the postwar years.

According to the organizing committee, the formation of the new Temple is an outcome of the rapid growth and spread of the Jewish population throughout the North Shore area, and the overflowing membership of Temple Emanu-El. The group invites the participation of those now affiliated and unaffiliated who wish to become part of the growing movement toward Liberal Judaism.

When 300 people attended a preliminary meeting at Whitefish Bay High School, the organizers knew their time had come. Before the year was out, they had named their temple Congregation Shalom, hired a rabbi (Harry Pastor, a former assistant at Emanu-El), and bought land on Santa Monica Boulevard at Calumet Road in Fox Point. Rabbi Pastor, whose name certainly fit his task, was thrilled to be guiding the new flock. "Few rabbis or laymen," he said in 1951, "have the rare privilege that we will have to build a brand new congregation, formed with such enthusiasm and out of such great need." As fund-raising proceeded,

Congregation Shalom worshiped at a Lutheran church in Whitefish Bay on most Sabbaths and rented the downtown Moose lodge for the High Holy Days. In 1954, with enough money in its building fund to ensure the project's success, Shalom broke ground for a V-shaped temple on its Santa Monica Boulevard property, with a school in one wing and a sanctuary in the other. It was an intentionally low-rise structure, designed "to conform to the ranchhouse style of architecture prevailing in the neighborhood." The synagogue was formally dedicated in 1956, and within three years Shalom's membership had risen to 464 households.

One year earlier, another group of North Shore families had decided to organize "a small congregation on classic Reform lines." Their goals were "revitalized religious expression" and "an intimacy of personal relationship between congregation and rabbi." Like Congregation Shalom, their progress was rapid. Before 1955 was over, they had chosen Congregation Sinai as their name and hired Jay Brickman as their spiritual leader. A former Army chaplain who had previously occupied a pulpit on

Two new Reform congregations emerged on the suburban North Shore: Shalom, whose founding rabbi was Harry Pastor ...

Staten Island, Brickman was a young rabbi with a taste (and a talent) for both poetry and psychology. His congregation met each Sabbath at Country Day School in White-fish Bay (the present home of the Jewish Community Center) and observed the High Holy Days at Fox Point Congregational Church. The arrangement was satisfactory but only temporary. In 1958, a group of thirty-three members purchased a four-acre parcel on Port Washington Road in Fox Point and donated it to the congregation. Their gift sparked a fund-raising campaign for a $300,000 temple that would accommodate 300 families; intimacy remained the community's overriding goal. Congregation Sinai's new home, built into a gentle slope on the Fox Point property, was ready for occupancy in 1962, when the roster had grown to 210 households.

Emanu-El B'ne Jeshurun, the senior member of Milwaukee's Reform trio, had no need to see the younger congregations as competitors. Its own facilities were taxed to the limit in the 1950s, and Shalom and Sinai undoubtedly attracted many North Shore families who had not been

affiliated with any synagogue. Members of all three temples shared the same ZIP Codes, the same social standing, and essentially the same religious outlook. They also took part in the same activities on occasion. One of the trio's more interesting collaborations was the Tri-Temple Institute, an adult education series whose 1960 presenters included the renowned rabbi and philosopher Abraham Joshua Heschel. Emanu-El, Shalom, and Sinai also maintained cordial relations with their nearest Reform neighbor: Emanu-El of Waukesha. In 1959, after worshiping in a converted residence for almost twenty years, the congregation purchased land northwest of downtown Waukesha and hired an architect. Jewish families had joined the movement to the western suburbs, but Emanu-El was still too small to afford a resident rabbi; neighboring clergy led monthly services on Sunday evenings, and faculty from Hebrew

... and Sinai, which took shape under the leadership of Jay Brickman.

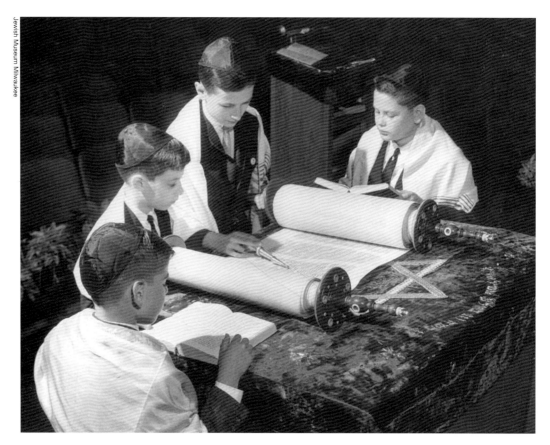

An Orthodox teen practiced reading the Torah for his Bar Mitzvah ceremony at Anshe Sfard. The adolescent rite of passage was one of several traditions to which Reform congregations were returning.

Union College in Cincinnati officiated during the High Holy Days. The little temple on Moreland Road was finally dedicated in 1963, providing a spiritual home for thirty-six families who traveled to Waukesha from eight communities in the region west of Milwaukee.

Whatever their geographic locations, the Reform temples were charting a common religious course after World War II. Like many of the Orthodox congregations, they modified their practices significantly, but Reform Jews were moving in an equal and opposite direction, one that would ultimately, and ironically, bring them much closer to traditional Judaism. On both ends of the spectrum, it was the children and grandchildren of eastern European immigrants who provided the impetus. Even observant Jews were pushing for greater freedom from the strictures of tradition, a fact evident in the liberalizations under way in the Orthodox synagogues and even more in the explosive growth of Conservatism. But the second and third generations had just as much influence on the Reform movement. There were simply not enough old-line German families to sustain the Reform congregations; their growth was due to an influx of upwardly mobile eastern Europeans who were leaving Orthodoxy behind. Those newcomers may have preferred the openness and flexibility of the Reform temples, but they also had a strong and continuing attachment to tradition; rabbis all over the country found themselves being pushed in the direction of greater observance. In Milwaukee and elsewhere, Jews as a body were moving toward a great American middle. Orthodox congregations were becoming less traditional, Reform congregations were becoming more traditional, and Conservative temples split the difference.

The trends had been apparent in the Reform temples since the 1920s, but they gathered new momentum after the war. In 1948, Emanu-El B'ne Jeshurun hired Milwaukee's first full-time cantor and started a Hebrew school, both of which would have been anathema to an earlier generation of members. With the rise of Israel, Zionism was no longer controversial in the least. Rabbi Samuel Hirshberg, who served Emanu-El from 1904 to 1947, had been active in the American Council for Judaism, a defiantly anti-Zionist group; Herbert Friedman, who took Hirshberg's former post in 1951, became one of the leading Zionists in America. Reform congregations, mirroring their Christian neighbors, had once focused on confirmation as the rite of passage for their adolescents; by 1960, more than 95 percent of the nation's Reform rabbis performed Bar Mitzvah ceremonies. Prayer shawls and yarmulkes, banned in the nineteenth century, began to reappear in the middle of the twentieth. Year by year, innovation by innovation, Reform congregations were making room for the ceremonial as well as the cerebral.

As Reform Jews rediscovered tradition, as Orthodox Jews showed a greater receptiveness to modernism, and as Conservative Jews held the center, common ground began to emerge. Although there were sharp differences among the traditions—one writer dismissed those who ignored religious distinctions as "Jewnitarians"—the fundamental unity of Judaism was just as apparent as its diversity. In 1954, Beth El Ner Tamid hosted an all-temple service to mark the three-hundredth anniversary of Jewish settlement in the United States. Nearly every rabbi and cantor in town took part in a ceremony that was broadcast live on local television, and Louis Swichkow found the perfect invocation from the Book of Psalms: "How goodly and how pleasant it is for brethren to dwell together in unity." In 1958, the assorted brethren organized the Milwaukee Council of Rabbis as a more permanent vehicle for intrafaith cooperation. One of the group's first projects was a calendar of Jewish holidays that was distributed to every school district in the region. The rabbis urged parents to take their children out of school during the major holy days. "By respecting the sanctities of our own faith," they wrote, "we will achieve not only greater self-respect, but we will earn the right to have our religious loyalties respected by the entire community." There was still plenty

Despite profound differences in doctrine and practice, rabbis from all three major movements could work together to make Jewish Milwaukee a community of interest. They are shown here after jointly endorsing the 1956 Welfare Fund campaign.

to disagree about—and would be in perpetuity—but relations among the various traditions were generally more collegial in Milwaukee than in other American communities. Amram Scheinfeld, whose father, Solomon, was once the leading light of local Orthodoxy, had become a distinguished author and journalist in New York, but he kept up with the social changes in his hometown. In a report to the *Wisconsin Jewish Chronicle* (September 9, 1966), Scheinfeld offered the observations of a native son:

> *I find increasing evidence that what was once a divided Jewry is now as unified a Jewish community as there exists anywhere.*
>
> *Familiar names of boyhood friends of immigrant, Orthodox stock—or the names of their sons—appear at least equally with those of German-Jewish backgrounds among the leaders of the Reform temples, the country clubs, and the most important of the city's Jewish institutions and organizations.*
>
> *The wedding announcements tell of alliances between descendants of forebears whom I knew as once having been far apart. News items tell of the graduation from the Ivy League colleges, and from Vassar, Wellesley and Smith, of the grandsons and granddaughters of sons of the humblest of my father's Orthodox flock.*

Milwaukee's spirit of unity—or at least peaceful coexistence—was nowhere more apparent than in the field of Jewish education. In 1944, after lying largely dormant since its establishment in 1929, the Bureau of Jewish Education was revitalized to "plan, direct, and stimulate" the community's scholastic activities—with financial support from the Jewish Welfare Fund. The bureau hired its first full-time director, Meyer Gallin, in 1947 and conducted a survey of the city's school-age Jewish children—excluding, for the time being, the Reform temples. The result was a card file bulging with the names of 4,500 kids, whose parents were contacted at the beginning of each school year and reminded of the importance of Jewish education. More often than not, those parents responded enthusiastically. The community's adults were riding the wave of postwar interest in all things Jewish, and they knew that the renaissance would falter unless their children caught the spirit—and the culture. Meyer Gallin appealed to that spirit in a 1951 plea for students:

> *Your children's happiness depends to a large degree upon the way they meet the Jewish aspects of their lives. Will you prepare your children to enter upon their rich heritage or will you disinherit them? By giving your children a good Jewish education you will open to them a fountain of strength. They will share with you the pride in Jewish living. They will learn about the glorious Jewish past. You will open to them the vast Jewish literature developed over a period of three thousand years. They will become familiar with Jewish customs and ceremonies of home and synagogue. They will learn the ideas and ideals of the Bible, Jewish prophets and scholars.*

Gallin also described what the community expected of its girls in the unconsciously sexist social climate of 1951:

> *Remember "Girls" are children too. The little girl of today is the young*

woman of tomorrow undertaking the responsibility of building a Jewish home. Will she know the meaning of a Jewish home? Will she be able to transmit to her children the true Jewish spirit? Not unless she is prepared. Not unless she is given a Jewish education now. Give your daughter a Jewish education. It will enrich not only her life, but the lives of her children. The survival of the Jewish people and its culture depends on a good Jewish education.

Never before had there been such an abundance of educational opportunities in Jewish Milwaukee. Every synagogue, even the smallest, had at least a Sunday school, and free-standing programs ranged from a nursery school (named for its founder, Edith Babbitz) to Hebrew classes for adults. On the very highest level was the Wisconsin Society for Jewish Learning. Organized in 1955 under Rabbi Joseph Baron's leadership, it was a permanent outgrowth of the state's celebration of the American Jewish tricentennial one year earlier. The Society for Jewish Learning brought in lecturers, supported scholarly research, and started the Wisconsin Jewish Archives, but its proudest achievement may have been the establishment of two chairs in Hebrew at the University of Wisconsin: one on the Madison campus in 1955 and the second in Milwaukee in 1961.

Higher learning was served, but the greater emphasis was on Milwaukee's young people. A short-lived day school was launched in 1949 at Beth Israel (when the congregation was still on Teutonia Avenue), and a more successful attempt followed at Anshe Sfard in 1960. Three

addresses later, Hillel Academy is still a proud fixture in Milwaukee's Jewish community. More typical were the half-dozen elementary schools supported by the Bureau of Jewish Education. Reflecting the collegial tone of Milwaukee Judaism, the same umbrella covered Orthodox, Torah-centered institutions and their secular, Yiddish-speaking cousins. Both types had once been confined to the North Side Jewish quarter, but no more. The East Side Hebrew School opened in

Jewish education assumed a new prominence after World War II. Opportunities ranged from Sunday schools like Shalom's (top) to the all-day program at Hillel Academy.

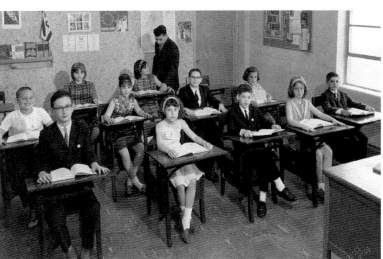

Jewish Museum Milwaukee

The East Side Hebrew School moved into a former church on Oakland Ave. in 1951.

The legendary Harry Garfinkel posed with graduates of his New Method Hebrew School in 1955.

The federated Jewish schools generally convened after public school classes had ended for the day, and the East Side Hebrew School's curriculum was probably typical: "modern and classical Hebrew and Jewish History, Customs and Ceremonies, Current Events, and Jewish Music." The teachers were all trained professionals who developed some novel curriculum materials, including *The Story of the Milwaukee Jewish Community,* a widely used 1954 textbook, and a set of Hebrew prayer flash cards that were sold to Jewish institutions across the country. The schools benefited enormously from a ruling by the community's leading clergymen. In 1953, nine Milwaukee rabbis, Orthodox and Conservative, issued a joint proclamation requiring "four years of satisfactory attendance at a recognized weekday Hebrew school" before a boy could become Bar Mitzvah. Temple Emanu-El B'ne Jeshurun, which

1948 and three years later bought an old church on Oakland Avenue in Shorewood. The school served "children of all backgrounds—reform, conservative, orthodox, or unaffiliated" and declared itself "independent of any temple and … run by the parents through an elected board under the guidance of the Jewish Bureau of Education."

Jewish Museum Milwaukee

ran its own Hebrew school, adopted similar requirements in the same year, and the Reform and Conservative synagogues soon extended them to girls who wanted to become Bat Mitzvah. Enrollment soared, and in 1964 a Hebrew high-school program was created for teenagers who wanted to continue their studies. By that time, an estimated 3,500 young people—an overwhelming majority of the community's school-age population—were receiving some form of Jewish education, whether in their own congregations or at free-standing institutions. Baby-boomers who attended those classes tend to recall their participation as more dutiful than meaningful, but they generally left the schools better-informed than their parents.

The Philanthropic Impulse

Synagogues and schools were perhaps the most revealing expressions of life in Milwaukee's Jewish community after World War II. Their locations highlighted the community's bifurcated geography, with distinct centers emerging in Sherman Park and on the North Shore. Their number and size suggested the widespread prosperity that underlay the community's expansion. And their programs and policies marked the continuing search for a sustainable balance between the pull of modernism and the demands of tradition. Temples and schools said a great deal about the state of the community between 1945 and 1967, but another set of institutions spoke just as eloquently: the array of health and human service agencies underwritten by Jewish donors. Some had been Milwaukee mainstays since the nineteenth century and others were recent creations, but all

showed the ancient philanthropic impulse hard at work, and all reflected the aspirations and achievements of a community rapidly on the rise.

The Hebrew Relief Society, a first line of defense against want since the mid-1800s, had evolved by 1921 into the Jewish Social Service Association (JSSA), which provided direct relief and casework services to the community's poorest members. After World War II, the community's poor dwindled to a relative handful; virtually everyone had entered the middle class. In 1948, the JSSA absorbed the Jewish Children's Home and adopted a new name: Jewish Family and Children's Service (JFCS). Rebecca Tenenbaum, who directed the institution from 1932 to 1964, noted that her staff no longer handed out blankets and rent vouchers. "Today we can say," she reported in 1949, "that we are becoming a service agency for the general Jewish community rather than the underprivileged few." There were still needs to be met, but most of them were psychological rather than material. It was painfully apparent that a suburban address and a healthy bank account were no guarantees of personal happiness; Jewish Family and Children's Service professionals found themselves counseling a sizable

A brother and sister separated during World War II were reunited with the aid of Jewish Family and Children's Service.

Jewish Museum Milwaukee

87th Annual Meeting

JEWISH FAMILY AND CHILDREN'S SERVICE

December 13, 1954
Milwaukee, Wisconsin

The Jewish Home for the Aged provided constructive activities, companionship, and three square meals a day for its residents.

number of individuals and families in both Sherman Park and the North Shore suburbs. Two smaller groups still needed the more traditional range of services: displaced persons from Europe, whose struggles were usually temporary, and a shrinking pool of dependent children. In 1951, after almost thirty years on Twenty-first Street, the old Children's Home moved out to Fiftieth Street—in Sherman Park, of course—and became a group home for youngsters awaiting adoption or foster placement.

A few doors south of the group home, and at the opposite end of the age spectrum, was an institution that had been on Fiftieth Street since 1929: the Jewish Home for the Aged. It developed a lengthy waiting list after the war, and in 1950 the home added a wing that boosted its capacity from roughly forty-five residents to ninety. The Jewish Home was a far cry from the dismal firetrap that had once warehoused elderly residents in the Haymarket neighborhood. "Bright colors and cheery designs take the institutional look away," reported the *Jewish Chronicle,* "and make each room look like home." The services, too, showed a progressive attitude toward geriatric care: physical and occupational therapy, a part-time psychiatrist, a beauty shop run by volunteers, thrice-daily chapel services, a newspaper, weekly movies, and a sheltered workshop that paid residents twenty cents an hour for light assembly work (including yo-yos). One November afternoon in 1962, chapel regulars were surprised to find a guest cantor leading their service: Jan Peerce, one of the leading operatic tenors of his day. Peerce, whose given name was Jacob Perelmuth, happened to be in town for a performance of *Rigoletto* and was looking for a place to pray. "Never before," gushed the *Chronicle*, "had the four walls of this small chapel been filled with so glorious a human voice."

Although they rarely had such distinguished visitors, other social service institutions showed the same steady growth in sophistication and professionalism. Jewish Vocational Service (JVS), established to help the community's young people find work in the late Depression years, broadened its mission to include Milwaukeeans, both Jewish and Gentile, with a variety of special needs: the developmentally delayed, the physically disabled, and the emotionally disturbed, as well as newly arrived refugees and older adults (including those at the Jewish Home). By the mid-1960s, Jewish Vocational Service had a staff of nearly 100 and enjoyed a reputation as one of the leading rehabilitation agencies in the country. Its annual meetings usually featured presentations on some aspect of the employment problems JVS addressed. The highlight of the 1949 gathering was a performance of the season's hit drama, *Death of a Salesman.* Playwright Arthur Miller might have been surprised to hear his masterwork described as "a powerful and poignant portrayal of the need for vocational guidance service."

Another community mainstay changed less dramatically. Since 1929, the Children's Outing Association (COA) had been giving local children "an experience in outdoor living" at Camp Sidney Cohen on Waukesha County's Upper Nemahbin Lake. In 1947, the Outing Association opened its facility to outside groups—Golden Agers, Scouts, church societies, and the physically handicapped, among others—during the long off-season, including the winter months.

The pace quickened when Norman Adelman became director in 1958. Under Adelman's leadership, COA bought more land, erected new buildings, and moved from boys' and girls' sessions to coeducational camping—a 1966 shift that anticipated the collapse in gender barriers and, as a practical matter, enabled the association to keep the same, coeducational staff all summer long. Perhaps the greatest change at COA involved the demographics of its campers. The Outing Association had been created to connect the impoverished children

Jewish Vocational Service was among the first agencies to serve Milwaukeeans with special needs.

Jewish Museum Milwaukee

Jewish Museum Milwaukee

Camp Sidney Cohen remained a favorite summertime destination for hundreds of happy campers.

Jewish Museum Milwaukee

of the Haymarket ghetto with the natural world. After World War II, there were still impoverished children and they still lived in the ghetto, but they were no longer Jewish. As a Red Feather (United Way) agency, the Children's Outing Association was open to everyone, and its orientation shifted steadily from the local Jewish community to the minority children of Milwaukee's inner city.

A newer institution had considerable difficulty getting off—or into—the ground. In 1949, a group of community leaders decided that Milwaukee needed a convalescent facility for patients who were not sick enough to be admitted to a hospital but not well enough to stay in their own homes. The Lubotsky family, a major force in Milwaukee's tire business, donated a piece of land on Fifty-first Boulevard near

Silver Spring, overlooking McGovern Park, and challenged the community to raise $100,000 for the project. Their challenge drew little interest until 1952, when the home's backers unveiled plans for a "ranch type California" facility. Those plans moldered on the shelf until the fund drive got off to its third and final start in 1960. The Milwaukee Jewish Convalescent Hospital (later Center), with forty-four beds and "a rehabilitative philosophy," was finally dedicated in 1961 on land donated by the Lubotskys twelve years before.

The community's leading health care facility had no such problems. Since its founding in 1903, Mount Sinai Hospital had been a pillar of Milwaukee's medical establishment, one of the city's leading institutions and the home of specialists who practiced nowhere else. Its most pressing problem after the war was a lack of space; as annual admissions surged toward the 10,000 mark, there were never enough beds. In 1948, Mount Sinai began a "speeded-up program" as a temporary expedient. The maximum stay for maternity cases, for example, was cut from eight days to five—still a luxurious stretch of time in comparison with the "drive-by deliveries" of more recent days. The effect was negligible. In all categories—patients, staff, equipment—everything was growing but the building, and the only permanent solution was a major expansion. In 1951, Mount Sinai's leaders announced plans to increase the number of beds from 197 to 322, introduce the latest laboratory and X-ray equipment, and thoroughly reconfigure the older sections of the hospital. The *Jewish Chronicle* called Mount Sinai's expansion "the largest capital improvement in the history of the Milwaukee Jewish community." Although the price tag was estimated at $2.4 million when ground was broken in 1954, the project ultimately cost nearly $4 million.

The Jewish Convalescent Center helped patients on the road to recovery.

Jewish Museum Milwaukee

Jewish Museum Milwaukee

As Mount Sinai Hospital expanded physically, it became a more visibly Jewish institution as well.

Jewish Museum Milwaukee

The United Hospital Fund, a non-sectarian community effort, provided $1 million, and Edith Greenwald, whose late husband, Oscar, had managed the Gimbels stores in Milwaukee, made a landmark individual gift of $600,000. The "greater" Mount Sinai Hospital was finally dedicated in 1956.

A subtle but important shift was evident in the rebuilt facility's cultural outlook. True to its German-Jewish roots, Mount Sinai had always maintained a carefully non-sectarian profile, but no longer. Although a relatively small minority of its patients were Jewish (16 percent in 1964), the hospital asserted its pride in being a Jewish institution—a change consonant with the resurgence of Jewish pride throughout the country. Observant patients could finally order kosher meals, light electric candelabras to start the Sabbath, read from Hebrew prayer books (as well as the ubiquitous Gideon Bibles), and even drink wine during the Sabbath kiddush prayer—with their doctors' permission, of course. In 1963, sixty years after the hospital opened, the Star of David was mounted above Mount Sinai's main entrance for the first time.

Milwaukee's Jewish residents, generally thought to number about 30,000, had their hands full between 1945 and 1967; the community sponsored a range of health, human service, educational, and religious institutions that seemed out of proportion to its actual size. Supporting them all required non-stop fund-raising, and annual drives and benefits were, for

many families, as much a part of the Jewish year as Rosh Hashanah and Yom Kippur—or at least Purim and Chanukah. Some organizations used clever themes to make their events stand out on the calendar, like the Matzo Ball for Beth El Ner Tamid or the Spring "Bawl" for the toddlers of the Babbitz Nursery School. In 1951, playing off the new vogue for Cinerama films, Mount Sinai Hospital held a "Sinai-Rama" to raise money; guests bid on a variety of items donated by movie stars, including Carol Channing's scarf and Hopalong Cassidy's neckerchief.

Individual fund-raising events brought in crucial revenue, but the real workhorse of local charity was the Jewish Welfare Fund. Established in 1938, it had become both the collector and the dispenser of money for more than forty member agencies—local,

From kickoff to final tally, the Jewish Welfare Fund's annual campaign functioned like a well-oiled machine.

Melvin Zaret, shown at center on a mission to Israel, became the Welfare Fund's director in 1955. Campaign events featured rising stars like Itzhak Perlman.

A Delightful Evening! ..
A Brilliant Program! ..

The Officers and Board of Directors Respectfully Request Your Presence at the

Annual Meeting

Featuring

ITZHAK PERLMAN
Israeli Child Prodigy of the Violin

ITZHAK PERLMAN

SUNDAY EVENING, APRIL 8
– 8:15 P. M. SHARP –
Jewish Community Center

8,000 Jewish households in search of funds. Kick-off events featured high-end entertainers as a way to attract high-end pledges. Some of the main attractions came from Israel, a major recipient of Welfare Fund dollars. In 1960, the young country sent across its stunning Miss Universe semifinalist (Miriam Hadar, who happened to be a military veteran) and two years later dispatched a teenaged violin prodigy named Itzhak Perlman.

The annual campaigns were a proving ground for volunteer leaders, and no unpaid post in town carried more prestige than the presidency of the Jewish Welfare Fund. Presidents were usually drawn from the ranks of business and the professions—men like attorney Benjamin Saltzstein, TV and appliance magnate B.J. Sampson, pathologist Norbert Enzer, liquor dealer Harry Epstein, and attorney Marvin Klitsner. Success in the Milwaukee effort was sometimes a prelude to even higher (but still unpaid) positions. Albert "Ollie" Adelman, whose family ran the region's largest dry cleaning business, chaired the Welfare Fund's 1960 campaign with outstanding results. In 1966, Adelman was named a national trustee of the United Israel Appeal, one of America's leading Israeli support organizations. Nor were the women of the community forgotten. In 1958, years before other cities saw the light, the Welfare Fund established a Young Women's Committee that sponsored leadership training classes for its members. The program's graduates rose to the top of numerous local organizations, and one of them, Esther Leah Ritz, became a power in both political and philanthropic circles. In 1965, Ritz was named the first woman president of the Jewish Community Center. "Since I regard myself as a

national, and international—and it was therefore without question the most powerful organization in the community. That was especially true after Melvin Zaret became its executive director in 1955. An Orthodox rabbi's son with a master's degree in social work, Zaret labored to strengthen the Welfare Fund's place at the center of Jewish life in Milwaukee. He tried, with limited success, to slow down the proliferation of independent campaigns, but his organization's annual drive was always the main event, and it was always executed with the intensity of a full-court press. Every segment of the community—businesspeople, doctors, attorneys, women—had its own chairperson and its own detailed list of prospects. Once a year on Stay at Home Sunday, canvassers visited nearly

person first and then as a woman," she told a reporter, "I saw nothing particularly extraordinary about my election."

The center that Esther Leah Ritz headed was clearly the Jewish Welfare Fund's pet community project in the postwar years. As essential as they were, the schools, hospitals, homes, and social welfare agencies each served a particular segment of the population with particular needs, from medical care to family counseling. The Jewish Community Center (JCC) served everyone. It was the one organization that aspired to cut across every religious, geographic, and age line to provide cultural sustenance for all. The existing facility, however, left much to be desired. Housed in a former high school on Milwaukee Street since 1931, the old Jewish Center was handicapped by its size, its lack of parking, and the age of its facilities. In the summer of 1945, even before the war was over, a community panel convened to discuss the agency's future. Their conclusion was plain: "With its present limited physical facilities, staff and equipment, the Center cannot adequately achieve that standard of service to and for

the Jewish community which the community desires." The committee recommended that the Jewish Center change its name to the Jewish Community Center—a more accurate reflection of its true mission—and find itself a new building "more centrally located down-town."

The first change was easily accomplished, but the second would take nearly a decade to make a reality. Higher priorities had surfaced overseas. Until Israel was reasonably secure, and until survivors of the Holocaust were out of harm's way, American Jews decided to put all purely local initiatives on the back burner. Work on Milwaukee's new Jewish Community Center did, however, continue at a low boil. In 1946, a lot was purchased on the northwest corner of Fourth and Kilbourn, nearly adjoining the Milwaukee Auditorium. JCC officials announced plans for a $750,000 building on the site and a branch facility "somewhere on the northwest side," i.e., Sherman Park. The old center was sold to the Milwaukee School of Engineering (MSOE), a growing presence on the east

Three community powerhouses of the 1960s and later (l. to r.): Marvin Klitsner, Ollie Adelman, and Esther Leah Ritz.

J.C.
FIFTH ANNUAL ATHLETIC BANQUET
MAY 28, 1942

The Jewish Center on Milwaukee St. was increasingly inadequate as a community gathering space.

side of downtown, with the promise that the Jewish Community Center would vacate the premises by early 1949.

Programming continued in the meantime. In 1947, the JCC drew more than 20,000 participants every month to activities that included "slenderizing" sessions for women, body-building workouts for men, an orchestra, a choir, a variety of dramatic groups, and classes that ranged from Invitation to Music to The Romance of Words. There were also new programs: a summer day camp for kids that took full advantage of Milwaukee County's parks and a Teen Town that offered music and dancing every Saturday night in the Milwaukee Street facility.

As it turned out, the teenagers had plenty of time to dance. In 1949, the JCC lost its site on Fourth and Kilbourn when the city acquired the property for construction of the Milwaukee Arena, a state-of-the-art venue for collegiate and professional sports

that opened in 1950. The JCC's leaders were forced to look elsewhere, and the site they found was a beauty: 120 feet of frontage on Prospect Avenue with a commanding "prospect" of Lake Michigan. Concerns about a "more centrally located" address went out the window when board members took in the view. Prospect Avenue had once been the most prestigious street in Milwaukee, but the mansions that housed the Adlers, the Friends, and other first families—Jewish and otherwise—were excess baggage after World War II, their original usefulness long outlived and their architectural details rapidly deteriorating. When the Jewish Community Center bought the property in 1949, the main building on the site, a brownstone built for grain dealer Charles Ray in 1877, was already condemned. Only after the parade of affluence had passed could the JCC and other institutions consider putting down roots on the lake bluff.

184

In the autumn of 1950, Milwaukee's Jewish households were asked to support yet another fund drive, this one for a $1.1 million community center on Prospect Avenue. The task was less daunting than it might have appeared; the JCC already had more than half the amount in hand from previous grants and the sale of its Milwaukee Street property. Support, financial and otherwise, came from all quarters. Mayor Frank Zeidler, a Socialist who had taken office in 1948, expressed his hope that the center would soften Milwaukee's industrial character:

> *The city being as it is, deeply active in mechanical and material things, needs a soul and a spirit to counteract the often-times brutalizing activities of a plain mechanical work center. The Jewish Center will serve to give tone and atmosphere, and opportunities for cultural achievements.*

An awkward interim followed the campaign kick-off. The center had overstayed its welcome on Milwaukee Street by nearly two years, and sharing space with the Milwaukee School of Engineering was proving unworkable for both groups. Taking advantage of the depressed market for lakefront mansions, the JCC purchased more property on Prospect Avenue, increasing its frontage from 120 feet to nearly 400 between Ogden Avenue and Curtis Place. In early 1951, the center moved into the fifteen-room Gallun house on Prospect and tried valiantly to continue its programming. Attention shifted to off-site activities, including a summer camp on Pelican Lake in northern Wisconsin. Donated by the Kesselman family, it was the first in a succession of JCC camps that stressed Jewish themes as the COA's Camp Sidney Cohen shifted its focus to inner-city children.

The Prospect Avenue project gained momentum when architect Maynard Meyer unveiled his plans in 1952. Meyer, who was

These aging mansions on Prospect Ave. came down to make way for a new center.

Its cornerstone was laid in 1953, and the gleaming new Jewish Community Center was dedicated two years later.

also working with Eero Saarinen on the nearby War Memorial Center, made full use of the blufftop site. He designed a building with four stories, two above street level and two below, that were packed with amenities: a full gymnasium, an auditorium, a swimming pool, club and class rooms, a library, handball courts, dining rooms, a fitness center, a drama workshop, off-street parking, a terrace overlooking the lake, and eight bowling alleys complete with automatic pinsetters. The *Jewish Chronicle* pronounced the plans "a pleasant surprise and wonderment to all," even if they did push the budget from $1.1 million to $1.75 million. Excitement continued to build when the cornerstone was laid on November 15, 1953. Nearly 600 people turned out, and the theme of inclusiveness was apparent in the event's rabbinical roster. Solomon

Schulson (Orthodox) gave the invocation, Joseph Baron (Reform) delivered the main address, and Louis Swichkow (Conservative) offered the benediction. Lizzie Kander had died in 1940, but she was present in spirit. Inside the cornerstone was a first edition of *The Settlement Cook Book,* the homespun culinary guide whose author had started it all.

After nearly ten years of planning and preparation, the Jewish Community Center was formally dedicated during a week-long series of events in January 1955. An estimated 100,000 people visited Prospect Avenue for sports exhibitions, plays, concerts, a youth night, Golden Age programs, a symposium on community-building, and the inevitable formal ball. Frank Zeidler called the building "breathtakingly beautiful," and Milton McGuire, the district's alderman, said it rivaled three recent civic acquisitions: the Milwaukee Arena, the Central Library annex, and the Milwaukee Braves baseball team. Edwarde Perlson, the *Chronicle's* managing editor, approached the point of rhetorical overload in describing the city's newest landmark:

> *No longer the nebulous, misty castle in the clouds, the Center today is the majestic achievement of two generations of men and women who dared to dream and hope. Though it was like a distant star to reach for, they—and those who followed after them—intertwined steadfastness and stamina as one fibre, courage and purpose as another, and with prayer and vision as the binding strength, they braided the cord that ever helped them bring closer and closer the star to which they hitched their dream and hope.*

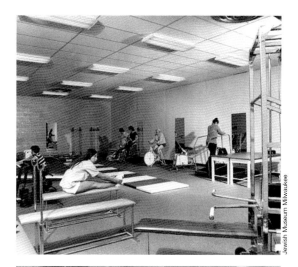

The JCC's amenities included a fitness center, a gymnasium, and a swimming pool as well as social and cultural facilities.

In the difficult pre-Prospect years, the JCC's paid membership had dwindled to 1,300. Although center officials tried to set a limit of 5,500 in the new facility, there was such a groundswell of demand that the roster soared to 8,400 by late 1955, and there were hundreds more on a waiting list. The new center's appeal extended well beyond Jewish circles. Like the Young Men's and Young Women's Christian Associations, the Jewish Community Center was a beneficiary of the annual Red Feather (United Way) drive, and as such was open to everyone. A significant number of Gentiles signed up, most of them to take advantage of the center's first-rate athletic facilities.

Jewish members, of course, were the center's mainstay, but not all of them remained active. After the first flush of enthusiasm had passed, membership dropped precipitously, sinking to 6,000 by late 1958. The problem, a survey revealed, was location. Although the site was spectacular, the building gorgeous, and the programming topnotch, the Jewish Community Center was simply too far removed from the Jewish community's centers: Sherman Park and the North Shore. "It was equally inconvenient

Camp Interlaken became the focal point of the Jewish Community Center's outdoor programs.

Jewish Museum Milwaukee

for East Side and West Side," joked Jack Weiner, a former participant who became the center's director in 1966. The JCC's location had been a compromise from the start, reflecting the community's bipolar geography, but sharp-eyed West Siders may also have noticed that twelve of the agency's eighteen board members lived east of the Milwaukee River. Before any more ground was lost, center officials launched a membership drive, initiated regular bus service from Fox Point and Sherman Park, and expanded programming beyond Prospect Avenue. "Extension clubs" were organized in the neighborhoods, but even greater emphasis was placed on JCC youth camps in outstate Wisconsin. A rented "country camp" opened on Green Lake in 1961, and it was followed in 1965 by the center's own Camp Interlaken near Eagle River, where the buildings bore Hebrew names, the kids put on clean clothes for Sabbath, and the Israeli flag waved proudly above the 150-acre complex. Three years after Interlaken made its debut, the Jewish Community Center added a facility near Fredonia, a small town just thirty miles north of downtown Milwaukee. Camp JCC, as the 95-acre property was known, served primarily as a summer day camp for city and suburban kids.

A judicious mixture of programs and policies kept people coming to the JCC on Prospect Avenue. Its location may have been less than ideal, but nearly 1,000 participants were using the center's facilities every day in the late 1950s. That was a multiple of attendance at any previous site, and it showed that, despite the inevitable shortcomings, the JCC was making steady progress in its efforts to be "the living room for the whole Jewish community."

A Time to Reap

The years between 1945 and 1967 are sometimes recalled as a golden age for the community that came together on Prospect Avenue. After the turbulence of the Depression and World War II, the institutions of Jewish Milwaukee, both religious and secular, were thriving. Landmarks like Mount Sinai Hospital and the JCC had raised the community's local profile, and all Jews basked in the reflected glory of a triumphant Israel on the world stage. On practically every front, conditions seemed to go from bad to better and from better to extraordinary. Harry Plous, president of the Jewish Welfare Fund in 1963, used the occasion of the fund's twenty-fifth anniversary to wax rhapsodic about the progress of his community:

The nature and character of Jewish life has undergone such remarkable, dramatic changes since [1938] that it would be difficult to describe them in this short writing. Suffice it to say that every one of the ... agencies is now on a sound financial footing, as well as enjoying a reputation for standards of service unmatched in our community. Our synagogues have had a rebirth, especially since the war, and religious life has never been more vibrant or more fulfilled. Our Hebrew and religious schools are bulging in their enrollments, with more pupils than ever before. Jewish organizational life has proliferated beyond anyone's wildest dreams in 1938. Our pre-school children, our youth, our teen-agers, our adults, and our aged now have opportunities for Jewish expression which is a source of pride to our entire community.

The role of the Jewish Welfare Fund in this "renaissance" cannot be overstated. Not only have the annual campaigns achieved remarkable success over the years, but the cohesion and sense of direction of our Jewish community is heartwarming.

What underlay this striking record of achievement was an equally striking pattern of economic growth. If residential mobility was one hallmark of the postwar Jewish community, the second, related trend was runaway prosperity. For thousands of families, the 1945-1967 period marked the payoff. All the immigrants' sacrifices, all the years of education they had funded for their children, finally found their reward. The long days of life on the entry level, when a newcomer would buy a box of apples or a gross of stockings and sell them from door to door, were most definitely over. There was no better sign of the times than the plight of the Independent Fruit Dealers Union. Organized in 1912 by immigrant peddlers who wanted a better shake from the wholesalers of Commission Row, the union had once boasted 145 members. By 1962, there weren't enough Jewish peddlers in town to fill a phone booth, and those who stayed in the business had become wholesalers themselves. Faced with extinction, the organization opened its membership to "merchants of all types and undertakings ... as well as professional men and other career men."

Nearly everyone was doing well, and some individuals were doing well indeed; a remarkable number of Jewish professionals and businesspeople rose to the highest tiers of the economic pyramid. In 1951,

Junior House continued the pattern of Jewish leadership in the local garment industry, and Florence Eiseman's designs won an international following.

Jewish Museum Milwaukee

Jewish Museum Milwaukee

Jewish physicians made up 20 percent of Milwaukee's medical establishment and 17 percent of its legal fraternity—at a time when Jews constituted less than 3 percent of the county's population. Individuals with the entrepreneurial itch sometimes fared even better, as small businesses of the prewar period grew large and new businesses found lucrative markets during the general postwar boom. In a throwback to the days of the Adlers and the Friends, Milwaukee was once again a garment center of considerable importance, largely on the strength of Jewish-owned giants like Junior House, Florence Eiseman, Reliable Knitting, Jack Winter, Eagle Knitting, and the Phoenix and Holeproof hosiery firms. The Kohl family parlayed a single corner store in the Bay View neighborhood into the largest grocery chain in the state. One of Kohl's suppliers was Peck Meat Packing, a family-run enterprise that served a national market. In the field of entertainment, Ben Marcus started with a single 500-seat movie theater in Ripon, then moved to Milwaukee and developed the largest theater circuit in

Wisconsin. Real estate moguls George Bockl and Joseph Zilber cut their teeth on Milwaukee projects and moved on to much larger things. Real estate attorney Max Karl, after deciding that he could insure home mortgages more efficiently than the federal government, founded the Mortgage Guaranty Insurance Corporation (MGIC) in 1957 and made it the largest firm of its kind in America. Harry Soref turned his idea for a laminated padlock into the Master Lock Company and in due time mastered the world market. Nathaniel Zelazo founded the Astronautics Corporation in 1959 and rocketed to a position of global leadership in aerospace electronics systems. Law partners Aaron Scheinfeld and Elmer Winter, who had seen what temporary workers could do for their business, began to offer the same service to other employers, founding Manpower in 1948. Aaron Scheinfeld's career was a stunning illustration of how much difference a single generation could make. His father, Solomon, had been the Yiddish-speaking chief rabbi of Milwaukee's Orthodox faithful when they were still

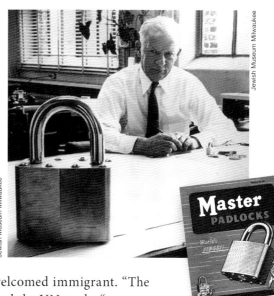

looking back to Europe. The rabbi's son learned American ways and capped his career as co-founder of the largest temporary-help company in the world.

Only a handful of entrepreneurs entered the economic stratosphere, of course, but the pattern of prosperity was general. The sole exceptions among the city's Jews were the approximately 500 displaced persons who had left the ruins of Europe for Milwaukee. Even though some had relatives in the city, it proved difficult to find housing and suitable employment in the tight postwar market. There were also thorny issues of adjustment—a problem for countless refugees before and since. A 1955 United Nations study described a pattern typical of the displaced persons: "So much of their energy had been channeled into the effort to reach the United States that, having at last gained admission, they were temporarily without any subsidiary goals and were too exhausted to plan further." As other obstacles surfaced—language, employment, housing, prejudice against "DPs"—there was often a cooling of relations between the welcoming

cousin and the welcomed immigrant. "The relative," continued the UN study, "came to consider the refugee unresponsive, ungrateful, and even demanding, not sufficiently impressed by the wonders of America…. The sensitive, disappointed refugee came to feel criticized, misunderstood, and once more unwanted." The same dynamic would play out for a different group of refugees one generation later.

Although the challenges were obvious, Milwaukee's displaced persons did find work, even if it meant that once-prosperous businessmen and professionals had to support their families, at least temporarily, as factory hands, clerks, shopkeepers, tailors, and grocers. The immigrants also helped themselves, particularly through the New Home Club. Organized before the war by Jews fleeing the Third Reich, the organization was revitalized by refugees fleeing the aftermath

Other stellar successes included (l. to r.) Ben Marcus in movies, Max Karl in insurance, Harry Soref in padlocks, and Elmer Winter and Aaron Scheinfeld in the temporary-help field.

Jewish Museum Milwaukee

Jewish Museum Milwaukee

Jewish Museum Milwaukee

*More recent arrivals prospered
as well. (Top) Harri and
Herta Hoffmann, shown in
Purim costumes, started a
thriving shoe-polish firm.
(Above) Alfred Bader founded
a chemical giant but still
made time to teach young
people about Judaism.*

*Joseph Peltz was one of several
Jewish scrap dealers who
recycled their way to success.*

of the Holocaust. The group had two goals,
said Sam Siegelman, its president in 1956:
"One is to help our members become
adjusted as good Americans, and the other
is to help them do this without losing what
is worthwhile in Jewish tradition." The
club was successful on both counts. Nearly
all the refugees made successful transi-
tions to life in America, and some rose to
positions of prominence in Milwaukee and
far beyond. Israel Feldman served with
distinction as Agudas Achim's rabbi from
1949 until 1994. Harri Hoffmann, one of
the New Home Club's perennial leaders,
built a highly successful shoe polish business—with significant help from his wife,
Herta, who concocted the first recipes in
her own kitchen. Alfred Bader, who had
spent part of his adolescence in refugee
camps, came to Milwaukee as a paint chemist and went on to start Aldrich Chemical
in 1951, making it America's largest sup-
plier of organic chemicals. Joseph Peltz,
following a more traditional path, began
as a junk dealer and became a regional
power in the recycling business, taking his
place with Miller Compressing, Afram
Brothers, and other Jewish-owned firms.
Interviewed in 1956, Peltz looked past the
obstacles to the opportunities:

> *There is no country like America. In
> what other country could people like us
> have the chance to be a success? Here
> religion or race does not matter. It's all
> up to you. If you have the spirit noth-
> ing can stop you. That's why we all love
> America, and want to do everything
> that we can to be good Americans and
> show our appreciation to this wonder-
> ful country.*

As they vaulted into and frequently over the middle class, Milwaukee's Jews, whether native-born or newly arrived, were changed in the process. They did not breathe the same air or have the same outlook as the rag-pickers and fruit-peddlers of memory. Economic success invariably meant social integration, particularly for those who spent their working days in non-Jewish business settings and their nights in largely non-Jewish neighborhoods. The temptation to assimilate was always there. Jewish kids participated in Little League and Scouting programs with as much enthusiasm as their Gentile classmates, and they might have just as easily become Americans, plain and simple, as Jewish Americans. There were, in fact, some subtle accommodations to the Christian majority. Chanukah, a relatively minor holiday on the traditional Jewish calendar, was inflated almost beyond recognition by its proximity to Christmas. An untold number of Jewish families put up trees in their living rooms every December and left plates of cookies for Santa Claus.

There was resistance as well. Being Jewish was increasingly a matter of choice after World War II, and it was a choice that most people embraced. The postwar decades were a high-water mark for Jewish organizational life, as they were for American organizational life generally. A 1954 study done by the Bureau of Jewish Education found 110 groups in Milwaukee, divided by happy chance into 55 for men and 55 for women. The Federation of Jewish Women's Organizations counted thousands in its collective membership, with Hadassah and Pioneer Women supplying the greatest number. The largest group on the men's side was B'nai B'rith, whose roster peaked at 3,773 in 1947;

Jewish organizational life rose to a new peak in the postwar years. The largest groups included Hadassah for women and B'nai B'rith for men.

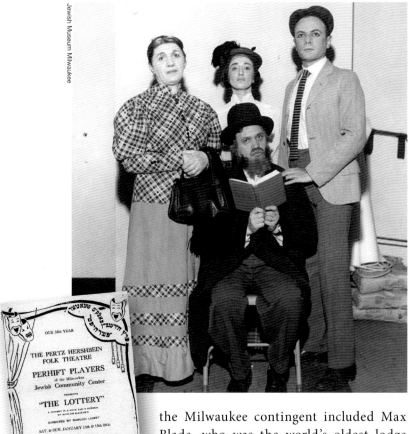

Jewish Museum Milwaukee

The Perhift Players made Milwaukee a center of the Yiddish theater long after companies had disbanded elsewhere.

back to life following the war. In 1948, shortly after beloved playwright Peretz Hirshbein's death, the group changed its name to the Perhift Players in his honor—an acronym for Peretz Hirshbein Folk Theater. "A speaking knowledge of Yiddish is desirable," wrote Perhift's president in a 1948 appeal for new cast members. "Appreciation of the arts and a genuine desire to grow, culturally, are far more important." Enough volunteer thespians signed on to keep the troupe viable when the Jewish Community Center moved to its new home on Prospect Avenue. Stage veteran Judah Bleich, who became the JCC's full-time drama director in 1956, carried the Perhift Players to new artistic heights. "One successful production after another," wrote the *Jewish Chronicle* in 1961, "won over a completely new type of patron, second and third generation young American Jews who sought out good theater though with only a scant acquaintance of Yiddish."

From Yiddish theater to Hebrew schools, the community's robust organizational life reflected an insistence on Jewish particularity. Economic success may have promoted social integration, but the process stopped well short of assimilation. In some respects, the opposite was true, as Jewish residents had a formative influence on their home communities. When the JCC's youth groups held a joint "Bar Mitzvah party" for Israel on its thirteenth anniversary of statehood in 1961, a *Chronicle* reporter was shocked by what he witnessed:

> *We listened, incredulous, while these youngsters sang songs in Hebrew, with as much alacrity and know-how as you'd expect them to sing jive and*

the Milwaukee contingent included Max Blade, who was the world's oldest lodge member when he died in 1959 at the age of 101. Many of the members played their golf at Brynwood Country Club, which, after spending the Depression and war years as a public course, became private again in 1948 and promptly filled to capacity.

Some organizations, of course, were more overtly Jewish than others. It was hardly a surprise that Milwaukee had supported Yiddish theater troupes as early as the 1890s. What made the city unusual was the existence of a Yiddish theater scene decades after World War II. The Young Literary and Dramatic Society, organized in 1921 as a Lincoln House program, was one of the relatively few American companies that came *jazz. They sang out the Hebrew lyrics and melodies as if they had been singing them in their everyday school music classes. And indeed, as we learned later while the boys and girls were hopping and stepping and swirling and whirling in horas and mayims, that these Israeli dances had been taught in gym classes (here at Nicolet High School, as we were informed!)*

The presence of a large (and growing) Jewish student population at Nicolet—the postwar generation's Washington High School—ensured at least some Jewish programming, but there were also tensions on the North Shore, particularly over the issue of Christmas celebrations. In 1961, after hearing from enough Jewish parents, the Fox Point-Bayside school district banned Christmas trees and ended the practice of gift exchanges during the Christian holiday, although "traditional music of all faiths" was still permitted as "a group activity." The Milwaukee Jewish Council (MJC) served as the community's point agency on all issues with potential for cultural conflict. Established in 1938 to combat Nazi propaganda of the domestic variety, the council became a full-time organization in 1944, working in "all phases of intergroup relations." The MJC's profile soared when Saul Sorrin was named its executive director in 1962. A native New Yorker and a veteran of the anti-defamation wars, Sorrin became one of the most powerful individuals in the Jewish community. Shortly after taking the Milwaukee post, he summed up the council's stance on both Christmas and Chanukah celebrations in plain language:

Adhering to the principle of church and state and to the Wisconsin constitutional provision that no sectarian instruction shall be allowed in the public schools, the Milwaukee Jewish Council believes that any holiday observances with sectarian content are out of place in the public schools.

The proper approach, in other words, was "neither manger nor menorah."

Tensions were bound to surface when different cultural groups shared the same schools and the same neighborhoods, but that was hardly the whole story. Although anti-Semitism never vanished, the resurgence of Jewish pride in the 1950s and '60s was accompanied by a new receptiveness to Jewish themes; there was, for a change, encouragement from the larger society. *Exodus*, first a novel by Leon Uris and then a 1960 film starring Paul Newman as a Haganah fighter leading Jewish refugees to freedom, rained down positive publicity on both Israel and America's Jewish community. *Fiddler on the Roof*, first a hit 1964 Broadway musical and then an award-winning movie, introduced American audiences to the richly human characters of author Sholem Aleichem's shtetl, and patrons generally left the theater humming. Israel, too—the little country that could—played a major role, both as a touchstone of identity and as a point of contact with the ancestral culture. Born in struggle and strife, Israel soon developed its own symphony orchestra and its own dance companies, as well

Saul Sorrin assumed a high public profile as head of the Milwaukee Jewish Council.

Jewish Museum Milwaukee

Music became one of Israel's most visible exports, particularly at fund-raising time.

as delicious oranges and fine wines, all of which crossed the Atlantic frequently. Milwaukee hosted groups ranging from the Israeli Philharmonic to the Israeli national soccer team.

Like most Jewish Americans, Milwaukeeans were proud of Israel, and proud of the role they had played in creating and sustaining the Jewish state. Those feelings were never stronger than when Golda Meir came to town. That this hometown girl had become one of the most powerful figures in Israel strained credulity, and the effect was especially vivid when she spoke about her childhood. During a 1960 visit to accept an honorary degree (and, as always, to raise money), Meir told the story of a Labor Day parade on Third Street some fifty years earlier. When a group of policemen rode by on horses, her sister, who had experienced the terror of pogroms in Europe, screamed, "The Cossacks are coming!" She was assured that, in Milwaukee, the police rode

to protect the people, not oppress them. In 1965, when Poale Zion was celebrating its sixtieth anniversary, the Israeli foreign minister sent a message of gratitude:

> *I owe a great deal to the Labor Zionist Organization—its members and friends in Milwaukee. From them I learned to cling to our ideals, and from them I learned the value of friendship. In all the walks of my life, I owe you thanks.*

The 1960s were a high point of pride and participation in Jewish Milwaukee, not least of all because "our Golda" was doing so well, but they were also a time of pervasive change. In 1963, determined to "know ourselves and take stock of where we are going," the Jewish Welfare Fund commissioned a painstaking community census. The results, released in 1966, contained a few surprises. A door-to-door canvass and an exhaustive follow-up had located 23,894 Jews in Milwaukee—not the 30,000 generally accepted

Jewish Museum Milwaukee

as fact—ranking the community sixteenth-largest in America, on the same tier as Providence, Rhode Island. Some of the occupational numbers were eye-popping. Fully 59 percent of all male breadwinners were self-employed, compared with just 7 percent for the metropolitan area as a whole, and 43 percent were engaged in some form of retail or wholesale trade. As a group, Milwaukee's Jews were older, better-educated, and more affluent than their neighbors—consistent with results elsewhere—but there was a sharp geographic divide. The West Side accounted for 52.4 percent of Milwaukee's Jewish residents, with the greatest concentration in Sherman Park, but the East Side, a category that included all the North Shore suburbs, was drawing closer with 44.7 percent. West Siders were predominantly Conservative by practice (58 percent) while the greatest number of East Siders were Reform (49 percent), but the vast majority of households on both sides of the river held Passover Seders and lit Chanukah candles every year.

The 1964-65 census offered a revealing snapshot of life in Jewish Milwaukee, but

Golda Meir met an admiring audience during a 1960 trip to her American hometown.

it did not begin to plumb the depth of the changes that were under way. American society as a whole was leaving behind the progress-driven agenda of the postwar years, and Jewish Americans were swept up in the same social currents as every other group. There was a climate of increasing dissatisfaction, first among those whom the march of progress had left behind and then among those who found something missing in what they perceived as the head-long materialism of the Fifties. As African Americans developed a highly disciplined and highly effective civil rights movement, white Americans were challenged to respond. Although sentiment was never unanimous, the nation's Jews were generally in the vanguard of support. By the early 1960s, every Reform and Conservative synagogue worth its kosher salt had formed a "social action" or "human concerns" committee. The case for Jewish participation was eloquently stated by James Farmer, head of the Congress of Racial Equality, in a 1963 address to the Women's Division of the Milwaukee Jewish Welfare Fund:

> *You know the meaning of suffering. You have suffered for thousands of years. We know that suffering for only two hundred years. In that suffering, in the seeking for freedom and tolerance, we—Jews and Negroes—have a great kinship.*

The veteran Freedom Rider said he could imagine "no greater natural alliance than between Jews and Negroes in the current civil rights crisis." In 1963, the Milwaukee Jewish Council voted to make "the current struggle of the American Negro" a "priority concern." MJC head Saul Sorrin

characterized the decision as a matter of enlightened self-interest: "A nation that is mature enough to grant equal opportunities to all is one that will also reject the social illness of anti-Semitism."

What followed was a round of discussions and conferences spiced occasionally with action. The Sisterhood of Emanu-El B'ne Jeshurun heard Vel Phillips, Milwaukee's first black (and first woman) alderman, tackle a provocative theme: "What would YOU do if a Negro moved into YOUR neighborhood?" The Jewish Council organized "buzz sessions" on human relations topics, and the local chapter of the National Council of Jewish Women sponsored an "inner city bus tour" that ended with soul food at the Urban League headquarters. A prominent real estate agent, Jack Lee, ruffled more than a few feathers when he urged his fellow Jews to sell their homes to black families as a mitzvah—both a righteous deed and a commandment. More direct was the witness of Clyde Sills, the associate rabbi at Emanu-El B'ne Jeshurun. In 1964, answering the call of Martin Luther King, Sills became one of seventeen Reform rabbis arrested during a demonstration in St. Augustine, Florida.

The social climate was increasingly volatile, and there were seeds of rebellion even closer to home. Young whites were beginning to launch protests of their own: against an unpopular war in Vietnam, against what they viewed as the hypocrisy of their parents' generation, against the status quo in general. Once again, Jews were in the vanguard. Raised in affluence and filled with great expectations, many of them embraced alternative music, alternative dress, and alternative lifestyles. The Jewish establishment tried bravely to adjust. Temple youth gatherings began to feature such novel entertainments as hootenannies and rap sessions. Nearly 500 young women wore "Jewish Power" pins to a convocation at Beth Israel. The Jewish Community Center introduced classes in rock guitar. Congregation Shalom allowed drums and guitars in its sanctuary for a rock-and-roll worship service in 1967. "Being an old fuddy-duddy, I had some misgivings," admitted Harry Pastor, but the rabbi professed to find the performance "inspiring." Attempts to keep young people within the fold were never-ending, but the central issues involved far more than songs and slogans. The ever-prophetic Abraham Joshua Heschel offered his own diagnosis in 1966:

> *Our young people are disturbed at parents who are spiritually insolvent. They seek direction, affirmation; they reject complacency and empty generosity. There is a waiting in many homes, in many hearts for guidance, instruction, illumination….*

For a growing number of young people, that search for authenticity would lead far beyond the temple life they had known since childhood.

The major currents of the decade came together memorably in the summer of 1967. Hordes of young people descended on San Francisco's Haight-Ashbury district for the "summer of love," and the director of the city's Jewish Community Center estimated that 20 percent of them were Jews. "Generally," reported Irwin Gold, "we feel we are not too successful in providing welfare services to Jewish 'hippies' essentially because of their estrangement from 'straight society.'" Milwaukee was certainly well-represented in the throng, but there were enough

local love-ins and live concerts to keep all but the most determined young people at home. For civil rights activists, the same long, hot summer produced spirited protests as well as demoralizing riots from coast to coast. Milwaukee experienced both: a series of open-housing marches led by Father James Groppi (with significant Jewish participation) and a "civil disturbance" on the North Side—the former Jewish quarter—that left three people dead. Night after night, newspaper headlines told of clashes in the customarily quiet streets of a city that had long considered itself above the fray.

One more headline-grabbing event from the frenetic summer of 1967 had particular significance for the Jewish community: the Six Day War between Israel and its Arab neighbors. Milwaukee's response to the crisis was nearly as swift as Israel's resounding victory. Although the Jewish Welfare Fund had just raised more than $1.6 million—its highest total since 1948—an emergency appeal netted another $1.75 million in barely a month. "Never in our history," declared campaign chair Julius Atkins, "has a response been of such magnitude—so quick, open-handed, massive! Of this we can be justly proud." The record-setting results showed just how firmly Israel had become entrenched in the American Jewish psyche. Rabbi Dudley Weinberg of Emanu-El was among the speakers who addressed an overflow crowd of 3,000 during an emergency rally at the JCC. "We Jews cannot afford to be without Israel," Weinberg said. "Their lives are at stake, but our souls are at stake." For a Reform rabbi to utter such words was a convincing demonstration of just how far American Jews had come. Even the young people,

Wisconsin Jewish Chronicle

Israeli soldiers placed the flag on Jerusalem's Temple Mount in 1967—a stirring declaration of victory in the Six Day War.

despite their multiple discontents, responded with pride. As 1967 drew to a close, the Jewish Youth Council organized a torchlight parade through the streets of downtown Milwaukee—not to protest America's involvement in Vietnam, but to celebrate Chanukah, Israel's twentieth birthday, and the country's triumph in the Six Day War.

In some ways, the 1945-1967 period ended as it had begun: with Israel in crisis and reaching out to its American cousins for help. The first crisis was one of creation, the second a matter of survival. Between those two bookends, however,

the world had changed enormously. Mirroring the experience of Jews around the globe, the Milwaukee community had moved from horror to hope, from tragedy to triumph. Riding currents that were both thoroughly American and uniquely Jewish, its members had soared economically, spread out geographically, prospered organizationally, and found new energy religiously. They had built a better life at home and helped to build a better life in their new second home across the sea. But the same currents that had washed in such a vibrant new order were washing out again, and the Jews of Milwaukee—and America—would follow them in new and unexpected directions.

Chapter 5
Testing the Limits of Diversity, 1967-

There is no question that the Jews of Milwaukee, with their peers across America, were at a pinnacle in 1967. By any conceivable measure—income, education, profession, address—they ranked at or near the top of the nation's social hierarchy, and their success had come with astonishing speed. Only a single generation separated most Milwaukee Jews from the social isolation and grinding poverty of their immigrant forebears, but the gulf was absolute. All the barriers seemed to have fallen for the children born in America; anti-Semitism, if not completely dead, was notably dormant by 1967. The children's children—the postwar baby-boomers—were so secure in their American bones that they felt free to protest the existing order with considerable, if temporary, vehemence. Israel, too, fed a rising sense of accomplishment. Once considered the vulnerable lightweight of the Middle East, the Jewish homeland had landed what appeared to be a knockout punch against its Arab adversaries in the Six Day War, and the American cousins who had helped underwrite the Israeli experiment shared in the victory.

By 1967, no sane Milwaukee Jew would have gone back to live in the Haymarket neighborhood, much less the shtetls of Europe. The community's material comfort and social confidence were both self-evident, but that very comfort, that obvious confidence, raised some troubling questions. The most serious was also the most basic: What does it mean to be a Jew? When you live your life as an American, when you succeed in America on America's own terms, what's left? What prevents your Jewish identity from melting away entirely? And what keeps you together as a people, set apart in any meaningful way from the cultural mainstream?

Staying together and apart has been a defining theme of the post-1967 period. Nearly everyone involved—rabbis, institutional leaders, community volunteers, parents—has wrestled with the same central questions and tried, with varying degrees of success, to answer them. Some, particularly in organizations like the Jewish Federation and the Jewish Community Center, have stressed the "together" side of the equation, while others, particularly in traditional religious circles, have placed the emphasis on "apart." Still others have felt the need to revise or even reject the customary understanding of what it means to be Jewish. Milwaukee retains a collegiality that has become conspicuously absent in other communities, but the result of all the together-and-apart exploration has been a thorough testing of the limits of diversity.

The fundamental questions have been answered so variously and in such vivid detail that two chapters are required to tell the story of Jewish Milwaukee in the post-1967 period. This chapter highlights some of the cultural challenges facing the community and charts the response of local synagogues and schools, with an emphasis on the religious dimension. Chapter 6 takes a broader view of the community's institutional life during the same years and chronicles the arrival of its newest members: immigrants from the former Soviet Union. A concluding section describes the present incarnation of Jewish Milwaukee in the lengthening context of its past. More than 160 years after their ancestors reached the shores of Lake Michigan, the Jews of Milwaukee, like the Jews of America, are a people enviably together on one level but distinctly, even painfully, apart on others—and searching, still searching, for the fundamental unity that underlies their obvious differences.

Israel at the Center

Israel was perhaps the most compelling answer to the question, "What does it mean to be a Jew?" Since its creation in 1948, the country had become an indispensable anchor of identity for America's Jews, and its stunning 1967 victory only intensified the emotions felt in Milwaukee and elsewhere in the Diaspora. "This community was as united as it could ever have been," said Melvin Zaret, executive director of the Jewish Welfare Fund. Max Karl, one of the Fund's leading volunteers, recalled the local mood in 1967 as "euphoric" and described Israel itself as a sort of latter-day utopia. More than half the money raised in the community's annual campaigns went

directly to Israel, and it was common for crowds of a thousand or more to attend the annual celebration of the homeland's independence. When Israel turned twenty-five in 1973, 3,500 people descended on the Jewish Community Center on Prospect Avenue for a day-long program of dancing, speeches, and song.

Israel did its best to keep the Diaspora fires burning. In the late 1960s, Milwaukee became one of numerous American communities with its own full-time *shaliach,* a resident emissary whose sole job was to promote interest in Israel, particularly among young people. There was also a procession of rising stars and seasoned veterans, including Yitzhak Rabin, Shimon Peres, and Abba Eban, who crossed the ocean to launch Milwaukee fund drives, and the Israeli Philharmonic made the same trip on a regular basis. Rabbi Herbert Panitch of Congregation Beth Israel offered a candid assessment of the orchestra's 1974 performance: "It was beautiful, beautiful, but even if it was lousy, I would have loved it." There was movement in the opposite direction as well. Elmer Winter, the co-founder of Manpower, not only opened a company office in Tel Aviv but also chaired the Committee for the Economic Growth of Israel, a group committed to developing industry in the Jewish state and markets for Israeli products in the United States. A more humanitarian effort began in 1977, when Milwaukee "adopted" Or Yehudah, a community of struggling Sephardic immigrants just outside Tel Aviv, as part of the Israeli government's Project Renewal. Within a decade, Milwaukeeans had invested $2.6 million—an amount matched by Israel's taxpayers—in housing projects, sports facilities, and

Milwaukeeans observed Israel's twenty-fifth anniversary with an all-day program at the Jewish Community Center.

Rebuilding the Or Yehudah community outside Tel Aviv was a more tangible statement of Milwaukee's support for the Jewish homeland.

Say Shalom to Milwaukee's Own
—With Tools of Peace and Development—

GOLDA MEIR

social services for Or Yehudah's residents. The town became a mandatory stop for local leaders on missions to Israel.

Milwaukee, of course, had an Israeli connection shared by no other community in America: Golda Meir. When Meir became prime minister in 1969, the mood in her old hometown was absolutely jubilant. The reaction of the *Wisconsin Jewish Chronicle* (September 26, 1969) bordered on disbelief:

> *A daughter, a Jewish daughter, of our community holds the supreme position it is in the power of her people to give her. Who in the whole history of Milwaukee has achieved greater station? What woman in all Jewish history has attained greater rank? What Jew has been entrusted with the reins of leadership at a period more crucial in the history of the young State?*

In October 1969, as part of a state visit to America, "our Golda" made a triumphant return in Milwaukee. No head of state has ever enjoyed a warmer welcome. The seventy-one-year-old addressed a full house at the brand-new Performing Arts Center, finishing to thunderous applause, but the emotional high point of her visit was a stop at Fourth Street School, from which she had graduated as valedictorian nearly sixty years earlier. The prime minister described her reception in *My Life*, her 1975 memoir:

> *They welcomed me as though I were a queen. Standing in rows on the creaky old stage I remembered so well, freshly scrubbed and neat as pins, they serenaded me with Yiddish and Hebrew songs and raised their voices to peal out the Israeli anthem "Hatikvah" which made my eyes fill with tears.... When I*

Prime Minister Golda Meir made a last nostalgic visit to Milwaukee in 1969. The day's highlight was a stop at her alma mater, Fourth Street School.

203

*"Our Golda" rose from the immigrant ghetto of Milwaukee's
North Side to play a prominent role on the world stage.*

204

entered the school, two little girls wearing headbands with Stars of David on them solemnly presented me with an enormous white rose made of tissue paper and pipe cleaners, which I wore all day and carefully carried back to Israel with me.

Meir took special note of the many African-American students at her alma mater, children who were "born, as I myself had been, into a minority and living, as I myself had lived, without much extravagance." She shared with them what she had learned at Fourth Street:

> *"It isn't really important to decide when you are very young just exactly what you want to become when you grow up," I told them. "It is much more important to decide on the way you want to live. If you are going to be honest with yourself and honest with your friends, if you are going to get involved with causes which are good for others, not only for yourselves, then it seems to me that that is sufficient, and maybe what you will be is only a matter of chance." I had a feeling that they understood me.*

It was this transparent idealism, coupled with her fierce advocacy and no-nonsense personal style, that earned Golda Meir legions of fans in Israel and far beyond. She was, according to the Gallup poll, the most-admired woman in the world during the early 1970s, and Milwaukeeans found themselves riding her coattails. Local activists who visited the homeland enjoyed unusual access to prominent Israelis, and even ordinary citizens took notice. "The community of Milwaukee has become identified with

Golda here," reported civic leader Gerald Colburn during a 1969 trip. Israelis who noticed the city's name printed on the delegates' badges flashed immediate smiles of recognition. "It gives us a very special relationship," said Colburn.

Golda Meir used her celebrity status at home and more especially abroad to advance one of the central themes of her long career. Israel, in her view, was not a nation unto itself but rather the tangible expression of an idea and an ideal that belonged to every Jew in the world. "If Israel did not exist," she said in 1972, "the Jews would lose their center.... They would be individual Jews but without a center—a focus." All Jews, therefore, owed Israel their loyalty, their financial support and, if possible, their physical presence. "Aliyah [immigration] is our lifeblood," she proclaimed. "Come to Israel and build the Land."

The existence of that Promised Land was tested once more during the Yom Kippur War of 1973, when Egyptian and Syrian forces attacked Israel on the holiest day of the Jewish year. Once more the Jews of the Diaspora were called upon to help. Milwaukee alone contributed $2 million in a single week, as hundreds of concerned residents sold stocks, mortgaged property, and took out bank loans. The city's Jewish community raised $9.6 million in the year following the conflict, nearly doubling all previous records, and the same extraordinary results were reported in other cities. Although Israeli forces were far better-equipped than they had been in 1967, the Yom Kippur War proved less decisive, and infinitely more controversial, than the Six Day conflict had been. The military outcome was

basically a stalemate, and more than 2,400 Israeli soldiers died in the effort. Although Golda herself was exonerated, there were questions about the quality of Israeli intelligence and the speed of the nation's military response. The Yom Kippur War marked the end of Israel's innocence and the beginning of a more complex relationship with the Jews of the Diaspora, particularly those in the United States.

The war also hastened the end of Golda Meir's stellar career of public service. She resigned as prime minister in April 1974, six months after the Arab attack, confessing that, at seventy-five, she could "no longer bear the burden." "Don't try to change my mind," she warned her comrades in the Labor Party. The first lady of Israeli politics remained an active participant in affairs of state, living long enough to see the Camp David accords signed in 1978. When Menachem Begin of Israel and Anwar Sadat of Egypt agreed, with President Jimmy Carter beaming his approval, to work for "a just, comprehensive, and durable settlement of the Middle East conflict," it seemed that peace was, for the moment, just around the corner. Golda Meir died less than three months later, on December 8, 1978. Israel is her enduring monument, but Golda was not forgotten in her American hometown. A few months after her death, two civic institutions—the Fourth Street School for the Gifted and Talented and the University of Wisconsin-Milwaukee Library—were named in her honor. These local landmarks, both dedicated to public service and both counting Golda Meir among their former students, preserve forever the memory of the prime minister who made Milwaukee famous.

Roiling the Waters

In 1972, near the midpoint of her term in office, Golda Meir sounded a prophetic warning to the Jews of the United States: "The big question is: Can Jewishness flourish in free societies? We now see that not only through hatred and oppression can the number of Jews be diminished, but also through love and freedom." Her choice of words was telling. "Love" and "freedom" were two of the American youth movement's favorite rallying cries, and much was being done in their name that would have horrified even the most open-minded ancestors. Although statistics are lacking—no one circulated a sign-up sheet—there is little question that young Jews were over-represented in the counterculture of the late 1960s and early 1970s. Their participation was a clear and profoundly ironic indicator of the Jewish community's success. In 1964, when only 27 percent of America's young Gentiles attended college, fully 80 percent of Jews in the same age group were enrolled—a condition that Rabbi Irving Greenberg, a Yeshiva University historian, described as "full college employment." In *Jewish Survival and the Campus*, a seminal 1968 essay, Greenberg called the phenomenon "unprecedented in world history," reflecting "the extraordinary achievement of the Jews in the modern, free society." But there was a cataclysmic downside to such remarkable success.

The Jewish press pictured the community's young people drowning in the cultural currents of the 1960s and '70s.

Study after study showed that college was a place where faith went to die, particularly during the heyday of the counterculture. "By and large," wrote Greenberg, "college is a disaster area for Judaism, Jewish loyalty and Jewish identity." In the 1960s and '70s, when there was such an abundance of alternatives, students found it much easier to identify with the youth culture than with their religious culture. Loyalty to Israel suffered, barriers to interfaith dating collapsed and, as the number of disaffected young people mushroomed, "Jewish survival" became a matter of urgent concern.

Some of those young people—the Abbie Hoffmans and Jerry Rubins of the day as well as legions of less-celebrated activists—dropped out of the mainstream entirely and devoted themselves to creating an alternative society. A much larger number maintained a semblance of loyalty to tradition, but not to the Judaism of their formative years. When members of Emanu-El B'ne Jeshurun's 1969 confirmation class sat down to write their required affirmations, the results may not have been exactly what the rabbis had in mind:

We affirm the synagogue. But the synagogue we affirm is not always the synagogue we have actually known. We want a synagogue that is really alive to the real world. We want a synagogue that has the courage of its Jewish convictions. We have been taught that a synagogue is a prayer house, a study house and a meeting house. Let our synagogue, then, be more concerned with prayerful aspiration than with what happens to be conventional respectability.

Jewish Museum Milwaukee

It was on the nation's college campuses that the desire to be "really alive" came to its fullest flowering. One Hillel center after another modified its worship services to incorporate Indian ragas, Bob Dylan songs, incense, modern dance, and "encounter sessions" rather than Torah commentary. The older generation often looked askance at such experiments—one thoughtful Hillel leader expressed concern that "the worship of relevance may ultimately destroy the relevance of worship"—but no one doubted that the hunger for authenticity was real. Even students who jettisoned religion continued to seek out specifically Jewish cultural alternatives. "The biggest radical rebellion is to become a Jew," said one young Milwaukeean. "It's doing your thing on the inside rather than the outside." That "thing" might have included reading journals like *Street Jew* or *Chutzpah*, joining the Messianic International Party (the Mippies), learning the songs of Rabbi Shlomo Carlebach, or absorbing *The Jewish Catalog*, a widely popular 1973

primer filled with ideas for "Jewish education and Jewish living in the fullest sense of these terms." This "do-it-yourself kit" offered instructions on how to crochet yarmulkes, make menorahs, prepare falafel, inscribe Hebrew letters, and even follow Jewish dietary laws. The cultural impulse occasionally took institutional form. In 1971, members of a kosher food co-op on the University of Wisconsin's Madison campus took over a vacant sorority house on Langdon Street and started Kibbutz Langdon, an experiment in "living together Jewishly." With help from one "kibbutznik's" sympathetic uncle, the twenty-five or so members of the collective purchased the home in 1978, and their successors kept the experiment going until 1985. A handful of Jewish activists went much farther—literally. Emigration from the United States to Israel peaked at nearly 9,000 a year in the late 1960s, and Milwaukee was represented in the flow. Most of the settlers were young people who viewed life on an Israeli kibbutz as the ultimate alternative.

Long hair for the boys, long dresses for the girls: the 1971 confirmation class at Emanu-El B'ne Jeshurun

Wisconsin Jewish Chronicle

Activities at the Finjan Coffeehouse included a countercultural sukkah built for the autumn festival of Sukkot.

The Jewish Student House at UW-Milwaukee served young people who remained in school.

Wisconsin Jewish Chronicle

"apart" members of the Jewish community, the most alienated, were their own children. Attempts to bridge the generation gap were never-ending. The American Jewish Committee, a pillar of group identity since 1906, made "alienated youth" its top priority in a 1970 policy statement:

> *In all probability, it is mainly these bright, currently disaffected kids who will speak for American Jewry in years to come. If they were to reject Israel for good, all our work in the larger community might prove to have been in vain. We must reach them now, lest Israel lose the source of strength it has found in American Jewry.*

Closer to home, Milwaukee's Jewish Community Center established the Finjan Coffeehouse in a Shorewood storefront in 1968. Named for a type of Turkish coffeepot popular in Israel, Finjan was described as "a place for high school youth to meet, greet and have fun," but it was much more than an after-school hangout. Center staff and volunteers led programs in film-making, macramé, photography, drama, bicycle repair, and poetry, as well as the obligatory "rap sessions" on topics ranging from Jewish identity to human sexuality. The coffeehouse moved to Whitefish Bay and then to Glendale before ending its run in 1975. Other community programs targeted the Finjan crowd's older siblings. In 1971, as mental and physical health problems multiplied in the city's youth enclave, the East Side Project was launched to connect those in need with the services of Mount Sinai Hospital, Jewish Family and Children's Service, Jewish Vocational Service, and other Jewish agencies. Those who stayed in college could visit the Jewish Student House,

Although some remained firmly, even militantly, within the ethnic fold, a far greater number of young people blended into the larger youth culture, keeping a wary distance from the "Jewish establishment." Adult members of that establishment had to face the unhappy truth that the most which opened in 1972 a few doors south of the University of Wisconsin-Milwaukee's student union. One of a sprawling network of Hillel centers on America's college campuses, the Jewish House offered consciousness-raising groups for men and women, vegetarian cooking classes, and more traditional fare like game nights and Sabbath dinners. The Jewish Community Center was less selective in its outreach. Brady Street was the heart of Milwaukee's "hip" community, and the JCC made full use of its location four blocks south of Brady. The center organized periodic Draft Teach-Ins to educate young men about their options (including conscientious objection) and hosted Free University courses that included How to Be an Activist, Human Potential, and surprises like Chassidic Mysticism and Music, taught by Rabbi Michel Twerski. The JCC also opened its extensive recreational facilities to youth-serving agencies from Milwaukee's central city.

It was the older generation, by and large, who paid for the various youth programs, and there was no limit to their concern for the welfare of their children. When Mount Sinai held a forum on "The Whys of Drug Abuse" in 1970, organizers were amazed to see 2,000 people turn out. Although there was a deep reservoir of good will, the generation gap was never far beneath the surface. In 1968, the Mr. and Mrs. Club of Temple Menorah heard John Kois, editor of the alternative newspaper *Kaleidoscope*, present "The Hippie Viewpoint." His talk was followed immediately by "colored slides of the Sweetheart Dinner-Dance" held at the temple a month earlier. The Jewish Community Center promoted its 1970 educational program as an "Adult Liberation

Jewish Museum Milwaukee

Movement," with classes in duplicate bridge, gourmet cooking, and needlepoint as well as tie-dyeing and guitar lessons.

Although its impact was permanent, the high tide of the counterculture was on its way out by the mid-1970s—the result of graduation, exhaustion, and the 1973 end of America's involvement in Vietnam. American society was not, however, even remotely close to settling down. The civil rights movement had broadened its focus to include the economic as well as the political plight of the nation's minorities, and the Jewish community was once again in the vanguard of support—a position it had occupied since the movement's earliest days. In 1968, B'nai B'rith became one of the few white groups in Milwaukee to honor Father James Groppi, the Catholic firebrand who had led marches for open housing the previous summer. The award was controversial, even among the city's Jews, but B'nai B'rith was undeterred. In the same year, the Jewish Welfare Fund formed an Urban Crisis Committee to bring

Despite criticism from some of its own members, B'nai B'rith gave civil rights leader Father James Groppi (third from left) its Human Rights Award in 1968.

the community's energy to bear on "the problems of the poor and the disadvantaged." Ollie Adelman, the Welfare Fund's president, described the group's activism as a particularly Jewish imperative:

> *The human values to which Jews are committed move them to seek rectification of social conditions which impose often crippling limitations upon many of our fellow citizens, black and white, Christian and Jew. This task is concurrent with our obligations to meet specifically Jewish needs both here and elsewhere. Neither may be reduced for the sake of the other. Both must receive maximum and effective response from us.*

Despite the lofty ideals, there was, in time, a definite cooling of relations between Jewish Americans and African Americans, both nationally and locally. Affirmative action, particularly the use of quotas, was a sticking point for a group traditionally over-represented on college campuses and in the professions, and there was a growing emphasis on separatism and self-determination in some segments of the black community. Despite frequent expressions of good will,

the relationship between the two historic allies assumed a new ambiguity.

There was no ambiguity at all in another movement of the 1970s. After spending decades behind the scenes or in the kitchen, more and more women were demanding the same access to power, the same compensation, and the same respect that men had long taken for granted. Betty Friedan, Bella Abzug, and Gloria Steinem imparted a strong Jewish flavor to the movement's national leadership, and American Judaism itself underwent a transformation. Reform seminaries began to admit women in 1968, and their Conservative counterparts followed in 1983. Sally Priesand, the first woman rabbi in America, assisted briefly at Milwaukee's Congregation Shalom, a Reform temple, in 1970, but it was not until 1982, when Dena Feingold joined Shalom, that a woman was hired on a full-time basis. Feingold was one of a few dozen trailblazers in the entire country when she became Ronald Shapiro's assistant. "I look forward," she said, "to the time when I won't be an oddity and people won't feel the need to point out that I'm a female rabbi." After three years in Milwaukee, Feingold took a pulpit of her own at Beth Hillel in Kenosha.

"A woman's place is in the pulpit." Rabbis Sally Priesand (left) and Dena Feingold both assisted at Shalom in Milwaukee before leading congregations elsewhere.

Jewish Museum Milwaukee

Conditions changed more rapidly for women who had a greater interest in social progress than congregational power. In 1972, the Jewish Student House at UWM became the home of the Jewish Women's Action and Consciousness Group, a free-wheeling association whose members wanted, among other things, "to investigate the Jewish community in their discriminatory practices toward Jewish women." A more resounding blow was struck in 1976. Women had been walking the corridors of institutional power in Milwaukee for years before the doors even opened in other Jewish communities, but they rarely did so on an equal footing with men. In 1976, three formidable women—Esther Leah Ritz, Betsy Green, and Betty Lieberman—presented a painstakingly researched, carefully composed "manifesto" to the leaders (all male) of the Milwaukee Jewish Federation, the umbrella group formerly known as the Jewish Welfare Fund. The trio pointed out that, although women constituted a majority of the community's population, they held only 20 percent of the lay leadership posts in Milwaukee's major Jewish agencies, ranging from 6.8 percent at Mount Sinai Hospital to 45 percent at Jewish Family and Children's Service. Within the Federation itself, they occupied barely 13 percent of the board seats and 28 percent of the standing committee positions. Ritz,

A trio of local dynamos (l. to r.)—Betty Lieberman, Betsy Green, and Esther Leah Ritz—stood politely but firmly for "equal representation of women" in community affairs.

Green, and Lieberman concluded, in rather understated prose, that "the potentials for the involvement of women are far greater than have been realized," and they formally requested "a plan for achieving equal representation of women on all committees." Although change did not occur overnight, the men of the community eventually saw the light. By the mid-1980s, women could be found virtually everywhere in Jewish Milwaukee, from agency board rooms to their executive suites and from temple presidencies to pulpits. Esther Leah Ritz and Betsy Green both served terms as head of the Jewish Federation, and Betty Lieberman became one of the organization's key administrators.

The opening of yet another front was apparent in 1984, when Milwaukeeans were among the delegates to the Midwest Regional Gay and Lesbian Jewish Conference held in Chicago. The gay pride movement had emerged some years earlier on the same wave of change that brought feminism to the surface of American social discourse, and Judaism was once again moved to respond—although never with unanimity. In 1990, the Central Conference of American Rabbis, the Reform movement's leading rabbinical body, endorsed the ordination of gays and lesbians. A decade later, the same organization acknowledged the right of individual rabbis to officiate at same-gender commitment ceremonies. Although groups elsewhere on the spectrum felt absolutely no compulsion to follow, the most liberal Jews were quite comfortable asserting that both homosexuality and heterosexuality were "normal expressions of human diversity."

Leaving the Middle Behind

The cultural currents that welled up in the late 1960s flowed in the same general direction. They washed away the assumptions of the post-World War II period and carried society out into the open, largely uncharted waters of freer expression, broader skepticism, and increased tolerance. The same currents swept in a relativism that was not universally embraced. If anything goes, where are the limits? What stars do you steer by when every viewpoint seems equally valid—or invalid? Gone were the calm and conformity of the Eisenhower years, but so were the certainties that had underpinned an earlier understanding. The result was an ambiguity of epic proportions. Where some saw liberation, others found only fragmentation. What some viewed as a long-overdue renewal of the American experiment was perceived by others as an impossibly risky abandonment of the status quo. The most insistent voices may have been young, but the social upheaval was by no means confined to the nation's college campuses. As the ground shifted beneath their feet, virtually every group and institution in America was forced to reassess its underlying principles and re-examine its place in the larger society.

After the falling apart, there had to be a putting together; the years of erosion were inevitably followed by a period of reconstruction. Responding to the same tectonic forces that were affecting everyone else, the nation's Jews moved in several directions at once. The central question remained the same—What does it mean to be a Jew, together and apart from other Americans?—but the answers varied enormously.

A significant number of Jews allowed the prevailing currents to wash them completely out to sea; they joined the broad American mainstream, retaining their ancestry but not their identity. Others became fervently Jewish without the slightest thought of becoming fervently religious. One of the most interesting responses to the post-1967 social ferment was a return to ancestral traditions so robust that it was dubbed the "new ethnicity." Klezmer music, described as "Yiddish bluegrass," enjoyed a spirited revival, and publishers released a never-ending stream of Jewish cookbooks. But a fondness for certain melodies, a taste for certain foods, and the observance of certain customs do not constitute a way of life. "Jewish," for many, became an adjective, and "Jew" gave way to "American" as the operative noun.

The cultural attrition was most apparent in the staggering rise of interfaith marriages. Intermarriage had been one of the most-feared bogeymen in American Jewish life for generations. Rabbi Samuel Hirshberg of Milwaukee's Temple Emanu-El stated the matter plainly back in 1909:

> *We Jews believe that we have a mission here, that we stand for certain things, and in order to fulfill that mission we must preserve our identity as Jews. Now we are in a hopeless minority and it would be simply suicidal if there was any considerable intermarriage.*

If Hirshberg had been able to revisit the scene sixty years later, he would have been horrified. The proportion of "suicidal" American Jews marrying non-Jews soared from 6 percent of the total between 1941

The Maxwell Street Klezmer Band, a Chicago group with multiple Milwaukee ties

Wisconsin Jewish Chronicle

213

and 1961 to 31.7 percent between 1966 and 1972, and the number kept rising. By 1983, according to a Milwaukee Jewish Federation survey, 47 percent of the community's married Jews under the age of thirty had taken a non-Jewish partner—soon to become an absolute majority. Rabbi Herbert Panitch of Beth Israel deftly described the prevailing pattern: "It begins as 'You can't date non-Jews,' then 'You can date non-Jews but can't marry one,' then 'You can marry one as long as they convert,' then finally, 'He/she's such a lovely person.'" The hazards were obvious. When a Polish-American man marries an Italian-American woman, they can both remain Catholic, just as a couple with German and Norwegian roots can wed without shedding their Lutheranism. No such continuity is possible for Jews. They marry within the faith or outside it; either one spouse converts (and the vast majority do not) or they live in a house to some degree divided. Couples who want a genuinely mixed marriage grow accustomed to compromises on everything from how to raise their kids to where to spend the holidays. The path of least resistance has been for both partners to drop formal religion altogether.

Although the challenges were clear, there was undeniably a positive side to the rising rate of intermarriage. After decades of striving for a genuinely open society—one that judged Jews as individuals rather than cultural clichés—the war was over. Jews and Gentiles could, and frequently did, fall in love, forming the most intimate bond imaginable without suffering ostracism or even criticism. Whether the ultimate cause was a dramatic decline in anti-Semitism or a subtler decline in Semitism itself, the result

was a degree of mutual acceptance that would have been unthinkable even one generation earlier. In a long view of the group's history, the moral was clear: Be careful what you wish for.

Intermarriage, assimilation, and secular surrender constituted one broad response to the currents circulating after 1967. Instead of sticking together, many Jews found it quite easy to live apart from the group that had nurtured their parents and grandparents. Choosing a course of retreat and even rejection, they left the Jewish middle behind. But there was an equal and opposite reaction from members of the religious community. Those who had always belonged to synagogues—or were joining them for the first time—went through the same sorting-out process as their unaffiliated peers, but they came up with an entirely different set of answers. In a world where everything had become relative, they migrated to the certainties of their ancient faith, and many who had belonged out of habit became Jews by choice. Their movement was related to the "new ethnicity," but it went far beyond the re-appropriation of folk culture; Jews alive to the spiritual currents of their time, including a sizable number who had intermarried, embraced the God of Moses and the Torah as the ultimate ground of their being. The result was a widely publicized (and widely praised) "Jewish renaissance" that was apparent across the country. "What all of us have become is more Jewish, " said Rabbi Harry Pastor of Milwaukee in 1975. "[We're] more loyal, more proud of Judaism." The American faithful as a whole shifted in the direction of stricter observance, more formal ritual, and greater reliance on Hebrew—a movement so pronounced that the newest liturgies came more and more to resemble their original versions. An old rift was widening in the American Jewish community. Secular Jews had already become more secular. As religious Jews became more religious, they, too, were leaving the middle behind.

The major division was self-evident, but there were obvious fissures within the religious community itself. Although the spirit of renewal was general, it affected the major movements differently. A great many Orthodox Jews had crossed over to Conservatism after World War II, bringing with them an inherited taste for tradition. A great many of their children kept right on going to Reform in the next generation, and their own traditional instincts helped to transform that movement. A 1993-1994 survey found that 80 percent of the nation's Reform temples provided yarmulkes to their members for worship, half made prayer shawls available, and every one sang or spoke at least 20 percent of its congregational prayers in Hebrew—all sharp departures from past practice. Reform Jews were, in effect, claiming territory that had long been a Conservative domain. The movement did not, however, abandon its long-standing latitude on matters of doctrine, a determination that

was obvious in its decisions to ordain women, to permit rabbis to perform interfaith weddings, and—the biggest one—to accept the children of Jewish fathers as authentically Jewish. Matrilineal descent had been the law since Talmudic times, and the Reform movement's 1983 decision to include the father's line as well as the mother's sparked endless controversy. Individuals struggling with what it meant to be Jewish faced an even more basic question: Who is a Jew?

With one foot in reclaimed traditions and the other in an insistent modernism, the Reform movement displaced Conservatism as America's largest in the post-1967 period. Conservatives struggled to find a similar balance—ordaining women, for instance, even as they encouraged stricter adherence to Jewish dietary laws—but the movement faced challenges from other quarters than Reform Judaism. Orthodoxy, in the years following World War II, had been widely viewed as an immigrant's faith, and many assumed that it would simply die with the last survivor of the European shtetl. Just the opposite occurred. For some Jews, the pervasive and accelerating changes that surfaced in the 1960s suggested, even

After a long series of English-only editions, the new generation of Reform prayer books included lengthy passages in Hebrew.

Rabbi Menachem Schneerson, the guiding light of the global Lubavitch movement

dictated, a particularly fervent return to the unchanging Judaism of Moses. Many of the newly observant—often referred to as the *ba'alei teshuva* ("masters of return")—were the children of Conservative or Reform families who had inhaled the atmosphere of the Sixties and wanted something more substantial, more permanent at the center of their lives. Orthodoxy became their new home, but they entered through more than one door. Some returnees found their way to old congregations whose leaders lived and breathed the joy of Jewish life—and knew how to communicate it. The *ba'alei teshuva*, in turn, re-energized those old congregations, a pattern strikingly apparent in Milwaukee's own Beth Jehudah.

Other returnees entered Orthodoxy through the Lubavitch movement, which gained significant momentum after 1967. Although it was rooted in eighteenth-century Russia, the Chasidic sect took a decidedly modern turn under Menachem Schneerson, the Brooklyn sage who became the seventh Lubavitcher rebbe in 1951. (According to one definition, rabbis have congregations, while rebbes have disciples.) A man of extraordinary charisma, energy, and vision, Schneerson did in fact build an empire of disciples that spanned the globe. They shared the core Jewish belief in the partnership between God and man—the covenant—but followed it to an unexpected conclusion. The Lubavitchers were certain that if all Jews, everywhere, faithfully observed every mitzvah, or commandment,

Milwaukee Lubavitchers provided instruction in the fine art of putting on tefillin.

contained in the Torah, the coming of the Messiah would thereby be hastened. Humanity, in other words, could influence divinity for the good of the entire world. The most visible commandments were high on their list: lighting Sabbath candles, keeping a kosher kitchen, using the mikvah (ritual bath), putting on tefillin (small leather boxes containing biblical verses), and putting up mezuzahs (similar cases affixed to the doorposts of a home). The movement was distinguished by the breadth and aggressiveness of its outreach efforts, which took in everyone from drug-addled dropouts to harried business executives. Lubavitchers tended to divide Jews from all walks of life into just two categories: the observant and the not-yet-observant. Menachem Schneerson oversaw a holy global army that worked with missionary zeal to turn the second category into the first.

As Orthodoxy claimed new adherents, Reconstructionism emerged at a much different point on the religious spectrum. Some Jews who had experienced the tumult of the Sixties concluded that the next stage demanded not a return to tradition but something quite the opposite: a new flexibility, a willingness to take the track of the past in fresh directions. One option was to join, or start, a *havurah*—a small group of like-minded seekers committed to growing and learning together as Jews, whether independently or within a larger Conservative or Reform congregation. The movement began as a countercultural phenomenon in the 1970s and quickly made the leap to established synagogues. Most *havurah* members sooner or later discovered the writings of Mordecai Kaplan, a seminal thinker who had developed an alternative understanding of his

faith. Kaplan viewed Judaism as an "evolving religious civilization" whose adherents were called to engage tradition but also to "reconstruct" it in ways that were relevant to the needs and concerns of contemporary society. "The past," Kaplan famously wrote, "has a vote, not a veto." Although he never intended to found a movement, his writings provided the intellectual foundation for Reconstructionism, which began to train rabbis in 1968 and grew to a network of roughly 100 American synagogues by 2000. Reconstructionists were a small fraction of the faithful, but their endlessly creative liturgies, concern for social justice, and basic egalitarianism added a distinctive voice to the Jewish conversation.

This, then, was the Jewish religious scene after 1967: the Reform movement was becoming more traditional without shedding its liberalism, Orthodoxy was enjoying an unexpected resurgence, Reconstructionism offered a hybrid alternative, and Conservatism was trying valiantly to hold a position at the center of them all. The middle ground was shaky terrain after 1967. Just as the gap between secular and religious Jews widened, there was a corresponding move to the poles within the religious community. As challenges mounted from both the right and the left, a grim joke made the rounds of the Conservative movement: "Our successes become Orthodox, and our failures become Reform." The situation was never that stark and hardly that hopeless, but tectonic shifts were under way within and between America's major movements. The result was an ongoing transformation of the Jewish religious landscape.

Rabbi Mordecai Kaplan, founder of the Reconstructionist movement

The View from the Synagogues

The ground was shifting in Milwaukee as well. The city was a compact microcosm of American Judaism, reflecting all the trends and pressures evident on the national level. But a closer look at the community's synagogues reveals just how complex the broad patterns were at the grassroots level, and how local variations could produce a thoroughly distinctive group identity. Like their counterparts in other cities, Milwaukee's Jews did become more devout, more diverse, and ultimately more divided, but they did so in ways that were not precisely duplicated anywhere else in America.

Mirroring national trends, the community's three Reform temples (four with Emanu-El of Waukesha) all rose to peaks of membership after 1967. Emanu-El B'ne Jeshurun was the oldest Jewish congregation in the state, and it remained the largest as well, particularly after the arrival of Rabbi Barry Silberg in 1974. A native of Baltimore with previous experience in Virginia, Silberg was hired as Dudley Weinberg's assistant and rose to the senior rabbi's post following Weinberg's untimely death in 1976. He quickly assumed perhaps the highest public profile of any rabbi in Milwaukee's history. As a religious leader, essayist, television host, liberal activist, poet, and banquet speaker, Silberg seemed to be everywhere in the 1970s and '80s, but he earned the widest notice for a distinctly non-rabbinical pastime. In 1975, 1976, and again in 1978, Silberg set the world record for continuous rope-jumping, slapping his way to a new mark of six straight hours and 50,180 revolutions, with two dozen distinct jumping patterns. The rabbi's comments after his 1975 performance were classic Silberg. Declaring that rope-jumping was "the world's most demanding and enervating activity," he paused to crow a little:

Rabbi Barry Silberg brought new energy to the pulpit of Emanu-El B'ne Jeshurun—and to the sport of rope-jumping.

Wisconsin Jewish Chronicle

It's exhilarating to know that I'm pushing the frontier of human achievement by an athletic technique I personally developed. I know I should try to be more humble, but I'm really very buoyant because I feel so doggone good.

The young rabbi's energy and eloquence helped boost Emanu-El's membership to an all-time high of approximately 1,600 households in the late 1980s. The congregation was practically a small city, and ministering to so many people presented unique challenges. In 1977, Emanu-El dedicated a $1.5 million addition to its limestone landmark on Kenwood Boulevard. The annex contained an array of classrooms, offices, music and art rooms, and a library named in honor of Dudley Weinberg. Programmatic changes were just as important. The congregation already had an award-winning educational program for its young people, and adult members received comparable attention. The synagogue staff developed small groups for young singles, senior citizens, college students, converts and—a response to the *havurah* movement—members who attended

monthly services in each other's homes. The intent of the group programs was to infuse a single large congregation with the warmth and intimacy of many smaller ones.

The vast majority of Emanu-El B'ne Jeshurun's members commuted to Kenwood from homes in the North Shore suburbs, particularly Shorewood, Whitefish Bay, Glendale, Fox Point, and Bayside. The distances would prove problematic in the 1990s but, for the time being, the faithful were willing to drive a few miles every weekend. The North Shore was already the home of two Reform congregations, both offspring of Emanu-El. Shalom had built a temple in Fox Point in 1956, with Sinai following in 1962, and they were beneficiaries of the continuing Jewish exodus to the suburbs. Harry Pastor retired as Shalom's senior rabbi in 1980, after twenty-nine years of service that had, in Pastor's words, "made my members my families." His successor was Ronald Shapiro, a former Minnesotan who had come to Shalom as Pastor's assistant in 1978. Shapiro had a warm, welcoming presence and a fondness for the life-cycle rituals—weddings, funerals,

A 1977 addition helped Emanu-El keep pace with its growth in membership.

219

Harry Pastor (left) and Ronald Shapiro are the only two senior rabbis Congregation Shalom has ever known.

The temple's stunning new sanctuary was dedicated in 1992.

circumcisions, confirmations, Bar and Bat Mitzvahs—that his members found particularly meaningful. Shalom's membership more than doubled under Shapiro's leadership, rising from approximately 600 households in 1978 to 1,200 in 2003. Space became a major problem in the late 1980s, when High Holy Day services had to be held in three shifts. Shalom's response was a $3.6 million building project that doubled the size of its temple on Santa Monica Boulevard. Formally dedicated in 1992, the rebuilt synagogue's focal point was a sanctuary constructed in the round and bathed in light from a glorious faceted-glass window that evoked both a menorah and the Tree of Life.

Congregation Sinai, a mile away from Shalom on Port Washington Road, had always prided itself on "intimacy and family feeling"—an emphasis that practically required a relatively small membership. That policy proved hard to maintain in the 1970s and '80s. The initial cap of 300 households was lifted to 350 in 1971, and demand was still so great that by 1989 only "first-degree relatives" of current members were

allowed to join. Membership peaked at about 460 in 2004, but that was enough to require a major remodeling and expansion of the original 1962 synagogue. Much of the growth was due to the quality of Sinai's rabbinical leadership. Jay Brickman spent nearly thirty-five years as the congregation's spiritual guide before moving up to "senior associate" status in 1989. His successor was Terry Bookman, who embodied the younger Reform generation's greater emphasis on ritual. Bookman tried to enlarge the temple's social role as well, working to develop "a sense of community that doesn't exist in our neighborhoods any

more." When he left in 1995 to lead a much larger congregation in Miami, another young rabbi, David Cohen, took charge at Sinai. A New Jersey native and Brandeis graduate who had been inspired by a teenage trip to Israel, Cohen showed a passion for Jewish education both in the classroom and in the pulpit.

Congregation Sinai, too, built a major addition as its roster swelled. Sinai has had only three spiritual leaders since 1955 (l. to r.): Jay Brickman, Terry Bookman, and David Cohen.

Temple Emanu-El of Waukesha was a center of Reform Judaism in the region west of Milwaukee, and its growth under Rabbi Steven Adams was steady.

The Milwaukee area's farthest outpost of Reform Judaism was Temple Emanu-El of Waukesha, sometimes referred to as "little Emanu-El." Although its members could easily have commuted to one of Milwaukee's Reform synagogues, the congregation maintained the keen sense of independence that had been its hallmark since 1939. It may have been smaller than its nearest neighbors, but Emanu-El experienced the same membership growth and physical expansion that typified the entire Reform movement. Its roster swelled from thirty-six households in 1963 to 120 in 2008—many of them interfaith couples—and they were scattered across the metropolitan area's western counties. Space concerns at the Moreland Road temple prompted a major renovation that was completed in 2006 under Rabbi Steven Adams' guidance. Emanu-El was even large enough to spawn a *havurah* in 1992 that continues an independent existence as Or Tikvah—"Light of Hope."

The Milwaukee area's Reform synagogues evolved in place; there was not the slightest geographic movement within the group until the late 1990s. For most Conservative and Orthodox temples, no such stability was possible. As their members relocated to newer homes in newer communities, the congregations were practically forced to follow. One of the sole exceptions was Beth Israel, and that was only because it was already in the suburbs; the Orthodox-turned-Conservative congregation had moved from its landmark building on Teutonia Avenue to Glendale in 1962. After a near-death experience associated with the change of address and affiliation, Beth Israel had made a complete recovery. Swimming against the prevailing Conservative tide, the congregation more than doubled in size, growing from 300 households in 1970 to 750 in the late 1980s. A larger membership enabled (and in fact forced) Beth Israel to finish the third phase of its long-range building program; the temple school had opened in 1962, the social hall followed in 1966, and the sanctuary was finally dedicated in 1980. Much of the growth was due to the leadership of Rabbi Herbert Panitch, who arrived in 1970 from a post in Pennsylvania and spent the next twenty-five years as Beth Israel's spiritual leader. Panitch was, among

Beth Israel finished the final phase of its original building program in 1980 under Rabbi Herbert Panitch, who served the congregation for twenty-five years.

Rabbi Jacob Herber became Beth Israel's spiritual leader in 2003.

other things, a certified family therapist, and he counseled his congregation to "live more Jewishly" in "a spirit of warmth and fellowship." One of his temple's more successful programs was Hebrew Blitz, a series of classes that helped members learn to read liturgical Hebrew in a matter of weeks. Panitch was also a tireless champion of Jewish schools, and Beth Israel's own educational programs were among the best in Milwaukee. When the rabbi retired to Florida in 1995, his successors were Lee Buckman, Paul Kerbel, and then, in 2003, Jacob Herber, a dynamic young leader whose activities have ranged from conducting conversion ceremonies for Jews in Uganda to overseeing an extensive renovation of the sanctuary in Glendale.

Beth Israel also served as the jumping-off point for the community's first Reconstructionist synagogue. (In Milwaukee and elsewhere, Reconstructionists were frequently former Conservatives.) Members of a Beth Israel *havurah* found themselves intrigued with the ideas of Mordecai Kaplan, particularly after a field trip to a Reconstructionist temple in Evanston, Illinois. They decided to affiliate with the movement in 1989 and one year later named their community Shir Hadash—"a new song." Keith Karnofsky, the congregation's first rabbi (who kept his day job as an airline pilot), defined Reconstructionism as "putting old wine in a new bottle." "When you change the bottle," Karnofsky said, "you let some air in, and that's what we're doing with Judaism. We're letting it breathe a little." The experimentation continued with the help of David Brusin, who followed Karnofsky as Shir Hadash's part-time rabbi in 1993. A member of the Reconstructionist Rabbinical College's very first graduating class, Brusin practiced "radical inclusiveness" and welcomed "the misplaced and displaced" from other movements. Meeting in rented quarters on the North Shore, Shir

Wisconsin Jewish Chronicle

Wisconsin Jewish Chronicle

Shir Hadash added an experimental flavor to the local religious scene. Rabbi David Brusin was among the first graduates of the Reconstructionist Rabbinical College.

Hadash grew from its original twenty-four households in 1990 to more than 100 in 2009.

Meanwhile, back in Sherman Park, the former heart of Jewish Milwaukee was beating more slowly every year. The West Side still had the city's highest concentration of synagogues in 1967—two Conservative and four Orthodox—but their days seemed numbered. Long-established Jewish families were leaving the neighborhood in droves, and they were doing so for the same reasons that had brought their parents and grandparents to Sherman Park in the first place: upward mobility, a desire for more room, and basic white flight. The original Jewish ghetto in the Haymarket district had long since become an African-American ghetto, and black Milwaukeeans were surging west along the same corridor the first Jews had followed.

Milwaukee's Jews were leaving the middle behind geographically as well as

theologically, but the path out of Sherman Park led in two very different directions. Some families, a sizable minority, extended the original corridor to the northwest, buying or building homes in areas of the city that had been cornfields or cow pastures a few years before. Marshall High School, just northwest of Sherman Park, had roughly 350 Jewish students in 1971, and Custer, a mile farther north, enrolled a smaller number. Neither was as densely Jewish as Washington High School had been in its heyday or Nicolet High School was in the 1970s, but both reflected the community's changing geography. McGovern Park, a few blocks north of Custer High School, was the location of choice for the West Side's congregational picnics and softball games. As the flow of residents to the northwest continued, a handful of community institutions followed. The Jewish Convalescent Hospital opened across the street from McGovern Park in 1961, Congregation Beth Jehudah established a short-lived Hebrew school on Eighty-fifth and Capitol in 1963, and Congregation Anshe Emeth built a small Orthodox synagogue nearby on Appleton Avenue at about the same time. (Founded by members of Beth Israel who opposed the older temple's 1957 switch to Conservatism, Anshe Emeth joined the Conservative movement itself before disbanding in the 1980s.)

The largest Jewish institution on the Northwest Side was, and still is, Temple Menorah. A fixture on Center Street since 1953, Menorah's leaders watched as the faithful drifted away to newer parts of town. "The present temple ... will be kept as long as we have people here who can be served," said Rabbi Isaac Lerer in 1977, but the reality, he noted, was that "92 percent of our people no longer live in the present neighborhood." The "traditional" Conservative congregation soon moved to a site on Seventy-Sixth Street north of Brown Deer Road—less than a half-mile from the northern border of Milwaukee County. The location was determined in part by the Kohl family, whose business interests had broadened from grocery stores to real estate development. The Kohls' largest project by far was Northridge, a residential and commercial complex that sprawled across both sides of Seventy-Sixth Street, practically surrounding the Menorah parcel. Confident that the temple would be a nucleus of growth, the Kohls donated the land outright, and the 400-member congregation began work on a $600,000 structure with a 400-seat sanctuary. Menorah dedicated its new synagogue—a relatively unadorned brick building—in 1978. On the temple's front lawn was a twenty-foot wrought iron menorah crafted by one of the community's metalworkers.

Temple Menorah marked the extreme limit of the Jewish presence on Milwaukee's Northwest Side, and it was to some extent an outlier, planted well beyond the nearest concentration of Jewish households. The second path out of Sherman Park, and by far the better-traveled, led across the Milwaukee River to the northeastern corner of Milwaukee County. Upwardly mobile Jews had been moving to the North Shore suburbs since before World War II, most relocating from the East Side but a significant number coming from Sherman Park. The movement became general in the 1970s, and its focus shifted from the close-in suburbs to the metropolitan edge. Seeking

Anshe Emeth was a short-lived Northwest Side congregation.

Temple Menorah, completed in 1978, was a more durable presence on the county's northern edge. Rabbi Isaac Lerer remained at the helm from 1964 until his death in 2009.

ever-greener pastures and ever-larger houses, affluent Jews and Gentiles alike gravitated to the northernmost Milwaukee County suburbs, particularly Fox Point and Bayside, and then crossed the Ozaukee County line into Mequon. Once known for its fertile dairy farms and German Lutheran churches, Mequon saw its population rise from 12,150 in 1970 to 21,823 in 2000 and its median income soar to the top tier of Wisconsin's rankings.

Mequon became a sort of Promised Land for Milwaukee's Jewish families, and it therefore exerted the same pull on their congregations. Beth El Ner Tamid led the exodus. The first and by far the largest of Milwaukee's Conservative synagogues, Beth El had been a West Side mainstay since 1923, but no more. Rabbi Louis Swichkow, interviewed in 1984, recalled his conviction that the future lay elsewhere:

After more than sixty years on the West Side, Beth El Ner Tamid spearheaded the migration to suburban Mequon in 1984.

> *We saw the handwriting on the wall. We were suffering a decline in membership because people were moving from that area into the suburbs. And this was a part of a national trend for U.S. Jews. We began watching the changes of addresses, and we found that for every three families that moved, two went to the northeast suburbs—Fox Point, Bayside, River Hills, Mequon. It was then we determined to buy a site for a new synagogue in an area where our people were moving.*

The new temple's sanctuary was among the largest in the Milwaukee area.

Wisconsin Jewish Chronicle

Wisconsin Jewish Chronicle

Wisconsin Jewish Chronicle

In 1972, Beth El Ner Tamid purchased nine acres on Mequon Road "for long-range planning." It took a full decade to find the right buyer for the landmark stone temple on Sherman Boulevard, but in 1982 Beth El accepted an offer from Parklawn Assembly of God and applied the proceeds to its new home in the suburbs. The $2 million temple was formally dedicated in June 1984. Although budgetary concerns forced the substitution of concrete block for brick, the Mequon synagogue was impressively light and airy, and it provided plenty of room for a congregation that had declined from more than 1,000 households in the early 1960s to roughly 600 at the time of the move.

Louis Swichkow announced his retirement soon after the temple was dedicated, ending a storied forty-eight-year

career at Beth El. His successor was Gideon Goldenholz, a young rabbi moving from a pulpit in Indiana. Proceeding carefully but deliberately, Goldenholz championed a "more user-friendly" liturgy, a more inclusive policy toward women, and a greater emphasis on outreach to intermarried families. "We have evolved to become progressive Conservative," he said in 1999. "We are not extreme. We are in the center, where we can serve the community best." When Goldenholz left to lead a Florida temple in 2006—after twenty-one years at Beth El Ner Tamid—the congregation hired Yitzchak Berman, a young scholar who held the post until 2009.

Beth El was a lonely outpost in Mequon for a few years, but other groups followed once the flag had been planted. The next congregations to arrive were Orthodox, and

Rabbi Gideon Goldenholz led Beth El Ner Tamid for twenty-one years after Louis Swichkow's retirement.

they represented an interesting blend of new and old. In 1982, Rabbi Dovid Rapoport moved to Milwaukee as one of the Lubavitcher rebbe's many *shluchim*, or emissaries. Targeting unaffiliated Jews on the North Shore, he began to hold Sabbath services in the basement of his family's home in Fox Point. Rapoport called his fledgling congregation Chabad of North Shore, using a Lubavitch acronym derived from the first letters of the Hebrew words for wisdom, understanding, and knowledge. When attendance approached 100 on some Saturday mornings, it was clear that Rapoport's basement shul had run out of room. In 1987, Chabad of North Shore purchased a 9.5-acre lot on Mequon Road—a half-mile east of Beth El Ner Tamid—and turned a home on the site into a house of worship. "I was afraid to go so far north," recalled Dovid Rapoport, but an unforeseen ally appeared at just the right moment: Congregation Agudas Achim. The Orthodox shul had anchored the west end of Burleigh Street in Sherman Park since 1954, but it was shrinking fast; there were only fifty members on its rolls in the early 1990s, many of them elderly widows and widowers. Rabbi

Israel Feldman, the Holocaust survivor who had led Agudas Achim since 1949, began to talk with Dovid Rapoport, and the result was a merger. In 1994, the old urban congregation and the new suburban shul joined forces as Agudas Achim Chabad.

The Burleigh Street building was sold to a community funeral home, and in 1996 the newly merged congregation completed a million-dollar synagogue on the Mequon Road property. Its approach was unabashedly traditional. "Agudas Achim Chabad," wrote the congregation's leaders in 2001, "is reminiscent of the way synagogue life used to be," which meant, in true Lubavitch fashion, an emphasis on the ancient commandments. Some congregations used membership figures or weekly attendance as yardsticks of progress, but Agudas Achim Chabad applied a different set of standards. The achievements highlighted in its report for the year 2000 included 23 men wearing tefillin every day, 40 families using the mikvah (ritual bath) regularly, 6 newly koshered kitchens, 8 large menorahs displayed, and 190 mezuzahs installed. Although its formal membership was never very large—175 households in 2008—the congregation's outreach programs touched a significant multiple of that number. In 2005, Agudas Achim Chabad became part of the much larger Peltz Center for Jewish Life on the Mequon Road site. Anchored by the synagogue, the Peltz Center was a full-service complex that included a Jewish preschool, a Hebrew school, an adult education institute, senior citizen programs, and a teen center—nearly all run by members of the Rapoport family. "We're more than just a shul," said Rabbi Menachem Rapoport, one of Dovid's sons. "We're really a continuum of Jewish services for the community at large."

Rabbi Dovid Rapoport, an emissary of the Lubavitcher rebbe, began to lead services in his Fox Point home in 1982.

John Gurda

As Agudas Achim merged into Chabad of North Shore, the old congregation's nearest neighbor on Burleigh Street was considering a move in the same direction. Anshai Lebowitz, a fixture at Fifty-second Street since 1953, had remained a sizable community—250 households in 1975—in large part because of Rabbi Bernard Reichman's welcoming presence. A fourth-generation Israeli whose great-grandfather had been the chief rabbi of Tiberias, Reichman had taken the pulpit at Anshai Lebowitz in 1965. "My goal," he said, "is to give people a warm feeling … that this is their home, this house of G-d. They should feel warmth, fulfillment and joy—these are all the things that make up a congregation." Although Anshai Lebowitz attracted its share of younger members who had developed a taste for tradition, very few of them lived in Sherman Park—or wanted to. The congregation began to discuss a move in the mid-1970s, but it was not until 1998, after various merger and partnership proposals had fallen through, that the congregation bought a former church on Mequon Road—squarely between the two earlier synagogues—and remodeled it to Jewish specifications. Anshai Lebowitz never regained the membership levels it had experienced in Sherman Park, but the shul played a distinctive role on Mequon Road. "In terms of where we stand on the spectrum," said congregation president Joel Guthmann in 2003, "Agudas Achim Chabad is to the east of us and Beth El is to the west. We're in the middle of those in our practice also."

One more congregation made the trek to Mequon Road. The Reconstructionists of Shir Hadash, after renting space in Mequon's Unitarian Church North for several years, moved into the lower level of Beth El Ner Tamid in 1999—a statement of religious pluralism that many found encouraging. When Shir Hadash became Beth El's tenant, the geographic transformation of Milwaukee's Jewish community seemed complete. There had been a "synagogue row" in the city ever since the early 1900s—first on Cherry Street in the Haymarket

After merging with Agudas Achim—one of the original Sherman Park shuls—Chabad of North Shore blossomed into the Peltz Center for Jewish Life on Mequon Road.

John Gurda

Led by Rabbi Bernard Reichman, Anshai Lebowitz left Sherman Park for a ranch-style synagogue that looked right at home in suburban Mequon.

neighborhood, then on N. Eleventh Street, and finally on Burleigh Street in Sherman Park. The progression had been gradual and its direction predictable for decades, but not so its latest incarnation. Between 1984 and 1999, Mequon Road became the Milwaukee area's new "synagogue row." The cluster was ten miles removed from the community's historic centers and light-years away from their social milieu. Its key quality was a diversity of expression that mirrored the larger Jewish faith. On a single Sabbath, a synagogue-hopper could experience liturgical dance at Shir Hadash, an old-fashioned kiddush table after worship at Beth El, a middle-of-the-road service at Anshai Lebowitz, and the holy hubbub of Orthodox davening (praying) at Agudas Achim Chabad. Within the same half-mile, four congregations offered a generous sampling of American Judaism as it existed in the early twenty-first century.

There wasn't room for every Milwaukee synagogue on Mequon Road, of course, but the pull to the northeast suburbs remained exceptionally strong—so strong, in fact,

that it nearly pulled one congregation apart. The Sherman Park shuls had made the jump across town with relatively little discord. It was somewhat ironic that the congregation whose members suffered the most from a move was the largest and in many ways the strongest in the state: Emanu-El B'ne Jeshurun. In 1956, aware that its center of gravity was shifting from the city to the suburbs, the local mainstay of Reform Judaism had purchased land in Fox Point. Many assumed that a move was inevitable, but in the early 1970s the congregation decided to stay on Kenwood Boulevard and build an addition instead. Rabbi Dudley Weinberg described the vote as a declaration of principle:

> *Emanu-El B'ne Jeshurun has always been an urban congregation with urban concerns. I was proud that an overwhelming percentage of our membership was willing to continue to maintain the presence of Reform Judaism in the city even at the price of some inconvenience.*

Although principle was involved, there was a more practical concern: Congregation Sinai had built its synagogue just up the road from Emanu-El's property in Fox Point.

Barry Silberg, who succeeded Weinberg as senior rabbi in 1976, declared that the congregation would stay on Kenwood "unless physical blight or crime in the streets makes the neighborhood unlivable." That decision was revisited as the northerly drift of the membership continued. In 1990, Emanu-El announced plans for a "twin campus," with the "flagship" temple remaining at anchor on the East Side and an "auxiliary facility" launched in one of the northern suburbs. After a three-year search, the congregation bought a ten-acre parcel—a former Nike anti-aircraft missile site—on Brown Deer Road in River Hills. "The River Hills campus will add to, not replace the space and activities of our Kenwood campus," the trustees promised in a letter sent to all 1,500 members, but they also mentioned the possibility of "a full-sized synagogue, if the need should arise." In 1993, Emanu-El presented River Hills zoning officials with plans for classrooms, offices, social space, and a 500-seat sanctuary. Barry Silberg stressed that his members wanted nothing more than "a satellite facility" on Brown Deer Road. "The congregation on Kenwood Boulevard is not leaving as long as I'm in Milwaukee," he said. "As long as that magnificent facility on Kenwood Boulevard is there, I doubt we'll ever have High Holiday services here."

Although the proposed facilities were relatively modest, River Hills did not exactly roll out the red carpet. The village was an extremely affluent enclave built around a historic country club, and many of its citizens resisted non-residential development of any kind. In a scene replayed with frustrating frequency in the post-1967 period, a Jewish institution locked horns with a municipality over land-use issues. The round of rejections, revisions, and recriminations lasted well over a year in Emanu-El's case. River Hills tried at one point to impose some rather novel conditions, including a ban on outdoor weddings except in winter and a stipulation that the congregation could not sell its temple on Kenwood without prior village approval. Those machinations prompted a lawsuit, and it was not until the autumn of 1994 that the issues were settled and construction could begin.

The drama was not over yet. When building costs exceeded the original estimates, Emanu-El decided to shelve its plans for a satellite synagogue and build instead a simpler "family worship and learning center" on Brown Deer Road. The colonial-style facility, featuring a combined chapel and social hall with space for 250 people, was dedicated in 1997, and for a time the center was used in tandem with the Kenwood temple. It was soon apparent that duplicate operating costs, mounting budget deficits, and the somewhat schizoid nature of the arrangement made a "twin campus" unworkable in practice. When the University of Wisconsin-Milwaukee, a dominant presence on the other side of Kenwood Boulevard for more than forty years, offered to buy the old temple in 1998, a majority of Emanu-El's members agreed to sell. A vocal minority, however, remained passionately attached to the East Side landmark. They sued their fellow congregants to stop the sale, and a vigorous round of protests and petitions generated a great deal of unwelcome publicity. The dissidents failed to derail the train. The Kenwood temple became UWM's Zelazo

After a tempest that nearly sundered the congregation, members of Emanu-El B'ne Jeshurun carried their Torah scrolls from Kenwood Boulevard to a colonial-style synagogue in River Hills.

Wisconsin Jewish Chronicle

Wisconsin Jewish Chronicle

Center for the Performing Arts in 2001, and the congregation gradually settled into its new home in River Hills—but not before membership had dropped from a historic high of more than 1,500 households in the 1980s to roughly 600 in 2003.

Barry Silberg retired in 1999 after a quarter-century at Emanu-El. His successor was Marc Berkson, an energetic Chicagoan who had previously led a temple in Skokie. "I wanted to come to Emanu-El B'ne Jeshurun," Berkson said, "because

it was an historic congregation that had encountered difficult times. It presented an opportunity to build a new kind of Reform Judaism." That meant, among other things, a more participatory approach to worship and innovations like Torah-palooza, a periodic Sabbath celebration that features joyful music from a full band. The congregation also moved forward under Berkson with long-standing plans to enlarge the River Hills facility. Emanu-El B'ne Jeshurun completed the project in 2009 and, with its physical needs met, resumed the harder work of rebuilding its membership and reaffirming its place as the historic heart of Reform Judaism in Milwaukee.

When Emanu-El moved to River Hills in 1999, Milwaukee's East Side was not left without a Jewish presence. The ongoing resurgence of Orthodoxy was felt in the very heart of the university district, and it was the Lubavitch movement that planted the seed. Milwaukee's first Lubavitchers were two Brooklyn rabbis, David Rimler and Abraham Stone, who visited the city in 1964. "We want to awaken a Jewish spark which may be dormant," Stone told a reporter. One of the pair's favorite strategies was to make the rounds of downtown office buildings, comb the lobby directories for Jewish-sounding names, and then drop in on their prospects unannounced. "Sometimes there is an unfriendly attitude at first," Stone admitted, "but most people try to cooperate after they hear what we say." The cold-calling continued under Rabbi Yisrael Shmotkin, who became Milwaukee's first full-time Lubavitch emissary in 1968. A native of Tel Aviv who spoke very little English when he arrived, Shmotkin began in Sherman Park, naturally, working with the neighborhood's Orthodox shuls, particularly Anshe Sfard.

The movement's emphasis on youth led him to the East Side in 1971. The rabbi and his allies opened their first outreach center in a house on Summit Avenue, and two years later, in a convincing demonstration of their growing financial support in the community, bought a thirty-room stone mansion on the busy corner of Lake Drive and Kenwood Boulevard. "To go to the East Side was like going to the Forbidden City," Shmotkin recalled years later. "It was like another country." But the East Side was where the young people congregated, including young Jews, and Lubavitch House, located five blocks east of the UW-Milwaukee campus, reached out to them with classes, counseling, and live-in weekend experiences called Shabbatons. "Those kids are looking for Jewish identity," Shmotkin said in 1974. "They know they are aimless…. What we do is, we give them a chance to *experience* Judaism, show its beauty and explain its depth." The outreach effort was broadened over the years to include a variety of family programs, but the emphasis was always the same: to lead Jews, mitzvah by

Rabbi Marc Berkson brought a fresh perspective to Emanu-El B'ne Jeshurun in 1999.

Rabbi Yisrael Shmotkin came to Milwaukee as a Lubavitch emissary in 1968 and established Lubavitch house in a Lake Dr. mansion just five years later.

mitzvah, toward a personal commitment to their religious traditions. Lubavitch House itself was a highly visible reminder of the ancient commandments. From the front-yard menorah illuminated each Chanukah to the king-sized backyard sukkah (open-roofed shelter) erected for the Sukkot festival each fall, the house was a beacon of observance to the larger Jewish world.

A different expression of Orthodoxy emerged a few blocks west. In 1982, a group of younger East Side families, including some who had been introduced (or re-introduced) to traditional Judaism at Lubavitch House, began to meet for worship in each other's homes. By mid-1983, the group had jelled sufficiently to form a brand-new congregation—Lake Park Synagogue—and to convert an old boarding house on Hampshire Street into a worship space. Located literally across the street from UW-Milwaukee, Lake Park Synagogue attracted a core group of highly educated professionals with a thirst for tradition. More joined the congregation after it moved into a fine old home just down the block in 1987. "There seems to be a trend afoot," said Jerry

Benjamin, one of Lake Park's early leaders. "Many couples want … to make Judaism their life—even couples who come from Reform or Conservative Jewish backgrounds." The synagogue offered a periodic "beginner's service" to ease that group's transition to Orthodoxy—"an anxiety-free, no-Hebrew-necessary prayer experience" that included traditional readings and songs in English. Worshiping with part-time rabbis for fifteen years, the faithful of Lake Park learned to rely on each other. David Fine became their first full-time spiritual leader in 1998 and Shlomo Levin followed in 2003, but the group had already come to resemble an extended family—one with a viewpoint all its own. "We're an Orthodox congregation of educated people that live in the day-to-day world," said Rena Waxman, the shul's president in 1998. The fact that a woman could serve as president set the community apart. Lake Park Synagogue became a stronghold of Modern Orthodoxy, a centrist movement rooted in Jewish law but more at ease with secular society than some of its close theological cousins.

Lake Park Synagogue and Lubavitch House represented two distinctly different faces of Orthodoxy in the same East Side neighborhood. A similar pairing developed a few miles north, and it reflected both the continuing Orthodox revival and the ongoing Jewish exodus to the suburbs. In 1985, shortly after the Lake Parkers got organized, a group of Glendale families, most of them Beth Israel members with children at Hillel Academy, began to gather for home worship on the Sabbath. Within a year, they had formed Kehillat Torah ("community of the Torah"), hired a rabbi (Nachman Levine, a popular Hillel teacher), and moved into

Lake Park Synagogue, a Modern Orthodox congregation organized in 1982, converted this former governor's residence on Hackett Ave. into an attractive house of worship.

Jewish Museum Milwaukee

the lower level of a small office building at the corner of Green Bay Avenue and Green Tree Road. Like Lake Park Synagogue, Kehillat Torah declared itself a Modern Orthodox community, which Nachman Levine described as "living in modern society within the halachic [Jewish legal] framework." The Glendale group's membership quickly rose to forty families—too many for the rented quarters on Green Tree—but building a genuine synagogue seemed well beyond their financial reach.

The solution to the community's problem materialized in Sherman Park. Anshe Sfard had been one of the old neighborhood's larger synagogues since moving to Keefe Avenue in 1958, and its rabbi, David Shapiro, enjoyed a national reputation for the depth of his Talmudic scholarship and his general intellectual acumen. No less a figure than Abraham Joshua Heschel called Shapiro "one of the half-dozen creative spirits of our time." Since taking Anshe Sfard's pulpit in 1948, the rabbi had seen his members move out and his neighborhood change, but Shapiro predicted in 1978 that Sherman Park "will remain a viable community for the next few years." What gave him hope in the short term was "an increase in young couples who want to lead a richer Jewish life and have a more intensive understanding of their Judaism." Those couples, however, were never an overwhelming presence, and their numbers diminished after Shapiro suffered a disabling stroke in 1983. Without their beloved rabbi actively at the helm, Anshe Sfard's membership plummeted from 265 households in 1983 to just 35 in 1989. Kehillat Torah, in the meantime, was moving in the opposite direction, and a merger became the obvious solution to both groups'

difficulties. In 1990, a new congregation was born: Anshe Sfard Kehillat Torah, soon generally known as ASKT. One year later, with an important financial boost from its Anshe Sfard contingent, the congregation completed a pleasantly understated synagogue on Green Bay Avenue, just down the road from its original Glendale home. As Anshe Sfard died into Kehillat Torah and Agudas Achim faded into Chabad of North Shore, two historic Sherman Park congregations disappeared, but their names lived on in the suburbs.

Teacher Nachman Levine (left) and scholar David Shapiro served two congregations that merged in 1990 as Anshe Sfard Kehillat Torah.

"ASKT," the area's second Modern Orthodox community, built a new shul in suburban Glendale in 1991.

Two miles north of ASKT, a second new synagogue completed the Modern Orthodox/Lubavitch pairing in the northeastern corner of the county. Shmaya Shmotkin, Yisrael's son, moved to Bayside in 1999 and made his home a northern satellite of his father's Lubavitch House. "We went to the North Shore because that's where the bulk of the kids live," said the young rabbi. "We want to be part of their neighborhood." Shmaya Shmotkin's Sabbath services were soon attracting a much broader age group than he had anticipated. Participants expressed a desire to form a permanent congregation, and so The Shul was born. In 2001, its members rented a pair of adjoining storefronts in Audubon Court, a shopping center on the Fox Point-Bayside border, and continued to grow. Plans for a free-standing synagogue a few blocks east of Audubon Court were postponed for financial reasons, but The Shul remained another busy outpost of traditional Judaism in the northern suburbs. A sister congregation had formed at Lubavitch House, and it was called, appropriately, The Shul East.

The broad geographic trends that emerged after 1967 were unmistakable. One by one, Milwaukee's older congregations moved to the northern reaches of the county or, in the case of Mequon's "synagogue row," some distance beyond. There they shared the Jewish religious landscape with newer congregations whose members had chosen to leave the city behind. Affiliation didn't matter; Reform, Conservative, Orthodox, and Reconstructionist communities all put down roots on the suburban edge. There was still a Jewish presence on the East Side, but by 1999 every synagogue in the metropolitan area was located east of the Milwaukee River or near the county's northern border—every synagogue but one. The sole exception, and in some ways the most exceptional community, was Beth Jehudah. Michel Twerski, who had become his father's assistant in 1961 and formal successor in 1973, faced the same pressures that confronted every other Sherman Park rabbi: an aging membership, too many empty seats each Sabbath, and a feeling that the neighborhood's days as a Jewish enclave were numbered. Twerski alone resolved to fight the prevailing trends and to build, if he could, a new community on the foundation of the old. Looking back in 1996, he recalled Beth Jehudah's challenge simply: "In order to survive, we had to introduce tradition to a new generation." In the late 1960s, Michel Twerski and his wife, Feige, a Brooklyn rabbi's daughter, began to host small groups of young couples—many of whom knew Orthodoxy only as the antique faith of their grandparents—for wide-ranging explorations of what Torah Judaism might mean in their lives. The Twerskis found a remarkably receptive audience. Their Orthodox Perspectives groups tapped a deep vein of discontent with both mainstream Judaism and the general drift of American society. The sessions also showed the way to a consistent, coherent world view that most participants had been unable to find elsewhere, either in their home congregations or in the grab-bag of countercultural alternatives. "These kids were never exposed to their roots," said Feige Twerski in 1976. "Their soul is looking for them." The charisma and human concern of the Twerskis—and the power of their message—helped turn a number of couples into what might be described as late-onset Orthodox Jews. These *ba'alei teshuva* decided that the only real alternative to drowning in the American mainstream was total immersion in the Torah world, and they proceeded to fashion lives so complete that there was virtually no room left for the distractions of secular culture.

What that meant, for many, was a move to Sherman Park; as old-timers left the neighborhood, the newly observant filed in behind them. They gravitated to the blocks north of Burleigh Street between Forty-eighth and Fifty-sixth Streets, in part because the Twerskis were there but also because the area had a particularly rich assortment of fine brick and stone homes from the 1920s and '30s, all selling for a fraction of what they would have cost in the suburbs. Beth Jehudah's faithful formed a highly visible enclave in a neighborhood that was changing both racially and economically. Just the faintest hint of Brooklyn's Williamsburg neighborhood was apparent on Burleigh Street, as bearded men wearing yarmulkes shared the sidewalk with young African-Americans listening to rap music and the Kosher Meat Club occupied a storefront next to Safee's African Hair Braiding. On Sabbath evenings, Sherman Park was a walking neighborhood once again, and during the autumn festival of Sukkot, as many as 150 backyard huts provided plenty of opportunities for "sukkah-hopping." Although the Orthodox became a distinct subgroup within the community, they were by no means completely isolated; members of Beth Jehudah took part in Sherman Park's crime watch efforts, interfaith programs, and economic development initiatives. Howard Karsh, an activist who played multiple

leadership roles in both the neighborhood and the congregation, explained the relationship between them in 1996:

> *This is an urban integrated community—nurturing, involved, a good place for kids. Part of our faith is a belief in working within the community to make it strong and safe, not just to meet our personal needs.*

Sherman Park's *ba'alei teshuva* were not particularly numerous—a few dozen families formed the original core—but they lowered Beth Jehudah's average age from about sixty-five in the 1960s to just over thirty in the 1980s. They also gave the congregation a vitality, both social and spiritual, that had been lacking in earlier years. Beth Jehudah became a rising star in the American Orthodox firmament, and Michel and Feige Twerski were much in demand as leaders of Sabbath seminars across the country. Before long, however, the Sherman Park experiment threatened to become a victim of its own success. As their commitment to Orthodoxy deepened, a number of families left for places where they could live even more Jewishly—some to Israel and others to North American cities with more abundant religious resources. By 1988, Michel Twerski recalled, "we were exporting more families than we were able to bring in.... Unless we ourselves could become a full-service Orthodox community, we would suffer the same fate as the Marinettes and Appletons."

The idea of fading away like once-proud Jewish communities in Wisconsin's smaller cities was unthinkable. "I called the remnant together, roughly thirty-five families,"

Rabbi and Rebbitzen Michel and Feige Twerski led "Orthodox Perspectives" discussion groups that ultimately revitalized the Beth Jehudah congregation founded by Twerski's father.

The scholars of the Milwaukee Kollel helped Beth Jehudah members and other adults grow in their Jewish faith. Rabbi Benzion Twerski (below), Michel's son and heir apparent, was a charter Kollel member.

Twerski told a reporter. "I said, 'You know what, folks? I have an aversion to presiding over a moribund community. It's very frustrating not to be able to build.'" And so build they did. In 1989, with funds raised both locally and through the Twerskis' national network, Beth Jehudah members established Yeshiva Elementary School (YES)—an institution described more fully in the following section. The school's location was familiar. As Sherman Park's sole Jewish survivor, Beth Jehudah was able to put the buildings of its former neighbors to new uses; when Anshe Sfard prepared to merge into Kehillat Torah of Glendale in 1989, YES purchased its former shul on Fifty-first and Keefe. In the same year and in the same

building, Twerski's group launched the Milwaukee Kollel, a community of scholars who helped local adults grow in their knowledge of Judaism. The young married rabbis of the Kollel studied during the day and offered informal classes at night, including Become a Seder Maven, Doing Purim and Pesach Right, Beginners Talmud, and Keep One Step Ahead of Your Kids—the last designed for parents whose children were learning Jewish traditions at YES. One of the Milwaukee Kollel's first members was Benzion Twerski, Michel and Feige's son, who was twenty-three at the time. The younger Twerski stayed in Milwaukee to become his father's assistant and heir apparent.

Yeshiva Elementary School and the Milwaukee Kollel were two key initiatives that enabled Beth Jehudah to become, in Michel Twerski's words, "a player in the Orthodox world." As its institutional base broadened, the next step was to grow the critical mass of congregants who used (and supported) those institutions. In 1995, Beth Jehudah launched its "Thinking Milwaukee" campaign. Ads appearing in national Orthodox publications trumpeted Milwaukee's "Big City Yiddishkeit—Small Town Warmth" and invited readers to visit "the family-centered community which is centered around the dynamic leadership of Rabbi Michel and Rebbitzen Feige Twerski." Those who responded were hosted by

Beth Jehudah was the first Orthodox congregation to move to the West Side and the only one to stay.

Beth Jehudah families, introduced to real estate agents, and even provided with job leads. The result was a small but steady stream of recruits from places like Denver, New York, and Toronto as well as Milwaukee and its suburbs. Within a few years, the congregation's 100-plus families needed a new home, and once again recycling provided the answer. When Anshai Lebowitz moved to Mequon Road in 1998, Beth Jehudah bought its shul on Fifty-second and Burleigh and invested $650,000 in a thorough remodeling. The result was a more attractive and more commodious building closer to the heart of Sherman Park's Orthodox population. In a clear sign of the neighborhood's cultural transition, Beth Jehudah's old synagogue on Center Street became an African-American preschool facility.

Sherman Park became a walking neighborhood again during the weekly Sabbath observance.

Opening schools and remodeling shuls required enormous amounts of time and money, but those activities advanced the goal that had been Beth Jehudah's reason for being from the start: building community. Although the world of evening prayers, kosher kitchens, and arranged marriages was clearly not for everyone, the congregation became what Michel Twerski called "an anchor in a storm" that enabled its members to weather the "spiritual holocaust" going on elsewhere in America. Twerski described Beth Jehudah more than once as a place where "we share our sorrows and multiply our joys," and his wife defined the shul as "one large extended family." Within and beyond their community-building efforts was an even broader purpose, one that went to the heart of the Jewish experience after 1967. The overarching goal, said Michel Twerski, was to transform every person in the community "from being a Jewish American to being an American Jew."

Conflict, Cooperation, and Curriculum

The Jewish religious scene, like the American religious scene as a whole, had always been fluid, but it was especially so after 1967. The nation's synagogues and the movements they represented were highly reflective mirrors of ferment in the larger society, and perhaps the clearest pattern that emerged, in Milwaukee and elsewhere, was a pronounced shift in identification. As the middle ground proved harder to hold, the number of Milwaukee Jews who described themselves as Conservative in community surveys dropped from 49 percent of the total in 1964 to 24 percent in

2000, while the Reform bloc swelled from 24 percent to 56 percent. The two movements were obviously headed in opposite directions. During the same thirty-six-year period, Reconstructionists grew from nothing to just over 1 percent of Milwaukee's Jewish population, and Orthodox identification slipped from 22 percent to 4 percent. The local statistics revealed a city more Reform and less Orthodox than the nation as a whole.

Why such a steep decline in Orthodox identification? Because the immigrant generation, Orthodox from birth, had largely died out by 2000, and the *ba'alei teshuva* who succeeded them were a relatively small group by comparison. But the resurgent Orthodox, from the aggressive Lubavitchers to the more inward-looking neighborhood shuls, had a significance that went beyond mere numbers. Their outreach efforts, particularly the full-bore mitzvah campaigns of the Lubavitch movement, reached thousands who never formally affiliated with a shul, and there was the larger dynamic of witness. The Orthodox faithful, including the close-knit community that developed around the Twerski family, represented Judaism in its original form; they stood publicly for a faith unchanged, and unabashedly so, for thousands of years. Less-observant Jews felt a connection to "Torah-true" Judaism through the Orthodox that was sometimes direct but more often vicarious. As long as the Lubavitchers and the Twerskis and their allies kept the faith, tradition was safe; the true believers preserved a religion that would surely withstand the onslaught of the secular world. The space the Orthodox occupied in the spiritual geography of

Jewish Milwaukee was therefore larger than their physical footprint, and so was their support among the community's financial elite.

As the relative strength of the various movements changed, so did the relationships between them. A certain hardening of viewpoints created abundant opportunities for conflict, and it was easy to find evidence of a new cultural chasm in Milwaukee. When the Jewish Community Center organized an inter-synagogue softball league in 1993, Emanu-El B'ne Jeshurun fielded a coed team and Beth Jehudah put only men on the diamond. Because Orthodox law prohibits men from competing against women and Emanu-El refused to bench its females, Jehudah forfeited its games with the Reform team. The JCC forestalled further conflict by organizing one league for men and a second for mixed teams. Other disputes were not so easily settled. In 1975, Barry Silberg of Emanu-El criticized Orthodox Jews for keeping their women "powerless." "I don't like the repression of women," the rabbi declared, which brought stinging rebukes from his Orthodox colleagues. The Union of Orthodox Rabbis, a particularly strident national group, returned the favor in 1997, dismissing Reform and Conservative Judaism as "erroneous" movements whose continued existence amounted to "a deception of innocent Jews." When the Milwaukee press picked up the story, Orthodox leaders were dismayed. "I saw years and years of work of trying to build up a sense of respect in the community going down the drain," said Michel Twerski. He was one of twenty-two local Orthodox rabbis who denounced the statement and publicly affirmed that

"a Jew is a Jew, period." There were also thorny issues of civil liberties. The Milwaukee Jewish Council for Community Relations was a staunch advocate for the separation of church and state, even on matters that were largely symbolic. When Lubavitchers persuaded the governor to light a menorah on the state capitol grounds each Chanukah, the Jewish Council spoke out vigorously against the idea, and its board was just as opposed when the Orthodox tried to secure public educational funding for their schools.

An inter-synagogue softball league became a source of contention rather than recreation.

Rabbi Michel Twerski ably presented the Orthodox perspective on issues facing the Jewish community.

241

There was more general discord over the issue of intermarriage. The Wisconsin Council of Rabbis, an umbrella group that had functioned smoothly for years, nearly came asunder in the 1980s, after one of its Reform members expressed a willingness to officiate at ceremonies uniting a Jew with a non-Jew. When disagreement continued over patrilineal descent and kosher dietary standards, the Wisconsin Council decided to abandon its policy-making role and concentrate, where possible, on networking and mutual support. In Milwaukee and elsewhere, theological disputes sometimes reached the point at which true believers considered each other either heretics or fanatics. "We're one people," said Marc Angel, a national Orthodox leader, in 1995, "but we've moved into a state where we're like different religions." Angel warned that, within a generation, the challenge would not be intermarriage so much as intramarriage. Those who took a longer view of history argued that dissension within the fold was an integral part of the Jewish experience, a pattern that had been in place ever since the Pharisees squared off with the Sadducees 2,000 years ago.

Although direct confrontations occurred frequently enough, they were probably less important than what might be described as firmly held differences of opinion. Members of the major movements occupied different religious spaces, and variations in the terrain of Judaism stood out more boldly than ever after 1967. For the fervently Orthodox, the possibilities for compromise were few; either the Torah was God's word—true to the last of its 613 commandments—or it was not. David Shapiro, the acknowledged dean of Milwaukee's rabbis, was anything but confrontational, but he felt the need to draw some lines in a 1978 interview:

While I regard Reform and Conservative Judaism as incomplete and more in the character of preparatory schools for total involvement in Judaism and complete fulfillment in Judaism, nevertheless, we have to recognize the value of each of these schools in retaining for Judaism the people who would be totally lost. Each of these movements is serving a purpose. It is incumbent on the Reform movement to recognize their incompleteness and to be aware of themselves as merely a stage in helping people obtain a fuller Jewish life, in study, prayer and practice.

Needless to say, few Reform Jews acknowledged their "incompleteness." Most of them found ample room for interpretation in the Torah, and they tended to view the Orthodox as terminally inflexible, thralls to a document that was divinely inspired but humanly constructed. Lubavitchers and West Siders were often lumped together as museum specimens whose men sported outlandish hats, whose women wore long skirts and long sleeves, and all of whom bore distinctly non-American names. You might find Batya and Yaffa, Shlomo and Tsvi at an Orthodox gathering, but rarely Emma or Susan, Steve or Pete.

The cultural gap was particularly ironic, and occasionally poignant, when the children of Reform or Conservative parents joined the Orthodox fold. In the 1920s, many American-born Jews had begun to abandon what they viewed as the Old World practices of their immigrant parents—a falling-away that created no end of family heartache and triggered sweeping congregational change. When the children of those assimilated Jews grew up, some embraced the very practices their parents had jettisoned in their youth. The *ba'alei teshuva* found themselves grappling with some novel questions, particularly if children were involved. Can Grandma take the kids out for ice cream? Does Grandpa have to wear a yarmulke when he visits? Is it impolite to bring your own kosher food to Thanksgiving dinner? When younger Jews embraced a future based on the past, the older generation often struggled to adjust.

There were intramural tensions as well. Although they read the same Torah and lived by the same laws, the various Orthodox groups were divided by matters of both substance and style. Some in the Torah community viewed the Lubavitch movement's outreach efforts as overly aggressive, while the Lubavitchers considered Beth Jehudah and other Orthodox shuls excessively insular. There were also concerns about the cultic aspect of the Chabad group, including a suspicion that some of its members considered their rebbe, Menachem Schneerson, the Messiah. When a young East Side rabbi flatly declared that Schneerson was God in 1998, his senior Lubavitch colleagues immediately dismissed the claim as "unmitigated idolatry" and "sheer apostasy."

There were parallel cleavages within the Reform fold. The most liberal wing of American Judaism was growing more and more traditional in its practice, but not everyone kept pace. Some felt that the knowledge required for intelligent participation in the Sabbath liturgy was overly specialized, bordering on the arcane. Hebrew was a typical sticking point; learning, even phonetically, a language that was read backward in strange

characters seemed impossibly foreign. Rabbi Jay Brickman of Congregation Sinai welcomed the much-ballyhooed "Jewish renaissance," but he also saw a downside:

> *The problem provoked by greater Jewish consciousness is a growing sense of alienation by those as yet uninvolved. For Jews who don't read Hebrew, don't find traditional ritual appealing or are not comfortable in the structure of Jewish organizations, the temptation to dissociate from the collective is increased.*

Although discord and dissociation were never far below the surface, there was plenty of room for cooperation as well. The city's "Jewish-Jewish" dialogue may not have proceeded entirely without rancor, but Milwaukee generally maintained a civility of discourse that had fled the scene elsewhere in Jewish America. The tradition had begun in the early 1900s with Rabbi Solomon Scheinfeld, a pillar of Orthodoxy who developed close friendships with the city's Reform leaders, and it continued with later lights like Samuel Hirshberg, David Shapiro, and Michel Twerski, all of whom could be cordial, even cooperative, without compromising their core beliefs. The result was a climate of mutual respect that could weather all but the worst storms. Reform, Conservative, and Orthodox rabbis took part in a 1987 symposium on "Who Is a Jew?" without descending to name-calling or fistfights—an exercise that would not even have been attempted in some other communities. Lay leaders were able to bridge the same gaps. The Milwaukee Synagogue Council, organized in 1970, succeeded for a time in uniting officers from all three major movements on issues of mutual interest. Individual congregations developed a strong appetite for joint programming. In 1973, for instance, Beth Israel, Sinai, Shalom, and Emanu-El B'ne Jeshurun formed the North Shore Institute of Adult Jewish Studies as "a meeting place for Jewish intellectuals." More recent collaborative efforts have ranged from Tikkun Ha-Ir ("Heal the City"), which combines social action projects with the study of Jewish texts, to Koach ("Strength"), a senior citizen program co-sponsored by six Reform and Conservative synagogues and the Jewish Community Center.

Tikkun Ha-Ir involved a cross-section of local Jews in its efforts to "heal the city."

One cause that united every religious Jew—and many of their not-so-religious peers—was education. As Jewish survival became a more pressing concern, study after study showed that early and frequent exposure to the ancient traditions was the strongest predictor of a robust ethnic and religious identity. "Individual Jews may be lost," Rabbi David Shapiro warned in 1978. "The only medium that can save them is Jewish education." As more of Shapiro's colleagues felt the same urgency, Milwaukee's Jewish community experienced an educational renaissance. As always, congregational programs were most numerous, but their enrollments declined with the end of the postwar baby boom in 1964, and some religious schools in the aging Sherman Park neighborhood closed altogether. The emphasis shifted to collaborative efforts—programs that

TIKKUN HA-IR

combined the resources of several or all to create more educational opportunities for everyone. No other field offered such rich possibilities for cooperation between the various communities—or a better expression of their diversity.

The renaissance was overseen and to some extent directed by the Board (formerly Bureau) of Jewish Education, an umbrella group that provided both technical assistance and organizational support to its members. In 1968, with backing from the Jewish Welfare Fund (soon to become the Jewish Federation), the Board of Education took over an old country school on four acres of land at Forty-Fifth and Good Hope. Surrounded by the postwar sprawl of Milwaukee's Northwest Side, the building was quickly remodeled to provide space for three organizations: the Board itself; Midrasha, a post-Bar Mitzvah Hebrew program; and Hillel Academy, the largest tenant by far. Established in 1960 by David Shapiro and his supporters at Anshe Sfard, Hillel was Milwaukee's first Jewish day school. It grew so fast in its new home on Good Hope—reaching an enrollment of 140 by 1970—that four trailers had to be hauled in as "classrooms." The student body ranged from kindergarteners to eighth-graders, and their school day was evenly split between Jewish studies and a general curriculum.

In 1974, with interest in Jewish education growing rapidly, all of the programs at 4515 W. Good Hope were relocated to much larger quarters in suburban Glendale. The new building, on Port Washington Road at the Milwaukee River, was a Georgian-style landmark that had originally been the administration building of the Eline chocolate bar plant—a business launched by the Uihlein family when Prohibition practically shuttered their Schlitz brewery. More recent occupants had included a Glendale public school and the Layton School of Art and Design. With a gym, an auditorium, and two floors of classrooms and offices, the facility made an ideal Jewish Educational and Cultural Campus (JECC), and it soon housed an abundance of community programs. The Board of Jewish Education expanded its role as a resource for local educators, opening a creativity center, building a media library, and upgrading its certification programs for Jewish religious school teachers. The Finjan Coffeehouse made its last stand at the JECC before winding down with the rest of the counterculture in 1975. The East Side Hebrew School took up residence in the same year. The Lubavitch movement opened a nursery school in 1977, and Jewish Family and Children's Service followed with a day care center in 1980. The most ambitious newcomer was Milwaukee

The Milwaukee Board of Jewish Education (MBJE) brought a number of programs together in a former chocolate factory in Glendale.

MILWAUKEE JUDAICA HIGH SCHOOL

חיכון

TICHON

TICHON IS SPONSORED BY
THE MILWAUKEE BOARD OF JEWISH EDUCATION
IN COOPERATION WITH CONGREGATIONS

ANSHAI LEBOWITZ   MENORAH
BETH EL NER TAMID   SHALOM
BETH ISRAEL   SINAI
EMANU-EL B'NE JESHURUN

TICHON is a beneficiary of the Milwaukee Jewish Federation.

Jewish Museum Milwaukee

*The Tichon program
gave local teens an
opportunity to further
their Jewish educations.*

Judaica High School, or Tichon, a joint venture launched in 1981 by Anshai Lebowitz, Beth Israel, Emanu-El, Menorah, Shalom, and Sinai—congregations from all three major movements. Tichon ("high school" in Hebrew) offered an intensive after-school program that included language classes, summer sessions in Israel, and seminars that helped students "discover new, personal meanings in their heritage."

The various programs housed at the JECC were made possible in part by increased educational funding from the Milwaukee Jewish Federation. In the 1950s, some lay leaders had viewed Jewish education, particularly on the congregational level, as too parochial to merit financial support; by the 1970s, the Federation considered it so essential that the group agreed to fund Jewish schools of nearly every description. When support was temporarily reduced during an Israeli emergency in 1975, the entire educational establishment protested. Speaking for the majority, Herbert Panitch said, "Jewish education is a world priority equal

perhaps to the needs in Israel." Two or three decades earlier, the rabbi's statement might have been blasted as high treason.

Hillel Academy was easily the largest program headquartered at the Jewish Educational and Cultural Center. The school's enrollment swelled from 174 in 1974 to 240 in 1979—four years after the move to Glendale. That, as it turned out, was Hillel's high point. From 1960 to 1981, Hillel Academy was the only full-time Jewish school in Milwaukee; it had the local educational market to itself. Although its orientation was basically Orthodox, other traditions were always welcome; the 1975 student body was 45 percent Orthodox, 29 percent Conservative, 10 percent Reform, and 16 percent unaffiliated. The academy was trying, in a sense, to be all things to all Jews. As the lines of demarcation across American Judaism were more boldly drawn, that approach caused defections from both ends of the spectrum.

The liberal contingent was the first to break away. In 1981, the Milwaukee Jewish Day School (MJDS) was established by a number of Reform and Conservative families who wanted a broader educational experience for their children. The school's principal founder was Philip Rubenstein, a successful businessman who had emigrated from Russia at the age of seven. Many Reform Jews were sending their kids to public schools, said Rubenstein, "because Hillel Academy was too Orthodox for their own beliefs." Milwaukee, in his view, had "a great need to provide an alternative Jewish school so children would not have to attend public school." MJDS opened with a total of eleven kindergarten students who attended classes in the educational wing of Emanu-El B'ne Jeshurun.

Although it was housed in a Reform temple, MJDS carefully cultivated a "pluralistic" image. It was open to all families who wanted a prep school education in a Jewish context, and by 1990, following a move to a larger facility, enrollment had grown to 350 students from kindergarten through eighth grade.

If Hillel Academy was perceived as "too Jewish" by some families, it was not Jewish enough for others. As described earlier, Beth Jehudah members established Yeshiva Elementary School (YES) in 1989 as part of their larger effort to become "a full-service Orthodox community." The congregation's leaders had observed that many of their young people needed remedial help when they graduated from Hillel Academy to yeshivas in other cities. "We felt compelled," said Rabbi Michel Twerski, "to start our own." YES enrolled sixty-five students in its first year, most of whom transferred from Hillel, and their surroundings in Anshe Sfard's old shul were anything but palatial. The textbooks were Milwaukee Public Schools castoffs, the desks and shelves came from a defunct Catholic school on the South Side, and the lockers were hand-me-downs from the Jewish Community Center. Spirits, however, were high. Growing with the West Side Orthodox community, Yeshiva Elementary School quickly ran out of room. In 1994, when Kramer's Kosher Corner vacated the building next door, YES moved in, reclaiming the old grocery store for its nursery school and primary classes.

Then came School Choice. In 1995, after prolonged debate (and over the objections of the Jewish Council for Community Relations), the Wisconsin legislature expanded its Milwaukee Parental Choice Program to include parochial schools; lower-income

city residents could send their children to virtually any Milwaukee institution of their choice, with the state paying a stipulated amount per student. Legal challenges delayed implementation of the new rule for three years, but YES families began to apply for vouchers in 1998. Within a decade, the proportion who met Wisconsin's income guidelines had grown to nearly 70 percent—a sure sign that Sherman Park's Orthodox community was richer in spiritual

The choices for elementary students ranged from the Milwaukee Jewish Day School to Yeshiva Elementary School, shown during a Purim assembly.

247

Saying "YES" to tradition, Yeshiva Elementary School gives its students a thorough grounding in Jewish life and learning.

blessings than material wealth. School Choice proved to be a godsend for Yeshiva Elementary School, accounting for more than half its operating budget by 2009. The vouchers also provided a stability that helped the school meet the challenges of continued growth. In 2000, when its student body reached the 170 mark, YES announced plans for a $2.8 million expansion of its home on Fifty-First and Keefe. Completed in 2001, the project transformed an old synagogue, a former grocery store, apartments, and a new structure into a single, well-integrated school facility, with amenities like a two-story indoor playground and natural light in every classroom. Rabbi Michel Twerski found the school's progress a validation of his central vision:

> YES is a symbol that the community is robust and in the major leagues Jewishly. It says Milwaukee has a young, vigorous Torah-based present in which observant families can thrive…. I believe YES has raised the standard of Jewish education overall.

By 1990, as YES took its place alongside Hillel and MJDS, Milwaukee had three Jewish elementary day schools, and there was general agreement that the community's young people deserved comparable educational choices on the secondary level—choices that went beyond after-school activities like Tichon. Although they were not as uniformly successful as the elementary programs, several thrusts were made in that direction. In 1984, aware that "yeshivas aren't for everyone," a group of activists founded Milwaukee Jewish Community High School, "an all-day coed high school offering a general studies program" that was integrated with "continuing Jewish education." Max Karl, an early supporter, expressed his hope that the fledgling institution would appeal to "all segments of the Jewish community … for the sake of Jewish survival." The Jewish Community High School opened with seven students in an old Fox Point elementary building, and its organizers projected an enrollment of 100 within a decade. Their estimates proved hopelessly optimistic. Hampered by doctrinal differences, staff turnover, financial struggles, and a general lack of interest, the Jewish Community High School closed its doors in 1991.

A more traditional institution had far greater success. In the late 1970s, when Hillel Academy was still the only game in town, the school's growth inspired some of its supporters to attempt a significantly bolder experiment. Why not, they asked, give Hillel's young people, specifically its males, a Jewish alternative when they graduated, one that offered an even more rigorous grounding in their faith? At the same time, as it happened, the Rabbinical Seminary of

America, an Orthodox institution based in New York City, was developing a network of affiliates across the country. This serendipitous convergence of local and national interests gave rise to the Wisconsin Institute for Torah Study (WITS), which enrolled its first students in 1980. Until a more permanent home could be found, they met in rented classrooms at Henry Clay School in Whitefish Bay. WITS was conceived as a classical yeshiva, rooted in intensive study of the Torah and Talmud, but it had two distinct components: a four-year boarding program for high school boys, who took general courses as well, and a college-level track for young men who focused on the foundational texts of Judaism. Their days were long from the start—religious studies in the morning, general subjects in the afternoon, with more religious work in the evening—but WITS attracted a solid core of scholars and would-be scholars from Milwaukee and far beyond. Enrollment rose to a total of forty in both programs by 1983, and winning full accreditation attracted even more. With major assistance from a national foundation, WITS purchased a mansion on Milwaukee's Lake Drive in 1984 and proceeded to grow. Built in 1913 as the home of lumber baron Henry Thompson, the lakefront property had done service as a Catholic retreat center and an Episcopalian convent before the Jewish institute took over. Located only two blocks north of Lubavitch House, WITS was a major addition to the Orthodox footprint on the East Side.

The Wisconsin Institute for Torah Study became the traditional choice for secondary and post-secondary male students, particularly after WITS moved from rented classrooms to a Lake Dr. mansion in 1984.

249

After weathering stiff resistance from some of its neighbors, WITS completed a sizable addition in 2000.

1996 that went all the way to the Wisconsin Supreme Court. The justices refused to hear it in 1998, finally ending the matter. The flap cost WITS nearly $2 million in extra legal, architectural, and construction costs, but it also rallied support for the school. "There was very significant bonding with very diverse sections of the community," said Rabbi Yehuda Cheplowitz, one of the school's founding heads. "It brought out for many people what the yeshiva stood for and what its purpose was." The addition was dedicated in 2000—minus its gymnasium—and Rabbi Michel Twerski, a staunch WITS supporter, called the school "a crown jewel for the community."

By 1995, enrollment had grown to 120 full-time students from cities across the United States, Canada, and even Israel. That was too many for even the largest Lake Drive mansion to accommodate comfortably, and WITS officials began to make plans for a two-story addition with a gymnasium, more classrooms, and a study hall. They could not have begun to anticipate the firestorm of protest that greeted their proposal. Preservationists objected to any changes that might have altered the historic character of the Lake Drive landmark, but the most vehement opposition came from neighbors, who were apparently uncomfortable with an educational institution in their well-heeled midst. Front yards began to sprout "Preserve" signs, and they stayed in place even after WITS scaled back its plans and moved the proposed addition to the back of the lot, where it was virtually invisible from the street. The revised plans were approved by city officials, but that failed to placate a core of angry neighbors; they filed a lawsuit in

With its specialized program and demanding schedule, the Wisconsin Institute for Torah Studies never attracted more than a relative handful of Milwaukee families; WITS did not put even a minor dent in Nicolet High School's Jewish enrollment. But the institution's growth did demonstrate a demand for Jewish education in its most rigorously traditional form, and it suggested that a similar approach might work for the community's young women. In 1984, when WITS students left their rented rooms in Whitefish Bay for a new home on Lake Drive, the Torah Academy of Milwaukee (TAM) moved in behind them. There were five girls in the first class and, despite the North Shore address, Feige Twerski of Sherman Park was dean of students. "Our religion is very much our lifestyle, a way of life," said Alice Lerman, one of TAM's founders. "In order to lead that way of life, we must know how, and our guideline is the Torah." The first attempt proved unsustainable after a year, but the

John Gurda

idea of a secondary religious school for girls had enough power to merit a second try, particularly after Yeshiva Elementary School emerged as a likely feeder. The Torah Academy of Milwaukee was reborn on the West Side in 1991. The school struggled with enrollment—its entire student body could fit into a Honda Civic in some years—and a desire for growth prompted a move to Glendale in 1996. TAM's leaders hoped to attract North Shore Orthodox families who might have been uncomfortable driving to Sherman Park every day. Enrollment did grow to forty girls in 2007—more than the rented basement on Green Bay and Green Tree could handle—and the board began to make plans for a genuine school building on the other side of the intersection. TAM's new home, faced with Jerusalem limestone and expandable as needed, was ready to receive its first students in 2008.

On both the elementary and the high-school levels, Milwaukee had a range of educational choices that did not exist in cities with much larger Jewish populations. Milwaukee Jewish Day School, the biggest and most liberal of the bunch, described itself as "Milwaukee's only pluralistic and egalitarian day school." Yeshiva Elementary School offered "a more intense immersion in Jewish religious texts."

The Torah Academy of Milwaukee (TAM) offers a "College Bound/Torah Bound" education for the Orthodox community's young women.

Wisconsin Jewish Chronicle

Wisconsin Jewish Chronicle

York-based research and advocacy group, called Milwaukee "one of the outstanding communities in terms of Jewish education." It was nearly as outstanding for the level of cooperation between schools. WITS and TAM were understood to be brother and sister institutions, but MJDS, YES, and Hillel had clearly divergent educational philosophies. Despite their differences, and despite the fact that they regularly competed for the same students, the trio launched the Day Schools Partnership Project in 2000, running joint ads, working together on curriculum improvements, and trying to raise both the professional standards and the pay scales of their teachers. Only in Milwaukee, said some observers.

Education was not solely for the young. Milwaukeeans whose Bar or Bat Mitzvahs were years behind them had plenty of opportunities, both formal and informal, to learn more about their faith and culture. The Jewish Community Center's programs included an annual book fair and a film festival as well as "Jewish U" classes like Judaism 101. The Lubavitchers were always ready to help their fellow Jews grow in observance; their most memorable campaigns included a "Suka Mobile" that traveled to local colleges during the fall festival and a "Mitzvah Tank" (a customized van) whose driver made the rounds of Jewish gatherings and invited men inside to put on tefillin and pray. The Milwaukee Kollel, the "community of scholars" launched by the Beth Jehudah community in 1989, created its own menu of outreach programs. They ranged from "lunch 'n' learn" sessions at local businesses to a

The Milwaukee Kollel moved into its own Sherman Park home in 1999.

Hillel Academy, despite some losses to both of its sister schools, held a place somewhere between the two, teaching "traditional Judaism without imposing Orthodoxy on the individual." True to its name, the Wisconsin Institute for Torah Studies promised "an intensive Torah education in addition to a complete general studies program," and the Torah Academy of Milwaukee advertised itself as "College Bound/Torah Bound." The combined enrollment of MJDS, YES, Hillel, WITS, and TAM approached 800 students in the mid-1990s. That amounted to more than 30 percent of the community's young people, and another 53 percent participated in supplemental programs at their synagogues. Few cities outside the East Coast were able to post such impressive numbers. In 1994, the Council for Initiatives in Jewish Education, a New

slow-motion Saturday-morning service affectionately dubbed "Davening for Dummies." Although the Kollel was rooted in Sherman Park, where it finally secured a building of its own in 1999, the scholar-teachers could not resist the call of the North Shore. "You need to be where the Jewish community is who needs this sort of uplifting education," said Rabbi Akiva Freilich of the Kollel. A Whitefish Bay branch opened in 1997, and it was succeeded in 2008 by a Fox Point learning center called Judaism Without Walls. Freilich himself started Ohr HaTorah (Jewish Heritage Center) in Glendale in 2001, offering a full schedule of classes, seminars, and one-on-one study to anyone who was interested. The point of all this activity was, in the words of Kollel rabbi Michael Stern, to help adult learners "reach their Jewish potential."

There were also opportunities in the realm of higher education. The Wisconsin Society for Jewish Learning (WSJL) celebrated fifty years of outreach and advocacy in 2005. The group's first campaign had been to establish Hebrew chairs at the University of Wisconsin campuses in both Madison and Milwaukee, but WSJL's focus shifted over the years to public programs—lectures, concerts, readings, exhibits, and even television documentaries, including an award-winning production on Wisconsin's smaller Jewish communities. At UW-Milwaukee, the original Hebrew chair evolved by 2007 into a full-fledged Jewish Studies major. The UWM program received a major boost two years later, when the Baye Foundation, a Milwaukee-based philanthropy, announced a $2 million grant to turn a former geology museum on campus into a new home for the Center for Jewish Studies.

The variety of educational opportunities in Milwaukee, from kindergarten through Kollel, demonstrated the breadth of what might be termed the religious marketplace after 1967. The same pattern was apparent in the evolution of Milwaukee's synagogues, whose liturgies ranged from the ancient to the experimental. Each of the three major movements and their various subgroups purveyed its own version of the ancestral faith—in the synagogue, in the classroom, and even on the street—with a firm conviction that the future depended on it. Their institutions thereby embodied the diversity of the Jewish community as a whole, and its capacity to work both together and apart on matters of urgent mutual concern. In developing those institutions, Milwaukee's Jews tested the limits of diversity and, more often than not, found them without rupturing the essential bonds of community.

By the early twenty-first century, the institutions of Jewish Milwaukee were spread throughout the northeastern quadrant of Milwaukee County and into Mequon.

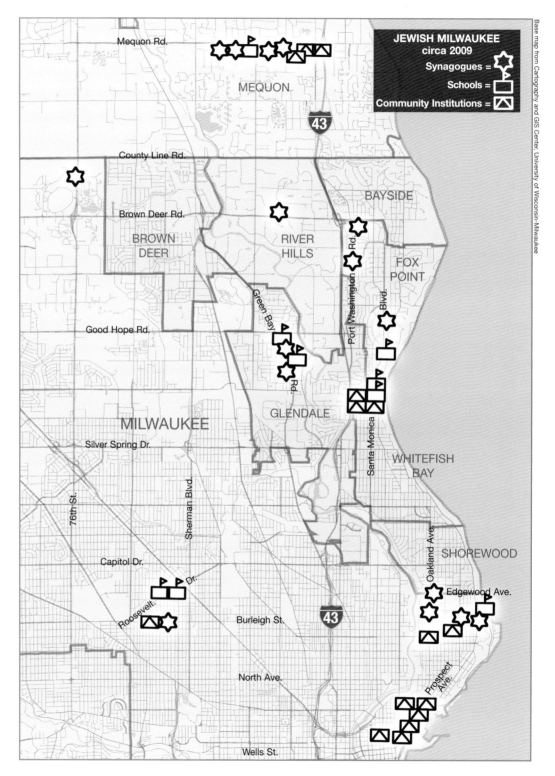

Base map from Cartography and GIS Center, University of Wisconsin-Milwaukee

JEWISH MILWAUKEE
circa 2009
Synagogues =
Schools =
Community Institutions =

Chapter 6
One for All, All for One, 1967-

Most people knew where they belonged. The majority of Milwaukee's Jews—nearly 67 percent in a 1996 survey—identified with one or another of the leading religious movements. The synagogues and schools described in Chapter 5 were, in one respect, their quintessential creations, speaking for them, to them, and through them. From Temple Menorah on the Northwest Side to WITS on Lake Drive, from "synagogue row" in Mequon to the Torah Academy in Glendale, Jewish religious landmarks dotted the Milwaukee landscape as highly public expressions of deeply personal beliefs. Together they formed a towering institutional superstructure with a distinctive blend of buildings, leaders, and programs.

That superstructure had a vibrant life of its own, but the view from the grassroots was significantly less clear. It was obvious, first of all, that identification and participation were not always the same thing. Although two-thirds of Milwaukee Jews called themselves Reform, Conservative, or Orthodox, only 48 percent actually paid dues to a synagogue in 1996, and there was impressive diversity among those who did. In some respects, the various movements are only points on a spectrum, each representing a particular "color" of Judaism within a given wavelength of religious expression. Individual members of a particular congregation might be any shade of purple between blue and red; there are declared agnostics attending Orthodox shuls and kosher-keepers worshiping with the Reform. Between the poles is a vast middle of nominally religious Jews without much appetite for introspection, individuals who are generally content to visit their temples twice or three times a year and leave the theologizing to their rabbis. A 2006 Gallup poll found that fewer than 15 percent of American Jews attended services on a weekly basis. The only groups in the country with lower participation rates were atheists, agnostics, and the unaffiliated.

Beyond the ragged circle of those who practiced, or at least professed, some religious belief was a sizable group who heard the theological conversation, if they heard it at all, as a distant rumble with no particular relevance to them. When asked what form of Judaism they espoused, thousands of individuals described themselves as "just Jewish"—an astounding 34 percent in the 1996 community survey of Milwaukee. These non-observant, frequently non-believing Jews, many of them married to non-Jews, formed no organizations and issued no manifestos, but they considered themselves part of the Jewish continuum just the same. Although they came to synagogue only for weddings and funerals, the "just Jewish" members of the fold felt a strong allegiance to Israel, took the Holocaust personally, gave to Jewish causes, and even sent their kids to Jewish camps. Their presence demonstrated just how big the Jewish tent could be, stretching to take in everyone from the ritually observant to the staunchly irreligious.

There was, therefore, a larger and more permeable Jewish circle than the tighter ring of believers, and Chapter 6 tells that circle's story since 1967. In Milwaukee and elsewhere, the Jewish community was broader than its shuls, more diverse than its schools. An entirely different set of institutions existed to serve the community in its total dimensions—the whole tent and nothing but the tent. Demonstrating the persistence of the ancient spirit of peoplehood, those institutions, most of them voluntary non-profits, addressed concerns that transcended every difference in doctrine, practice, or lack thereof. Their specialties ranged from education to health care, and they formed a second institutional superstructure, one significantly less complicated and more broadly focused than the religious establishment.

One for All: The Jewish Federation

At the top of that superstructure was the Milwaukee Jewish Federation, part of a network of Federations that spanned the nation. Organized in 1902 as the Federated Jewish Charities and reorganized as the Jewish Welfare Fund in 1938, the group adopted its present name in 1970. The change was more than window dressing. It signaled a much-expanded role for the Federation: from a bank account whose funds supported worthy causes to nothing less, in its leaders' minds, than the collective will of the Jewish people. The Federation functioned as a unified umbrella organization committed to serving all segments of the Jewish population. The shift in focus marked the community's growing affluence and increasing sophistication, but the one-for-all approach also reflected the priorities of Melvin Zaret, the former social worker who served as the Federation's head from 1955 to 1984. "I always felt," Zaret said, "that it might be possible to build a model community, ... the kind of community that might be an example for others." At the center of his vision was, of course, the Jewish Federation.

Mel Zaret was convinced that Milwaukee had enormous potential for unity under Federation auspices, and he believed that it should be expressed physically. In the late 1960s, with vital assistance from Ollie Adelman, his board president, Zaret began to contemplate a building that would serve as "the

As the Jewish Federation broadened its mandate after 1967, three individuals played key roles (l. to r.): Melvin Zaret as director, Ollie Adelman as board president, and Evan Helfaer as a major donor.

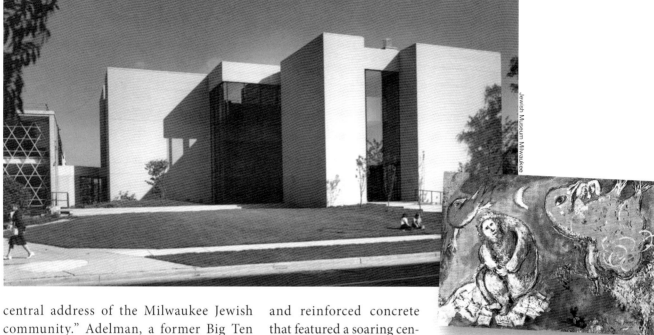

Jewish Museum Milwaukee

central address of the Milwaukee Jewish community." Adelman, a former Big Ten football star and head of a thriving family laundry business, used his contacts and his chutzpah to assemble an all-star team of players for the project. Edward Durell Stone, already famous as the architect of such icons as the Museum of Modern Art in New York and the Kennedy Center for the Performing Arts in Washington, agreed to design the building. World-renowned artist Marc Chagall consented to create a tapestry for its interior, and Evan Helfaer said he would pay for it all. Helfaer was a Milwaukee chemist who had transformed a small medical supply business into Lakeside Laboratories, a global pharmaceutical firm that he ultimately sold to Colgate Palmolive.

Plans for the Helfaer Community Service Building were announced in 1971, and its site was familiar to everyone: the former parking lot just south of the Jewish Community Center. Edward Durell Stone designed a four-story block of brick and reinforced concrete that featured a soaring central atrium and rhythmic banks of windows angled away from the proposed freeway next door. (Although the land was cleared, the freeway was never built.) The Helfaer Building was formally dedicated in 1973, and the focal point of its interior was the bold and whimsical Chagall tapestry in the atrium. The focus of the building itself was community service; its tenants included the Jewish Federation, Jewish Family and Children's Service, the Milwaukee Jewish Council, the career counseling unit of Jewish Vocational Service, B'nai B'rith Youth Organization, and the offices of the *Wisconsin Jewish Chronicle*, which the Federation had purchased from founder and publisher Irving Rhodes in 1972. Bringing so many agencies together under one roof was "not only convenient and central," said Mel Zaret, but "ideal and cooperative."

The Milwaukee Jewish Federation was clearly the new landmark's leading tenant.

Completed in 1973, the Helfaer Community Service Building became the "central address" of Jewish Milwaukee. A colorful tapestry by Marc Chagall dominated its interior.

Wisconsin Jewish Chronicle

Super Sunday volunteers made certain that no one missed an opportunity to support the Federation's annual fund drive.

The Federation became the Jewish community's chief planner, coordinator, and communicator after 1967; its staff worked to nurture a sense of shared purpose, strengthen a common identity and, through its constituent agencies, meet a broad range of human needs. That required money, more often than not, and the annual fund drive remained the Federation's signature activity. Year after year, Milwaukee's drive was among the most successful in Jewish America, placing the community at or near the top of the nation in per-capita giving. Annual contributions passed the $3 million mark in 1968, exceeded $5 million for the first time in 1972, and crossed the $7 million threshold in 1982. Giving invariably spiked whenever Israel faced a threat to its existence—$9.6 million was pledged after the Yom Kippur War of 1973 and $8.4 million following the 1982 conflict in Lebanon—but generosity was more the

rule than the exception in every season. During a single two-year period in 1990-1991, the regular campaign and a special refugee resettlement appeal brought in a total of $25 million—more than $1,000 for every Jewish man, woman, and child in Milwaukee.

Why such singular success? Milwaukeeans obviously took the principle of *tzedakah* to heart; giving, from a Jewish perspective, is an obligation rooted in justice, not simply an act of charity stemming from kindness. It was also apparent that the collegiality, or at least the peaceful coexistence, that characterized relations between the various religious communities carried over to the non-religious sphere. Most Milwaukeeans viewed the annual campaign as a genuinely joint effort, and they trusted Federation leaders to make sound decisions with the money entrusted to them—a level of confidence not found in every American city. Well-run campaigns were a given, of course. The Federation moved away from glitzy kickoff events and celebrity speakers, but the annual appeal was painstakingly orchestrated, and innovations like Super Sunday, a phone-a-thon first conducted in 1981, helped to keep interest high.

All of these ingredients were vital, but they wouldn't have mattered much if local residents had lacked the capacity to give. The success of the Federation campaigns was, on one level, graphic proof that the entire community had, simply put, made it. Jewish families had entered the middle class as a body after World War II, and their incomes kept rising against the local and national medians, some to heights beyond the imaginations of the first arrivals. A growing number of entrepreneurs were able to make the hefty lead gifts so critical to each campaign's success. Their names became familiar: Gerald Colburn, head of a local toy company (Jak Pak) with an international market; Max Karl, founder and guiding light of Mortgage Guaranty Insurance Corporation (MGIC); Ollie Adelman, who built and then sold one of the nation's largest laundry firms; the Kohl family, who did the same thing with groceries and then department stores; Elmer Winter, co-founder of Manpower; Phil Rubenstein, a national distributor of plastic bags; and the Marcus family, a major presence in movie theaters, restaurants, and lodging. Just as influential were the Sorefs of Master Lock; the Pecks of meatpacking fame; real estate developer Joseph Zilber; Sheldon Lubar, a banker who became one of the region's leading venture capitalists; and Martin Stein, who began with pharmacies, moved on to optical stores, and succeeded splendidly in both fields.

A significant number of these moguls and magnates provided leadership as well as lead gifts. Gerald Colburn, Ollie Adelman, and Max Karl, who served on multiple boards and in multiple campaigns, were revered as community role models in the years after 1967. Marty Stein, who called the trio "my three idols," was practically in a class by himself. The immigrant peddler's son served as Federation president and campaign chair at various times, but he seemed to be everywhere in the 1970s and later: running community meetings, supporting at least a half-dozen synagogues, leading trips to Israel (a total of sixty by 1993), and raising funds for causes that ranged from the Jewish Home to Israel Bonds. "My overriding goal," Stein said in 1986, "is to live my life in such

A quartet of Jewish community quarterbacks— (l. to r.) Gerald Colburn, Max Karl, Marty Stein, and Phil Rubenstein— gathered in the 1980s.

Marty Stein stood virtually alone in the intensity of his commitment to the community's welfare.

Jewish Museum Milwaukee

Wisconsin Jewish Chronicle

Wisconsin Jewish Chronicle

(L. to r.) Esther Leah Ritz, Bruce Arbit, and Rick Meyer were three more mainstays of Jewish Milwaukee.

a way that it has a positive impact and that it helps people to realize their full potential." A man of enormous compassion, Marty Stein did not give from a distance; whether he was putting inner-city youngsters through school or making sure that senior citizens had decent housing, Stein took an intense personal interest in the lives of those he helped.

Such commitment was not lost on national Jewish leaders. Success on the local level was often a prelude to national office, and Milwaukee became a source of lay leadership completely out of proportion to its size. Marty Stein, after playing a key role in the airlift of Somalian Jews to Israel, became board chairman of the United Jewish Appeal in 1988—one of the most prestigious posts in world Jewry. Gerald Colburn and Ollie Adelman both served as national UJA officers, Elmer Winter became president of the American Jewish Committee, and real estate developer Avrum Chudnow chaired the Jewish National Fund's American arm. There were also younger leaders like Bruce Arbit, whose direct-mail firm, A.B. Data, provided crucial help to Jewish charities and whose

volunteer posts included chairmanship of the United Israel Appeal. Nor were the contributors limited to men; Esther Leah Ritz headed both the National Jewish Welfare Board and the World Confederation of Jewish Community Centers in the 1980s. Ritz was taught from an early age that Judaism meant "doing as well as believing"— "and so," she said, "I've done."

Whatever roles they played, Milwaukeeans who were called to the national stage found that their city's reputation preceded them. Marty Stein remembered traveling to his first United Jewish Appeal meetings as president of the Milwaukee Jewish Federation:

Coming from Milwaukee, which is one of the all-time great Jewish communities, and saying that you're president, is a great honor and a great privilege. I feel very honored to have been president of Milwaukee. It's one of the great positions one can have in the American Jewish community process.

Esther Leah Ritz seconded the motion. "This community has always been special in terms of its sense of community," she said in 1989, and at its heart was the Jewish Federation she had chaired from 1978 to 1981. Ritz described the national Federation network as nothing less than "the voluntary polity of the American Jewish community." "There isn't a better game in town," agreed Bruce Arbit, who became Milwaukee's president in 2006. "The Federation *is* the Jewish community." Its role remained central despite frequent changes in volunteer leadership

WE CAN'T GIVE THEM PEACE.

WE CAN GIVE THEM PEACE OF MIND.

The people of Israel have more problems than we can imagine. Overcrowded hospitals. A shortage of doctors and trained nurses. Wounded who need immediate care. Aged and infirm who need continual care. War widows who need education and training. Absorption centers which are strained to the hilt ... and more immigrants coming daily. Homes that must be rebuilt. Education that must continue. And more...

But it doesn't take much imagination to know that the people of Israel cannot do it all alone. They don't have a cent to spare. We must help. With more dollars than we've given before. With more than we can afford. In cash.

GIVE TO THE ISRAEL EMERGENCY FUND.

BECAUSE
IF YOU DON'T...
WHO WILL?

MILWAUKEE JEWISH FEDERATION
1360 N. Prospect Ave., Milwaukee, Wis.   271-8338

and significantly less-frequent changes in professional staff. When Mel Zaret retired in 1984, after nearly thirty years at the helm, his successor was Robert Aronson, a native Milwaukeean (and former Zaret assistant) who came back to his hometown after a stint in New York. Aronson left in 1989 for a larger Federation job in Detroit, and Rick Meyer moved up from the campaign director's post to succeed him. A California native with a master's degree in social work, Meyer has managed the Federation's affairs with a cool professional hand ever since.

Fund-raising may have been the Jewish Federation's signature activity, but the point of raising money was, naturally, to spend it. When the last phone call had been made and the last pledges tallied, Federation professionals sat down with lay officers to begin the arduous allocation process—a yearly balancing act that was political by nature and cautious by design. Federation leaders had the unenviable task of considering every viewpoint, reflecting every interest,

and steering a course down the broad middle way without leaving behind those on the edges. After 1967, that meant staying within sight of the most religious Jews without alienating the most secular—a job that did not get easier as the gap between them widened. Although allocating funds was hardly a democratic process, the Federation's decisions did reflect, at least in broad outline, the entire community's priorities. What that meant in the years just after 1967 was an urgent concern for the welfare of Israel. The Jewish state absorbed more than half the funds raised by the Federation in most years, and an even greater share when Arab forces attacked or waves of refugees threatened to swamp the country. During military or humanitarian emergencies, Milwaukeeans willingly suspended all other campaigns and reduced support for their own programs to channel money to Israel.

Personal missions to Israel and generous gifts to the annual campaign underscored Milwaukee's commitment to the Jewish state.

The balance began to shift, almost imperceptibly at first, in the late 1980s, and it shifted in response to changes taking place on both sides of the ocean. Although taxes were onerous and inflation could soar into the triple digits, Israel became economically self-sufficient in the late twentieth century. As the nation matured, the forced consensus of its pioneer period evaporated. Years of Labor Party dominance gave way to governing coalitions that seemed to be held together by hope alone, and there were painful distinctions within Jewish society, some based on skin color, as well as new signs of restiveness in the Arab minority. Conflicts between hawks and doves, the observant and the secular, Ashkenazim and Sephardim were transparent and intense—all signs of a living democracy, perhaps, but hardly conducive to civic contentment. With the beginning of the Arab intifada, or uprising, in the occupied territories in 1987, tensions ratcheted to an even higher level, and terrorism began to make more news than tourism. These developments were viewed with considerable alarm in the United States. Year by year, the stereotype of the Israeli populace as a hardy band of wholesome young men and women turning the desert into a garden was replaced by something far more ambiguous. The Reform and Conservative Jews who dominated the American Diaspora were particularly uncomfortable with Orthodox control over religious affairs in the homeland, and their worst fears were realized when the rabbis tried to exclude non-Orthodox converts from citizenship. The emergence of the Palestine Liberation Organization as a voice for the region's displaced Arabs changed the political equation as well. Some Americans, including some Jewish Americans, began to see the Palestinians as the Mideast's new underdog, a role filled admirably by Israel not many years before. America's Jewish leaders found the shift in sympathies galling, but shades of gray were starting to appear in a picture that had long been rendered in black and white.

As Israel lost its innocence, the American Jewish community was undergoing changes of its own. The simple aging of its population had brought a new generation to the fore that had no memory of Israel's birth and knew the Holocaust largely through books and movies. The baby-boomers found support for the Jewish homeland far less reflexive than it had been for their parents. American Jews were also facing a crisis within the extended family. The forces of assimilation had been galloping merrily along for decades, but it took the 1990 Jewish Population Survey, the largest study of Jewish America ever done, to bring their impact into focus. The survey revealed that more than half the Jews married since 1985 had taken a non-Jewish partner, and that most children born to intermarried couples were not being raised in the faith. As stories about the "silent Holocaust" multiplied in the Jewish press, American Jews looked to their backs. Shoshana Cardin, who chaired the Conference of Presidents of Major Jewish Organizations, provided a terse description of the new perspective in 1992: "The reality is that the American Jewish community, while accepting the centrality of Israel, is primarily concerned now with our own continuity." Two years later, the Council of Jewish Federations made "identity, affiliation and intermarriage" the focus of its annual assembly. "After rescuing Soviet, Syrian and Yemenite Jewry," concluded one reporter, "the U.S. Jewish community is trying to save itself."

In Milwaukee and elsewhere, "Jewish survival" became the new buzzword. Although Israel remained a touchstone of identity, financial support for the Jewish state declined from more than half the Milwaukee Federation's budget before 1985 to only a quarter in 2009. Educational programs absorbed most of the difference. There was universal agreement that the only way to stop the bleeding was to start early, developing in each child a Jewish identity so secure that it could withstand the erosive power of mainstream culture. The Federation was already funding Hillel Academy and the Jewish Day School, but its leaders, doggedly following the middle path, had a long-standing aversion to more overtly denominational programs. A growing sense of crisis overcame their reluctance, and in the 1990s the Federation began to support Yeshiva Elementary School, the Lubavitch preschool, and even family education programs at individual synagogues—an effort that Federation officials hoped would "inspire Judaic expression in the home." Private philanthropists answered the call to support education as well, none more vigorously than the Helen Bader Foundation. Created with funds from Aldrich Chemical, a firm founded by Helen Bader's former husband, Alfred, the Foundation began to make grants in 1992, and education was a priority from the very beginning. The Helen Bader Foundation has provided millions of dollars in scholarships to Milwaukee's Jewish day schools over the years—an initiative that Daniel Bader, Helen's son and the Foundation's president, traced to his family's passion for parochial education. Bader attended

Wisconsin Jewish Chronicle

The Helen Bader Foundation began to make grants in 1992 and quickly became an important source of funding for both Jewish and non-Jewish education and social welfare programs.

Hillel Academy from kindergarten through eighth grade, and his own Jewish survival was never in question. "Jewish education at Hillel," Dan Bader said in 1991, "is the base of my personality."

As education for survival became the new priority, the Milwaukee Jewish Federation showed its ability to adjust to changing conditions. Other changes proved more difficult to manage. Giving flat-lined in the early 1990s, never rising much above $8 million a year and sometimes falling well below that figure. The stagnation, which mirrored national trends, had multiple causes. Major givers were growing old and dying or moving away. Assimilated Jews were shifting their charitable dollars from Jewish causes to broader community programs. Individual agencies were siphoning money away with their own campaigns—a recurrent problem since the nineteenth century. In 1998, after months of work, the Federation adopted a Strategic Renewal Plan to help its leaders regain lost momentum. The plan was rooted in an elemental understanding of the group's mission: "The Milwaukee Jewish Federation leads and unites the community in addressing the needs and aspirations of the Jewish people."

Simple enough, and the Federation had an indispensable ally in its efforts to fulfill that mission. The Jewish Community Foundation, established in 1973 as the Federation's endowment arm, had quietly become one of the largest funds of its kind in the United States. Relying almost entirely on bequests, the Community Foundation saw its assets swell from $38.5 million in 1995 to $100 million in 2004 and $143 million in 2008. Income from those assets supported a variety of specific programs, but the Foundation also helped bridge the gap between the Federation's annual campaign goals and the community's annual giving. Even with those shortfalls, Milwaukee ranked among the top five American Jewish communities in per-capita giving at the turn of the twenty-first century. The city's reputation for generosity endured.

That spirit of generosity was sorely tested when the American economy began to founder in 2008. As foreclosures multiplied and the unemployment rate soared, the Jewish Federation, like philanthropies all across America, was hit with a double dose of bad news. Not only were donors less able to give as their own finances deteriorated,

but staggering investment losses severely compromised the Community Foundation's ability to make up the shortfall. The Federation's campaign revenues dropped 15 percent from 2008 to 2009, and the Foundation's assets shrank 27 percent in the same year. Faced with an extraordinary situation, the Jewish Federation made some extraordinarily difficult decisions, laying off staff, cutting or eliminating programs of many years' standing, and introducing a new climate of austerity. Community agencies were forced to adjust as they could and to wonder when, and if, there would ever be a return to normal conditions.

All for One: Jewish Community Agencies

Those agencies had already made multiple adjustments in the years preceding the meltdown; since 1967 a number of them had changed their names, changed their addresses, and even changed their missions. With expertise in fields that ranged from counseling to community relations and from geriatric care to youth recreation, the agencies had almost nothing in common, but they did have a common purpose. Just as the Jewish Federation was one organization promoting the welfare of all, the many non-profits served one community with programs that promoted the well-being of each individual. The voluntary agencies were in some ways the non-religious counterparts of the shuls and schools, and they helped make Jewish Milwaukee a full-service community.

In the procession of changes that followed 1967, a few agencies left the Jewish orbit altogether. Jewish Vocational Service (JVS) had been a pioneer in its field since the darkest days of the Depression. Under

Music therapy was one of several Jewish Vocational Service programs that served clients with special needs.

director Michael Galazan, it became the first rehabilitation agency in America to work with the Jewish handicapped, and its programs kept expanding to take in refugees, the elderly, long-haired dropouts, welfare recipients, and anyone else—Jewish or Gentile—who needed help making productive use of their lives. Galazan was a devout believer in the redemptive power of work:

> *Any work is of value if it contributes to the good of society. Those who begin work, or resume it, find they have a productive place in society, or at least can contribute. There is a pride and feeling of self-respect they never had before.*

By 1980, JVS was the largest Jewish rehabilitation agency in America, with a staff of more than 600 and a budget swollen to $16 million by government welfare-to-work grants. Such rapid growth nearly swamped

the organization, and it carried JVS miles away from its early Jewish identification. In 1990, the reorganized Jewish Vocational Service became the Milwaukee Center for Independence— a name more in keeping with its renewed emphasis on clients with disabilities. Although a majority of its board members were Jewish, the center's formal ties to the Jewish community ended.

COA Youth and Family Centers, the former Children's Outing Association, followed the same path to independence with fewer detours. Established in 1906 to expose low-income children to a healthier, more wholesome world than the one they knew in Milwaukee's inner city, COA maintained a remarkable fidelity to its mission. A century after its founding, the agency was still working with kids from the inner city, but their backgrounds

Michael Galazan directed JVS for more than forty years.

John Gurda

COA Youth and Family Centers evolved from an agency serving Jewish youngsters to one with an African-American and Latino clientele. Its in-town center crowns the Milwaukee River bluff south of North Ave.

had shifted almost completely from eastern-European Jewish to African-American and Latino. Although outdoor activities remained a central focus, their location changed from the venerable Camp Sidney Cohen in Waukesha County to the much larger Camp Helen Brachman in central Wisconsin. There was, at the same time, a growing emphasis on serving children where they lived—in the heart of the city. In 1967, COA began to offer year-round programming in a rented building on the west end of the North Avenue bridge. The agency outgrew that facility and then another before erecting a state-of-the-art center on the nearby Milwaukee River bluff in 1991. By the early 2000s, COA was serving nearly 8,000 inner-city youngsters and their families every year with programs that ranged from early childhood education to GED preparation. Although the agency was officially independent, COA continued to rely heavily

on Jewish staff, Jewish board members, and Jewish philanthropists.

The largest organization to leave the fold was Mount Sinai Hospital. Founded in 1903 as a place for Jewish doctors to treat patients of any faith or no faith, Mount Sinai had become one of the leading health care facilities in the region, and its growth after 1967 was particularly rapid. It grew, however, in its downtown location, rather than following some of its peers out to the suburbs. The hospital's board did consider a move, reported chairman Joseph Rapkin in 1971, but its members ultimately chose to keep faith with the past:

In order to maintain the tradition and philosophy of the hospital founders, which is to serve the entire community, the board of trustees decided that we best serve the community and its growing health needs by staying at our present location.

Jewish Museum Milwaukee

In the salad days of the 1970s, when federal grants were plentiful and health care was a growth industry, Mount Sinai developed a campus on Twelfth Street that covered nearly three square blocks. Completed in 1976, the $30 million complex featured 454 patient beds, a comprehensive suite of specialties, technology worthy of *Star Wars*, and one of the largest teaching programs in the city. Its Jewish identity was obvious in the mezuzahs on the doorposts, the Star of David on the stationery, and the rabbi in the chaplain's office.

The 1980s were a different story entirely. As health-care costs spiraled out of control, there was general agreement that the medical establishment had overbuilt. The industry's focus shifted to outpatient services, and hospitals across the country, their

occupancy rates plummeting, went through a painful round of mergers, downsizings, and closings. Mount Sinai did not escape the epidemic. Despite the mezuzahs, only 8 to 10 percent of the hospital's patients were Jewish in any given year, and there were no major impediments to an institutional intermarriage that offered some hope of financial relief. After considering a union with Columbia, Mount Sinai joined forces with nearby Samaritan Hospital in 1987. Samaritan was a former United Church of Christ facility that had been purchased by St. Luke's Hospital, a Lutheran institution; the addition of Mount Sinai created an ecumenical giant. The parent organization soon changed its name to Aurora Health Care and closed the Samaritan campus, leaving the old Jewish hospital—now Aurora Sinai

Mount Sinai Hospital was another institution that left the Jewish orbit. It merged with a nearby facility in 1987 to become Aurora Sinai Medical Center.

Jewish Museum Milwaukee

Jewish Museum Milwaukee

Activities at the Beth Am senior center in Sherman Park ranged from shuffleboard to paid work projects.

Medical Center—as the last comprehensive health-care facility in downtown Milwaukee. Mount Sinai loyalists, including a number of physicians, were saddened and angered by the moves, but they could hardly deny the financial realities. A philosophical few viewed the merger as a sign of progress; with Jewish doctors free to practice anywhere, they argued, there was no longer any need for a Jewish hospital. The old connections weren't lost entirely. The Jewish Federation continued its annual support at a modest level, and the Ladies Auxiliary of Mount Sinai, a pillar of polite Jewish society for decades, turned over its entire $750,000 treasury to the hospital when the group disbanded in 1997.

The Milwaukee Center for Independence, COA Youth and Family Centers, and Aurora Sinai Medical Center are all gifts of Milwaukee's Jews to the community as a whole. Each provides vital services to thousands of people every year, and none would exist if Jewish volunteers hadn't provided leadership and support over the decades. Like many gifts, the institutions are too often

taken for granted, but Milwaukee would be the poorer for their absence. The fact that so many Jewish households continue to support them long after they have outgrown any meaningful Jewish connection demonstrates that the tradition of *tzedakah*, or sacrificial giving, is still very much alive.

As one set of institutions moved away from their old Jewish identities, another set simply moved away from their old addresses. The same post-1967 exodus that emptied Sherman Park of all its synagogues except Beth Jehudah affected non-religious institutions as well. Beth Am Center, the labor Zionist temple on Burleigh Street, declined with the labor Zionist movement in general, and in 1973 the facility was turned over to the Jewish Federation for use as a senior center. Nearly 250 West Siders came to Beth Am every weekday for current events classes, Golden Age Club meetings, gentle exercise routines, and a county-funded kosher meal. Dwindling numbers and a deteriorating facility prompted the Federation to close the center in 1987. The senior program was relocated to Anshe Sfard, then

Jewish Museum Milwaukee

The new Jewish Home for the Aged, completed in 1973, marked a giant step forward in geriatric care.

to Anshai Lebowitz, and finally consolidated with its East Side counterpart in 1994. The relative handful of participants who still lived in Sherman Park were bussed across town to Prospect Avenue every day.

The 2400 block of N. Fiftieth Street had long been the address of two institutions that served opposite ends of the age spectrum: the Jewish Children's Home and the Jewish Home for the Aged. Both quit their premises in the 1970s. The Children's Home closed entirely in 1976, a casualty of the shift from group homes to foster care placement for dependent children—and the corresponding drop in public funding. The Home for the Aged, a fixture on Fiftieth since 1929, relocated in 1973 to a gleaming new facility on Prospect Avenue, just north of the Jewish Community Center. The move had been in the works for years. Not only was the southern section of Sherman Park rapidly shedding its Jewish character, but there was a new interest in consolidating community

services, and the lakefront location seemed ideal at the time. The new Jewish Home, which took two years to build and cost a total of $6 million, was superior to its predecessor in every way: larger rooms, spectacular views, and an array of services that ranged from podiatry to physical therapy. On move-in day, the staff greeted all 115 residents with a carnation and a smile, and Yiddish-speaking social workers stayed overnight to calm any adjustment jitters. "Always new is better," concluded one happy resident.

The lower end of Prospect Avenue was fast becoming the institutional heart of Jewish Milwaukee. The Helfaer Community Service Building and the Jewish Home for the Aged opened within months of each other in 1973, and Golda Meir House, a federally subsidized apartment complex for the low-income elderly, opened across the street in

Golda Meir House, practically across the street, provided apartments for the low-income elderly.

1980. At the core of the ensemble, flanked by the Helfaer Building and the Jewish Home, was the Jewish Community Center, a 1955 landmark that was selectively upgraded in the 1970s. Volunteer leader Ollie Adelman praised the entire Prospect Avenue campus as "one of the most comprehensive groupings of communal services under Jewish auspices in the country." Federation head Mel Zaret was typically more expansive:

> *When you get agencies together physically, they tend to work together collaboratively, augmenting and strengthening each other rather than duplicating services or competing. It becomes much easier for them to communicate, cooperate and interchange ideas.*

There was something for practically every age and interest group on Prospect Avenue. The Jewish Home and Golda Meir House both provided a full array of services for their elderly residents, and the Home added an adult day care program in 1984. The JCC's

The B'nai B'rith Youth Organization's signature activity was a Walk for Israel that generated thousands of dollars in pledges every year.

Wisconsin Jewish Chronicle

activities began with a new nursery school on the lower level—where the bowling alleys had been—and moved up to four floors of cultural and recreational programs for both youngsters and adults. The Helfaer Community Service Building had the broadest reach. The Jewish Federation, its lead tenant, worked for the welfare of the community at large, and other groups in the building played more specific roles. The *Wisconsin Jewish Chronicle* published a weekly digest of news and features, as it had since 1921. The B'nai B'rith Youth Organization sponsored groups for young men and women that encouraged a stronger sense of Jewish identity; one of BBYO's major events was an annual Walk for Israel that raised hundreds of thousands of dollars over the years.

Another Helfaer Building tenant, the Milwaukee Jewish Council for Community Relations, was the public face of the Jewish community, particularly in the area of human rights. Saul Sorrin, the formidable figure who led the Council from 1962 to 1984, was encouraged by the relative scarcity of anti-Semitic incidents during his tenure. "Overt discrimination against Jews exists but is at an all-time low," Sorrin reported in 1983. There was still plenty to do. The Jewish Council represented the community in interfaith efforts, built support for Israel, promoted equal rights for all minorities, and lobbied for strict separation of church and state—a policy that sometimes put it at odds with other groups in the Jewish community. In 1993, as Arab-Israeli relations deteriorated in the Mideast, Council officers sat down with their Arab-American counterparts in the Midwest to hammer out a statement calling for "a just and lasting peace" based on

Jewish Family Services programs ranged from a Jewish-themed child development center to individual and family counseling.

"non-violence, tolerance, [and] mutual respect." Drafting the statement had required fifteen meetings over a period of two years. True to its emphasis on equal rights, the Jewish Council was also an important platform for female leadership. When Saul Sorrin retired in 1984, Judy Mann moved over from Planned Parenthood to take the director's post, staying until she moved to Israel in 1990. Mordecai Lee, a former state legislator, succeeded Mann, and in 1997 Paula Simon, a Jewish Council veteran, took charge of the agency. When Simon retired in 2009, the Council entered talks to become a department of the Jewish Federation—a cost-saving arrangement more typical in communities of Milwaukee's size.

The remaining tenant at 1360 N. Prospect was Jewish Family and Children's Service (JFCS). No voluntary agency in the community had served so long or changed so much. Established in the mid-1800s to provide impoverished newcomers with food and shelter, the organization had shifted its focus over the decades from material relief to casework services and then to family and individual counseling—changing its name multiple times in the process. As American society continued to evolve after 1967, JFCS evolved with it. With more women entering the work force every year, the agency opened a day care center in 1977. With life expectancies rising steadily, five full-time social workers were assigned to work exclusively with the elderly by 1986. As thousands of newcomers arrived from eastern Europe—a development described later in this chapter—resettlement services regained their old importance, and there was a new awareness of the needs of people with mental illnesses and physical disabilities. Under Ralph Sherman, JFCS director from 1966 to 1989, the organization's staff swelled from eight to forty-five and its annual budget from $235,000 to $1.5 million.

With such a variety of programs and services under its administrative roof, the agency underwent one more name change in 1987: Jewish Family and Children's Service became the broader Jewish Family Services. When Ralph Sherman retired in 1989, Elliot Lubar, his longtime deputy, took over the agency and

Ralph Sherman (top) *directed the agency for twenty-three years before Elliot Lubar took the reins in 1989.*

continued to provide what Lubar called "a safety net for the Jewish people." By 2001, his staff had grown to seventy-two—far too many for the cramped offices in the Helfaer Building—and Jewish Family Services moved into a home of its own: the former Bryant & Stratton College on Jackson Street, a few blocks west of Prospect Avenue. Purchased with the help of a $1 million gift from attorney Robert Habush and his wife Mimi, the facility was named the Habush Family Center in their honor.

Moving North

In the 1970s and '80s, hundreds of people visited the Prospect Avenue campus every day of the week, some to receive counseling, others to play racquetball or hear lectures, and still others to attend community board meetings, place ads in the *Jewish Chronicle*, or visit their elderly parents. The Jewish Community Center, the Jewish Home, Golda Meir House, and the manifold institutions in the Helfaer Building created a critical mass that made Prospect Avenue the Jewish community's central address. Not for long, however. Although traffic was heavy, the configuration of the

Jack Weiner, who spent much of his childhood at the old Jewish Center on Milwaukee St., ran its successor on Prospect Ave. from 1966 to 1982.

Jewish Museum Milwaukee

campus in its 1970s format was relatively short-lived. The Jewish community's migration to the North Shore and beyond—a trend apparent before World War II and dominant thereafter—was transforming the religious landscape of Jewish Milwaukee, and it was about to transform its institutional scene as well.

The Jewish Community Center felt the pressure most directly. The elderly residents of Prospect Avenue were already home, and the agencies in the Helfaer Building could have done business almost anywhere, but the JCC depended on its members to drive downtown for virtually every activity. The center's location had been a compromise from the start; Jewish leaders of the 1950s had simply split the difference between the West Side and the East Side, between Sherman Park and the North Shore, choosing a site that left neither geographic faction especially happy. Nearly 8,400 people had joined the JCC after the facility opened in 1955, but membership quickly subsided to 6,000 individuals (or 2,000 households) when the novelty wore off. The losses would continue. As Sherman Park emptied out and the tide of Jewish settlement turned decisively toward the North Shore, the JCC was farther and farther away from its core constituency.

The center's directors—Jack Weiner from 1966 to 1982 and Mort Levin from 1982 to 1985—launched any number of new programs to keep their members interested: teen sports nights, singles clubs, Yiddish readings, cardiac rehabilitation, a full kosher restaurant, Bible study, classes in self-defense, and special series like Summer Evenings of Jewish Music. One of the more successful new activities was Jewish Jubilee, which debuted in

1981 as the community's entrant in the parade of ethnic festivals that had begun to crowd Milwaukee's summer calendar. Prospect Avenue was closed for Jewish Jubilee, and more than 3,000 people came to the center for street dancing, entertainment, games, historical displays and, of course, food. The JCC also developed programs miles away from the center, including a nursery school at Congregation Sinai in Fox Point, cultural programs at Northridge Lakes, and athletic activities at North Shore gyms. "As the need arises," said director Mort Levin, "JCC staff implements programs and services to meet the needs of young and old throughout the city." It soon became clear that no amount of innovation could stem the center's decline. Despite frequent membership drives and steep discounts for first-time applicants, the JCC's roster sagged from 2,000 households in 1964 to 1,800 in 1971 and 1,400 in 1987—30 percent of them

non-Jewish. Center officials reluctantly came to the conclusion that their facility, dedicated with such fanfare in 1955, had become something of a white elephant.

As the status quo grew increasingly untenable, community leaders began to explore alternatives. A task force assembled in 1979 had no trouble diagnosing the problem: "Distance from the present Center location, possibly related to use of other facilities and cost, seem to be predominant factors in dropping Center membership and/or limiting use of Center services." After a careful look at the addresses on the roster, task force members were just as sure about their next step: "to research the need for and feasibility of a JCC satellite to be located in the North Suburban area." No thought was given to a complete relocation of the center, at least initially, but the community's thinking changed when its scouts found a most unusual

Hands-on Rosh Hashanah programs and the annual Jewish Jubilee couldn't halt the erosion of the JCC's membership base.

273

The former Country Day School campus in suburban Whitefish Bay emerged as the new hub of the Jewish community.

piece of property for sale in Whitefish Bay. It was the former Milwaukee Country Day School, a prep school for boys that had been a fixture on Santa Monica Boulevard since 1917, when the campus was quite literally in the country. The school had erected two major classroom buildings, both Tudor-style landmarks with slate roofs and exposed beams, on opposite ends of the twenty-seven-acre property, one for its junior classes and the other for its senior division. Financial pressures had forced Country Day into a three-way merger with Milwaukee University School and Milwaukee Downer Seminary in 1964. The resulting entity, University

School of Milwaukee (USM), operated the Country Day facility as its south campus until 1985, when all classes were consolidated at USM's present home in River Hills. The Whitefish Bay parcel went on the market even before the consolidation, and the Milwaukee Jewish Federation, alive to its potential, bought the entire property—gym, ball fields, and blackboards—for $2.7 million in July 1983.

The Jewish community was not a complete stranger to the Country Day campus. The American Council for Judaism, an anti-Zionist group, had sponsored gatherings there in 1952, and Congregation

Sinai worshiped at the school until its temple was completed in 1962, but no one had ever imagined owning the complex. Its size and the quality of its buildings suggested possibilities that went far beyond a "satellite" of the Jewish Community Center. It became obvious, first of all, that there was plenty of room for a completely relocated JCC, one even larger than the Prospect Avenue facility. While that prospect was being mulled, what might be described as the Jewish nesting instinct took over. The tendency was apparent in the succession of "synagogue rows" that had materialized at every point in the community's outward migration, and it was apparent in the cluster of agencies planted on Prospect Avenue. With the acquisition of the Country Day property, the nesting instinct entered a new dimension. The Federation's planners looked beyond the needs of a single organization to envision a something-for-everyone campus that would meet the recreational, educational, and cultural needs of the community for years to come. What they proposed, after considerable thought, was a grand northerly procession of Jewish institutions from the older part of town to Whitefish Bay. The Jewish Community Center would move from its quarters on Prospect Avenue, the Milwaukee Jewish Day School would relocate from Temple Emanu-El, and the B'nai B'rith Youth Organization would leave its rooms in the Helfaer Building. The Jewish Educational and Cultural Campus (JECC) on Port Washington Road would close, and all its tenants—Hillel Academy, the Lubavitch nursery school, the Jewish Family Services day care center, and the Milwaukee Association for Jewish Education

(formerly the Board of Jewish Education)—would join the parade to the north.

It was difficult to imagine a geographic juggling act on the scale proposed, but the idea of a one-stop campus had broad appeal once the community had taken the time to digest it. In 1984, the Jewish Federation board approved the plan and launched a $10 million fund drive to make the "Jewish Community Campus" a reality. Marty Stein, the Federation's president, expressed high hopes at the kickoff event:

> *The beginning of this campaign signifies a new era for the Jewish community in Milwaukee. The new campus, located in the midst of the North Shore, will serve as the hub of the Jewish community. Our dream of a central facility, serving all ages and interest groups, is about to become a reality.... It [will] be able to handle our needs for virtually forever. There is so much room for expansion here, there is no limit as we go on.*

Neither the $10 million price tag nor Stein's promise of "virtually forever" would prove accurate, but there was enough initial support to begin construction in 1986. The task of turning a prep school into a Jewish campus was not especially easy. The south building, the larger of the two Country Day structures, was laid out like a large capital "E," with a long main corridor and three wings extending to the east—hardly a design conducive to community programming. The north side of the building was radically modified to become the new Jewish Community Center, with two gyms, a fitness center, a weight room, a raised running track, dance and yoga studios, classrooms, lounges, and

Jewish Museum Milwaukee

Wisconsin Jewish Chronicle

Jewish Museum Milwaukee

The reconfigured campus featured a multi-purpose south building (top) *with a chlorine-free indoor pool and a north building* (bottom) *devoted entirely to Jewish education. Jewish Day School students* (center right) *were among the hundreds who used the complex every day.*

Jewish Museum Milwaukee

RUBENSTEIN CENTER
HILLEL ACADEMY
LUBAVITCH NURSERY SCHOOL

a swimming pool that used ozone rather than chlorine to keep bacteria at bay. The south end of the 1917 landmark was reconfigured to house the Jewish Family Services day care center, the B'nai B'rith Youth Organization, the Association for Jewish Education (which became the Coalition for Jewish Learning in 1997), and a suite of administrative offices. The north building, which had once housed Country Day's junior school, was devoted entirely to education. The 1931 structure, much altered, became, in its final form, the home of the Milwaukee Jewish Day School, Hillel Academy, and the Lubavitch preschool—three institutions in one facility. Despite marked differences in their educational philosophies, MJDS and Hillel shared a gymnasium, a library, a lunchroom, and the outdoor playground—an arrangement found nowhere else in North America. Once again, Milwaukee's penchant for cooperation, or at the very least coexistence, came shining through.

The entire project's final price tag was nearly $20 million, twice the original estimate, but donors stepped forward to finish the job. More than forty families made gifts of at least $100,000, and those who gave $1 million or more had major facilities named in their honor, including the Marcus, Peck, Rubenstein, Soref, and Zilber clans. The most generous supporters of all were Max Karl and his family, who contributed $2 million. Although it was far from finished, the Whitefish Bay complex was formally dedicated in September 1987. "I can remember the discussions we had concerning the purchase of the campus," Max Karl recalled at the ceremony. "At first we envisioned a very circumscribed project—not more than a branch of the downtown JCC."

The ultimate reality exceeded everyone's expectations. "This is a true campus," Karl declared, "a true community center." It has been known ever since as the Karl Jewish Community Campus.

Nearly 3,000 people showed up for an open house soon after the dedication. There were plenty of smiles, and they grew even wider as patrons familiarized themselves with one of the largest Jewish community campuses in the country. Not everyone was pleased, of course; some explorers got lost repeatedly in the south building's multi-level maze, and racquet enthusiasts complained about the lack of facilities for their sports. But most users loved the Karl Campus, particularly its new Jewish Community Center. Jay Roth, a Brooklyn native with fifteen years of experience in the JCC network, had taken charge of the Milwaukee operation in 1985. After rebuilding the staff and

The entire Tudor-style campus was named in honor of Max Karl and his family, who wielded the shovel at the 1986 groundbreaking.

Jay Roth directed the Jewish Community Center in its new home on the Karl Campus.

balancing the budget, Roth led the move to a facility that he promised would offer "a level of service that this community has never seen before." His patrons obviously agreed with him. The JCC's membership exploded from 1,400 households to 1,950 during the 1987 inaugural year, and the roster kept growing to 3,300 households in the mid-1990s. Neighboring institutions on the Karl Campus reported the same response. "The new location couldn't have been better," said Gerald Stein, the Federation's president in 1996. "How well the entire campus is used by kids to senior citizens is beyond our wildest anticipation."

That left the matter of what to do with the old campus on Prospect Avenue. The JCC had been a premier facility in its day, but it was severely underutilized after the move to Whitefish Bay. The Jewish Home for the Aged next door was experiencing no such drop-off in demand. As people lived longer, they also wanted to live better, and they inevitably had more needs as the years passed. Nita Corré, the Gibraltar-born dynamo who became the Jewish Home's director in 1978, began to think in terms of a "continuum of care"—a concept gaining currency

in the geriatrics field. The continuum began with independent living units that would allow seniors to "age in place" without having to move. As they "accumulated disabilities"—a rather frank description of aging—elderly residents would move on to assisted living, skilled nursing care and, depending on need, dementia or rehabilitation units. The logical place for the Jewish Home to create such a continuum was right next door, on the site of the nearly-empty JCC. In 1988, the Jewish Federation approved the sale of the property to the Jewish Home, and in 1991 the old center came tumbling down. The *Jewish Chronicle* (July 5, 1991) waxed philosophical:

> *It is bittersweet to see, with the building's demise, the passing of an era in which the Jewish community ventured from its neighborhoods and declared its presence to Milwaukee.... For 35 years, Jewish groups and sometimes a broad cross section of the community gathered in that building to learn about Jewish issues, express their opinions or enjoy plays and concerts. Some people wistfully remember time spent with friends while bowling or playing handball, or learning how to swim or dance. Others celebrated there a bar or bat mitzvah, a wedding, an anniversary. Thousands of pounds were gained while eating in the various incarnations of the kosher restaurant, and probably almost as many were shed in the athletic facilities downstairs.*

The reconfigured Jewish Home, which was renamed the Jewish Home and Care Center after a 1993 merger with the old

Convalescent Hospital on Fifty-first Boulevard, was soon earning praise as a model senior citizen community. A new north tower housed residents with special needs, including Alzheimer's patients. Its Helen Bader Center, named for the philanthropist who spent her last years as a full-time social worker on Nita Corré's staff, provided a comfortable, home-like setting for patients suffering from memory loss. Chai Point, "a ten-story luxury retirement community" with floors for both independent and assisted living, dominated the former JCC site to the south; its amenities included an indoor pool, a full-service dining room, and spectacular views of the lake. Between Chai Point and the north tower was a "community activity center" that featured a spacious domed hall, day care services, and a drop-in facility for seniors from the neighborhood. The entire $30 million ensemble was finished in 1994 and named the Harry and Jeanette Weinberg Jewish Terrace, after the Baltimore couple whose foundation made a $2 million gift to the project. There

was nothing institutional about the complex, particularly Chai Point. As Prospect Avenue filled in with high-rise, high-priced residential towers, Chai Point—"not just a place to live but a *way* to live"—looked right at home.

With the Karl Jewish Community Campus buzzing with activity from morning till night and the senior campus on Prospect buzzing a bit more sedately, the community might have rested on its institutional laurels for a time. There was a lull in the 1990s, but it didn't last long. As Jewish families kept leapfrogging from the older North Shore suburbs to Mequon, there was a strongly felt need to provide them with services. Mequon Road emerged as the Milwaukee area's "synagogue row" in the 1990s, and it seemed that an "institution row" might not be far behind. Two familiar agencies were in the vanguard: the Jewish Community Center and the Jewish Home and Care Center. Jay Roth, interviewed in 1996, was looking to the future:

The old JCC was torn down in 1991 (left) to make way for a new Jewish Home and Care Center. The facility is connected to Chai Point (above), the "high point" of luxury housing on lower Prospect Ave.

Executive director Nita Corré won praise as a skillful administrator and a gifted fund-raiser.

Once before the JCC was caught in the wrong location, and I believe location is critical to our continued usage. We are not concerned about now and even ten years from now, but our population is continuing to move north. We have to be ready.

In 1998, true to the prevailing spirit of collaboration, the Jewish Community Center and the Jewish Home and Care Center jointly purchased seventy-three acres of land near the intersection of Mequon and Port Washington Roads. They envisioned an "intergenerational campus" on the site, with a variety of services for every age group, including the senior citizens who would live on the premises. Neither organization had any intention of abandoning its almost-new facilities farther south; the Mequon project was viewed as a complementary campus for Ozaukee County residents and a potential foothold for future growth. As the nesting instinct asserted itself, Congregation Anshai Lebowitz was provisionally added to the mix. Marty Stein, the Jewish Home's board chairman, explained the logic behind the alliance:

Why should the home build a chapel when we can use the synagogue's sanctuary? And why should the synagogue build a community room when the JCC will have one? That the community has operated independently and separately in the past will not work in the future. There just isn't enough money to do it.

The concept of a three-way partnership had considerable appeal to Milwaukee's Jewish leaders, but it had considerably less to Mequon's city officials. Determined not to let sprawl overwhelm one of the suburb's most strategic intersections, they imposed a development moratorium on the site in September 1998. By the time it was lifted in 2000, Anshai Lebowitz had moved from Sherman Park to Mequon Road, less than a mile west of the proposed campus. The original partners continued to pursue their intergenerational idea without the synagogue's participation—and with mixed results. When the city raised questions about the scale of the project and the traffic burden it might impose on "the heart of Mequon," JCC officials cut the size of their proposed facility in half and reduced parking spaces accordingly. That was not enough for the local plan commission, whose members rejected the scaled-back proposal by a vote of seven to one. "This is a wonderful project," said Mayor Christine Nuernberg, "but I think it's in the wrong place." Rebuffed in Mequon, the JCC's leaders decided to upgrade their Whitefish Bay campus instead. That left the Jewish Home and Care Center to forge ahead on its own. Mequon had always favored residential development on the site, and there were few objections to a home for seniors. The result was the Sarah Chudnow Campus, a little jewel of a retirement community that opened in 2005. Named for the matriarch of a family that had done well in both recycling and real estate development, the Chudnow Campus offers a full spectrum of residential choices: independent and assisted living, dementia care, a rehabilitation unit, and a hospice. The focal point of the complex is an enclosed "town square" surmounted by perhaps the largest Star of David in Wisconsin.

The Jewish Community Center did eventually have a presence on the Mequon campus, but hardly in the form originally proposed. In 1990, responding to the call of its members for outdoor sports facilities, the JCC had purchased a struggling swim and tennis club in Bayside. Upgraded with a gift from Lillian Smith in memory of her husband and son, the club was reborn as Smith JCC Family Park in the following year. Some members used the pool and courts every day during the summer months, but in 1998 JCC officials sold the property to a developer who had made them an irresistible offer. Their hope was to replace the Bayside facility with an outdoor pool on the Karl Campus—an idea that the Village of Whitefish Bay rejected outright. Thwarted in its own backyard, the JCC eventually looked north to Mequon as the site for its aquatic center. In 2007, after what had become the customary round of rejections, modifications, and appeals, the second incarnation of Smith JCC Family Park opened across the road from the Sarah Chudnow retirement home.

It had taken the Jewish Community Center nine frustrating years to come up with less than half a loaf on the Mequon property it had co-purchased in 1998. That odyssey, as it turned out, was a cakewalk in comparison with the difficulties the Jewish Federation faced in upgrading its Whitefish Bay campus. There had been no inkling of resistance in the early years. The village, in fact, had issued $6.2 million in tax-exempt bonds on the Federation's behalf to develop the JCC's recreational facilities—a neighborly gesture that saved the Jewish community nearly $750,000 in interest costs. The bond issue also helped to create a first-class facility that was used by a sizable number of Whitefish Bay residents, Jewish and Gentile alike. The Karl Campus was widely viewed as a community resource—an amenity rather than an irritant. That attitude began to change as the number of daily visitors exceeded the original projections. The runaway success of the Karl Campus, on both the recreational and the educational sides, brought more people to Santa

The Sarah Chudnow Campus in Mequon offers a comprehensive range of residential choices for seniors. The south wing was built around an indoor "town square" capped by an oversized Star of David.

Wisconsin Jewish Chronicle

Despite rabid local opposition that forced a number of changes in the architectural plans ...

Monica Boulevard every year, and it also exposed deficiencies in the original campus design. In 1991, the Federation proposed an eight-room addition to the Milwaukee Jewish Day School, more parking spaces, and a handful of other upgrades. Those changes were approved, but only after angry neighbors had circulated a petition against the project and Whitefish Bay had imposed a new cap on daily usage.

A proposed expansion on the JCC side proved even more contentious. The center was still in sound shape, particularly after banker and developer Harry Samson made a $2 million donation in 1998; the Whitefish Bay facility was immediately named the Harry and Rose Samson Family Jewish Community Center in his honor. Such generous support helped, but the confusing layout and the lack of a genuine gathering space had been concerns from the beginning, and a gradual dip in membership was starting to worry Jay Roth and his staff. The number of households on the JCC's roster fell from roughly 3,300 in 1995 to 2,700 in 2001, largely as the result of competition from newer and nicer health clubs elsewhere on the North Shore. In April 2001,

JCC officials unveiled plans for a substantially rebuilt center with a 400-seat community hall, updated fitness facilities, new classrooms, a kosher café, an indoor playground, a family locker room, and a lengthy list of other improvements. Jane Gellman, president of the JCC board, declared the project a top priority:

> We have outgrown our building and are facing increased competition from other facilities and therefore decreasing membership. We view the project as a necessity, not a luxury. To provide outstanding programs, we have to have outstanding facilities. And we are committed to reinforcing the centrality of the Jewish community on the Karl Campus.

The announcement touched off a small-scale war that raged for the next two-and-a-half years. "Stop JCC Expansion" signs began to sprout on local lawns soon after the plans became public, and more than 400 people turned out for a hearing at Whitefish Bay High School. Some residents supported the center, but others railed against "excessive land use," "JCC creep," and the catastrophic collapse in property values they were sure would follow the center's expansion. A seemingly endless round of accusations and recriminations followed the first salvos. The JCC scaled back its plans repeatedly, only to face the same intractable opposition every time. The project became a major issue in the 2002 race for Whitefish Bay village president—the first contested election since 1945—and the ferment spread to Fox Point, which had jurisdiction over 3.4 acres at the northern end of the campus. Despite studies

showing that property values near the Karl Campus had kept pace with those elsewhere on the North Shore and that traffic patterns would actually improve with a new campus layout, the skeptics were unmoved. They conjured up images of a Six Flags amusement park in the heart of a tranquil residential enclave—an exaggeration that Federation officials found exasperating.

The dispute seemed close to resolution in March 2003, when JCC officials agreed to reduce the size of their proposed addition once more, limit the number of "outside" events like weddings and Bar/Bat Mitzvahs, and accept a twenty-five-year moratorium on new construction. After signaling their preliminary approval, Whitefish Bay's trustees demanded even more concessions, which was the last straw for the Federation's negotiating team. Blasting the board's action as "unfair, arbitrary and discriminatory," they began legal proceedings against the village in June 2003. Arguing that no other institution in Whitefish Bay had been subjected to such intense scrutiny, the Federation started a legal defense fund and began to air television ads telling its side of the story. In November 2003, at long last, the controversy was settled out of court. Whitefish Bay agreed to the March iteration of the campus plans—the version in place before the lawsuit—and the parties signed a statement committing both to "a positive long-term working relationship." The voices of the NIMBY faction—"not in my backyard"—had been heard, but they had not prevailed.

Work began almost immediately. The project affected virtually every institution on the Karl Campus, but its most visible component was a multi-purpose wing attached to the south building. Not only did the west wing create a new primary entrance, but it also featured a "Main Street" concourse connecting a spacious community hall, a play area for toddlers, the long-planned kosher café, a library, and cultural offices that helped put the "Jewish" in "Jewish Community Center." More than 1,700 people attended the grand opening in October 2007, and they were just as impressed as an earlier group had been when the facility opened twenty years before. As memories of the dispute began, ever so slowly, to fade, everyone involved with the Karl Campus returned to the vision articulated by Federation president Judy Segall Guten in 2003:

> *We acquired the campus to provide a gathering place at the heart of our community—to create a setting where we can learn and share with one another. Indeed, the campus has become the focal point of our Jewish community for close to two decades and has provided the setting for essential services that benefit the total community. The federation remains dedicated to this vision and to the role of the Karl Campus in our Jewish community.*

... the Jewish Community Center was extensively remodeled in the early 2000s. A new "Main Street" concourse helped to unify the sprawling complex.

283

Here Come the Russians II

As battles were being won and lost on the institutional front, as buildings went up and came down, and as the community's voluntary agencies changed their locations and their programs to meet the changing needs of their constituents, another thread of Milwaukee's Jewish story had been unspooling all the while. In a movement that recalled a much earlier influx of immigrants, thousands of Soviet Jews made their homes in Milwaukee between roughly 1973 and 1993. Their arrival affected the full spectrum of local organizations, from synagogues to social service agencies, and they added a distinctive new layer to a community that was already a specimen of diversity.

Although the original immigrants were long gone and their stories were rapidly fading, Milwaukee had experienced an eerily similar movement in the late 1800s and early 1900s. At least 10,000 Jews came to the city from the lands of tsarist Russia during that period, fleeing chronic poverty and recurrent pogroms. German Jews were present to welcome the new arrivals—or at least receive them—but the eastern Europeans quickly outnumbered their hosts to become the dominant element in Milwaukee's Jewish population. It was their descendants, by and large, who were building the fine homes on the North Shore, working out at the JCC, and worshiping on "synagogue row" in Mequon.

The Soviet Jews, by contrast, were descended from eastern European Jews who had never left. The gap between them and their distant American cousins—and the difference in their historical experiences—could hardly have been greater. As the immigrants of the early 1900s prospered in their new homes, those who had stayed behind suffered, first under the tsars, then through the horrors of World War I, and ultimately in the dislocations that followed the Russian Revolution of 1917. Religious expression of any kind was discouraged in the Soviet Union. Generation after generation grew up in a society that dismissed religious belief as superstition and places of worship as anachronistic museums. Tradition slowly starved to death, and yet the anti-Semitism of an earlier era did not die with it. All Russians suffered terribly during World War II, but Jews were singled out for abuse after the conflict, particularly under Josef Stalin, the mustachioed strongman who ran the country from 1929 to 1953. Synagogues were confiscated, cemeteries closed, rabbis arrested, and services prohibited. There was a brief respite in 1948, when the USSR actively supported Israel's bid for statehood. The two nations established full diplomatic relations—Golda Meir was her homeland's first ambassador to Moscow—but Stalin's ardor cooled when Israel cast its lot decisively with the Western powers. Soviet propagandists were soon dismissing Zionism as "a reactionary nationalist trend of the Jewish bourgeoisie."

Jews elsewhere took notice of the repression taking place behind the Iron Curtain. In 1950, only two years after independence, David Ben-Gurion implored Stalin to permit free immigration to Israel. He also defiantly proclaimed Israel's solidarity with Jews suffering under Soviet rule: "Your hopes are our hopes. They are constantly present in our minds." The Israeli campaign, interestingly, invoked the words of Moses to Pharaoh: "Let my people go." American Jews began to show concern not long after. When a delegation of U.S. Zionists visited the Soviet Union in 1956, Rabbi Emanuel Rackman filed a sobering report that was widely circulated in the Jewish press:

What we have seen and heard leads us to the melancholy conclusion that Judaism in Russia is seriously threatened with extinction. The core of devout Jews, despite heroic and sacrificial efforts to preserve their faith, is waging a losing battle against Communism's fundamental hostility to religion....

We were shocked to find that the major institutions of the Jewish religion and the vehicles of expression of Jewish culture had all but vanished, leaving a Judaism that is anemic and moribund.

We found no Jewish cultural institutions, no religious literature of recent origin, no community organizations, no Yiddish or Hebrew press, no national Jewish bodies, no Jewish social service institutions, without which Jewish life cannot long endure.

Soviet Jews did, in fact, have the worst of two worlds. For many of them, "Jew" signified neither a religion nor a cultural tradition; it was simply a name stamped on their identity papers, one that had been stripped of its rich historical context years before and yet retained all the toxic associations acquired during centuries of anti-Semitism. Most Soviet Jews had never known the ritual pleasures of a Seder meal

or felt the warm glow of Sabbath candles; they suffered the paradoxical pain of being penalized for their Jewishness without knowing what it meant. And yet a saving remnant endured, preserving the Hebrew language, observing the ancient holidays, and living, as best they could, an authentic Jewish life. It was this group, and their persecuted brothers and sisters, who became the focus of a world-wide liberation movement.

The American phase of the movement began in the early 1960s, slowly at first and principally among the young. It drew from the same well of righteous outrage that was fueling the civil rights movement, and the two campaigns presented a fascinating case study of cultural exchange. Just as civil rights leaders borrowed some of their most powerful imagery from the Torah—casting off shackles, climbing to the mountaintop, seeking the Promised Land—Soviet Jewry's advocates borrowed from the arsenal of tactics that African Americans and their allies were using to bring about social change: marches, petitions, demonstrations, letter-writing campaigns, and non-stop lobbying efforts. The cause of Soviet Jewry sparked one of the longest sustained human-rights campaigns in American history, and it was all the more remarkable because it focused on the rights of complete strangers who spoke a different language and lived thousands of miles away. American survivors were determined not to let another Holocaust occur, but there was an even deeper reason for involvement: the ancient sense of peoplehood that bound all Diaspora Jews. United across the centuries, they were united across oceans as well.

Jewish Museum Milwaukee

WISCONSIN
Marches in Washington D.C.
for
SOVIET JEWRY
December 6, 1987

The campaign to free Soviet Jews was one of the most sustained human-rights efforts in modern history, and Milwaukeeans were enthusiastic participants.

Milwaukee's activists kept pace with the national movement. During the High Holy Days of 1966, virtually every synagogue in town posted the Declaration of Rights for Soviet Jewry, a document that expressed "protest and indignation" against Soviet policies designed to "weaken the fabric of their lives as Jews by systematically destroying its unique threads." Later in the year, more than 1,200 people turned out for a protest rally at the Jewish Community Center on Prospect Avenue—one of thirty-two held across the country. The Milwaukee crowd heard Sen. Gaylord Nelson in person and Dr. Martin Luther King by phone from Atlanta. King had been an active ally for years, declaring in 1965 that he deplored anti-Semitism "as we deplore discrimination and segregation in Mississippi and Alabama."

The campaign reached another level in 1967. Emboldened by Israel's stunning victory in the Six Day War, a number of Soviet Jews applied for exit visas to Israel, a move that put their livelihoods, their educations, and their personal safety at serious risk. Most applicants were refused, and they suffered the consequences, which sometimes included imprisonment. These "refuseniks" became international celebrities for their courage, and they helped to put a human face on the continuing tragedy. The drumbeat of protest activities—the rallies and the parades and the phone calls—continued all the while. American "tourists" smuggled religious materials (as well as blue jeans) into the Soviet Union and smuggled out videotapes that reached large audiences. Indignation rose to new heights in 1972, when the Soviets imposed a confiscatory "diploma tax" on anyone who wanted to leave. The exit fee was supposedly a reimbursement for all the years of education provided by the state, but it was set so high—a multiple of each applicant's annual income—that it became simply another form of refusal. When moral suasion proved inadequate, the United States began to link the treatment of Soviet Jews to the Soviet Union's trade status—an approach codified in the Jackson-Vanik Amendment of 1974.

The campaign to liberate Soviet Jewry was consistent, coordinated, relentless, and global in scale. It was like water dripping on a rock, and in time the first cracks began to appear. The number of Jews released by the Soviet Union rose from roughly 1,000 a year in the late 1960s to 13,000 in 1971 and 35,000 in 1973—a minuscule portion of the 3,000,000 stuck behind the Iron Curtain but a significant gain nonetheless. Most went to Israel, but many came to the United States, and Milwaukee absorbed its share of newcomers. Then the gates were closed again, prompting a new wave of protests. One of the more creative took place in 1987, when Milwaukeeans, as part of a national effort, deluged the Soviet embassy in Washington with 1,185 boxes of Passover matzos intended for Jewish families in the Soviet Union. They were returned, predictably, but each box, said organizer Jerry Benjamin, was "a telegram" that carried an unmistakable message: "Stop oppressing our people."

Finally, in the late 1980s, the rock began to split wide open. When Mikhail Gorbachev came to power in 1985, he attempted to revive a moribund economy and quell growing civic discontent by easing restrictions on private property and lifting social controls that had been in place for decades. A taste of freedom quickened an appetite for more. Gorbachev's policy of *glasnost*, or openness, touched off a landslide of social changes that

swept away the settled Soviet order and ushered in a period of new possibilities that some found exhilarating and others considered terrifying. Free emigration was suddenly an option for Jews, Roman Catholics, evangelical Christians, and other religious minorities. The floodgates opened in 1989, releasing a torrent of Jewish emigrants that ultimately swelled to 1.5 million. The United Jewish Appeal, chaired by Milwaukee's own Marty Stein, promptly launched Operation

Some protesters prepared Passover matzos for delivery to the Soviet embassy (top), while others, including Marty Stein, marched on Washington to draw attention to their cause.

Wisconsin Jewish Chronicle

All the hard work paid off when Soviet Jews began to pour into the city, some rejoining relatives and others starting entirely new lives.

Exodus, a $420 million campaign to aid resettlement efforts. Stein underlined the urgency of the appeal:

> *I think all of us involved in leadership understand this is the single greatest moment in modern Jewish times. This is the opportunity to rescue 1 million Jews without bloodshed. We have to mobilize even more than during a war.*

Milwaukee, like virtually every other Jewish community in America, braced to absorb the surge, and a surge it was: the number of Soviet Jews who settled in the city jumped from 41 in 1988 to more than 400 in 1989. The scene was strongly reminiscent of the summer of 1882, when volunteers scrambled to prepare for the Russians, the mayor issued

a proclamation, and everyone wondered what the newcomers would need. This time, however, the Milwaukeeans who received the immigrants were not volunteers with bars of soap and barber's shears in hand but the trained resettlement workers of Jewish Family Services (JFS). Director Ralph Sherman had retained a skeleton staff even in quiet times—"Jews have always had their bags packed," he said, "and we have to be ready"—and the number of resettlement specialists rose with the tide of immigration, from two to ten in 1989 alone and eventually to eighteen. There was also a mayoral proclamation, but this time it was not John Stowell pleading for money and compassion but John Norquist praising the city's Jews for taking care of their own:

288

It's in Milwaukee's interest to welcome immigrants from all over the world. They add to Milwaukee's diverse culture and economy. I compliment the Jewish Federation for its active concern for Jewish refugees from the Soviet Union.

Nor was there confusion about what the immigrants needed in 1989. Jewish Family Services—whose direct ancestor, the Hebrew Relief Association, had provided material aid to the immigrants of the nineteenth century—coordinated a multi-step approach to resettlement. New arrivals were welcomed at the airport; matched with anchor families (if possible their own relatives) who helped them find housing, furniture and food; given (later loaned) $1,800 to get them through the first few months; scheduled for physical exams at Aurora Sinai Medical Center; enrolled in English classes at Milwaukee Area Technical College; informed about school choices for their kids; counseled by employment specialists; and provided with a year's free membership in the Jewish Community Center. The multi-pronged approach required a great deal of energy; JFS functioned, in effect, as two agencies, one dealing with Soviet Jews and the other with everyone else, and the community's other organizations struggled to keep up with the same demand. It was also expensive; the cost of resettlement was so high that it forced periodic cutbacks in other services funded by the Jewish Federation. But leaving the immigrants to their own devices was not an option; if you considered yourself part of the community, you accepted your obligation to help its newest members without undue resistance or resentment.

The Soviet newcomers would ultimately number between 3,000 and 4,000 individuals—roughly 15 percent of the Jewish community's current population. During the flood tide of immigration, from 1989 through 1993, Milwaukee absorbed 400 to 500 Soviet Jews every year, a figure that tapered off gradually until the late 1990s, when the only significant additions were elderly relatives of immigrants who were already established in their new homes. The Soviet Jews were numerous enough to constitute a world of their own, one that stood out clearly both within the Jewish community and in the larger community. They were, first of all, clustered geographically. Golda Meir House, the senior apartment complex on Prospect Avenue, became a haven for older immigrants, and a number of other newcomers found homes on the East Side. The vast majority, however, settled in Shorewood, Milwaukee's nearest North Shore suburb. JFS specialists channeled them to Shorewood because of its abundance of relatively affordable apartments, excellent schools, easy access to public transportation, convenient

A number of new programs helped to speed the resettlement process, including English-language tutoring sessions arranged by Jewish Family Services.

John Gurda

With its abundance of apartments, convenient location, and fine schools, Shorewood became the community of choice for the first wave of Soviet Jews.

neighborhood shopping districts, and its location in the general vicinity of other Jewish families. JFS workers prepared Russian translations of Shorewood's municipal pamphlets on everything from garbage pickup to police services, and the school system (with assistance from the Jewish Federation) hired English as a Second Language instructors to help kids understand their lessons. In 1992, school superintendent Lynne Moore declared that enrolling Soviet Jewish students had been "a wonderful experience for us"—a cultural infusion that "reflects a global world, which is unusual for a suburban district." For both the young people and their parents, Shorewood was what the Haymarket neighborhood had been for their eastern European predecessors: a place to start.

The Soviet Jews stood out culturally as well. As the first sizable group of Europeans to settle in Milwaukee since the Hungarian refugees of the 1950s, they were bound to attract attention, and cultural misunderstandings, or at least adjustments, were common. Immigrants accustomed to waiting in line for everything were astonished to find that they could simply walk into a store, pick

any item they wanted off the shelf, and give the cashier money for it. When coaches introduced the rudiments of softball to them, youngsters raised on soccer instinctively tried to stop the ball with their feet. One woman, taking her cues from the multicultural world around her, put up a Christmas tree in December with a menorah beneath it. Milwaukee's host families had some learning of their own to do, including how to make toasts with vodka—copious quantities of vodka. And there was the family who studiously learned what they thought was the Russian word for "Hello" to try on their new guests. When the immigrants got off the plane, they were surprised to find a group of American strangers shaking their hands energetically and wishing them a hearty "Goodbye."

For many host families, the characteristic that most clearly set the newcomers apart was, ironically, their lack of Jewishness. Most did not share the passion for Jewish learning and Jewish identity that marked the famous refuseniks. A number of immigrants did indeed make up for lost time once they had landed in America, devouring every scrap of knowledge about their ancestral culture and religion as if they were newborns. Those inclined to observance were generally surprised by the internal diversity of American Judaism. They had experienced their own Jewishness as little more than a label, and a negative one at that; the abundance of choices in America came as a shock. Most immigrants, however, made no choice at all. When the Milwaukee group was surveyed in 1996, 86 percent of its members identified themselves as "just Jewish," in comparison with 34 percent of the community as a whole. After generations in the acid bath of Soviet Communism, their Jewish identities had been largely stripped away. Only the very oldest spoke Yiddish or remembered Seders; the rest were members of a mistreated minority, but they were a Soviet minority who had been immersed in Soviet culture. The immigrants underwent a curious metamorphosis in the New World: in Russia they had been Jews, and in America they became Russians.

Milwaukeeans involved in the resettlement effort often found the newcomers' lack of enthusiasm for their cultural heritage at least a little disconcerting. "Some people here," said Elaine Appel of the Jewish Federation, "thought the Russians were going to get off the airplane and run to the synagogue." When they did not, there was inevitably disappointment. Without realizing it, Milwaukee's Jews were echoing the reactions of their ancestors to the mass immigration of the late 1800s. In both cases, the initial passion to free the oppressed gave way to cooler emotions once the oppressed were actually on the scene. In the late 1800s, the Russian newcomers had been too Jewish for their assimilated hosts; in the late 1900s, they were often perceived as being not Jewish enough. A visiting rabbi

gently reminded his Milwaukee audience that their expectations might have been too high. "We want them to be like us," said Yehiel Poupko in 1992, "but the majority of us are marrying non-Jews, go to synagogue three times a year and don't regularly celebrate Shabbat. I think we want them to be more than we are."

However observant they were—or were not—the immigrants received plenty of encouragement to involve themselves in the life of the local community. The *Jewish Chronicle* included a periodic Russian-language page in its weekly edition. The Jewish Community Center organized a Russian Club and offered classes on rituals, holidays, religious garments, kosher cooking, and other fundamentals. "We want them to know what they have lost," said specialist Gert Kozak. Individual congregations translated their liturgies into Russian, hosted model Seders, and provided religious instruction. The Lubavitch movement, not surprisingly, initiated the most aggressive outreach efforts. In 1991, Rabbi Yisrael Shmotkin and his staff started REACH—the Russian Education and Aid Center House—for Soviet newcomers. Its classes, social programs, and worship services evolved into a congregation, the Synagogue for Russian Jews, on Oakland Avenue, and a former REACH rabbi founded another small shul a few blocks south. One Lubavitch educational program put a new twist on an ancient command: "Let My People Know."

There were plenty of religious success stories, from families who decided to maintain kosher homes to young men who chose to undergo ritual circumcisions. For every immigrant who became a more observant Jew, however, several more threw themselves into what constituted a religion for many Americans: succeeding economically. It was lack of opportunity, not religious persecution, that drove many Soviet Jews to leave their homeland. Once they had overcome their initial exhaustion and shed their early illusions, most discovered that America was indeed a land of second chances. The employment counselors of Jewish Family Services provided crucial assistance from the start. At the peak of immigration, they placed 85 percent of the newcomers in paying jobs within four months of their arrival—one of the highest success rates in the country. True, those jobs were typically several rungs down the occupational ladder from what the immigrants had known across the ocean. Physicians found themselves drawing blood at local plasma banks, graduate engineers worked as draftsmen, and Ph.D.s spent their days painting houses or making donuts, but those initial placements were nearly always temporary. The jobs they landed through JFS gave them a foothold, and the newcomers took it from there, putting in long hours and shouldering heavy class loads to improve their prospects. Some excelled in their old professions, others launched new careers, and more than a few started their own businesses, from gift shops to real estate development firms. The adjustment was not painless—older adults and adolescents showed particular strain—but there is no doubt that, as a group, the Soviet Jews were making it on America's terms. As a result, many left Shorewood—their generation's version of the Haymarket neighborhood—for bigger, greener lawns farther north. Much like the original Haymarket, Shorewood retained a concentration of elderly Jews, while younger families joined the general exodus to Fox Point, Bayside, and Mequon.

If the Soviet Jews were not exactly what their American hosts had in mind, neither was America precisely what the Soviet Jews had expected. Both groups adjusted. The interface between old and new revealed yet another dimension of the together-and-apart theme that permeated the post-1967 period. Like the eastern Europeans of the late 1800s, the immigrants led lives parallel to the native population's at first, finding emotional security in their own company while they worked for economic security in the marketplace. As the years passed, and particularly as their children entered adulthood, the parallel lines began to converge. As the twenty-first century progressed, more and more of the newcomers were not only in but of the larger community.

Dayenu

In 1993 and 1994, just after the peak years of immigration for its newest members, the local Jewish community celebrated 150 years of life in Milwaukee. The observance included concerts, plays, publications, film showings, panel discussions, and art exhibits, but its most ambitious component was "The Golden Land," a full-fledged exhibit in the Milwaukee Public Museum. Featuring photographs, artifacts, and a life-size replica of a street scene from the old Haymarket ghetto—complete with peddler's cart, butcher shop, delicatessen, and grocery store—the temporary installation looked right at home in a museum widely considered one of America's best. The sesquicentennial celebration was judged a success on all fronts, and it whetted the community's appetite for more remembrance of

things past. The Milwaukee Jewish Historical Society, founded in 1986 as the Milwaukee Jewish Archives, took over a portion of the reconfigured Helfaer Building on Prospect Avenue and proceeded to fill it with materials, manuscripts, and memories; a home-grown oral history project has generated more than 400 hours of recorded interviews with community notables. But the centerpiece of the Historical Society's efforts was another museum installation, this one permanent. The Jewish Museum Milwaukee, which opened on the first floor of the Helfaer Building in 2008, is one of the finest facilities dedicated to a single group in the region. The little gem uses barely 5,000 square feet to tell the story of the local Jewish community in its national and international contexts, and it has attracted a steady stream of

The highlight of Jewish Milwaukee's 150th-anniversary celebration was "The Golden Land," a full-scale re-creation of a Haymarket street scene at the Public Museum. As interest in the past swelled, so did the volume of materials collected and sorted by Jewish Museum volunteers.

Xibitz, Inc.

The Jewish Museum Milwaukee, dedicated in 2008, puts the community's rich heritage on permanent display.

visitors, including school groups. Marianne Lubar, the community activist who has been a driving force behind both the Historical Society and the Jewish Museum, spoke to the broader significance of both: "Without our cultural heritage we have nothing…. We must preserve it so the next generation will learn from the past."

Jewish Milwaukeeans were clearly in the mood to remember, but they were also looking ahead, and the future of their community seemed, in some respects, more challenging than ever. There were few worries from a bricks-and-mortar perspective, at least in the early years of the twenty-first

century. In 2004, the Jewish Federation launched a $40 million capital campaign to "renovate, expand and develop our existing, yet aging, facilities," notably the Karl Jewish Community Campus (after the Whitefish Bay flap had been settled) and the Helfaer Community Service Building. The fund drive was the most ambitious in the history of Jewish Milwaukee, and it was, to the surprise of many, the most successful as well; gifts and pledges totaled $41.24 million by the middle of 2006. As construction crews descended on the Karl Campus and the Helfaer Building, several other community anchors underwent similar transformations.

The Jewish Home and Care Center was rebuilt from top to bottom, a new Hillel student center took shape near the UW-Milwaukee campus, and several synagogues—Sinai, Shalom, Beth Israel, Emanu-El B'ne Jeshurun, and Emanu-El of Waukesha—launched major remodelings or expansions. Milwaukee's Jewish establishment found itself in the throes of a genuine building boom in the early 2000s. The boom reflected the community's affluence, certainly, but it was symbolic on another level. As support for Israel became somewhat less automatic and their own cultural survival seemed somewhat less certain, American Jews were, in effect, shoring up their home defenses; the procession of rejuvenated buildings marked the community's determination to remain relevant and viable for decades to come. Steve Marcus, one of the Federation campaign's co-chairs, described the effort as a debt owed to the past and paid to the future: "Somebody spent money and spent time so that my generation had the benefit; it is now up to our generation to renew those facilities and make them available to the next generation."

In a masterstroke of timing, the bricks-and-mortar projects were largely completed—or at least completely paid for—by the time the bottom began to fall out of the national economy in 2008. The financial meltdown raised serious questions about the long-term health of Jewish Milwaukee's institutions, but there were equally pressing concerns about its heart, its soul, and even the size of its body politic. In 1996, the community had completed one of its periodic demographic studies. Some of the results were heartening—a stable population (second only to St. Louis in average length of residence),

high educational attainment, and superior economic status—but there were some red flags as well. Milwaukee's Jewish population dropped from 23,894 in 1965—the year of the last authoritative count—to 21,180 in 1996, despite heavy emigration from the former Soviet Union. As the population shrank, it also aged; like their counterparts elsewhere in America, Milwaukee's Jews were simply not replacing themselves. The tally rose to 25,400 if every non-Jewish partner in a mixed marriage was counted, but that strained the common-sense understanding of "community." Where will it end?, local leaders asked themselves. How do we stop the bleeding?

So much had already been lost. B'nai B'rith, a fraternal fixture in Milwaukee since 1861, had dwindled from fourteen active lodges to two by 1978. The survivors, Gilead-Memorial and Shofar, merged in 1993, with a membership whose median age approached sixty-five. The Perhift Players, after years as the oldest Yiddish performing group in America, staged

The new Hillel Student Center at UW-Milwaukee makes a forward-looking statement about the local Jewish community.

La Dallman Architects

their last full-length play in 1973. Yiddish became a dying language, and periodic attempts to revive it were laced with irony. In the late 1800s, Jewish immigrants had abandoned Yiddish in order to become more American; in the late 1900s, their American descendants studied Yiddish in order to become more Jewish. There were more fundamental threats to Jewish identity. The social currents of post-1967 America pushed some toward the safe but demanding haven of "Torah-true" Judaism, but those currents left an even greater number adrift without an anchor on a secular sea, moving with the tide toward identities as Americans, pure and simple—citizens of the realm who married with little regard for tradition, shared the passions and pastimes of their neighbors, and no longer insisted on their particularity as a religious and cultural minority. The fervor of the *ba'alei teshuva* at Beth Jehudah and other Orthodox centers was impressive indeed, but it was not enough to counterbalance the basic indifference of their non-observant peers. The Jewish community seemed at times to be under a silent siege, and there were fears, rarely vocalized, that Jews and Judaism faced a finite number of tomorrows.

The truth is that those fears had always been present, and the truth is that they had always been groundless. The demise of Judaism had been predicted from the dawn of the Diaspora, and yet Jews had persisted while Hittites and Etruscans, Sumerians and Phoenicians had all slipped beneath the waves. That is the basic paradox of the Jewish people: they have for millennia seemed on the verge of dying out or imploding or splintering beyond repair, and they have for

millennia survived to add something of value to the world around them. Under any number of rulers in any number of regions, they have been hounded and exploited, lulled to sleep and put to death, and yet they have endured. "I am not concerned about the future of the Jewish family," Rabbi David Shapiro of Anshe Sfard once said. "We are an eternal people. We have always outlived our enemies and we will continue to do so"— whether those enemies were Haman or Hitler, persecution or prosperity.

Even in America, the land where so many ancestral traditions came to die, Jews have not only survived but thrived. They have resisted the corrosive freedoms of a modern, materialistic democracy and the equally acidic force of their own vivid internal disagreements to play a formative role in the life of their host society. In Milwaukee and elsewhere, the Jewish community exists as a fractious and often fragmented conglomeration of conflicting viewpoints, its contradictions held in permanent suspension, but it is a community for all that. Many paths indeed, but still one people.

The impact of the Jewish people on Western civilization is incalculable, but their impact on Milwaukee, Wisconsin, is a good deal easier to assess. One of the most popular songs of the Passover Seder meal is *Dayenu*, generally translated as "It would have been enough." If God had only brought us out of Egypt, the song begins, it would been enough—Dayenu—but He didn't stop there. God gave His people the Sabbath, He gave them the Torah, and He gave them the Temple. Any one of these would have been enough—Dayenu—but God continued to bless His people with grace upon grace, favor upon favor. An earthbound version of the same sentiment might apply to Milwaukee's Jewish community. It is doubtful that any ethnic or religious group of comparable size has ever had such a significant impact on the life of the metropolitan area as a whole. From Golda Meir and Lizzie Kander to Marty Stein and Max Karl, Milwaukee-born or –bred individuals have made a crucial difference, some on the world stage and others closer to home. Social scientist and presidential advisor Wilbur Cohen is widely considered the father of Social Security. A Washington High School alumnus named Jerome Silberman found fame in Hollywood as Gene Wilder, blazing the same comedic trail that Jim Abrahams and brothers David and Jerry Zucker followed to glory. Allan "Bud" Selig brought the Milwaukee Brewers to town in 1970 and went on to become commissioner of Major League Baseball. Herb Kohl moved from running the family business to buying the Milwaukee Bucks basketball team and winning multiple terms in the U.S. Senate. Ateret Cohn's passionate commitment to Jewish education made her a legend far beyond Milwaukee. Ben Barkin was the public relations kingpin who brought the Great Circus Parade to the streets of downtown Milwaukee. Florence Eiseman designed children's clothes that became collector's items. Norman Gill kept generations of local politicians honest as head of the non-profit Citizens Governmental Research Bureau. Spiritual leaders from Solomon Scheinfeld and Joseph Baron to David Shapiro and Michel Twerski carried Milwaukee's fame to a much larger audience. Dayenu.

In business, too, the Jewish imprint has been indelible. The Adlers in clothing, the Friends in manufacturing, the Sorefs in padlocks, the Marcuses in movies, Alfred Bader in chemicals, Max Karl in mortgage insurance, Elmer Winter in temporary help, and dozens of other entrepreneurial giants have brought untold wealth and employment to their hometown. On the retail side, local families were fed by Kohl's and clothed by Gimbels, Schuster's, Goldmann's, and the Grand. Dayenu.

The community has benefited more broadly from institutions that were started by Jewish volunteers and now serve a broader population: Aurora Sinai Medical Center, the Milwaukee Center for Independence, COA Youth and Family Centers, the Helen Bader Foundation, and the Jewish Community Center itself, to name only a few. Jewish philanthropists have also played decisive roles in creating or developing Milwaukee's cultural and civic infrastructure—a role preserved in the names of the Sheldon B. Lubar School of Business at UW-Milwaukee, the Marcus Center for the Performing Arts, the Peck Welcome Center at the Milwaukee County Zoo, and the Zilber Neighborhood Initiative. And there are thousands of nameless benefactions that have nurtured the arts, helped the poor, and shaped public policy. Dayenu.

The Jews of Milwaukee have been an extraordinarily productive group whose contributions to the community far outweigh their share of its population. Any number of individuals or institutions could be singled out for praise, but together they form a critical mass that indicates the scale of the Jewish impact on Milwaukee. Jewish residents have been building the city since the city began, and their greatest contribution is not the achievements of a relative few but the ongoing, creative presence of the entire community. Rooted in an ethical tradition, eager to engage, and accustomed to discourse, they form a distinctive and indispensable thread in the fabric of local society.

The story of Jewish Milwaukee has been, in the long view, an odyssey, both geographic and historical. The community's Jewish residents traveled a long road from the shtetls of Europe to the ghettos of the North Side, and they kept on moving from Sherman Park to the North Shore and beyond. Their general movement has been upward economically and outward geographically, and along the way they have added something distinctive to Milwaukee's sense of civic possibility. Their story, then, is one not of exodus but of arrival. The Jews found a home in Milwaukee, and they have enriched that home beyond measure.

A Note on Sources

Anyone who attempts a history of Jewish Milwaukee stands squarely on the shoulders of Rabbi Louis Swichkow. His magnum opus, *The History of the Jews of Milwaukee* (co-written with Lloyd Gartner, Jewish Publication Society of America, 1963) is a painstakingly researched and exhaustively footnoted chronicle of the community's development to 1950. I did not always follow the historical record to the same conclusions as Swichkow (and in fact read him last in my research for Chapters 1 through 4), but his account is essential to understanding the community in its first century.

Primary sources were just as important. Digitization has not affected history as profoundly as it has other disciplines, but the revolution is under way. The *Milwaukee Sentinel* index, a manual reference tool compiled by WPA workers during the Depression, was once a key to daily life in the nineteenth century. It has been largely supplanted by the Nineteenth-Century Newspapers Database (Thomson Gale Co.), which is widely available through public library systems. The entire run of the *Milwaukee Sentinel* from 1837 through 1899 has been digitized by Thomson Gale and thus rendered searchable by keyword, name, and date—an invaluable resource for the formative years of the Jewish community. Entering a single keyword—"Jewish"—yielded a grand total of 5,106 hits from the *Sentinel* and led me to articles that probably hadn't been seen since they were published.

More sharply focused coverage begins in December 1921, when the weekly *Wisconsin Jewish Chronicle* began publication. The entire run is bound by year in the *Chronicle* offices on Prospect Avenue in Milwaukee, and no better source exists for the community in its second century. In the course of researching *One People, Many Paths,* I spent weeks poring over old newspapers, and in the process became perhaps the only person in the world who has turned every page of every issue of the *Jewish Chronicle* from the first in 1921 to the last paper copy in 2009, when the *Chronicle* "went digital."

The gap in newspaper coverage from 1900 to 1921 is partially bridged by the clippings files in the Milwaukee Public Library Humanities Room and the Milwaukee County Historical Society. Both institutions also have an abundance of more general resources, from insurance atlases to city directories, that put Milwaukee's Jewish history in context. The University of Wisconsin-Milwaukee Library Archives contains some wonderful materials on both Golda Meir and Lizzie Kander—the reigning queens of Milwaukee's Jewish history.

By far the single richest resource for this project was the archives of the Jewish Museum Milwaukee. The Museum's collection is a treasure trove of congregational minutes, institutional records, family papers, business materials, oral histories, published accounts, photographs, and artifacts, all painstakingly cataloged and overseen by Jay Hyland, the finest archivist with whom I've had the pleasure to work.

As an outsider, I felt the need to learn as much of the larger Jewish story as I could in order to understand the framework of Jewish Milwaukee. The most helpful general studies I read, and ones I consulted frequently, were Jonathan Sarna's *American Judaism: A History* (Yale University Press, 2004) and Rabbi Joseph Telushkin's *Jewish Literacy* (William Morrow, 2001). And there was, of course, the Bible—the best Jewish history of all.

John Gurda

A Basic Jewish Glossary

by Jody Hirsh, Judaic Education Director, Harry & Rose Samson Family Jewish Community Center

aliyah
"Going up"—either going up to the Torah in a synagogue or immigrating to Israel

ba'al teshuva
"Master of return"—a non-religious Jew who returns to the faith

Bar/Bat Mitzvah
"Son/daughter of the commandment"—a status celebrated in the coming-of-age ceremony in the synagogue for boys at 13 and girls at 12 or 13

bris (brit milah)
Circumcision, as required on the eighth day of a baby boy's life

cantor
The musical leader in the synagogue who chants the prayers during public services

Chanukah
The winter holiday commemorating the victory of the Jews over their Greek oppressors in the second century BCE

Chasidic
Mystical Jews who trace their form of Judaism to the 18th-century spiritual leader known as the Baal Shem Tov

chutzpah
Nerve, impudence (Yiddish)

Conservative Judaism
The form of Judaism which is committed to halacha (Jewish Law), yet seeks modern ways of adhering to it

daven
To pray (Yiddish)

dreidel
A spinning top used in a gambling game during Chanukah

Haggada
The book which contains the service for the Seder, the ritual Passover meal

halacha
Jewish Law, derived from the 613 commandments of the Torah

hamentashen
"Hamen's pockets"—the triangular cookies eaten at Purim

havurah
A communal group which meets for Jewish ritual meals, prayer, and/or study

Kaddish
A prayer said as a memorial for the dead

kashrut
The dietary laws and practices dictating which animals and vegetables can be eaten, how kosher meat is slaughtered, and how milk foods and meat foods are to be separated

kibbutz
A Zionist commune in the land of Israel

kiddush
The blessing over wine used on the Sabbath, holidays, and at other joyous rituals

kollel
An institution devoted to constant study of the Torah

kosher
"proper", referring to the Jewish dietary laws

Lubavitch movement
A Chasidic sect that specializes in outreach to non-religious Jews

matrilineal/patrilineal descent
The controversy in contemporary Jewish life that seeks to define "who is a Jew." According to strict Jewish Law, Jews are defined as having a Jewish mother (matrilineal descent), but many Jews today (including those in the Reform Movement) include Jews who have a Jewish father and non-Jewish mother (patrilineal descent).

matzo
The unleavened bread eaten at Passover

menorah
A multi-branched candelabra. The Chanukiah, or 9-branched lamp used at Chanukah, is often called a menorah.

mezuzah
A small parchment containing passages from the Torah, including those that command writing the words of the Torah "on the doorposts of your house." The parchment is usually enclosed in a small, ornate case.

mikvah
A ritual bath that women are required by Jewish law to visit after menstruation. The conversion ritual also includes immersion in a mikvah.

minyan
The quorum of 10 men required to have a religious service

mitzvah
A commandment, specifically one of the 613 commandments of the Torah. The word has also come to mean "a good deed."

mohel (Hebrew) or moyel (Yiddish)
A man who performs the ritual circumcision

Orthodox Judaism
The strictest form of Judaism. Although there is a broad spectrum of belief and practice, Orthodox Jews believe in strict adherence to Jewish Law, which they hold was received by Moses from God on Mount Sinai.

Passover (Pesach)
A week-long holiday (8 days outside of Israel) which commemorates the exodus of the Israelites from Egypt

pogrom
A violent attack against Jews, particularly one carried out in the 1880s and later in tsarist Russia, often at the instigation of the Russian government

Purim
The spring holiday which commemorates the events of the Book of Esther in which the Jews were saved from destruction

Reconstructionism
A movement begun by Rabbi Mordecai Kaplan in America that focuses on Judaism as an evolving civilization

Reform Judaism
A movement begun in Germany in the 18th century that focuses on the "spirit" of Judaism rather than strict adherence to Jewish Law

Rosh HaShanah
The Jewish New Year, a major holiday occurring in autumn

Sabbath (English)
Shabbat (Hebrew)
Shabbos (Yiddish)
The weekly day of rest, imitating God's resting on the seventh day after creating the world. Strict Jewish Law prohibits many activities on the Sabbath, including cooking, driving, and handling money.

Seder
The ritual meal at Passover. The word is derived from the Hebrew for "order," referring to the meal's 15 parts.

shaliach
Emissary from the Israeli government who lives and works in the local Jewish community for an extended period of time

shochet
A ritual slaughterer who kills animals for food according to the strict laws of kashrut

shofar
The ram's horn sounded at the Jewish New Year

shtetl
A village in eastern Europe in which Jews constituted a large part of the population

shul
A synagogue (Yiddish)

sukkah
A hut or "booth" with branches for a roof that Jews eat or even sleep in during the holiday of Sukkot

Sukkot
The autumn Feast of Booths, commemorating the wandering of the Israelites in the wilderness for 40 years

tallit, tallis
The fringed prayer shawl worn by Jewish men (and increasingly by women) during the morning prayers

Talmud
The monumental, multi-volume book of Jewish Law which contains the rabbinic interpretations of the laws of the Torah

tefillin
Small leather boxes that contain passages from the Torah, including those that command wearing the words of the Torah "as a sign upon your hand and . . . between your eyes." The tefillin are strapped on the forehead and on the left arm.

Torah
The Five Books of Moses. Torah can also refer to the whole Jewish way of life as well as the laws of the Talmud.

treyf
Not kosher

tzedakah
Charity, rooted in the Hebrew word for "justice." In the Jewish tradition, giving charity is a commandment, not a choice.

yarmulke (Yiddish)
kipa (Hebrew)
A skullcap

yeshiva
A Torah school, usually for boys and young men

Yiddish
The Eastern European Jewish language derived from medieval German, Hebrew, and other languages

Yiddishkeit
The Yiddish word for "Jewishness"

Yom Kippur
The Day of Atonement—Judaism's most solemn holiday, occurring 10 days after Rosh HaShanah

Zionism
The national liberation movement of the Jewish people, started by Theodor Herzl in 1897 and focused on creating a Jewish homeland in Palestine

Index

[Page numbers in *italics* refer to illustrations.]

About the Author

John Gurda is a Milwaukee-born writer and historian who has been studying his hometown since 1972. He is the author of nineteen books, including histories of Milwaukee-area neighborhoods, industries, and places of worship. *The Making of Milwaukee* is Gurda's most ambitious effort. With 450 pages and more than 500 illustrations, it is the first full-length history of the community published since 1948. Milwaukee Public Television created an Emmy Award-winning documentary series based on the book in 2006.

In addition to his work as an author, Gurda is a lecturer, tour guide, and local history columnist for the *Milwaukee Journal Sentinel*. He holds a B.A. in English from Boston College and an M.A. in Cultural Geography from the University of Wisconsin-Milwaukee.